JEWISH MARITAL CAPTIVITY

Jewish Marital Captivity

The Past, Present, and End of a Historic Abuse

Shulamit S. Magnus

NEW YORK UNIVERSITY PRESS
New York

NEW YORK UNIVERSITY PRESS
New York
www.nyupress.org

Library of Congress Cataloging-in-Publication Data
Names: Magnus, Shulamit S., 1950–   author.
Title: Jewish marital captivity : the past, present, and end of a historic abuse /
Shulamit S. Magnus.
Description: New York : New York University Press, [2025] |
Includes bibliographical references and in
Identifiers: LCCN 2024040438 (print) | LCCN 202404 (ebook) |
ISBN 9781479835546 (hardback) | ISBN 9781479835553 (ebook) |
ISBN 9781479835560 (ebook other)
Subjects: Classification: LCC KBM550.5 .M34 2025 (print) | LCC KBM550.5 (ebook) |
DDC 296.3/63—dc23/eng/20240905
LC record available at https://lccn.loc.gov/2024040438
LC ebook record available at https://lccn.loc.gov/2024040439

The manufacturer's authorized representative in the EU for product safety is Mare
Nostrum Group B.V., Mauritskade 21D, 1091 GC Amsterdam, The Netherlands.
Email: gpsr@mare-nostrum.co.uk.

Manufactured in the United States of America

10 9 8 7 6 5 4 3 2 1

Also available as an ebook

For Susan Weiss

Eshet hayil

ציון במשפט תפדה ושביה בצדקה

Zion will be redeemed through justice
And those who return to her, through righteousness

You shall not deal deceitfully or falsely with one another. . . .
You shall not defraud your fellow. . . .
You shall not insult the deaf or place a stumbling block before the blind. . . .
You shall not render an unfair decision. . . .
Do not profit by the blood of your fellow.
—Leviticus 19:13–16

Keep distant from falsehood.
—Exodus 23:7

Justice, justice, you shall pursue.
—Deuteronomy 16:20

רש"י על דברים ט"ז:כ':א: צדק צדק תרדף (ספרי, סנהדרין ל"ב) הַלֹּךְ אַחַר בֵּית דִּין יָפֶה
Rashi's commentary on Deut. 16:20—"Justice, Justice you shall pursue"
Follow a worthy *beit din* [court of law].

Justice, justice you shall pursue: With justice, you shall pursue justice.
Even the pursuit of justice must employ only just means.
—Rabbi Simhah Bunim of Pshischa

Justice, justice you shall pursue: Justice alone is not enough. The Torah,
therefore, stresses, "Justice, justice you shall pursue," namely the *musar*
(ethic) of justice, where both the means and the end are just.
—Derashot El Ami[1]

Did you know? She wanted to be a rabbi. Because a rabbi pursues justice.
—Margaret Frisch Klein, In Memory of Ruth Bader Ginsburg

A man who wishes to divorce his wife is not like a woman who seeks
divorce from her husband.
—Mishna Yevamot 14:1

Halakhic marriage is an exclusive conjugal
servitude of the bride to the groom.
—Rabbi J. David Bleich

You know why the *dinnim* (laws) are the way they are, don't you? Because
the men made the *dinnim*.
—Leah Juda Grossman, z"l, my Hasidic grandmother, as conveyed to me
many times by my Orthodox mother, Liba Grossman Magnus, z"l

The problem with power is that there is no speaking truth to it when it
holds all the cards.
—Dahlia Lithwick

Clearly, we are living in an era of unworthy rabbinic authorities. We
should not abdicate the tradition we love because of their weakness.
—Rivka Haut

פוק חזי מאי עמא דבר :
Look around, see what people are doing; then, legislate.
—BT Berakhot 45a

CONTENTS

List of Figures   xi

Preface   xiii

Introduction   1

PART ONE: HISTORY

1. Origins: Foundations and Early Reforms   21

2. Why Did Reforms Happen?: Iggun and Agunot in
   Historical Perspective   31

3. Agency and Authority: Real Women and Rabbinic Law   54

4. Using Non-Jewish Courts, and Rabbinic Courts   74

5. Socioeconomic and Halakhic Realities in Early Modernity   82

6. Backlash   88

7. "Agunot, Halakhic Decisors, and Suffering" in
   Mid-Seventeenth- to Mid-Nineteenth-Century Europe   110

8. Agunot vs. Iggun: Strategies   124

9. Iggun in Modernity   134

PART TWO: THE PRESENT

10. The Present State of Jewish Marital Captivity   157

11. Divorce in the Conservative/Masorti and Other Movements:
    Evasions and Illusions   174

12. Intradenominational Politics and Rivalries Abort Solutions
    within Orthodoxy   190

PART THREE: DENYING IGGUN A FUTURE

13. Thinking outside the Chains to End Jewish
Marital Captivity   225

Conclusions   251

Acknowledgments   259

Appendix   263

Notes   267

Bibliography   303

Index   329

About the Author   349

LIST OF FIGURES

Figure 3.1 Cover image of Monique Susskind-Goldberg and
Diana Goldberg, *Za'akat Dalot*.   55

Figure 3.2 Halitsa document of the daughter-in-law of Rabbi
Joseph Karo.   67

Figure 11.1 Nitzan Caspi Shiloni, Tzviya Gorodetsky, and
Shulamit Magnus, hunger-strike vigil at the Knesset,
Summer, 2017: "Pass the law that will free me!"   187

Figure 11.2 Annulment of Tzviya Gorodetsky's marriage in the
court of Rabbi Professor Daniel Sperber (seen from behind),
with Attorney Nitzan Caspi Shiloni and court recorders.   187

Figure 11.3 Tzviya Gorodetsky testifying in Rabbi Sperber's
court in the hearing for annulment of her marriage.   188

Figure 11.4 Tzviya Gorodetsky with Attorney Nitzan Caspi Shiloni,
with the document certifying annulment of her marriage
and her marital freedom.   188

Figure C.1 "He who differentiates between darkness and light."   255

Figure C.2 Rachel's Tomb.   256

Figure A.1 Flyer circulating in Jerusalem neighborhoods, 2022,
calling for shunning of a get refuser's father for abetting
his son's fifteen-plus-year get refusal, against the rabbinic
court's ruling.   263

Figure A.2 "Proclamation" (2005) of a Cleveland, Ohio,
rabbinic court summoning a man who has ignored the
court's prior summons, authorizing sanctions against him
for this defiance.   264

Figure A.3 Letter of the Joint Law Conference of the Rabbinical
Assembly and the Jewish Theological Seminary of America
(1966) requesting a man's attendance in its rabbinic
court regarding his wife's request for a get.   265

Figure A.4 Natalie Lastreger and supporters as she awaits arrest
by the Chief Rabbinate for seeking to use a haredi rabbinic
court and not that of the Chief Rabbinate for her divorce.   266

PREFACE[1]

This book presents a history of Jewish marital captivity (*iggun*), and of women chained in marriage against their will (*agunot*), from early medieval times to the present and across the Jewish world—the Middle East and North Africa, Europe, the Mediterranean, the United States, and Israel. It is the first work to attempt such a narrative across time and space, studying an enduring, if also evolving, social institution and women's responses to it.

The book also assesses the present state of this problem, its victims, perpetrators, and enablers, in the United States and Israel, critiques current policy about it, and makes proposals to end the abuse. It has a programmatic goal: ending policies that manage, rather than end, iggun. Implicitly or explicitly, consciously or not, these policies accept women's marital captivity as a given in Jewish society, an inevitable fact of life, rather than as a complex and embedded but solvable problem. Assumptions that dismiss iggun as an Orthodox or an Israeli rather than as a Jewish problem also perpetuate the abuse.

The purpose that motivated my work was this programmatic one, underlain by personal experience and prompted by the invitation of Rabbi Rachel Adler to write a chapter on iggun and agunot for a proposed anthology. The writing quickly outgrew the dimensions of an article. I realized that historical grounding was essential and subsequently, that a perfunctory history of iggun against a near-total absence of historical inquiry about it would neither suffice the programmatic goal nor do justice to a huge untold story, a significant chapter in Jewish history that has not been recognized as one. Thus was launched the historical part of this project.

Feminist historians and epistemologists long ago established that there is no such thing as objective scholarship and that pretensions to have produced such only reveal an unacknowledged, profound bias. All scholarly work is driven, first, by interest—an immediate bias in the sheer selection of a subject to the exclusion of others. Without a focus, a point motivating and driving the work, there would be nothing but a collection of data. Bias itself is not a bad thing; on the contrary, it is essential to meaningful scholarship. What is required is transparency about one's purpose; rigorous, transparent method; and substantiation of assertions. These have been my guidelines.[2]

In keeping with the mandate of transparency, I share the following.

My mother was an agunah.

My father became mentally ill, paranoid to the point that he posed a threat to others— enemies he perceived all around him, in his coworkers in the printers' union, in neighbors—until he was hospitalized when I was four.

My parents were both immigrants to the United States, my mother from Czechoslovakia, my father from Poland. My mother was the only survivor of her large family, who were all murdered by the Nazis except one brother, who left for Palestine in the 1930s and was killed in the siege of Jerusalem in 1948. My father fled interwar Poland as a youth after Jew-hating hooligans threatened to kill him after he ripped off placards they had put up on my grandparents' store in their town, Mlawa. Cousins in the United States took him in. Explaining his later behavior regarding these cousins and their influence over him, my mother reported him saying that he owed them his life. They did not believe that my father was ill (nor did he), and wanted my mother to take him home from the hospital. When she did not do that, they spoke ill of her to him and turned him against her, accessing misogynist tropes readily available in the Jewish and wider cultures he and they knew. She then became the chief object of his paranoia. When, some eight years after he took ill, she sought to get a get, a rabbinic divorce, he refused; what, give her a divorce so she could pursue boyfriends? My father was beleaguered and ill; a year after he was hospitalized, he suffered a stroke and was paralyzed on one side. He was physically crippled as well as deeply troubled. But he could act on his right as a Jewish man, however nonobservant he was (he had grown up in a religious, Zionist home), and deny my mother freedom. And he did.

At some point my father's cousins, authorized to sign him out for day visits, did so but did not return him to the hospital. From this point commenced years in which my father wandered, living in different places. He also would materialize near our apartment from time to time. My mother was terrified that if he got inside she would never be able to get him out, that he would take us children. Her terror passed to me. My father had been a wonderfully engaged, loving father before he became ill. I adored him. But this other entity, whom my mother perceived as a threat, was a stranger to me and frightening.

My mother grew up in a Hasidic family in a mountain town in northern Slovakia, near the Polish border. She was a devout, pious Jew, in the United States, becoming what would be termed modern Orthodox. She did not have a phony or sanctimonious bone in her body and could not abide those who did. I davened (prayed) next to her in the synagogue; she was the real deal. When she said "sh'ma kolenu" ("Hear our voice"), she meant it. She was Sabbath-observant and kept a strictly kosher home, the only such home in our cooperative Veterans' Administration development, which was otherwise populated almost exclusively by Jews, but nonobservant American-born Jews, speaking nonaccented English. She was aware, of course, that our lifestyle was, in that context, literally singular, but that was who she was and she never wavered. She was in shul (synagogue) every Shabbat, first in a Conservative shul whose rabbi was Orthodox, and then, when an Orthodox, Young Israel shul opened, there, my older sister and I with her. When a yeshiva day school opened up within bus and subway distance of our neighborhood in the outer reaches of Queens, New York, near the city limits, she enrolled my sister and me in it after getting dispensation from the principal about the tuition she could not pay ("Send me the children," Rabbi Baruch Charney said, "and never speak of money again"). I began bus and subway transportation to yeshiva while in kindergarten, struggling to keep up with the older, bigger children, who walked and ran faster than I could to get to the stations. I attended Orthodox schools, yeshivas, from kindergarten to college.

There were, indeed, men who were interested in my mother. One was the widowed nephew of the woman who saved her from Europe. His family were fine, *heimish* (friendly and warm) people she liked; Yiddish-speaking, religious people from "home" who understood her and her way of life, who admired and liked her. They lived in Israel, where she had some surviving cousins and friends from home. But she was a married woman. She would not so much as date, nor would that man proceed. She needed a get and could not get one.

She tried for the first time when I was twelve. Her rabbi was head of the Rabbinical Council of America. He had connections, knew influential people, the biggest-name rabbis in that world. My mother was surely not aware of that and its potential importance. It just made sense that she would turn to her own rabbi for help.

This rabbi did make efforts. My father had not seen my sister and me, nor we him, of course, for years, except for furtive, terrified glances when he materialized near our apartment, his scheduled Sunday visits home from the hospital having ceased after his stroke. Either my father asked for, or perhaps the rabbi offered to arrange, a meeting between us, and it happened one Sunday in the rabbi's office in the shul. It was a heartbreaking encounter for me. The man I saw was not the handsome, vigorous father I remembered from my young childhood but aged, crippled. To see him as he now was broke my heart and I could not keep from weeping in his presence throughout the meeting, pitying him, imagining how he would have to struggle to board buses or navigate the steps in subway stations, as I had seen other people with disabilities struggle to do; how people would see him and recoil, or pity him as I now did. My father.

I wonder if, at the time of that meeting, my father was under the impression that the rabbi was trying to arrange a reconciliation with my mother, not a get; that all this was preliminary to him coming home. He was certainly very benign in that meeting, saying nice things about us, including my mother. (He had wanted to send us to Yiddish-speaking socialist schools but my mother insisted that the schools be religious and Zionist. And she was right, he said; look at the Hebrew we knew.) When he understood that the rabbi wanted him to give my mother a get, my mother would later report, he became furious and cursed the rabbi (my father had served in the US Army in World War II and surely had a repertoire). The rabbi then cut off contact with my father, who refused to give my mother a get.

So matters stood until I reached college.

There, I resolved that I would get my mother a get, as I put it, if it was the last thing I did. And I was sure I would succeed. My mother was a beleaguered immigrant; I was US-born and knew how to fight. The facts of the case, after all, were so outrageous. She was the only survivor of her family, observant, Orthodox, raising two children alone, sending us to yeshiva. He kept nothing. Surely the rabbis would find the egregious injustice of the situation intolerable and act on her behalf.

It was quite an experience. I interacted primarily and repeatedly with my mother's rabbi, but when I found his engagement lacking, I sought out others, the biggest names in American modern Orthodoxy. Some responded with sympathy but had nothing to offer. Some reacted impatiently. Nothing can be done, what don't you understand? I went back to my mother's rabbi again and again. What was he doing? What was happening? When would things move?

Once I called him from university, shoveling quarters into a pay phone. When I heard, yet again, that in fact nothing was happening, I exploded, yelling at him, "This is a hillul hashem!" (desecration of God's name). "A hillul hashem! You know who she is! She lives a few streets from you, how do you sleep at night!"

The rabbi responded by telling me about a woman in upstate New York who could not get a get, so got a civil divorce. He said this to me knowing full well that my mother would not so much as carry a tissue outside the house on Shabbat (transporting anything within the public domain, or from the private to the public domain, or vice versa, is prohibited on the Sabbath). A civil divorce would do nothing for her.

I reported regularly to my mother about the proceedings, or lack of them. We would have these discussions on *shabbes* (Sabbath) afternoon. I would explain and she would say, "Der hez to be anodder vay," some other way aside from him giving her a get, because "he vil never give me a get." There is no other way, Ma, I would say, looking into her enormous brown eyes, unbearably, being the vehicle of more pain, more helplessness.

My father by this point had gotten himself to a Veterans Administration hospital in South Dakota. I maintained contact with him, sending letters about my studies and daily life. I sent him a *tehillim'l*, a book of Psalms, and chocolates once when he asked for this (I did not know that he was diabetic; I got a note from the hospital saying never to do this again).

In one of my conversations with Rabbi B., pressing him to do something, he told me that it was up to me to get my father to agree to give my mother a get. "Shulamis," he said (using the Yiddish pronunciation of my name), "you are the ace in the hole," a phrase about whose literal meaning I had no clue but whose upshot I did understand. I was to go to South Dakota.

It is hard to convey what "South Dakota" meant to an Orthodox girl from New York. Going there on my own, on such a mission, to my father yet, was a terrifying, unimaginable proposition.

When I told my mother what the rabbi said, she exploded. "Whose get is this?!" she yelled. Outrageous that the rabbi would put this on me. That idea went nowhere.

The whole effort was going nowhere. I spoke with my mother on yet another *shabbes* and said, "If you want me to continue, Ma, I will, but at this point, what would you get out of it?" Meaning, if she were somehow to get a get.

She thought a minute, then said, "Vell, I vudn't hef to sit shiva" (the seven days of in-house mourning after the death of an immediate relative).

For this, I was not going to get a stroke, as I put it, and I gave up.

When my father, z"l, died, my mother and I sat shiva together. She had him buried in Israel, in a double plot she had purchased. They are buried next to one another.

* * *

My experience trying to get my mother a get confronted me with a stark and painful conflict. I had been a very religious child. On Shabbatot (Sabbaths), I began returning to shul for minha and maariv (the afternoon and evening services), the only female in the place. The late afternoon light filtering into the then largely empty synagogue, and the sweet, haunting melody (*nusach*) of *shabbes* minha prayers created an enchanted, deeply peaceful space I craved. The Torah reading in that service is short, its ceremonial aspects abbreviated. Up against the latticed division, the *mehitsa*, in the women's section, I could see and hear clearly all that was done—how the men took the Torah scroll out of the *aron* (Torah ark), removed its mantle, and laid it on the reading table. I heard the thud of its circular wooden handles hitting the velvet-draped wood of the table and the click-click sound of the reader scrolling to the place for the afternoon reading. After minha, I would accompany the men to *shalosh shides*, the third Sabbath meal, in the shul's basement–social hall, and heard the *z'mires*, the table songs that accompanied this meal, something I never heard at home. On the first days of the new month, after the Sabbath had ended and the men had made havdalah, the ritual that ends the Sabbath and inaugurates the new week, I would go outside with them to the steps of the shul for *kiddush halevana*, the blessing of the just-visible crescent of the new moon. They sang, rose up on tiptoe, dancing to the moon. When it was over, we went our separate ways and I walked home alone in the dark. "Git vokh," from and to my mother. Wishing a good week in Yiddish.

In school, *limmudei kodesh* (study of sacred texts) was my favorite subject. I dutifully learned *dinnim*—laws of Sabbath and festival observance, and of kashrut, the ritual diet, and followed them rigorously. I would hasten to the synagogue for the early part of the Sabbath morning *tefilla* (prayers), noting the difference in style and melodies between different prayer leaders, happy when my favorites led; alert to the difference in the *leining* (chanting) of the week's Torah portion by different men, who enunciated precisely and could be heard well in the women's section. When, much later, I asked one of the men whose voice and davening were beautiful to tape for me his version of Kol Nidre, the inaugural prayer of Yom Kippur, he replied, "Yes, I know, you like to sing." "How do you know?" I asked, surprised. "Because I hear you, from the women's section," he said.

I brought my religious connection home. In second grade, the teacher taught us how to daven the Friday night service, with the distinctive tunes for those prayers, as well as how to make kiddush, the sanctification of the day over wine. There was none of this in my home. My mother was raised in a Hasidic home; these were men's rituals. But I had learned them, and I now did them. I made kiddush from the age of seven, and to this day am uneasy when I am a guest at the table of others and do not make my own kiddush. We were an Orthodox family, without a man.

I remember studying the story of Elijah the prophet (1 Kings 18) and how he confronted and defeated—crushed!—the false priests of Baal, publicly exposing their falsehood. There was Truth and there were Lies, Right and Wrong, and Truth and Right would out. It was enormously important to me, the child of a woman who had lost everyone, people who should have been my grandparents, aunts, uncles, cousins, that this was so. And I learned it in yeshiva.

I also learned there that God is a God of justice, *mishpat*. While rabbinic commentaries say about the biblical Abraham that he was a pioneering monotheist among idolaters, the text itself shows him experiencing God as the ultimate Arbiter of Justice, and acting on that perception. "השופט כל הארץ לא יעשה משפט?"—"Will the Judge of all the earth not do justice?"—Genesis 18:25 has Abraham protesting to God, even admonishing God with, "חלילה לך!", which in any other context would translate as "God forbid!," when Abraham pleads Sodom's case to God. And God accedes to Abraham's plea, on those terms.

But all that came crashing up against the reality I was encountering as I tried to get my mother a get. I was in Barnard College (of Columbia University) in the 1970s, a very feminist place and time, and this was a rude, fierce new education in applied, not theoretical, feminism. I was taking courses in Jewish history and in Talmud at Columbia, for the first time encountering the sacred in a secular setting and from an academic perspective, and it began to undermine the ideational bases of my Orthodoxy. And then, the failure of the system to deliver justice to my mother—that the system, the rabbis I'd so revered, were content to leave it at—Sorry, nothing we can do. Where was the zealotry for justice they were supposed to embody and implement? This was not a past outrage, perpetrated by enemies—the murder of my mother's family—but a present one, within the gates, and they could do something about it and weren't.

Then I learned, to my shock and despair, that my mother's predicament was not hers alone nor confined to her so egregiously wounded generation. I will never forget telling my mother, stunned, that someone who had been a close friend of mine in elementary school, starting in kindergarten, had become an agunah. Then I learned that someone I had gone to high school with had become an agunah. And then that the first cousin of one of my closest friends had become an agunah, in Israel. This was not some other generation's plague.

One day, when I was in graduate school, it struck me suddenly with unerring clarity: Whatever the rabbis have to say about women does not apply to me. And I knew in that instant that I was no longer Orthodox, regardless of what I did or did not do on the Sabbath, or ate or not. Orthodoxy is about accepting rabbinic authority and there is no saying I don't accept it about anything.

That moment was terrifying. If I was no longer Orthodox, what, who was I? What would become of all I had been and lived my whole life? How would my family now relate to me? Outside the Pale, the phrase kept repeating in my mind. Would they write me out? Cut me off?

I was studying for doctoral exams in Jewish history, which, at Columbia, were in all periods; one's chosen era and area of specialty were irrelevant. The pressure was enormous and the time very pressed. We had huge reading lists to absorb. I was observing *shabbes* as I had always done, meaning I would write nothing, take no notes that day, though I continued reading, putting paper clips at something to note. A full day, every week, of impaired preparation—and why, if I no longer believed that God would either punish me if I did not keep *shabbes* or reward me if I did? Keep *shabbes*, or stop?

One day, I decided on a mental experiment. I stood in the doorway of the kitchen of my apartment and imagined that it was Friday night. But instead of the white tablecloth, the wine for kiddush, the special meal— the same food my mother prepared for *shabbes*, which I'd eaten all my life and continued to prepare for myself—and, heavens, the quiet!—no radio, TV, phone calls—there was none of this. Friday night would be just like—Tuesday night.

I felt devastation. What was so wonderful about Tuesday night that I wanted another one? Why inflict loss of *shabbes* on myself when I was already in pain and feeling much other loss?

So *shabbes* stayed. Tref (not kosher) food never drew me and I knew that if I stopped keeping kosher, my mother would never step foot in my house again. So *kashrus* stayed, too.

But there was an emptiness, the loss of larger meaning for what I was doing. I understood far better what I was not, no longer Orthodox, than what I now was, except that I knew I was a feminist, that it and traditional Judaism—patriarchal Judaism—were in conflict, and that I was going to tell the truth, to myself above all, and be all of who I was.

I found (and also helped to found) communities in which, over time, all this got much more worked out. In these settings, with serious, thoughtful, committed people from varied backgrounds who were also searching, I learned a new vocabulary for embracing all of who I was in all its complexity. The bottom line was that I was a religious Jew and a feminist and that I would tell the truth and be whole. No one had the power to write me out of anything. The tradition was mine, all of it, along with the responsibility to create something whole for myself as a woman and to participate in the larger project of creating feminist Judaism.

All this is the genesis of this book. As a friend said when she read an early draft of it, "Shulamit, you have been writing this all your life."

I do not, of course, condone what my father did, which included cutting off my mother's receipt of Social Security and veteran benefits he got for the support of his minor children; this was yet another means of pressuring her to take him home, another of his relatives' ideas. That certainly produced additional hardship and for me, lifelong anxiety about money. My mother qualified for welfare, which she refused to take. She got a job she hated as a seamstress, traveling hours daily by bus and subway to and from Manhattan's garment district, and we made our way.

What I say about my father's bad behavior, in the Jewish and secular spheres, is that larger systems allowed it. My father did what those systems allowed him to do. He was mentally ill (and manipulated by misogynistic relatives); the rabbis, presumably, were/are not. What is their excuse?[3]

It is easy to focus on bad men, bad husbands and bad rabbis, as the target of agunah advocacy, but to do that is a terrible displacement of attention that perpetuates iggun. Such men are the end result, not the cause, of the abuse.

There has to be another way, my mother, z"l, said.

And there is. To get to it, we must first speak the truth about the origins and causes of iggun, and it is not bad husbands or bad rabbis. We must understand the deep history of how iggun has operated, historically, in Jewish societies across the long eras and vast regions of Jewish life because, like any other social institution, it has a history. Without informed historical consciousness, agunot cannot grasp the systemic nature of their victimization, without which neither they nor anyone else can respond effectively. We must understand how women have strategized and operated, creatively and vigorously, to protect themselves and advance their interests and with what, often notable successes in the distant past. We must probe why significant reforms that enhanced women's protections in marriage and divorce emerged and operated for centuries during the medieval era, and also why the dynamics that underlay those protections ceased to function, were suppressed and de-activated in a backlash that continues and has worsened in our day. We must explore the operating assumptions and tactics of agunah-advocacy organizations because, if these aimed at ending, rather than managing, iggun and freeing all agunot, that should long ago have occurred. These are the aims of this book, focusing on the United States and Israel, where 85 percent of the world's Jews live, while also citing cases in other countries, since the same system operates in rabbinic courts everywhere.

I am the daughter of an agunah but I am also a social and cultural historian of the Jews, with a particular interest in the history of Jewish women. When I began my research, I was shocked to find that there were no institutional histories of Jewish marital captivity or of women held as marital captives. Even encyclopedia entries were lacking. Although they have entries on "Divorce" and "Family," focusing on legalities, and on "Family" and "Marriage," respectively, the *Encyclopaedia Judaica* and the *YIVO Encyclopedia of Jews in Eastern Europe* have no entries on iggun or agunot. Neither does the encyclopedic compendium *Jewish Women in America*, nor did the first edition of *Jewish Women: A Comprehensive Historical Encyclopedia*, have such entries. An article on "Agunot," which I authored, is in the revised edition of the latter work.[4] Volumes on the Jewish family, such as *The Jewish Family: Myths and Reality*, edited by Steven M. Cohen and Paula E. Hyman, and *The Jewish Family*, edited by David Kraemer, have no chapters on this subject.[5]

As was the case in the 1980s, when I was just starting my teaching career and developed and taught a course on "The History of Jewish Women" at the Reconstructionist Rabbinical College, the first time, to my knowledge, that such a course was taught in a rabbinic school, and was reduced to combing the indexes of books for references to "women," I now sought references to agunot or iggun. Some works, such as Jonathan Sarna's *American Judaism*, have passing references; the English translation of Margalit Shilo's *Princess or Prisoner?* contains no mention of the terms, though the Hebrew original does.[6] Other works where one would expect such mention, such as Hasia R. Diner and Beryl Lieff Benderly's *Her Works Praise Her: A History of Jewish Women in America from Colonial Times to the Present*, contain none.[7] When I sought scholarship about agunot in Sephardi and Middle Eastern Jewries, Aron Rodrigue, the foremost historian of Sephardi Jewry during the Ottoman era, wrote me that, "As far as I know this is not a topic that had been studied when it comes to Middle Eastern Jewries."[8]

Much critically important material for the medieval era appears in the Hebrew original and English translation of Avraham Grossman, *Pious and Rebellious: Jewish Women in Medieval Europe*, and, for Ashkenaz, in Simha Goldin, *Jewish Women in Europe in the Middle Ages*.[9] I use both these works extensively, as well as Elisheva Baumgarten's *Practicing Piety in Medieval Ashkenaz*,[10] in order to construct the history of significant reforms in Jewish marriage and divorce practices that benefited women and the eventual rabbinic backlash against them, the latter of which set regressive precedents enacted in rabbinic courts to this day. Scholars of the medieval documents in the Cairo Geniza—S. D. Goitein, Mark R. Cohen, Eve Krakowski—reference abandoned wives and the prevalence of this problem in Geniza society. The word "agunah" is not used in Geniza sources, but the term *armalat al-hayat*—"widows of living husbands"—appears abundantly. Those references were invaluable for conveying specifics of cases, including names and details of the lived realities of these women, as well as information about efforts to mitigate women's vulnerability in marriage and divorce. I extracted significant information about agunot in the Land of Israel (as contemporaneous sources referred to it), Syria, Egypt, and other Middle Eastern communities in the sixteenth century from the works of Ruth Lamdan and Minna Rozen.[11] Regarding Italy I drew from Howard Adelman's studies, in particular *Women and Jewish Marriage Negotiations in Early Modern Italy*.[12]

A major contribution to the history of agunot, indeed, the first such history, is Noa Shashar's *Vanished Men: Agunot in the Ashkenazi Realm, 1648–1850*.[13] Haim Sperber's data-filled *The Plight of Jewish Deserted Wives, 1851–1900: A Social History of East European Agunah* and related articles contributed by delineating specifics to gauge the dimensions of iggun in the period and area he studies.[14]

I use primary sources—rabbinic material, communal records, memoirs, diaries, letters, newspapers, and entries in various media—but, given the scope of what I set out to do in the historical section of the book, it relies heavily on secondary scholarship. I much hope that what I have done will spur others to probe primary sources in all geographic and cultural realms and periods of Jewish life so that this huge and virtually unexplored chapter in the history of Jewish societies and in the history of Jewish women will receive the cross-cultural, cross-geographical, and cross-era study it warrants.

The sources about agunot in the past are largely rabbinic. To some extent in this book, this means normative (prescriptive) pronouncements in law codes and commentaries (Mishna; Talmud). More important are rabbinic ordinances (takkanot), which amended or overrode prior rulings in response to changed circumstances, and subsequent rabbinic (re)interpretation and application of those ordinances. Similarly, important are rabbinic responsa (*teshuvot*) addressing theoretical or actual situations posed in questions (*she'elot*) to rabbinic authorities. These provide details of cases and show sometimes clear social and political motivations in the rulings of halakhic decisors (*poskim*). More important still are records of the actual outcomes of agunah cases brought to rabbinic courts or otherwise notated in rabbinic and communal records and cases reported in journals, the press, and other media. The problems with using rabbinic sources for historical reconstruction are well-known. I address them, noting what we can and cannot learn from them in the cases I examine and in the larger conclusions I draw. It should be clear that my interest in and use of rabbinic sources is historical, or when I address the contemporary situation, is geared to an assessment of policy and is not legal/halakhic per se. I seek to illuminate the historical circumstances that underlay change in women's actual rights in marriage and divorce: why such change—whether reforms that benefited women or backlash against women's rights—happened how and when they did. In particular, I seek to highlight the behavior of Jewish women in the face of severe liability in marriage and divorce and the impact of their actions on rabbinic and larger Jewish practice.

This book is dedicated to tracing the origins and workings over time of Jewish marital captivity and the reasons that Jewish women continue to be victimized by it, because this knowledge, and its application, are essential to ending the abuse.

Introduction

Until very recently, agunot, Jewish women unable to get a rabbinic divorce (get), and iggun, the marital captivity that results, have been treated all but exclusively as problems in rabbinic law (halakha). Agunot (sing., agunah) have not been seen as a class of Jewish women with a history, nor has iggun been addressed as a social institution and pathology, like slavery, with a history.[1] When "the agunah problem" has been addressed, this has been largely by rabbis, writing apologetically of the "problem" as a "tragedy," which, in an oft-employed usage, rabbis have "left no stone unturned" to address "compassionately."[2] That desire for "compassion" is stymied, however, apologists explain, by the limits of the rabbinic law they practice; one such hugely influential apologist, Rabbi Joseph B. Soloveitchik, even makes an elaborate case for privileging halakha over acting "compassionately" toward agunot. Indeed, not coincidentally, I will argue, he makes severity in ruling on agunot the proof case for his overarching argument for halakha as a "metahistorical" entity, impervious to human, much less women's, considerations.

Halakha makes divorce—that is, control of women's marital status and freedom—the unilateral act and prerogative of husbands. It stipulates that the husband's giving a get must be by his free will and specifies elaborate technical requirements about all this that only men (rabbis) adjudicate. Among other things, these stipulations mandate stringent requirements for the identification of dead husbands who, in the past, often perished on business trips or in criminal incidents or wars. If their bodies were never found, which was typical, or lacked identification meeting elaborate Talmudic criteria, their wives, lacking gittin (plural of get), became agunot, unable to remarry. There is no time limit to this state.

Since halakha does not recognize the efficacy of conversion out of Judaism and rules Jews who convert to another religion still Jews (if bad ones), women whose husbands converted were also agunot unless they managed to get valid rabbinic divorces from them—unless, that is, somehow, prominently, through paying bribes or extortive demands, they got converted men to initiate and enact get proceedings in rabbinic courts. The insistence on rabbinic divorces from such men persisted even during the era of the Inquisition, which targeted, precisely, suspected "Judaizing" converts and in the absence of openly functioning rabbinic courts in Iberia. Wives who fled Iberia to remain openly practicing Jews remained chained in marriage to converted men. A widow from a childless marriage was, and in communities that enact rabbinic law, still is, held in marital reserve (*yibbum*) to any and all brothers (*levirs*) of the deceased husband, required to marry the levir unless he releases her through the ritual of *halitsa*. If such women are unable to locate levirs, obtain halitsa from them, or meet extortive demands for release, they too become agunot—widows chained in marriage to men all acknowledge are dead.

Noa Shashar's *Vanished Men*, which studies iggun and agunot in Ashkenazi communities from 1648 to 1850, first historicized the discourse about Jewish marital captivity. Shashar also quashed any claim that rabbis in the huge region and era she studied ruled leniently in cases of agunot, as the Talmud twice enjoins they should (BT Gittin 3a; Yevamot 85a). She, scholars of medieval Geniza (Middle Eastern and North African) Jewries, and scholars of other Jewish communities establish that, in Geniza terminology, becoming "the widow of a living man" meant poverty, social limbo and ostracism, loneliness, and vulnerability to further abuse, including employment discrimination. Falling into marital captivity was catastrophic for women, a vulnerability shared by all women who marry under *kinyan* and kiddushin, the legal rituals of rabbinic marriage, in the past and now.

This book is the first attempt to offer a comprehensive history of iggun and agunot across the chronological and geographic sweep of Jewish history.[3] It spans from seventh-century-CE Iraq to the present and treats communities in the Middle East, North Africa, Franco-Germany (Ashkenaz), Iberia (Sepharad), Italy, the Mediterranean, Europe east and west, Israel, and the United States. It is meant to firmly historicize this subject by applying to it the fundamentals of historiographical methodology: chronology, and assessment of causality, agency, continuity, and change. In this book, I show significant similarities and continuities—anywhere

Jews lived, there was marital captivity and chained wives—as well as changes over time and place. Several historians have studied some of these specifics, including significant reforms in rabbinic marriage and divorce law that emerged in the medieval era, but did not focus on women's marital captivity or on agunot per se. Drawing on the work and integrating the findings of these scholars, I date a decisive turning point for the worsening of the actualized rights of Jewish women in marriage and divorce in rulings of leading, late medieval, rabbinic authorities. These ranking legal decisors (*poskim*; sing., *posek*) nullified previous rulings and long-established practices that had offered important protections to women, substituting precedents that suppressed women's ability to protect their most fundamental bodily, financial, and psychological interests in marriage and divorce. Those precedents, originating in a concerted and explicit rabbinic backlash against women and the power of women, continue to be applied in rabbinic courts to this day. Long usage has shrouded the patriarchal anxiety and misogynistic impulse behind these precedents, cloaking them in the authority of antiquity and seemingly impervious law. Such shrouding and imputed imperviousness serve ongoing abuse. The historian's task is to reveal the circumstances and impulses behind law and social institutions.

We have become inured to Jewish marital captivity, opposing positions converging in its acceptance. Some, compliant with halakha, see iggun as tragic but inevitable; others, not thus compliant, think themselves immune to it, the problem not their concern. Both these positions, conscious or not, see iggun as someone else's problem: because it only victimizes women; or only the halakhically observant; or only Israeli Jews, who have no alternative to rabbinic courts for divorce. The fact that there has never been a lived reality without women's marital captivity contributes immeasurably to it continuing. Retrospect on such a reality "conveys a sense of inevitability,"[4] but there is nothing either inevitable or irresolvable about Jewish marital captivity.

This book draws agunot out of the abstraction of rabbinic legal discourse and shows them as living Jews, whenever possible, with names, dates, places, and other life details, as they sought to prevent themselves falling into iggun or the requirement of levirate marriage and, when in those states, acting when they could not obtain a get or halitsa. I situate this behavior in the larger context of an entirely normal pattern of economically vital, assertive, traditional women, whose economic activities were critical not just to their natal and marital families but to their communities. In Ashkenaz, women's activities were also critical to the very existence of Jewish communities under Christian rule, where the privilege of settlement was conditional upon Jews providing rulers economic and financial benefit. Both women and their communities, I argue, particularly in medieval Ashkenaz, understood that importance and embraced it as a communal good, a necessity so self-evidently critical to the welfare of the community that it overrode Talmudic injunctions defining (literally—limiting) women's rights and space. I show that women knowingly leveraged their economic importance to force protections for themselves in marriage and divorce, translating economic power into political power. I call the latter behavior "politically engaged economics." Aside from being part of Jewish women's history, this record should also be recognized as a chapter in Jewish political, economic, and communal history.

Jewish women acted within and outside the boundaries of normative behavior—that is, prescribed rabbinic law—to protect their interests in marriage and divorce. These efforts included robust recourse to non-Jewish courts, both Muslim (sharia and those of the state), and (nonecclesiastical) Christian courts. Jewish women treated action to protect and advance their rights in marriage and divorce as self-evident behavior, no different from actions they took to advance any of their other economic interests—marriage and divorce, of course, being preeminent economic institutions. They did not hesitate to apply pressure, including going outside the Jewish community for rulings that would override or better the outcomes of their cases in rabbinic courts (*batei din*), behavior that defied Talmudic and repeated later rabbinic injunctions against taking intra-Jewish disputes to Gentile courts. Such actions involved bringing Gentile pressure on the legally recognized community (kehilla), which was the Jews' official representative to the non-Jewish authorities and supremely sensitive to the messages of the latter. Their communities not only tolerated these actions but integrated their outcomes into normative, rabbinic pronouncements and communal practice. Recent scholarship has shown that recourse to Gentile courts was common premodern Jewish behavior, including by prominent rabbis. The repetition of injunctions forbidding this behavior itself testifies to broad noncompliance, not confined to women. But women in both Christian and Muslim realms, systematically disadvantaged in rabbinic law and clearly understanding that they were thus disadvantaged, made disproportionate use of non-Jewish courts in divorce cases. Women's recourse to Gentile courts in divorce cases was widespread for centuries across Jewish ethnic boundaries—in Ashkenaz, Sepharad, Italian, Mediterranean, Middle Eastern, and North African communities—and efficacious, achieving outcomes in individual cases and becoming part of living Jewish practice.

In investigating this dynamic, I make a distinction between rabbinic law and Jewish law. The latter encompasses the former but also takes into account what I call a loop mechanism by which premodern Jewish behavior, in this case, that of women, stretching and violating normative pronouncements, looped back and became normative—reflected in rabbinic and communal rulings. I maintain that women pressing their rights in marriage and divorce played a significant role in this dynamic.

The women who acted in these ways were entirely "traditional," living in premodern communities: there was nothing else. It is, therefore, impossible to attribute their actions to (some would say, blame) modernity, "the Reform movement" ("*reformim*" or "*reformiot*," as the contemporary Hebrew parlance of Israeli Orthodox demonizers puts it), or feminists, a term used by some in similarly demonizing language. Active, assertive, aggressive, and transgressive behavior by women on behalf of their rights in marriage, divorce, and related property disputes was not only normal, using that term in its sociological sense, but entirely traditional. In contrast to Avraham Grossman, who in his book *Pious and Rebellious* distinguishes between "pious" and "rebellious" women, I contend that they were one and the same. Premodern, traditional Jewish women saw themselves as entitled constituents of the Jewish legal system and expected and demanded that Jewish law encompass and serve their interests. When it didn't, it was self-evident to them to press their claims on the system with all means at their disposal. In so doing, they were simultaneously "rebellious" and pious. Truly "rebellious" behavior would have been conversion—desertion of Jewish religious belief and practice and betrayal of an oft-beleaguered community, recourse some agunot indeed took in response to their situation. We know of no women converts who also instigated against the Jews and Judaism from their new privilege within the majority religion, while it is well-known that a class of male converts did this, to their benefit: true rebellion and revenge were available options.[5] For women to stay within and demand that the Jewish system serve their needs was an act of fealty and piety.

Numerous scholars have established that women in medieval Ashkenaz were disproportionately among the martyred and self-martyred during violent anti-Jewish persecutions. Women and their religious fealty and martyrdom factor so heavily in valorizing accounts of Ashkenazi behavior during the Crusades that Jewish martyrdom in such situations seems to have been heavily gendered female.[6] Yet I have not encountered a single instance, cited in any source (all written by men), in which a woman, much less, women, were said to have validated, much less valorized, their own or other women's martyrdom on the altar of rabbinic marital and divorce law, or accepted a pious, martyred plight as agunot. Even the male authors of hagiographical martyrologies did not think to attribute such behavior to actual women. Effectively, there was a Jewish women's worldview of entitlement to having their interests served by Jewish law, which Jewish women enacted in assertive behavior. Both the worldview and its resulting behaviors were entirely traditional. Any demand that women today in halakhic communities, or in Israel, where Jewish citizens can get divorced only through rabbinic courts, accept compliant martyrdom as agunot not only lacks any precedent but utterly contradicts Jewish tradition and history.

The mechanisms by which women knew of their disabilities in marriage and divorce under rabbinic law and acted on their own behalf are largely unexplored subjects in Jewish history. Probing the history of agunot offers insights and suggests directions for that inquiry. Of course, these disabilities were common, lived knowledge within families and communities, and women in the families of the rabbinic and mercantile elites surely knew more than the lived basics. Since S. D. Goitein's pioneering scholarship on the Cairo Geniza, we have known that male kin in medieval Geniza society negotiated detailed prenuptial agreements meant to protect daughters, sisters, and other female dependents from marital abuse, including forms of harassment and excessive control by husbands and having to endure a husband marrying additional wives. Such agreements always established financial arrangements in case of divorce. The work of subsequent Geniza scholars Mark Cohen and Eve

Krakowski has refined our understanding of this male behavior by highlighting the class and social standing of such men and the reciprocal, all-male networks operating in rabbinic and Islamicate courts on which it was based. Such behavior by male guardians, forged in discussions overheard by or including women, taught girls and women realities of rabbinic marriage and divorce law and about protective expedients.

Research on women in sixteenth-century Ottoman Palestine and elsewhere shows that such patterns continued well past the medieval era. Several remarkable cases from Safed, one involving daring action by the daughter-in-law of Rabbi Joseph Karo to avoid a levirate marriage, document it. Women clearly both conspired to help other women in evading pitfalls in rabbinic marriage practice and extended actual such help, having been educated about the needed specifics by men.

If for no other reasons, men acted to protect female kin in marriage and divorce in order to protect their own financial interests, since abandoned and divorced women returned to their natal, male-led families as dependents. Levirs and their families had significant financial interests in the levir marrying his brother's widow. Doing so meant him and his family retaining the deceased's assets, rather than these going to the widow (and to an unrelated, new husband) via her widow's settlement. The opposing interests of the widow and her family were equally compelling and spurred creative and assertive actions on their behalf. Concerns about abandoned women and children becoming burdens on the male-administered communal purse led to the enactment in medieval Ashkenazic and Middle Eastern communities of such reforms as conditional divorce required of men before they undertook long journeys, or enactments barring foreign men from marrying local women without proof or sacred oath that they were not already married. In both the familial and the larger, communal cases, such actions served male interests but benefited women. Indeed, there was probably no better possible scenario for women—then and now—than that the benefit of the collective, both familial and communal, be perceived as tied to the welfare of women. There is much evidence that this, in fact, was a widespread premodern Jewish understanding, made operative in protective expedients that were enforced.

When women's male kin and the male-led community enacted protections for women in marriage and divorce in order to protect their own financial interests, they were acting on patriarchal imperatives. Such behavior complicates our understanding of Jewish patriarchy. Men, full citizens in oligarchic, patriarchal, premodern Jewish societies, acted to protect themselves from certain patriarchal norms—divorced women becoming wards of their natal homes—when such disability threatened them, the men. Marital disability, after all, was the rightful lot of women, denizens of the patriarchal system. Other than this self-protection, men acted to enjoy male privilege in marriage and divorce—the right to grant or withhold a divorce or halitsa, and make demands for its delivery—as well as advantage in rabbinic property and inheritance law. In effect, men opted in and against patriarchal privilege as their interests dictated. Women had no such latitude and could only elaborate and deploy clever navigations and manipulations to extract whatever protections were extractable for denizens, working through the agency of men and male institutions. Such actions by women are a major focus of this book. Clearly, however, Jewish patriarchy operated in complicated ways and sometimes worked to protect women. Such interventions were "teaching moments" for women about their disabilities in the system and methods to mitigate them. Study of the history of agunot opens this additional line of inquiry in the history of Jewish societies.

There is evidence that women, particularly those in families of the rabbinic and/or mercantile elites (which often intermarried), communicated about protective expedients to one another. Clear indication of such communication is rabbinic denunciation of it and threats of dire punishment to women giving such assistance to other women. Other indications, however, are seen in rabbinic recommendations for leniency in rulings on cases of transgressive agunot, as happened in the case of one sixteenth-century woman from Safed who married without rabbinic dispensation after her husband (in a group of other Jewish men) was lost at sea. Rabbis feared that her behavior—in necessary collusion with her marital partner, male witnesses, and a marriage officiant—would set off a wave of transgressive behavior among the other agunot from the incident. Rather than maintain the standard ruling in cases when no bodies were recovered or identified to Talmudic specifications—that the women were agunot—some decisors argued for declaring the other agunot to be widows free to remarry, before they and male accomplices acted on their own. These cases show that, as we would expect, news of transgressive behavior was communicated. They also illustrate the dynamic relationship, the loop mechanism, between premodern Jewish behavior and rabbinic ruling.

Given the geographic realities of Jewish life, women's communication within the family about expedients to help evade disability in marriage and divorce could mean communication across very far-flung locations and subethnic lines—between Sephardi, Ashkenazi, Mediterranean, and Romaniot (Byzantine) communities. Rabbinic denunciations served then as now to convey information about transgressive behavior. Women themselves, however, lacked systematic means to relay the fruits of their own experience or those of other women—methods of communication that the rabbinic elite enjoyed even before the invention of printing. This meant that generation after generation of Jewish women lacked knowledge of the experience of other women and had to reinvent the wheel in efforts to protect themselves in marriage and divorce, perhaps with the benefit of advice from an experienced local female relative. The evidence, awaiting further research, suggests that women reinvented this wheel continuously and also communicated such information to one another as they could. After a certain point, or points—this too awaits time-and-place-specific research—such efforts became increasingly less efficacious. Gradually, the rights of Jewish women in marriage and divorce underwent significant and ruinous decline, as Shashar documents for the period and region she studies and which, I contend, the contemporary record in the United States and Israel depicts.

A focus on agunot yields other insights into Jewish history as a whole. One such insight illuminates gendered conceptions of "the people," its needs, and means to meet them, expressed by rabbinic authorities processing group trauma after the persecutions, mass conversions, expulsion, and flight of Iberian Jews in the fifteenth and sixteenth centuries. A new, large subclass of agunot was created in that era. In a reversal of the typical Jewish pattern of men moving and leaving women behind, these women fled Iberia for Jewish communities in Ottoman lands in order to avoid forced conversion and remain openly practicing Jews, while converted husbands and levirs stayed behind. If they had managed to obtain gittin from converted husbands, would the validity of those divorces be recognized in their new communities and they be allowed to remarry? And if they had fled without receiving a get, or were widows from childless marriages and their levirs were converts back in Iberia, would they be agunot without hope of release? Rabbinic rulings in such cases privileged the presumed sensibilities of converted men in Iberia and the rabbis' hope for their return to the Jewish fold in Ottoman lands over those of loyal Jews who actually fled to those lands. There would be no leniency in releasing agunot from marriage to converted husbands, or, when the men were levirs, from their obligation to it because, in the minds of these rabbis, the ties of marriage—bonds that kept pious Jewish women in marital captivity—were those that bound these converted men to "the people"— a construct gendered male. Agunot bound to converts in Iberia would be the adhesive for a shattered society, binding converted men to it.

Such thinking was inconceivable without presumption of agunot as a normal, available fixture in Jewish society. Indeed, it was predicated on a perception of agunot not as "Jews," as were men—converted men, at that—but merely as agunot. Agunot were not a "tragedy," to be treated with "compassion." They were an always-available resource in the service of "group" needs, gendered male.

Such new insights about Jewish society and its leaders, about unconscious working paradigms of group identity and the hierarchized status of men and women within the group, brought out of relief to full expression in a traumatized time, emerge from a focus on the experience of agunot.

This book traces the entry of iggun and "the agunah problem" into public awareness as a Jewish communal and intercommunal, global concern in late nineteenth- and early twentieth-century Western, Central, and Eastern Europe, Britain, and the United States. This awareness was aroused through the work of two new institutions in Jewish society in an era of unprecedented Jewish migration and an upsurge in women made agunot by the desertion of husbands: women's organizations and the Jewish press. Jewish public awareness across geographic and cultural lines was also ignited when a traditional Jewry, that of Algeria, came under French rule and law after the country's annexation in 1834. France had instituted civil divorce and Algerian Jewish men began to divorce civilly without giving wives gittin, or widowed sisters-in-law in childless marriages, halitsa. Such women appealed to French authorities, who pressed the issue with the state-controlled, modernized, but still Orthodox French rabbinate. The latter made remarkable excuses to explain its inaction about levirate marriage, which left such widows agunot for lack of halitsa but did suggest preemptive reforms regarding divorce, including conditional marriage. Prominent rabbinic authorities in Eastern Europe fiercely opposed these proposals, threatening French Jewry with herem—ostracism, including prohibition of marriage with them at a time of substantial Eastern Jewish immigration to France—if the proposals were implemented. All this was reported in the French Jewish and other media, which gave the "agunah problem" potentially threatening political implications for newly emancipated French Jews, unsure, despite legal equality, of their acceptance in French society.

It would be a mistake to consider this episode a confrontation between tradition and modernity since the Jews who sought relief from marital victimization were traditional women, seeking it because they abided by halakhic norms, and the men denying that relief were acting on these same norms. Rather, the relevant distinction between the parties in this case, as in iggun altogether, is that of gender. The tradition-bound agunot of nineteenth-century Algeria were behaving as had their medieval forebears in appealing to non-Jewish authorities to try to compel relief inside the Jewish world. The nature of those authorities, however, now servants of a militantly secular state that had abolished Jewish autonomy and insisted on rabbinic subservience to the state, had changed radically. The women's attempt foundered on the shoals of modern Jewish politics about halakha, in particular about the halakhic status of women, a politics articulated and conducted entirely by men, at whatever location on the religious spectrum, about women and their rights.

I address the proposals made then, over a century ago in France, Germany, and Poland, to mitigate the "agunah problem" through halakhic measures and the refusal of rabbis to implement any of them. The same proposals and the cited reasons for rejecting them have been repeated regularly since then by advocates largely bereft of knowledge of their long precedent and failure. Lack of public awareness of this history enables the perpetuation of iggun, with new generations of would-be activists and defenders of the status quo reinventing worn proposals and rejections in an exercise of utter futility.

But the dance of proposal and rejection of means even to mitigate iggun through preventive measures serves other purposes. Such proposals and their rejection since the Algerian episode have served as a means for internal Jewish religio-political demarcation and branding: the drawing of boundary lines between modernizing and stridently traditionalist rabbis in Europe, and between new Jewish denominations—Conservative and Orthodox—in the United States in the early and mid-twentieth century. That use has only expanded since and is not confined to interdenominational struggles. "The agunah problem" has also been extremely useful, and utilized, in intra-Orthodox wrangling over legitimacy and supremacy. Its usefulness as a wedge issue is seen in boundary drawing between competing groups, such as ultra-Orthodox (haredi) rabbinic groups and the modern Orthodox, Zionist rabbinic organization Tzohar in Israel regarding halakhic prenuptial agreements. In the United States, its usefulness was evident in the struggle between Orthodox Rabbi Moshe Morgenstern, who in the 1990s operated a rabbinic court that freed agunot on a wide halakhic basis, and a long list of rabbis in the United States and elsewhere who repudiated, denounced, and anathematized him for this. Morgenstern's fate was shared by Rabbi Emanuel Rackman, a major figure in modern Orthodoxy in the United States and Israel, for operating a similar court. All those who take significant action about the "agunah problem"—in Israel, currently, Professor Rabbi Daniel Sperber—are denounced as lacking authority to act, their actions dismissed as without halakhic validity, while those opposing them claim superior authority for themselves and their rejection. Real, living women are marginal in these power and authority struggles. As a halakhic issue, a "problem," however, agunot represent a precious opportunity for posturing about "true" as opposed to "false" halakhic rulings and authorities. Perpetuation of iggun, not ending it, serves vital interests. The problem, I contend, is not halakhic but political.

Premodern Jews in Christian and Islamic realms lived in corporate, self-governing communities (kehillot) whose internal legal system was rabbinic law, halakha. A defining characteristic of Jewish modernity is the demise of this communal structure and with it, the authority of halakha as a mandated legal system. From a mandatory (though never hermetic) legal system of the Jewish minority, halakha became a system of voluntary compliance with supposedly heteronomous Divine Will and Command, the contradictions of which stance are the subject of much scholarly writing. This sea change made rabbinic marital law irrelevant for many, eventually for most Jews and continued adherence to it voluntary by those born into or choosing any version of halakhically observant life—meaning all versions of Orthodoxy and observant Conservative/Masorti Judaism. In the state of Israel, however, which lacks civil marriage or divorce, all "personal status" matters are handled by the respective religious authorities of citizens, Jewish, Muslim, Christian, and Druze, regardless of an individual's religious orientation. Jewish women in Israel can be divorced legally only in rabbinic courts, officially those of the state-recognized Chief Rabbinate, staffed by ultra-Orthodox rabbis, or in technically illicit but de facto recognized, independent ultra-Orthodox rabbinic ones.

While there is a fundamental difference between the legal systems and status of religion in the United States and Israel, I argue that iggun is a Jewish, not an Orthodox or an Israeli—a sectoral or geographically defined—problem.[7] This is so because people move, physically as well as ideologically-religiously, and can and do find themselves or their children ensnared in systems they did not envisage having control over their or their children's marital freedom. Beyond that practical issue, I maintain that it is ethically untenable that Jews living outside the parameters of rabbinic law would assume a triumphalist stance or behave indifferently to those within it, whether they are there by birth, choice, or Israeli law, who find themselves in marital captivity. Jews engage prominently on behalf of social justice causes within and outside Jewish boundaries under the banner of *tikkun olam*—"repairing the world"—which is a driving force for many in their Jewish identity. Such a commitment applies in this case, too. It is equally untenable to express an expectation that Jews born into and/or choosing to live a life bound by halakha should "just" walk away from such lives because they are marital captives. This holds, too, for those, including large segments of Israeli society, whom I call "tradition-friendly," who are not Orthodox or consistently observant of religious law but have traditional understandings about "authentic," that is, efficacious marital and divorce rites and fear stigmatization for their violation. Liberal Jews defend the right to individual conscience as a basic human right, to which halakhically observant and tradition-friendly Jews are also entitled. Victims of abuse should not be blamed for being abused or told to give up being who they are because of abuse. In Israel, moreover, there is no legally recognized alternative to rabbinic divorce, though there are workarounds, which I discuss.

This book distinguishes between "managing" iggun and ending it. Agunah-advocacy organizations, all of which work under Orthodox rabbinic auspices of some kind, do the former. To manage iggun is to perpetuate it, to accept it as an inevitable and necessary, if unfortunate, "tragedy" that can, at best, be limited. That position must be rejected.

Iggun originates in the manner in which rabbinic marriage is enacted: via the groom's "acquisition" (kinyan) and "sanctification" (kiddushin) of his exclusive access to his wife's sexuality and reproductivity, all done in unilateral, nonreciprocal actions by the new husband. This being the case, divorce is also unilateral, enacted by the husband. This is the origin of iggun.

Every woman married in this way is an agunah-in-waiting, betting on luck. But aside from creating the possibility for iggun, marriage enacted in this manner sexually objectifies and commodifies women and should be terminated on that ground alone. To retain this manner of marriage enactment, as all agunah-advocacy organizations do, and propose the illusory, deceptive "solution" of prenuptial agreements is to participate in and enable the perpetuation of iggun. There are many versions of prenuptial agreements. Some are worse than none. None are guarantees. All that accompany marriage enacted by kinyan and kiddushin are part of the problem. They are an expedient akin to having an antidote on hand after taking poison and hoping it works.

This book argues that bad husbands and bad rabbis are by-products, not causes, of Jewish marital captivity. Rather than focus on late-stage manifestations of marital abuse—get refusal, get extortion, and (sometimes) on rabbinic collusion with such extortion—as do agunah-advocacy organizations, this book focuses on the origin of iggun in the manner in which rabbinic marriage is enacted. Any approach other than one that addresses the root cause of marital captivity will necessarily result in measures, such as prenuptial agreements, that manage, and thus perpetuate, rather than end the abuse.

There are alternatives, which involve adapting other rabbinic legal constructs to enact marriage on the basis of equal status, rights, and obligations of both members of the couple. Such rituals eschew any notion of "acquisition," entitlement, power, or control in the enactment of marriage or its dissolution. I discuss two such alternatives, one proposed by Rabbi Rachel Adler, the other by Dr. Tzemah Yoreh, as well as legal workarounds in Israel to avoid the traditional rabbinic wedding ritual and prevent future ensnarement in rabbinic divorce courts.

Vital political interests operate to perpetuate iggun. There are also substantial financial benefits to rabbinic courts in adjudicating gittin and in perpetuating marital captivity as an ongoing "problem." The precise dimensions of such benefits are unknowable since no rabbinic court, including the state–authorized and funded ones in Israel, makes its records available—in Israel not even to the country's parliament, the Knesset. The benefits, however, are clearly substantial, given court fees for hearings that routinely extend over months, years, and even decades. There are also allied financial benefits, as in court-mandated *shalom bayit*, reconciliation sessions in facilities associated with the courts that charge their own fees, and to which couples are routinely sent as a condition of the court handling the divorce request—when Jewish citizens have no option but rabbinic courts for divorce. The purpose of such counseling is not to determine, in the neutral manner of professional services, the best interest of the parties but to maintain the marriage, whose burden, in the conception of rabbinic courts and counseling facilities, is the wife's. Rabbinic courts mandate reconciliation sessions even when wives have experienced physical and/or emotional violence by the husbands and there are police and criminal proceedings against them, including for sexual abuse of the couple's children. Sessions are mandated when the women seeking divorce have been separated from their husbands for years and when husbands have been convicted and jailed for violence against them.[8] It is a known tactic by abusive, violent husbands to claim that they wish to maintain the marriage and seek counseling to this end. They thus reabuse the wives by forcing them into proximity with them in futile processes, while inflicting irremediable harm through lost life-time and added costs, all enabled by rabbinic-court mandate. All this abuse within the divorce system itself increases pressure on wives to accept extortive get deals, written and enforced by the courts. An ongoing, reliable flow of agunah cases, not the termination of iggun, serve the interests of this entire system.

But there is yet another, massive benefit to rabbinic nonresolution of iggun. As noted, since the advent of modernity, compliance with almost all areas of halakha for the vast majority of Jews, including those living in Israel, is voluntary. The one area of rabbinic jurisprudence that retains its premodern authority, in the Diaspora as much as in Israel, is divorce law—that is, rabbinic control of women's marital freedom. There is no rational expectation that any rabbinic authority will cede this one, last corner of premodern power and authority, which also just happens to coincide with essential patriarchal claims about women.

Rabbinic courts not only fail systematically to be avenues to end marriages in cases when husbands refuse gittin but have sought to reinstate, and at times have succeeded in reinstating back into iggun, women who, after massive effort, succeeded in escaping chained marriages. Rabbinic courts routinely refuse to publicize their grounds (*nimukim*) in the rare instances where they release a woman from a chained marriage because they do not wish such exceptions to become precedents applied to free women more generally. An example is what became known as the case of the "agunah of Safed" in Israel. A young woman's husband was in a persistent vegetative state after a motorcycle accident. After years of proceedings in which the woman sought release from the marriage, a local Chief Rabbinate court in Safed finally annulled it. Only months after that ruling came under withering criticism from other rabbinic authorities and action to overrule it did the Safed court release the halakhic basis (*nimukim*) of its ruling. The agunah in this case was forced to endure a further ordeal, ultimately terminated by Israel's Supreme Court, when the Chief Rabbinate's superior court, in Jerusalem, sought to invalidate the annulment of its own lower court and return the woman to permanent iggun (the Israeli Supreme Court is loath to engage cases of religion and state and acted in this case solely on a technicality).[9] While her ordeals finally ended in her release from marriage to a brain-dead man, this woman lost many years of the prime of her life to this wrangling and suffered inestimable anguish as well as financial costs on its account. Her circumstances may have been particular, but her vulnerability to this abuse was anything but. Had the effort of the Chief Rabbinate succeeded, moreover, no divorce would ever be final. The very term "divorce" would have been emptied of meaning—and an endless stream of cases would have been sent to rabbinic courts.

There was similar behavior regarding agunot freed by the aforementioned Morgenstern and Rackman courts in the United States, which used established halakhic methods, broadly applied, to free agunot. Multiple rabbinic authorities opposed to such use declared any divorces issued by these courts invalid and the women thus freed, still married and hence still agunot—reinstated to iggun. Any new relationship the women would enter, they labeled adulterous; any children born to them in such relationships they would stigmatize as *mamzerot/im*—a term mistranslated as "bastards" but with specific meaning and serious consequences in halakha and in Israeli law.

There have been two book-length critiques of rabbinic, communal, and state policy about iggun and agunot, focusing on the United States and Israel, respectively: Susan Aranoff and Rivka Haut, editors, *The Wed-Locked Agunot: Orthodox Women Chained to Dead Marriages*, and Susan M. Weiss and Netty C. Gross-Horowitz, *Marriage and Divorce in the Jewish State: Israel's Civil War*.[10] I, too, focus on the United States and Israel and note the fundamental difference in their respective legal systems regarding rabbinic divorce. For all that difference, however, there is more in common than not when women, either legally, in Israel, or effectively, because of belief in the authority of rabbinic marriage and divorce law and/or profound socialization, and/or intimidation, lack alternatives to Orthodox rabbinic adjudication of divorce. This book, moreover, focuses not only on the legalities and administrative failures involved in the perpetuation of iggun in these countries. It treats marital captivity as a Jewish, not an Orthodox, problem (cf. the subtitle of Aranoff and Haut's book), which crosses borders between the United States, Israel, and other countries—get refusers often flee locations to escape pressures and marry polygynously—as well as religious and denominational lines.

There are complicated reasons why "tradition-friendly" women, particularly in Israel, pursue traditionally enacted rabbinic marriage despite not being otherwise halakhically observant (that they become trapped when they seek divorce is not the result of any kind of choice but of Israeli law). Any ability of such women, Diaspora or Israeli, to leave the system cannot be treated on the individual level, with the burden of difficult action and onerous consequences placed on the individual woman. Rather, real choice is possible only with systematic communal support, specifically for this problem. For iggun to end, it must move from being treated as the episodic misfortune of individual women to being addressed as a systemic problem, met by a coherent, comprehensive, cross-border, Jewish communal response.

There is no engaging the material documenting the behavior of rabbinic courts, whether independent in the United States or state-authorized in Israel, and maintaining any illusion that these function even rationally or professionally, much less fairly or justly, to adjudicate women's marital rights, and this book makes no appeal to rabbis or such courts. Such appeals are not only futile. Every act of making them reconstructs and reifies the authority of these courts despite their failure to free agunot and end iggun. My book also makes no appeal to rabbis whose actions show a courageous wish to help but who truly feel that their hands are tied by halakhic constraints. They themselves say that there is no global solution, that iggun will continue, and that agunot will continue to be created and remain captive.

Meaningful change will come only from informed consciousness and, as was true in medieval times, from the actions of women based on that consciousness—but crucially and necessarily, with active, effective, and ongoing cross-border, communal support, informed by a full history of this problem and understanding of its workings, past and present.

In focusing on the actions of women working to prevent their ensnarement in iggun or in get or halitsa extortion, and, when already in these predicaments, to extricate themselves, I move agunot from object—a halakhic "problem"—to subject. Doing that is consistent with historical purpose and methodology and with the historical record. But reclaiming the record of Jewish women's agency in matters of marriage and divorce is also necessary to forge an effective strategy to end Jewish marital captivity.

PART ONE

History

1

Origins

Foundations and Early Reforms

כִּי יִקַּח אִישׁ אִשָּׁה וּבְעָלָהּ וְהָיָה אִם לֹא
תִמְצָא חֵן בְּעֵינָיו כִּי מָצָא בָהּ עֶרְוַת דָּבָר
וְכָתַב לָהּ סֵפֶר כְּרִיתֻת וְנָתַן בְּיָדָהּ וְשִׁלְּחָהּ
מִבֵּיתוֹ
וְיָצְאָה מִבֵּיתוֹ וְהָלְכָה וְהָיְתָה לְאִישׁ אַחֵר
וּשְׂנֵאָהּ הָאִישׁ הָאַחֲרוֹן וְכָתַב לָהּ סֵפֶר
כְּרִיתֻת וְנָתַן בְּיָדָהּ וְשִׁלְּחָהּ מִבֵּיתוֹ אוֹ כִי יָמוּת
הָאִישׁ הָאַחֲרוֹן אֲשֶׁר לְקָחָהּ לוֹ לְאִשָּׁה
לֹא יוּכַל בַּעְלָהּ הָרִאשׁוֹן אֲשֶׁר שִׁלְּחָהּ
לָשׁוּב לְקַחְתָּהּ לִהְיוֹת לוֹ לְאִשָּׁה

A man takes a wife and possesses her [sexually]. She fails to
please him because he finds something [sexually] indecent
about her, and he writes her a bill of divorcement, hands
it to her, and sends her away from his house; she leaves
his household and becomes the wife of another man; then
this latter man rejects her, writes her a bill of divorcement,
hands it to her, and sends her away from his house; or the
man who married her last dies. Then the first husband who
divorced her shall not take her to wife again. . . .
—Deuteronomy 24:1–4 (*New JPS Translation*, 1985; "sexually," my insertion)

This text is a perfect example of descriptive and prescriptive statements
in the Hebrew Bible. It depicts a case and everything is descriptive until
the very end, when we get the text's one prescription, its law, and the
point of the case described: prohibition of remarriage of a divorced

couple if the woman had remarried and was divorced by or widowed from a second husband.

The rabbis would halakhize—legalize—every descriptive detail in this text, turning them into rabbinic law—halakha, and define a basic element of rabbinic marriage—the man "takes," the woman is taken; he acts, she is acted upon—as well as procedures and requirements of divorce. All that is descriptive in the biblical text is made prescriptive in rabbinic ones: there must be a written document of divorce, a get, which the husband writes (or, the rabbis would rule, which he delegates another man to write and possibly, deliver, on his behalf) and must put into the woman's hands.[1]

But this is the bare beginning of punctilious detail about every aspect of how marriage and divorce must be handled under rabbinic law. The Mishna—the first rabbinic law code (redacted ca. 200 CE)—devotes an entire tractate, Gittin (plural of get), to the subject, which the Gemara, the commentary on the Mishna (together, the two are Talmud), parses at length. The discussion continued in rabbinic commentaries, codes, and responsa (queries and rabbinic responses about cases), from that day to this, all flowing from these few biblical lines. The literature on this subject is vast and constitutes an area of halakhic specialty. The Talmud[2] (Kiddushin 6a, 13a) states that only those conversant in divorce law should adjudicate it, so complex are the particulars, down to the materials with which the get is handwritten, its wording, the exact layout of lines and letters on its page, the manner of the husband's dropping it into in the wife's hands and their precise position for its receipt, the credentials of witnesses for the procedure, and so on.[3]

Why such punctilious detail? Understanding the anxiety driving the particulars of the get is basic to understanding why the problem of agunot, "chained women," who cannot obtain freedom from rabbinically enacted marriages, exists.

As even cursory reading of the text in Deuteronomy shows, its assumptions are patriarchal. The text is androcentric, its perspective and lens wholly male. It reflects male experience and the privilege of acting and enacting, of creating and changing marital status. Women are objects. There is no indication, either in the descriptive elements or in the prescriptive upshot, of the woman having any agency. When she is married, she lives in her husband's "house." When she is divorced by him, she is "sent out" of his, not their, house. She is divorced because the husband has found something indecent in her; the Hebrew, *ervat davar*, points to sexual transgression. Men divorce women at will. We hear nothing about women divorcing husbands in whom they have found "something obnoxious."

Patriarchal marriage is inextricably bound to the desire for "legitimate" progeny, that is, progeny born of the husband's seed, to whom his inheritance is to be passed. Why should a man bestow his means on another man's child? Until very recently, with DNA testing, there was no way for a man to be sure a child was his own offspring, short of permanently locking up his wife. Anxiety about paternity underlies the entire institution of patriarchal marriage and leads to legal and physical restrictions on women's bodies and freedom of movement and to the powerful taboo of adultery—which, in rabbinic law, is an offense based on the marital status of the woman involved. The marital status of a man having extramarital sex is irrelevant. He commits "adultery" only if his partner is another man's wife: the offense is against that man and his rightful claim to sexual and reproductive exclusivity with his wife.[4] A married woman, however, who has sex with any man but her husband, whatever his marital status, is guilty of adultery and subject to severe punishment.[5] Under halakha, a child born of such a union bears the worst of stigmatized status: a "mamzer/a" (a child born of a Jew who is not another man's wife, a child born to two unmarried Jews, or to non-Jews of any marital status, is not a "mamzer/a").

Male anxiety about paternity leads to the staggering detail about divorce in halakha. It is imperative for the woman's marital status to be unambiguous because if she is not properly divorced according to halakha and marries (or just has sex with) someone other than her husband, halakha deems her an adulteress and any children born of the second union, mamzerot/im. Such offspring are permitted to marry only other mamzerot/im, or converts and their descendants, and (in theory, at least) are stigmatized for generations.

But consider: in a system that was matriarchal—emanating from and built on women's experience—the strictures just enumerated would not exist, because the anxiety that underlies them would not, indeed, does not, exist: any child that issues from a woman's body is hers. Only by grappling with this starkly gendered reality can we begin to grasp that women's marital captivity is no "tragedy" (though it is certainly that), caused by abusive husbands, or even by uncaring, corrupt, and/or incompetent rabbis. Such captivity inheres in the patriarchal foundations of halakhic marriage and divorce and is an inevitable outcome of it. Iggun is not a failure of the system but a fulfillment of it. Not the only fulfillment, of course, but certainly one, not an aberration but an inherent possibility that occurs necessarily and inevitably.

Agunot are a subclass of women whose ranks any Jewish woman who married under halakha, regardless of her economic class, social status, or lineage, her educational level or professional profile, can join in an instant.

Rabbinic Marriage and Divorce

The Deuteronomic text cited above is the biblical source of rabbinic law about enactment of rabbinic marriage and divorce. As noted, the only action it describes, reflecting already established practice in biblical antiquity—it does not prescribe, but assumes this—is that a man "takes" a woman and "possesses" her: this constitutes "marriage." "Possesses" is polite English wording for what the Hebrew says. The Hebrew says, literally, that he "masters" her via sexual intercourse. The word for this sexual act and "mastery"—ownership of a woman—the verb is never used with regard to a man except a slave—is the same, from the root b'al.[6] It is also the source of the biblical and rabbinic terms for "husband," baal, meaning "master" or "owner." Put politely, this is about "consummating" the marriage. The difference between this act and random sex is that its context and purpose are marriage. The difference between this act and rape is that the woman, or a male guardian on her behalf, or both, have given legal consent.

Since the time of the Mishna, rabbinic marriage has been enacted via kinyan, the baal's "acquisition" of the right to exclusive sexual and reproductive access to the woman, and kiddushin (also called erusin), his "sanctification" of her as his exclusive sexual and reproductive preserve. We readily see the connection between the manner in which marriage is enacted and the implications for divorce. In halakhic marriage, authority over the woman's sexuality and reproductivity passes from the woman's father or other male guardian to her husband via kinyan. She signals assent to the transaction passively by being present for it and accepting an object of minimal value from the baal (by long-established custom, this is a simple ring), but otherwise plays no legal role. The act of marriage is unilateral—he marries, she is married—a status change enacted by the husband.[7] This being the case, so is divorce.

Divorce, enacted through the giving of a get document, is the husband's exclusive prerogative under halakha to give or withhold, at his free will. If the husband is unwilling or physically or mentally unable to grant a get, or if he goes missing on a trip, in an accident, criminal incident, or war without halakhically valid witnesses to his death, which has to be established in detailed and far from self-evident ways set in the Talmud,[8] his wife's status remains "married." She is an agunah, chained, from the Hebrew word *oggen* or "anchor." There is no statute of limitations to this condition (also referred to as *aginut*) under halakha, no automatic presumption of death after a certain amount of time and no out for her if he refuses or is unable to give a get.

As noted earlier, a widow in a childless marriage is held in marital reserve to the deceased husband's brother(s) (levir; levirate marriage); the biblically stated reason for this is to continue the deceased's memory and to preserve his line of inheritance.[9] If the levir cannot or will not marry the widow and does not release her in a ritual (halitsa) to marry someone else, she, too, is an agunah—chained in marriage to a man all acknowledge to be dead.[10] A woman who received a get whose validity someone later challenges based even on a technicality—for example, a misspelled name (common in eras when there was no standardized spelling), or a calligraphic error by the rabbinic scribe, or a problem in the manner of its delivery, or a myriad of other possible grounds, including the husband changing his mind or deliberately using get renunciation as a form of abuse—she would be deemed an agunah, unfree to remarry. If a divorced woman had remarried and her get was then challenged, she would be forbidden to her second husband as well as to her first, required to obtain a get from both, and would likely remain an agunah. All the men implicated in the technical errors or in deliberate abuse of the process would suffer no consequences. These would fall entirely on the woman and, if she had children with a second husband, on them, stigmatized as mamzerot/im; she and they, enveloped in scandal and its emotional, financial, and social consequences.

Husbands regularly demand extortive payment from wives in money, property, and custody of children in return for a get; this, as well as halitsa extortion, are ancient practices. In a much-publicized case in 2019 that spanned from California to Israel, a husband refused, for what were then fourteen years, to give his wife a get unless she paid him a half million dollars and relinquished custody of their minor child to him. He claims that he is not withholding a get but offering one, which she refuses to accept. As we shall see, this tactic is widely practiced, enabled, and justified by rabbinic courts, which label women who refuse get extortion not agunot but get refusers—shifting this designation from abusive husbands onto their victims.

A halakhic ordinance in medieval Ashkenaz (Franco-Germany) allows the husband, in cases where the wife refuses to receive a get or is incapable of receiving one, to marry a second wife without divorcing the first if one hundred rabbis in different locations agree to lift the ban against polygyny (*heter meah rabbanim*) instituted sometime between the tenth to the twelfth century for Jews who followed Ashkenazi halakhic custom.[11] That is what the man in the above-mentioned case, Israel Meir Kin, did, marrying an additional wife. His first wife, Lonna Ralbag, remains a marital captive, hostage to Kin's extortion.

The nature of rabbinic marriage and all that has been described thus far is clear in the second of the blessings recited under the huppah, the marriage canopy (which symbolizes the groom's domain, which the bride is entering through the marriage ceremony). The *birkat erusin* blessing enacts halakhic betrothal, stating:

> Blessed are You, Lord our God, sovereign of the universe, who has sanctified us with your commandments and has commanded us concerning forbidden relations [*arayot*; literally "nakedness," in this context meaning nakedness outside of licit, that is, married, relations]; who has forbidden us those betrothed to us, permitting us those who are wedded to us through huppah [the wedding canopy, meaning rabbinic marriage] and kiddushin. Blessed are you, Lord, who sanctifies his people Israel through huppah and kiddushin. (my translation)

The setting for this blessing is the start of the marriage ceremony. The bride is standing right there, next to her groom. Yet the wording is all about men, not the one she is about to marry but men, plural, who represent the community of Israel. It speaks of "us": who is forbidden "us," sexually, and who is permitted "us," how, when. Men are the community, women their othered possessions, sex objects, their sexuality acquired through the proper, public rituals.[12]

As the Talmud (Shabbat 33a) puts it with bracing honesty in the name of Rabbi Hanan bar Rava, " 'Everyone knows why the bride enters the marriage canopy' ": to be acquired by her baal for licit, that is, married sex, which act confirms and establishes the marriage legally, and for a necessary public, communal (male) declaration of the change in her sexual status vis-à-vis all other men and her legitimate, exclusive possession by her baal.[13]

It has become the unfortunate custom in marriage ceremonies for the assembled to proclaim, "mekudeshet, mekudeshet!" (sanctified) to an upsurge of music, just after the new baal has effected kiddushin by putting a ring on the bride's outstretched index finger (to facilitate witnessing her acquiescence to kiddushin), and pronounced the formula: "harei at mekudeshet li betaba'at zo kedat moshe ve'yisrael": "With this ring you are hereby sanctified to me, according to the law of Moses and Israel."

About all this one can only cite the words of the Talmud itself (Ketubbot 10b), which, unlike contemporary apologetics, speaks honestly of what is transpiring. It quotes Rabi/Rebi saying to a man who came questioning the virginity of his new wife: "Go and enjoy your acquisition."[14] A moment of degradation, of sexual objectification and ownership of the woman—of women, the parallel "us" to the words of the *erusin* blessing—celebrated with music and fanfare.

Rabbi J. David Bleich, on the far-right wing of modern Orthodoxy in the United States, states quite unapologetically what halakhic marriage is and why divorce, as the sole prerogative of the baal, flows from it. In his words, halakhic marriage is "an exclusive conjugal servitude" of the bride to the groom. "Understanding that the essence of marriage lies in the conveyance of a 'property' interest by the bride to the groom serves to explain why it is that only the husband can dissolve the marriage. As the beneficiary of the [wife's] servitude, divestiture [divorce] requires the husband's voluntary surrender of the right that he has acquired," via kinyan and kiddushin.[15] To be clear: the "property interest" that Rabbi Bleich references, which is the baal's possession during the marriage, is his wife's body.

Halakhic marriage—"conjugal servitude"—is the source of women's marital captivity. To ignore the source of the problem and focus on later, necessary consequences as if they—abusive husbands and rabbis who enable them—were causes rather than consequences of the system is to guarantee that iggun continues. It is to deceive the unknowing and to lead new victims to harm. Tinkering with the problem with measures that manage rather than end it ensures its continuation.

The Ketubbah and Other Reforms

Halakhic apologetics emerged in modernity, which, according with the work of many historians, I define as the era when the autonomous, premodern community (kehilla) declined or was abolished and obedience to rabbinic law became voluntary, followed by mass decline in its observance.[16] Such apologetics quickly became a hefty genre of its own, with a major focus on arguments directed against the criticism that traditional, rabbinic Judaism is misogynistic.[17]

Apologists and scholars alike note that reforms ameliorating the status of women in halakhic marriage emerged already in early rabbinic times.[18] Foremost among these was the ketubbah (plural: ketubbot), the marriage contract. Emerging from customary law—that is, from lay practice, surely at the behest of women's kin—it had become a necessary component of rabbinic marriage by the Mishna's time; formulaic, set language for it emerged in the late Second Temple period. The ketubbah is a unilateral prenuptial agreement given by the husband to the wife.[19] It stipulates a husband's obligations to his wife during the marriage—to provide food, clothing, and household needs; and sex (requirements based on Exodus 21:9, which states the rights of concubines, with the reasoning that if these are due a concubine, they are surely due a wife).[20] Sexual intercourse is a basic expectation and requirement in rabbinic marriage, as is the wife's cooperation in producing children, behavior that, if withheld, deliberately or otherwise (infertility, blamed on the woman), constitutes grounds for divorce and withholding the ketubbah payment. But, in a striking act of reasoning, the rabbis placed the religious obligation (mitzva) of procreation (*pru urevu*) on men, not women,[21] whose cooperation is of course essential and, as noted, whose bodily functions to this end are a prime concern and claim of Jewish patriarchy.

The ketubbah seeks to address women's assumed economic dependence on a husband caused by patriarchal restrictions on women's movement and economic activities and discrimination against women in halakhic inheritance law. It recognizes the assumed negative financial consequences of divorce to wives and states an amount due the wife in case of divorce—unless she commits adultery or fails to perform domestic duties that the Mishna, Ketubbot 5:5, defines as wifely, in which cases the law prescribes forfeiture of the payment, a serious consequence in times when the ketubbah was an actionable document. The rabbis stated a standard amount for this payment for a virgin at marriage, half this for a divorcee or widow. As long as the halakhic system regulated the lives of pre- and early modern Jews and, in Middle Eastern communities, the lives of Jews well into chronological modernity, the amount of this payment and of ancillary ones, articulated in other, detailed prenuptial agreements, was negotiated by the families of the bride and groom, reflected their respective economic and social standings, and were meaningful sums.[22] The ketubbah was not, as it is now, a symbolic relic but a legally actionable and enforced document, as were other prenuptial agreements. Since the biblical text stated no limit on men's right to divorce wives, the financial stipulations of the ketubbah could operate to limit rash marriage and divorce, offering women the possibility of important protections, subject, always, to specific situations and actual enforcement.[23]

Although halakha stipulates that valid divorce is effectuated only through exercise of the husband's free will, it allows a wife to request a divorce and, under certain circumstances, theoretically and at times in practice, rabbinic courts could pressure or force a husband to grant one "willingly."[24] Formal grounds for such a request by a wife are the husband having an illness with repellent symptoms or practicing an occupation that leaves him reeking of a repellent odor—that is, if he becomes sexually repulsive to her; if he is impotent or infertile; withholds her rights under the ketubbah; abuses her physically; becomes an apostate; or seeks to move to a location she does not wish to inhabit.[25] In fact, there were other grounds on which rabbinic courts actually forced a divorce, including with the active assistance and coercive powers of Gentile authorities, when the husband was persona non grata to both Jewish and non-Jewish authorities.

A rabbinic court might or might not investigate claims by the wife seeking divorce and might or might not pressure the husband to grant one. In the latter event, the premodern Jewish community had powers of coercion that could be employed to pressure a refusing husband to give a divorce "willingly." These included corporal punishment, fines, and ostracism (herem), which, if fully applied, could make economic, religious, and social life for a recalcitrant husband untenable.[26] After apparent implementation from early medieval times through the twelfth century of rabbinic powers to force divorce at the request or demand of wives, application of such power was severely curtailed and became a great rarity.[27]

A medieval halakhic ordinance (takkanah), binding only on Jews following Ashkenazic decisors, attributed to Rabbenu Gershom Me'or Hagolah (Gershom ben Judah, 960–1028), instituted a further legal limit on a husband's prerogatives by prohibiting divorce of a woman against her will. We have already noted another ordinance attributed to him which barred polygyny, again, only for men of Ashkenazi halakhic practice (minhag).[28] Combined, these were significant reforms affording women the possibility of leverage with which to try to negotiate protections for themselves in marriage and divorce, though we caution against any assumption that they necessarily operated as written. Enforcement was always subject to rabbinic interpretation and the system was weighted in favor of established male privilege in divorce. Thus, if a husband following Ashkenazi custom (that is, bound by the ordinance prohibiting divorce against a wife's will), succeeded, through deceit, in delivering a halakhically valid get to a wife who had not consented to divorce, the divorce took effect. In non-Ashkenazi Jewries in Ottoman lands in the sixteenth century, even where clauses against divorce of a wife against her will were written into the ketubbah, when the husband wished to divorce and the wife did not, it was invariably the husband's will that prevailed, even when he could not pay the wife's ketubbah settlement.[29]

In short, the record shows a patriarchal system that established sacrosanct male privilege in divorce, originating in the manner of enacting marriage, which also introduced some potential brakes on that privilege. The question is why such reforms came into existence.

2

Why Did Reforms Happen?

Iggun and Agunot in Historical Perspective

What prompted reforms that created the possibility of protections for women in rabbinic marriage and divorce and, however unintentionally, openings for women to exercise power in those areas so critical to their lives, and to patriarchy and patriarchal privilege? How did women respond to, influence, and participate in the rabbinic legal system concerning marriage, divorce, levirate marriage, the release of widows in childless marriages from the requirement to marry the levir, and release from marital captivity? There is much evidence from the medieval and early modern eras in Ashkenazi, Middle Eastern and North African, Italian, and Mediterranean Jewries with which to address these questions; a record very relevant to contemporary concerns.

Women, Economics, and the Premodern "Community Paradigm"

Contrary to popular conceptions that premodern women, Jewish and not, "traditionally" did not work for income to support themselves and their families, the opposite is true. The only social class in which such idleness was possible, for women and men both, was the aristocracy, whose wealth derived from the labor of peasants working aristocratic lands. Discriminatory taxation and legal measures in Christian and Muslim realms excluded Jews from this class.[1] Until the creation of the modern middle class in industrializing England and Europe, all women, of all classes except the aristocracy, and certainly Jewish women, worked from girlhood on to produce income for their families of origin and those they created after marriage.[2] Elisheva Baumgarten notes about the schooling of Jewish girls in medieval Europe that they "remained within the home with their mothers, preparing themselves for their roles as mothers, wives, and financial supporters of their future families"—the last-named pursuit as normal and expected as the others.[3] Dispensing with the productive labor of half the population was inconceivable for most of human history, including that of the Jews. It was a major innovation of industrializing Europe, and even then was possible only for those either with sufficient means to dispense with women's earnings or who, lacking such means, could pretend to have dispensed with them in order to assert middle-class social status, while women, in fact, continued income-producing work behind the scenes. Marion Kaplan amply illustrates this behavior in the German Jewish middle class of nineteenth-century Germany.[4]

In medieval Franco-Germany (Ashkenaz) and Christian Spain (Sepharad), Jewish women commonly engaged in commerce and moneylending at all levels. We see evidence of this already in the time of the great French biblical and Talmudic commentator and halakhic decisor Rashi (Rabbi Shlomo Yitzhaki, 1040–1105). One of his responsa includes reference to women who managed businesses, made loans to Christian authorities, negotiated on collateral, received vineyards and lands in pledges, sued other Jews in court, bought and sold property, made deals with non-Jews (men) over properties and fees owed them, and dealt in wine, all of which Rashi relates as unremarkable.[5] Scholars note that widows played an important role in commerce, moneylending, and managing estates left by husbands.[6] Such practices, however, were not confined to widows, who could continue them as widows because they had engaged in them during their husbands' lifetimes, alongside and separate from them. Jewish women also supported family income through weaving, spinning, and leather work for home consumption and for sale and through other petty commerce.[7] Husbands not only made no effort to bar wives from economic enterprises but encouraged this.[8]

We also see no evidence that norms about "modesty" prevented Jewish women in Christian realms from leaving their homes as part of normal business behavior, including frequenting markets to obtain and sell goods. Grossman notes that when husbands were away from home, a routine occurrence given male Jewish concentration in long-distance trade, women discharged the family's commercial and financial business. This situation, he says, was common in Ashkenaz, with sources describing women bargaining with both Jewish and Gentile men, suing them and being sued, appointing emissaries, and traveling to the courts of feudal lords and negotiating with them, with no hint in any source that such functions were seen as entailing "immodesty"[9]—an indication of the cultural embeddedness and malleability of that concept. Goldin, too, attests that no notion of a requirement for women's "concealment," from fear of transgressive sexual behavior, existed in medieval Ashkenaz.[10]

Socioeconomic realities were reflected in rabbinic rulings. The ranking Talmudic authorities from the twelfth to the fifteenth century, the tosaphists, ruled that "it is impossible that a woman not be left alone with a non-Jew [meaning a man] at some time," although this contradicted a ruling of the Mishna, echoed by Maimonides (1135–1204).[11] Clearly, as Grossman states, underlying this ruling was the economic prominence of Jewish women in Ashkenaz in commerce and money-lending,[12] an importance, he notes, that led to a radical change in halakha, something that later decisors attempted to explain and defend not on halakhic but economic grounds. Thus, Rabbi Yair Bacharach, in seventeenth century Germany, "stated that the source for this leniency [lay] in economic reality":

> Because our main livelihood is from [the Gentiles] and we need to negotiate with them, and because our women also engage in business negotiations, and we are much preoccupied with our livelihood and it is very difficult to make a livelihood . . . the sages of past generations did not . . . protest [against Jewish women being alone with Gentile men during business transactions], because they realized that *it is impossible to [oppose] this edict.* And it may be that because of their desire to make money through business *the women disobeyed their husband's orders concerning this* (my emphasis).[13]

Clearly, it was not only economic but social and gendered family reality that undergirded this and other departures from rabbinic prescriptions.

Acting in response to these exigencies, medieval halakhic decisors overrode other halakhic norms that limited women: rules that prohibited administering oaths to women lest they be compelled to appear in court, which halakha considered an offense to women's "dignity"; and women acting as their husbands' business agents, which would entail them bearing responsibility for damages or bodily injury they might cause. As the major twelfth-century decisor Rabbi Eliezer ben Nathan (Raban) of Mainz, one of the early tosaphists, stated in one ruling, "In these days, [when women] are bailiffs and money changers and negotiate and loan and borrow and repay and receive payment and make and take deposits, it is to their benefit [rather than an offense to the women's dignity] to require them to take an oath, for otherwise people will refrain from doing business with them."[14]

Any such loss to the women would be an intolerable loss to their husbands and families and to the Jewish community as a whole. Raban gave explicit voice to this reality and to the perception of change in Jewish historical circumstances as altering the status of women when he dismissed one husband's claims, based "entirely on the Talmud," that "what a woman acquires belongs to her husband" and that she could not be sued or appear in court. Rather, he ruled that "there is no substance in what the husband is saying . . . *now, at a time when women act for themselves*, run shops, deal in commerce and money lending and banking, making and repaying pledges. . . . If we were to say that they may not commit themselves to undertakings and promises concerning commerce and business, others could not conduct business with them" (my emphasis).[15] Acknowledging changed circumstances, Raban also ruled that women could undertake business activities on their own, acting as independent agents, because "now [in the twelfth century] *that women are guardians of their husbands*, we accept anything [from them]" (my emphasis).[16]

Such behavior continued in Ashkenaz, Martha Keil notes. Whatever the reservations of some rabbis, women's business activity

> made their capacity to appear in court and to swear oaths indispensable. We find them in all relevant legal transactions, in trials with Jewish men or women before rabbinical courts as well as before Christian courts, alone or with their . . . legal counsel. . . . Independent women merchants active in the urban economy . . . enjoyed, even when married, almost unlimited transaction and court capacity, as well as preference in inheritance law. . . . Women were able to assume guardianship for minor children or for their grandchildren. . . . All of this means that they must

have been considered legal persons and that they could dispose of their own property.[17]

Jewish women in medieval England, Provence, Spain, Italy, and Sicily typically also engaged in trade and moneylending and were healers and midwives, likely in combination with other economic pursuits.[18] Simha Goldin sums up the impact of all this by saying that women "had become a vital element of the general economic force that could not be ignored; . . . the tone of the response [of Raban, cited above], makes it quite plain that at that time and place, things had changed."[19] By "things," Goldin means not just economic circumstances but halakhic rulings in accordance with changed circumstances. Such accommodation in medieval Ashkenaz occurred in other areas, for instance, regarding Talmudic restrictions on economic relations between Jews and non-Jews before or on the holy days of the latter. But the changes we have seen in halakhic rulings were not just about economics. They also involved the supremely sensitive status of women in a patriarchal system and have specific significance on that account.[20]

Legal, political, economic, and social circumstances in medieval Middle Eastern Jewries differed from those in Ashkenaz, but here too women were not only economically active but economic actors, that is, they used their economic heft to secure betterment of their circumstances. Significant protections for women emerged in this sphere, too.

Notices about women's earnings begin to appear in the early twelfth-century documents in the Cairo Geniza—a trove of hundreds of thousands of writings, including everyday materials like letters and business and marriage contracts, deposited in synagogues in Fustat—old Cairo—over centuries. This material is a major source about Middle Eastern Jewish societies from antiquity to modernity.[21] By the mid-thirteenth century, says Mordechai A. Friedman, marriage contracts noted a wife's earnings as a matter of course, indicating that economically productive work by women was common and expected.[22] Although in households of modest means, the professions open or specific to women were limited and produced sparse income, in such settings women's earnings were the more significant and even pivotal. Since most Jews were not wealthy, such economic significance marked the community as a whole.[23]

Various factors have operated to obscure the economic impact of girls' and women's activities in Geniza society. Eve Krakowski notes that unmarried girls had little to no economic control over property given to them but were economically productive in other ways. She describes a "not unusual" orphan

> who had embroidered fabric intended for her dowry and thus increased its value [and with it, her own value on the marriage market]. . . . Geniza documents and [rabbinic] responsa alike suggest that girls could per-form economically significant work from a young age, contributing to their household economies through housework and textile production, and in the case of textile work, to their own future assets as well . . . texts that mention [the labor of girls] illustrate the distance between social ideas about unmarried girls' economic agency and their actual economic capacity.[24]

The domestic and often exclusively female contexts of women's labor also rendered such work less visible in documentary sources and its eco-nomic importance more likely to be overlooked than typically male pur-suits. The urban economy of medieval Egypt was rigidly gendered, with women performing housework and working for pay in a limited range of occupations. Many of these involved caring for other women's bodies, serving as midwives, hairdressers, and corpse-dressers. Other women worked in service jobs also performed by men, as brokers, peddlers, and elementary religious teachers. By far the most important area of paid female labor was textile production, with women of all classes involved in producing clothing and textiles for household consumption. Women also did specialized textile work—spinning and embroidery, for wages or sale. "Whether or not they received payment for their labor," says Kra-kowski, "women in medieval Egypt seem nearly always to have worked within private homes . . . [which] may explain why neither the Geniza nor contemporary literary Arabic sources provide . . . detailed descrip-tions of women's textile work, despite its clear economic importance."[25]

Women in textile trades, midwifery, and hairdressing learned their skills from women, often though not always from their mothers. This function, too—unsalaried, vocational teaching within the home—clearly of significant economic value, does not appear as such in Geniza documents.[26] Still, the end product of such training—the teaching and the being trained—was that Jewish women contributed to family income through spinning, weaving, embroidery, and other occupations made typical for women, contributions the more significant in economically marginal families. If the value of such work did not register in written records, it registered in the communal mind, particularly, as we will see, in the consciousness of the male keepers of the communal purse.

In families with some means, women's economic worth was based on property ownership and its use rather than on earnings from commercial activities. Women of all classes, Goitein established, appear in Geniza documents as owning immovable property, which they inherited and bequeathed, donated, bought and sold, rented, or leased. Such property included houses or parts of houses, stores, workshops, flour mills, and other urban properties. Women also managed the upkeep of properties. They acquired possessions through gifts, dowries, inheritance, or communal charity; precisely whose derivative character, Goitein notes, brought women into constant contact with the world of men.[27] This means, of course, that men were in constant contact with the world, and economic worth, of women.

Women in the societies depicted in Geniza documents did not necessarily practice only domestic professions or ones conducted exclusively within the home. Krakowski shows that Rabbanite (as opposed to Karaite) court officials in late tenth-century Iraq who wished to summon a woman to court would first ascertain if she was accustomed to being out for business—buying, selling, and speaking with men.[28] Many Geniza documents mention women appearing in court cases involving property and inheritance disputes, as well as being represented by male proxies.[29] Jews of the Geniza world followed the established norm in the surrounding Muslim society, what Krakowski terms "Islamicate cultural assumptions," which accorded social status to women who did not regularly appear in public (one surmises that this status came with wealth, meaning that such seclusion was a minority behavior)—and finds that this social accommodation, rather than "modesty," drove the seclusion of women. But she also notes that commercial legal documents make clear that not all wealthy and well-connected women stayed indoors, since some describe women contracting substantial business transactions with nonkin men outside their households.[30]

Under Talmudic law, wives owned the dowries they brought into the marriage, whose usufruct, commonly enjoyed through use as security in business loans, was the husband's right during the marriage. Wives' earnings were to go to husbands in exchange for husbands providing clothing (that they would provide wives food and housing was obligatory under the ketubbah).[31] But there is evidence that women in medieval Palestinian and Egyptian communities often arranged to keep their own earnings and supply their own clothing, and that some kept their earnings even while husbands provided clothing.[32] Goitein notes numerous documents that show women taking charge of properties that were part of their dowries (dowries were typically given in goods, not money). He also notes that, because women often possessed commercial experience, they were frequently appointed as legal guardians of their children and executors of estates, meaning that they were legal persons. Barred from large-scale production and exchange of goods in which only men engaged, women were active in all the other productive endeavors we have described, including trading in items in their dowries and entering into business partnerships.[33]

Economic Importance and Expanding Rights and Protections

With economic importance came expanding rights for Jewish women in both Christian and Muslim realms. The nexus between women's economic importance and enhanced rights may have been particularly pronounced in Christian Europe, where Jewish existence was anomalous, Jews being the only non-Christian group to exist there openly and officially.[34] Jewish existence, justified theologically with arguments from Augustinian doctrine, was anchored in economics—in the commercial and financial benefits Jews were required to provide rulers, secular and ecclesiastical, in return for permission to settle, with promised protection and the privilege to live under "their own," meaning rabbinic law.[35] These understandings were specified in charters, contract-like documents issued by rulers to Jewish communities for stated periods of time. Economic contributions were not just a self-evident, mutual interest of Jews and rulers but a condition for a community's permission to settle, with specific privileges, in given locales, for a specified duration. In this context, Ashkenazi women's economic contributions had not only material but vital political importance to their communities and gave women, directly and via their male kin, clout to demand and receive expanding protections in marriage and divorce and in ownership and disposition of property, which were always central in deliberations and disputes about marriage and divorce.

The dynamics of Jewish status in the medieval Middle Eastern world differed in that the Jewish presence there was acknowledged as indigenous and predating Islam, if also requiring theological justification and management. In Islamic realms, however, Jews were not alone in this status, sharing it with other recognized non-Muslim minorities deemed monotheistic—Christians and Zoroastrians. These groups, classed together as "dhimmis," were sworn to subservient loyalty to Muslim rule and bore discriminatory burdens but were permitted their own religiously defined communities and governance.[36] Economic vibrancy in the areas Jews could practice, trade and crafts, was not freighted with the threat of expulsion if not delivered, though poverty and, in particular, appeals by impoverished Jews to non-Jewish sources for assistance were a drawback of which Jewish communal leaders were cognizant and a consideration with direct bearing on the clout of women regarding iggun.

In Islamic realms, too, economics factored in patriarchal dynamics that created protections for Jewish women in marriage and divorce, or rather, that counterbalanced to some extent other patriarchal dynamics that disadvantaged women at these critical points in their lives. We see these dynamics in detailed prenuptial negotiations and agreements that go well beyond or contradict Talmudic law to protect a wife's rights in several pivotal areas and gave women significant protections. These included the right to refuse a husband's wish to relocate (he could not use her refusal as grounds for divorce with financial penalties); stop him from marrying an additional wife (unlike the situation in Ashkenaz, there was no halakhic ruling prohibiting polygyny in these communities, so any such limitation resulted from negotiation between the parties); prevent him from interfering with her visiting her family (from whom women often got assistance in marital disputes); and from demanding that she give an accounting of household possessions upon the husband's return from business trips. Such behaviors—cutting women off from family and friends and exerting extreme control over finances and possessions—are now recognized forms of marital abuse but clearly were also recognized as such centuries ago.

Some negotiated prenuptial agreements directly contradicted Talmudic law, such as a stipulation that the value or profit of a wife's labor accrues to the husband. One such document Krakowski cites granted the wife rights to the fruit of her own labor but required her to provide her own clothing. Several others, however, required the husband to supply her clothes even though she kept her own earnings.[37] These agreements were instituted by women's male kin on their behalf, to better their rights during the marriage and in case of divorce. Spousal stipulations were inserted on behalf of both parties to the marriage and "could make a difference to both . . . but especially to women."[38]

Travel for business, including long-distance travel lasting months or years, was a central feature of the medieval Jewish world everywhere Jews lived. This reality, however, was gendered. Women were concentrated in local trade and in finance—moneylending. Long- distance business travel was men's business. This posed obvious problems to betrothed girls and women, and to wives and family life, because of the long absences themselves and because men often failed to return from trips, having deserted, or fallen victim to accidents, attacks, or illness, all of which sent women into marital captivity.[39] Difficulties deriving from travel and moving for the sake of business rank first in Avraham Grossman's list of grounds for divorce from the eleventh through the thirteenth century, when the Jewish divorce rate in Ashkenazic and Geniza societies alike was very high, with problems caused by abandonment plaguing Jewish societies in Egypt and North Africa, Spain, and Ashkenaz—the entire Jewish world.[40] Such difficulties led to a mid-twelfth-century edict by Rabbenu Tam (Rabbi Jacob ben Meir, 1100–1171), the ranking French tosaphist, prohibiting a merchant from being absent from home for more than a year and a half and mandating that he remain home for a minimum of six months upon return.[41] An earlier ordinance, attributed to Rabbenu Gershom (960–1040), prohibited married men from setting out on long journeys if there was marital tension and required the assent of wives for the travel in order to (try to) ascertain that the trip was for business and not abandonment. Before marriage, women in Spain would ask future husbands to swear a sacred oath, which bore more force in traditional societies than written agreements, that they would not depart for travel without their wives' agreement. Communities in eleventh-century Spain levied heavy fines on men who abandoned wives or fiancées and defaulted on contracted financial arrangements for them. Rabbinic responsa and ordinances reference such fines in the twelfth century as well, all of which testifies to wife-desertion and the often desperate economic straits in which this left wives-made-agunot.[42]

We gain insight into the plight of one such woman, as Krakowski details a case from Fustat:

> Sometime between 1046 and 1090, a woman named Hayfā' bt. Sulaymān submitted a petition to an unnamed Jewish official in Fustat. She had arrived in the city alone and friendless, "a feeble stranger" with a two-year-old son in tow, desperately seeking the runaway husband who had deserted her in Jaffa. Rejected by her . . . relatives . . . and finding no help from a brother-in-law in the north Egyptian town of Malīj, she told the official that he was her last hope: "I have no one to whom I can turn with my complaint, except God and your honor." She asked him to write on her behalf to a Jewish court in Palestine, where she believed her husband had now returned, to pressure him to either return to her or divorce her—an outcome that would at least permit her to remarry.

This story was not unusual, Krakowski notes, continuing:

> *Geniza documents mention abandoned wives so often that the topic easily deserves a book of its own.* Constant mobility meant that many men spent more time apart from their wives than with them. Men traveled for many reasons: business, religious pilgrimage, simple wanderlust, or to evade the poll tax, poverty, debt, and the financial burden of family itself. "I was bankrupted in Alexandria (by debts owed to) Muslims," a man writes from Fustat in an early twelfth-century charity petition; "My children and old mother were starving. I could not bear to sit and watch them in that state, so I fled" (my emphasis).

For abandoned wives like Hayfa, there were but a few options. Women, of course, could not enact divorce, much less assure themselves any ketubbah settlement if divorced (indeed, abandoning wives allowed husbands to renege on premarital agreements and was a factor encouraging abandonment). A woman "without adequate means of support," says Krakowski,

> could seek help in two arenas: first and ideally, among her birth (and sometimes marital) relatives, or if this failed, from the government, writ small or large—either the class of administrative and legal authorities who ran Jewish courts and synagogues in the Fatimid and Ayyubid empires, *or the Fatimid and then Ayyubid states* [that is, non-Jewish authorities] *themselves* (my emphasis).[43]

While the term "agunot" is not stated here (the term in Geniza documents is *armalat al-hayat*—a "widow during [his] lifetime"),[44] every married woman whose husband abandoned her or who disappeared (as opposed to men who traveled and returned), and who did not receive a get, was an agunah. If mention of abandoned wives in the Geniza documents is abundant enough to fill its own book, we get a measure of the dimensions of iggun in the world of medieval Jewry of the Middle East and North Africa—Egypt, Palestine, Lebanon, Syria, Iraq, and Iran—then by far the most numerous Jewish population in the world.[45] Mark Cohen hints at the prevalence of this reality when discussing the terminology used for women recorded in communal charity records: women listed as "widows" who were also noted as being "married." "Sometimes," he writes, "the word *mara* [wife] is paired with the word for 'widow,' a tautology unless we assume that the writer thought it would otherwise be taken in its . . . meaning of 'wife of a living person.'"[46] Wives of apostates—converts to Islam, one case of which Cohen mentions—who were left without being divorced were also agunot, and like others in this state fell into poverty and onto the patriarchal family or the male-administered, communal, or non-Jewish state resources with appeals for help.[47]

Until quite recent times, when education and professional degrees could enable agunot to support themselves reasonably, throughout Jewish history becoming an agunah meant economic liability—loss even of the claim to food and board that are a husband's responsibilities under the ketubbah, as well as loss of a husband's commercial connections and assets—or outright, often dire, poverty. Cohen relates the following case, illustrating these consequences in Geniza society:

> A Hebrew letter of recommendation [for communal support] on behalf of an abandoned wife says she has been "in widowhood during the lifetime (of her husband) (*be-almenut hayyut*) more than three years." The "widow" lived in Damascus (where the letter was penned) and had four children to support (they are "dying from hunger," she says). Her husband had converted from Karaism to Rabbanite orthodoxy and had headed for Fustat for a handout (hence the letter was sent there). She wants him to come home, or, if he has moved on or is rumored to have died, wants a letter to that effect. Two eyewitnesses to his death would free her from being "anchored" to her marriage and permit her to remarry.[48]

Yet another social problem visited upon women, deriving from men's long-distance trade, was that of them marrying a second wife while on such travel, in order, as Grossman puts it, to "take care of [their] personal needs."[49] This was a legal privilege categorically denied women during a husband's absence under penalties for rabbinically defined "adultery," which, as noted, establishes "adultery" based on the marital status of the woman, not the man. While technically what Grossman describes was polygyny, whose practice was not barred in non-Ashkenazi Jewries, in reality such temporary marital liaisons were a form of prostitution that devastated the women involved as well as their families and communities, since such "temporary" second wives were typically deserted and not divorced. Left unsupported as wives yet without the divorce settlement in their ketubbot, and unable to remarry, they were agunot, dependent on their male-led natal families and/or the male-led community for support. While halakhic discussion in such cases focused on polygyny and the technical means and authority to limit it (or not),[50] desertion of wives had manifold, destabilizing social consequences. These included abandoned wives taking lovers, a social phenomenon documented in the denunciations of decisors in France, Germany, Spain, and Egypt, which they attempted to combat through bans and fines. Accordingly, Maimonides issued edicts stating that "no woman be married to a foreign Jew, who is not from the community of Egypt, unless he brings proof that he is not married or takes an oath to this effect on a Penta-teuch. And any foreign man who married a woman here and wished to go out to another country is not allowed to leave, even if his wife agrees to this, until he writes her a divorce writ and gives it to her"—an action, presumably, accompanied by payment of her ketubbah settlement and any other support commitments undertaken by the husband.[51]

A major reform came as a result of communal perception of this problem: a requirement that husbands going on extended trips deposit a conditional bill of divorce. Should they not return within a specified time, it took effect automatically so that wives did not become agunot. Rabbinic sources quote women explicitly demanding such divorces, or the regular (unconditional) kind, prior to the husband's departure for travel.[52] Geniza records show that conditional divorce was common practice.[53] It was also common, or in some circumstances required, in Middle Eastern Jewish communities of the Ottoman era (thirteenth to early twentieth century), and in sixteenth-century Istanbul and Italy.[54]

Childless men who were gravely ill also gave conditional divorces to prevent their wives' entrapment in the requirement of levirate marriage in case of their deaths, in extortion for release from that obligation, and in other, related abuse, such as the levir vindictively demanding sums he knew the widow could not pay simply to prevent her from remar-rying. Conditional divorce meant that, if the husband succumbed (in halakhic terms, *skhiv mira*), the status of his wife was "divorced" rather than "widowed in a childless marriage," foreclosing all the above en-tanglements (if the husband recovered, the divorce could be retracted).[55] Clauses were also inserted into ketubbot requiring—subject, as always, to enforcement and often observed in the breach—that levirs enact the ritual of release (halitsa) in case the marriage was childless.[56] Given the far-flung nature of Jewish life, with prospective grooms coming from distant locations—Ruth Lamdan cites the case of a groom from Kurdis-tan marrying in Safed—families of prospective brides in that sixteenth-century town would investigate a man's family background—did he have brothers?—or make the man swear a sacred oath about this and would write precautions into prenuptial agreements against the woman be-coming beholden to a levir.[57]

Such measures did not necessarily accomplish their purpose. Cases of contested levirate marriages were rife, even when protective clauses had been inserted in prenuptial agreements or levirs had sworn oaths against victimizing the widow. The point is that communities across the Jewish map and over centuries instituted these and other measures, and that they were an established, normal, and normative practice in premodern Jewish communities, offering women at least the possibility of some protection.[58] The fact that such measures were contested shows that they were not simply legal formalities.

In the far-reaching prenuptial contracts that Goitein and Krakowski have analyzed in their respective works on the Cairo Geniza—not normative (theoretical) pronouncements but actual documents negotiated between marital parties in Egypt, Palestine, Syria, and elsewhere in the Middle East between the eleventh and thirteenth centuries—we see fathers, brothers, and uncles insisting on extra-Talmudic protections for their female kin—their legal wards. Such documents do not give insight into affective motivations (love for kin), but the material motivations for such actions are clear. If the woman was divorced or became an agunah, she and any children of hers, especially in families of any means, would return to her natal home and become its financial dependent. Women without such family would become wards of the male-run community, which extended alms, bread, and clothing to the needy, making such women, too, the concern of male householders, whose taxes financed communal expenditures.[59]

Goitein, Mark Cohen, and Krakowski show that deserted or neglected wives indeed expected and sought help from communal authorities. Cohen cites the following case, transcribed in the voice of the woman and recalling that of Hayfa, encountered above: "My husband, Abbas b. Khalaf, left for an inn in the Land of Isr(ael) eight years ago, leaving me naked and hungry, lacking everything, having to rely on the community" (meaning: the communal dole).[60]

Significantly for our purposes, Cohen and Krakowski note the gendered difference in the address for appeals for help by men and women in medieval Egyptian Jewish society. Men could establish mutually beneficial relationships outside of kin networks and so, when in need, were more likely to petition private individuals or bring them letters of recommendation asking them to help the letter-bearer directly than to turn to communal sources of support. Gendered socioeconomics limiting women's spheres of interaction prevented women from having such nonkin associations. Women in need turned to communal officials, such as judges and "heads of the Jews" (as communal leaders were called), or to the community as a whole.[61]

Krakowski's analysis supports and enlarges this conclusion. As we have seen in the cases cited above, she demonstrates that male kinship protection did not always materialize and that desperate, deserted women—agunot—would appeal not only to Jewish communal but to Muslim state authorities—to an Islamic religious court or to the Islamic state—for support,[62] not a desirable outcome for the community. Krakowski identifies several classes of women who were particularly vulnerable, structurally, in medieval Egyptian Jewish society (though women as a class, of course, were structurally vulnerable). These were orphans, older women, and women who either lacked male kin or whose kin had abandoned them.[63] Although Krakowski does not specify abandoned wives, agunot, among the structurally vulnerable who would turn to male sources of support, whether familial, communal, or Islamicate, of course agunot were in that class. Given the widespread occurrence of wife-abandonment that she, Cohen, and Goitein document (Goitein devotes ten pages to this in his work),[64] they may well have been much or most of it. Whether Jewish communal or Islamicate, society's institutions were male-run, which gave them strong incentive to try to force back onto individual marital agreements measures to prevent women becoming dependent on them. The same patriarchal structures (not least, rabbinic marriage) that made women structurally vulnerable, establishing limits on their economic function and their dependence on men and on male-run institutions (including the family), created individual and communal male self-interest in instituting protections for wives. The structures of patriarchy itself, and in Islamic realms, Jewish dhimmi status in addition, made iggun—women becoming agunot and the financial difficulty or outright poverty and dependence on communal support this typically caused—a male and communal concern. In creating a structural need of women to resort to appeals for communal sustenance, the same patriarchal structures that created this gendered vulnerability made iggun a problem for men, individually and communally, and not just the women's personal misfortune.

Krakowski shows that prenuptial agreements with protective clauses for women had standing in rabbinic courts and that claims based on them were pressed there. She also shows that rabbinic authorities and courts had very weak administrative capacities, their power to enforce rulings directing a husband to give a divorce or pay sums due the wife in the case of divorce, or pay fines levied for defiance, very limited. About the latter reality and its implications for women, consider this "unusually frank" letter from a husband from Fustat, likely from the early thirteenth century, to a Jewish communal official named Hisday about his divorce case being adjudicated in a rabbinic court. In it, the husband

> baldly states that if Ḥisday does not issue him a divorce deed immediately [that is, confirm that the divorce would proceed on terms the husband demanded], he will walk away from the case—and from his wife: "Either you yourself divorce me from her, or I will leave her and travel far away, never to see her again, and she will be left chained in living widowhood [iggun]. But if you give her a divorce deed from me, and set her deferred dower on me in installments, as you rule . . ."

The letter breaks off here but Krakowski notes that the author's intent is clear: He wants the communal official to agree to let him repay his wife's dowry in installments after the divorce—effectively allowing him to default on repayment. Denied his demand, he threatens to leave her an agunah, impoverished and dependent on the community. "This threat," says Krakowski, "illustrates not only how a husband's desertion could harm his wife, but also the power this option gave men in divorce negotiations. Men's freedom to walk away from the *beit din* [rabbinic court] made it risky for women to press too hard for their dowers, no matter how impeccable their legal claims on paper."[65] Use of the poverty entailed in a woman becoming an agunah was a weapon with which husbands could threaten the community.

Mark Cohen, Oded Zinger,[66] and Krakowski all emphasize that the ability of women to actualize any written claim they had was determined by the existence, strength, and credibility of the intervention of male kin, given women's lack of associations outside of kinship circles that could help their prospects in court. The rabbinic-court system not only enforced patriarchal law but, Krakowski shows, equally important for outcomes, was a male network.

Because Jewish leaders depended on their male subjects for political support,

> they inevitably favored legal outcomes that could help them cultivate social associations with other men: networks of patronage shared among litigants, scribes, and judges alike, in which women could not directly participate. In this climate, court officials were naturally predisposed against women who approached them to sue a husband without another man's support—which is to say, without anything to offer in the "calculus of benefit" on which Geniza society ran.[67]

The fact that women lacking the support of male kin were structurally disadvantaged in rabbinic courts did not stop them from appealing to them—there was hardly an alternative—as well as to Muslim religious and civil courts, as numerous petitions threatening such action establish.[68] Cohen cites the following such case, in which a

> letter of appeal to the community [for support] comes from the young wife of an older man who had failed to live up to his marital obligations, neither supporting her financially nor observing her conjugal rights (he rarely came home at night, she says). Her mother, who took care of her for ten years during which time her husband gave her "no clothing except one wimple," had died three years earlier. She had then sold her dowry [items] to make ends meet, but all of that was now gone . . . she threatens, if she did not get help from the [Jewish] community . . . [to] resort to the Muslim court.[69]

All this evidence complicates and tempers our assessment of legal reforms that benefited women. It mandates consideration of class and social status as variables affecting, even determining, the efficacy of any benefits actually accruing to women, whether from rabbinic rulings or negotiated agreements between parties to a marriage. But there is no question that both promulgated reforms and negotiated agreements opened at least the possibility of ameliorating women's disability in marriage and divorce. And there is overwhelming evidence that women across the Jewish map, across eras and lines of class and status, used both in efforts on their own behalf. How often women succeeded, how economic class, social status, male kin, and other factors beyond women's control affected outcomes, is a separate question, and we must distinguish between efforts and results. We need to consider the former in their own right, not least because the sources often do not state and we do not know the outcomes of cases, while we can assess the behavior of women in pressing their cases. It is also possible that the weak enforcement capacities of rabbinic courts could have operated on behalf of women with powerful male kin. All this is material for future inquiry. What the record clearly shows, however, is a fluid, dynamic environment, which meant opportunity for resourceful, inventive, and assertive women to try to press their interests, which we see that they did.

Similar patriarchal dynamics to those of the medieval era operated in sixteenth-to-eighteenth-century Ottoman Jewries. Husbands and other male kin took measures not just beyond but conflicting with Talmudic law, including using the Muslim waqf, the religious charitable trust, to circumvent Talmudic restrictions and give wives, sisters, and mothers means to inherit or enjoy perpetual use of property.[70] When men of means left wives and widows in charge of significant assets, women contracted deals, extended loans, acquired property, and engaged partners, suing and being sued. It was common in Ottoman regions for women's male kin, their legal guardians, to insert clauses into the engagement agreements of the latter barring prospective husbands from taking a second wife—though bigyny remained a husband's legal privilege in non-Ashkenazi practice—and stating the couple's place of residence. The latter specification meant that a husband could not simply move to a location far from an often very young bride's family and their protections and require her to follow or be deemed "rebellious," a designation that posed severe legal and fiscal consequences. Since marriages typically were patrilocal, the bride, often barely in her teens or not even that, went to live with her new husband's family, and her family acted to construct protections.[71] While, as always, the existence of such stipulations cannot be taken as evidence that they were enforced as written—disputes and litigation about such contracts, in and outside of rabbinic courts, abounded—it is significant that such protections for women, beyond and even contradicting normative halakha, were created, normal, and expected in this era as in earlier ones. That they were litigated shows that they were not just theoretical but applied. They are prime evidence of Jewish legal norms and realities emanating from "below," from economic, social, and familial exigencies pressed by women and men.

In this setting, too, concern about the consequences of women left unsupported by husbands could affect rabbinic and communal policy to women's benefit. Rabbi Moshe Mitrani (Hamabit, 1505, Salonika–1585, Safed),) justified a woman's appeal to a Muslim court in Beirut about her husband's lack of support. Rabbi Yomtov Zahalon (Maharitz, ca. 1559–1638, Safed) upheld the divorce a man tried to revoke, acting because, while married, the man had threatened to abandon his wife and run off "to the faraway lands of Ashkenaz," leaving her a dependent agunah (having previously extorted large sums from her). That Muslim authorities shared this concern with Jewish ones is seen from their active collusion in the case of another man whose imprisonment for various crimes Muslim authorities commuted on condition that he be expelled from Safed—but only after giving his wife a divorce, whose suit the qadi (Muslim religious judge) supported so that she would not be left a destitute agunah there. The man later claimed that the divorce was invalid for being given under duress—which claim Mitrani and Rabbi Yaacov Berav, ranking decisors, rejected.[72] In all these cases as in earlier ones we have seen, communal patriarchal concerns took priority over those of individual men—and over Talmudic law. Particularly in divorce cases, when women could be left destitute by their husband's actions, such concerns also led to open, frequent, normal recourse to non-Jewish courts and authorities—qadis, who could impose imprisonment as rabbis could not[73]—regardless of Talmudic strictures forbidding this.

Concluding: On the Emergence of Protections for Women in Marriage and Divorce in the Medieval Era

Medieval Jewish women's economic contributions at all economic and social levels gave them traction to demand and receive enhanced protections, or at least the possibility of such protections in marriage and divorce. As we saw in the case of the orphan who embroidered a garment in her dowry, thereby increasing its value, and hers, on the marriage market, women across class lines understood economics and tactics for upward mobility, as well as the workings of legal systems that could hinder or advance their interests. For economic as well as social and religious reasons, marriage—an economic partnership to which both partners contributed and from which each sought tangible benefit—was almost always women's preferred option (very wealthy widows could prefer to remain in that state). For this reason, being an agunah—married in status but not in reality, without a husband's economic partnership, business connections, and basic support (room and board), but unable to contract a new marriage and the assets and connections that came with it—was always economically harmful, when not catastrophic, for women. Women's economic value was best realized in marriage. Whatever that value in individual cases, marital captivity, which commonly caused women to fall back on their natal families or on community resources—both of which were male-administered and funded—was an undesired outcome for families or communities, however much it could benefit the husband who abandoned a wife.

Abandonment, divorce, and iggun in the world of premodern Middle Eastern and European Jewries, therefore, were not simply women's problems, from whose consequences male kin and the male-led community felt, or actually were, immune. They were not moral (soft) problems but financial (hard) ones that affected men, individually and as lay leaders of communities, responsible for communal finances and social order. Abandonment—women left unsupported by husbands, whether through accident, desertion, sexual opportunism, or vindictiveness—had financial and social costs that fell on male-led families and the male-led community as a whole. These they were unwilling to bear unchallenged. Accordingly, measures had to be and were taken to limit such costs, however imperfectly implemented given the available means of enforcement. Men exercised both the right of full citizenship to benefit from patriarchal privileges and the right to protect themselves from injury when patriarchal structures imposed consequences that fell rightly, in patriarchy, on denizens of the system, women. Thus, we find twelfth-century Ashkenazi fathers appealing to the highest contemporaneous authority, Rabbenu Tam, in one case to extract from iggun a daughter whose husband had converted and, in another case, to allow a daughter, divorced after being suspected of having had an adulterous relationship, to marry her lover—this, in violation of clear halakhic prohibition and extreme taboo—in both cases winning the appeals.[74] For a long period of Jewish history, the latter dynamic—of men seeking to shield themselves and their interests from negative consequences of certain patriarchal structures, could and did help women—if the women had financial and/or status resources, including male kin, who acted to protect them.[75] This did not stop brothers and other male kin from seeking to apply established male privilege in their own marriages and divorces, of course, or in rabbinic inheritance and property law against women kin in asset disputes.[76] The common denominator in the behavior was patriarchal privilege.

Simha Goldin posits reasons motivating the reforms that benefited women in medieval Ashkenaz, citing a "community paradigm" he says operated there. He discerns in the rabbinic sources a conviction that the vulnerability of the medieval Ashkenazi community and its need to withstand existential crises required that communal interests be given the highest priority. It was this concern, Goldin asserts, that underlay the ruling limiting the period of time a man could be absent from home and barring him from setting out on another trip for at least six months after his return. "This ruling," he says, ". . . is based on *the communal concern that any harm that befalls a woman also harms the community*" (my emphasis). Accordingly, not only were the duration and frequency of men's absence limited and inquiries made to assure that there was marital harmony and consent of wives to the travel. Prior to departure, a man was also required to prove that he was "leaving behind sufficient funds and assets to pay his debts and to ensure the maintenance of his wife and children for the duration of his absence." The male-led community demanded of such men coverage not just of subsistence needs but funds to pay teachers for their children's education, so that the family (obviously, the one assumed in the ruling had means) would not fall into poverty and become a financial burden on the community in the near or later term.[77]

Such communal considerations persisted in other realms and in the later Ottoman period (1300–1922), a time not associated with existential anxiety but with refuge and opportunity, and not only for people with means. Thus, we hear of the financial officers (*parnassim*) of the community (kehilla) in sixteenth-century Jerusalem absolving poor widows of communal taxes and debts because this bettered the low remarriageability odds of such women, whose remarriage would lessen the community's support burden in the longer run. Such considerations underlay the appeal by the *parnassim* to a certain man (of means or standing—a *gvir*) for help to a widow in obtaining funds being contested by her late husband's family, who were threatening to take the case to non-Jewish courts. In remarkable language, the *parnassim* appealed to the man "to facilitate the outcome [on the woman's behalf], *because in her welfare is the welfare of the city* . . . and let a word to the wise suffice" (my emphasis—referencing Jeremiah 29:7).[78]

This verse in Jeremiah imparted a revolutionary and foundational political strategy for no less than Jewish survival in and of Exile—a teaching put into practice in medieval Jewish communities across the map of Jewish existence. There could be no more powerful expression of the premodern Jewish understanding that the predicament of women, victimized by patriarchal structures (however much these were not then understood as such), was an essential communal concern than the appropriation of this verse by the financial officers of Jerusalem's community on behalf of a woman—and of the community's interest in preventing non-Jewish interference in its affairs. That expression speaks powerfully, too, to the efficacy of precisely such appeals to non-Jewish authorities in intra-Jewish disputes, efficacy that Jewish women in divorce disputes understood very well and employed to their benefit.

It bears noting that the limited ability of rabbinic courts to enforce rulings and the reliance on voluntary compliance, which sounds archetypally modern, is actually ancient, long predating movements of modern Judaism that, in Orthodox apologetics, are responsible for the demise of effective rabbinic rule and traditional life.

3

Agency and Authority[1]

Real Women and Rabbinic Law

From Object to Subject

Works on women and rabbinic law routinely essentialize women, referring to them as "woman" or "the woman" (often capitalized); that is, as halakhic "problems," or as a category. Such and other works also routinely refer to halakha as "Jewish" rather than as "rabbinic" law and treat "Jews" and Jewish men as synonymous, referring to Jews as men and to men as "Jews," and to women (when this is done) as "women" or even as "Jewesses."[2] These categories and terminologies are entirely uninterrogated and work after work has perpetuated them and the patriarchal assumptions underlying them.

This study foregrounds women as Jews, half the Jewish population, past or present; as people in historical contexts and situations along with the rest of their communities and the larger, non-Jewish worlds that women and men inhabited, and in the specifically gendered predicament of iggun. "Jews" were women as much as they were (or are) men. To use a different referent for women is to insinuate into the analysis patriarchal constructs that establish men as the norm, which marginalizes women as "Other" in a hierarchical, androcentric scheme. It is to distort and impede analysis.

It is this distorted perception that gave rise to, perpetuated, and perpetuates iggun as a normal and inevitable, tragic condition. Such perception precludes treatment of marital captivity as a problem not of women, however much women are victims, but of the Jewish society that creates and tolerates it. It prevents seeing iggun as a tractable, solvable problem rather than as an intractable one, subject at best to "management." However inadvertently, for some at least (for some it is intentional and defended), such perception perpetuates the stereotype of women as

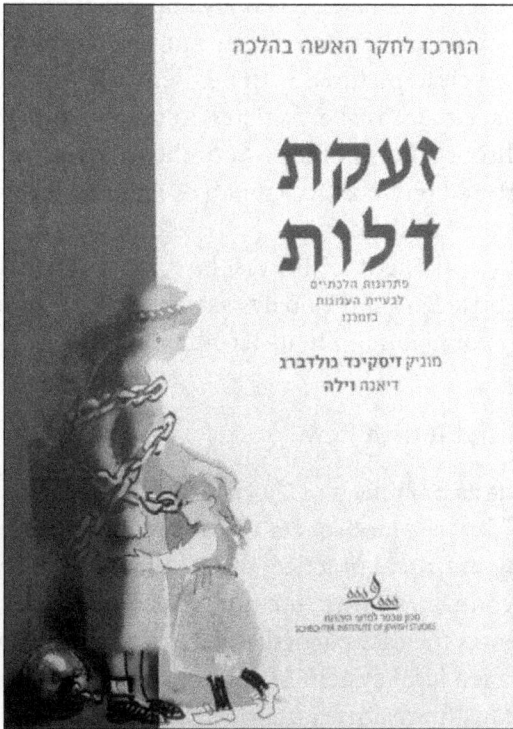

המרכז לחקר האשה בהלכה

זעקת
דלות

פתרונות הלכתיים
לבעיית העגונות
בזמננו

מוניק זיסקינד גולדברג
דיאנה וילה

Figure 3.1. Cover image of Monique Susskind-
Goldberg and Diana Goldberg, *Za'akat Dalot*. Credit:
Maureen Fain.

natural or inevitable victims, worthy of pity, perhaps of concern and
compassion as agunot, a status even the most sincere advocates admit
some will not escape because iggun is an inevitable, unavoidable "tragedy."[3] That stereotype, founded on the Otherness of Jewish women and
the gendered power imbalance that is patriarchy, is circular, deriving
from that perception and perpetuating it.

We see that perception and its perpetuation even in the most unintended expressions, as, for instance, in the illustration on the cover
of Monique Susskind-Goldberg and Diana Goldberg's *Za'akat Dalot*
(The Cry of the Wretched), which analyzes the rabbinic sources about
iggun and agunot and presents halakhic solutions.[4] The pose depicted,
of a modestly dressed, hair-covered, head-bowed woman, her torso

encircled by chains, a ball and chain around her foot, conveys victim-hood, wretchedness, and impotence meant to elicit pity. The similarly, modestly dressed child pictured with her, seeking her mother's comfort or protection, is female, as she, initiated to the realities of pious Jewish womanhood through her mother's victimhood, contemplates her own future in a martyred plight as an agunah or vulnerable to it.

It is not just the facts about iggun, therefore, that need attention but the approach to studying it. This must be done through a gynocentric, not an androcentric lens, if the analysis itself is not to be another tool in the perpetuation of iggun but in its termination.[5]

Rabbinic Law and Jewish Law

I refer to halakha as rabbinic, not "Jewish" law because that is what it was, and is. "Jewish" law is a far broader category that expresses the range of Jewish religious and ritual practice, that is, practice by Jews in dynamic discourse and connection with, but not synonymous with, rabbinic law. Such discourse was the case particularly in premodernity, when halakha was the recognized legal system of and for the Jewish minority in both Christian and Muslim realms, authorized by rulers to govern Jews living in autonomous, corporate Jewish communities. Interaction with rab-binic law was not a choice but necessary, a given, in Jewish life.

Jewish practice was the result of dynamic interaction by Jews, half of them women, with the always evolving rabbinic legal system. It was not simply the product of rabbinic pronouncement from above, a "top-down" conception of halakha that does not accord with historical reality, as study of women's (and men's) behavior regarding halakhic strictures about women in marriage and divorce shows. A study that even be-gins to approximate historical reality must encompass both "authority," as expressed in normative rabbinic pronouncements, and women's ac-tions; and the effects of such actions upon halakhic decision-making and pronouncements. Lay engagement with the rabbinic legal system influenced and changed that system, as Rachel Furst argues. Lay liti-gants coming to the rabbinic courts of medieval Ashkenaz about di-vorce cases, she found, understood "the legal requirements they needed to meet in order to advance their cases . . . and were often shrewd enough to recognize developments in the law and adapt their tactics accordingly." Important for our purposes, such behavior, she notes, not only gave these litigants—prominently among them, women—a fighting chance in court, but was a

> significant way in which litigants—and not only the rabbinic elite—affected the functioning of the Jewish courts and contributed to the development of the legal system. . . . In adopting the legal scripts available to them and following the guidelines that enabled them to litigate effectively—and in the course of so doing, prompting rabbinic authorities to continue debating the application of changing legal norms—[litigants in divorce cases] not only participated in the justice system that governed their lives but also actively contributed to its development.[6]

Jay Berkovitz makes a similar argument about Jewish businesswomen's use of rabbinic and French courts in eighteenth-century Metz. Not only did the women's economic heft factor in their reception in these courts, but their use of them caused non-Jewish legal categories and norms to feed into and alter Jewish/halakhic practice.[7]

Rather than conceive of halakhic functioning as two-dimensional and vertical, proceeding "down" (or even horizontally, "out") from rabbinic pronouncement, its more accurate representation is as a loop of exchange and mutual influence, influence that normative decisors themselves sometimes acknowledged explicitly. We see one instance of this in the actions of Sherira Gaon ("Gaon" was the title for a head of a Talmudic academy from the sixth to the eleventh century) in tenth-century Iraq, who reinforced, or reissued, a takkanah (rabbinic ordinance) that instituted a major change in the handling of divorce cases of women deemed "rebellious." In it he cited the fact that Jewish women encountering difficulties in obtaining rabbinic divorces were turning for help to Muslim courts (and, he said, had been doing so for centuries) as grounds for diverging from punitive Talmudic rulings about "rebellious" women seeking divorce and facilitating the divorces. He and other Babylonian geonim "explained" that the takkanah was "a conscious innovation in legal procedure [in] response to social conditions" and feared loss of rabbinic authority and control.[8] We see another instance of such reasoning in the statement of the fifteenth-century rabbi Jacob Moellin (Maharil) of Mainz, who records in his book of customs that he had been asked "why he does not reprimand Rabbanit Bruna [who lives] in his city for wearing tzitzit at all times. And he said: '*Perhaps she will not listen to me*'" (my emphasis).[9]

Maharil expressed severe disdain and disapproval of "women wearing four fringes—as a woman in our neighborhood does," labeling such behavior "arrogance." He did not, however, forbid the behavior, which would have had a very different, binding status. As Baumgarten shows, halakhic rulings on this and related matters followed and were prompted by de facto behavior or at times, as in this case, were withheld and not pronounced because of rabbinic fear that people would defy them. Such withholding not only allowed de facto behavior to continue but to set precedents in lived life and norms.

In an earlier period in medieval Ashkenaz, Baumgarten shows, a time when most Jewish men did not observe the commandment of donning tefillin (phylacteries) or enveloping themselves in the tallit (prayer shawl), some women began practicing these and other positive, time-bound mitzvot. This was not an expression of some kind of protofeminism—decisors had not yet labeled these acts "arrogant" and otherwise disapproved of for women—but because such acts were conspicuous religious practices in which the women wished to participate (Baumgarten speculates credibly that the women adopting such practices were family members of the scholarly elite who practiced them).[10] Tefillin, tzitzit (the shirtlike fringed ritual garment), tallit, the rituals of the Sukkot holiday (lulav, sukkah), and hearing the ram's horn (shofar) blown on Rosh Hashanah were all behaviors conspicuous to Jews and to non-Jews alike. Those, including women, who participated in these sacralized acts "communicated piety through visible symbols."[11]

Halakhic decisors responded to this behavior with discussions, beginning—the order is significant—not with the question of whether such acts were permissible, which was assumed, but only about whether women should pronounce the prescribed blessings when performing them. On this question, the most authoritative decisor, Rabbenu Tam, declared that such blessing was not even optional but required, as would be the case for blind (that is, defective) men (whose full obligation to positive, time-bound commandments, like that of women, was debated); or slaves[12] (a category, along with minors, in which women were classed from the Mishna on). Only much later, for reasons Baumgarten

illuminates, did discussion shift to whether authorities should pronounce such acts deviant, discouraged, or even prohibited.[13] As she
puts it, in these and other cases, such as women being called up to the
Torah—behavior mentioned as an aside, "a matter of course," in a mid-
eleventh-century source—"*the rabbis were responding to the women's initiative and attempting to regulate their practice*" (my emphasis).[14] Women
also innovated practices, such as refraining from synagogue attendance
when menstruating, "leaving the rabbis to endorse or rebuke their behaviors" post facto. Rabbinic "elucidat[ion] and standard[ization]" followed women's initiatives.[15]

Early medieval rabbinic responses to women donning tallit and tefillin and practicing the rituals of the Sukkot festival were matter-of-fact
and forthcoming. Awareness of gender was diffuse and without anxiety or urgency. Rabbinic responses, however, grew more restrictive and
gender-inflected with time, becoming pronounced in the thirteenth
century, giving rise to rigid rabbinic categories defining Jewish gender.
Constructed Jewish gender—normative maleness and femaleness—did
not precede and drive these developments but was constructed through
and because of them, as medieval Ashkenazic rabbinic authorities advocated expanded men's observance of the mitzvot of tallit and tefillin,
exhorting that these rituals become normative, male-gendered behavior
and not just that of the rabbinic elite.[16]

We have seen that rabbinic ordinances and prenuptial agreements
between the parties were not necessarily enforced as written, or at all,
a conclusion many scholars have reached about pronouncements in
rabbinic texts and historical reality altogether. Apologetic works often
conflate the two, asserting, for instance, that institution of the ketubbah, or in Ashkenaz, prohibition of polygyny and divorce of a woman
against her will, establish that Jewish society (often claimed to be in positive contrast to non-Jewish societies in this regard) protected women
against abuse in divorce, from polygynous marriages, or from spousal
violence.[17] Normative pronouncements, whether prescribing or forbidding behavior, are often in inverse relation to the behavior they address,
testifying to transgressive or "lax" behavior or to a desire to establish a
practice. Repeated prohibitions testify to failed efforts of control; repeat
exhortations to a desired behavior evidence the failure of efforts to produce changed practice or, as in the case of the commandments of tallit

and tefillin in medieval Ashkenaz, indicate that such behavior is being promoted for men against a norm of nonpractice.

Eve Krakowski argues similarly about the emergence in early twelfth-century Egyptian Geniza society of the elaborate prenuptial agreements we have discussed, showing that the authority of these agreements derived from "below," from the legitimacy that Jewish litigants accorded them, however much this authority could be reinforced from "above," by Muslim religious judges and state officials. While recourse to rabbinic courts and the exercise there by scribes and judges of their expertise demonstrated their "hierarchical authority as technical experts," she emphasizes that "rabbinic officials needed to remain flexible about what litigants wanted their agreements to say in order to attract them as litigants in the first place."[18]

We hear similar evidence of the consumer influence in rabbinic actions in the concern expressed by Joseph ben Abraham, a member of the rabbinic court in Avignon, to Solomon ben Abraham ibn Adret (Rashba, d. ca. 1310), a senior rabbinic authority in Barcelona. The question was whether both litigants to a court dispute were to pay court costs (there were paid lawyers) or whether only the losing party should compensate the victor for these. Ben Abraham expressed concern that denying the prevailing party his remuneration might cause litigants to avoid coming to rabbinic courts.[19] Rabbinic authority was in dynamic play with circumstances and pressures, Jewish and not, a reality to which rabbinic figures in medieval Ashkenaz, Provence, and the Jewish East were supremely sensitive. This was true in Jewish communities of the later, Ottoman era as well.[20] As Esther Benbassa and Aron Rodrigue state about Jewish juridical autonomy under the Ottomans, it "was entirely relative. Jewish society could not enforce total compliance with its laws within the community when this same law was not considered absolutely binding by the dominant ruling non-Jewish authority."[21] Howard Adelman demonstrates a similar reality for rabbinic authority in early modern Italy.[22]

We can conclude that reforms such as we have described, both de jure (rabbinic-normative) and de facto (prenuptial agreements negotiated by the parties), conditional divorce being an example of both, emerged in response to several factors: economic realities, the behavior of women in pressing their interests, and the adaptiveness of the rabbinic system, given its operational limits. Women grasped the power that wealth or economic contributions—or the threat of falling needy—gave them to demand protections for themselves and their interests.[23] They applied that power, using rabbinic as well as non-Jewish courts as means of pressure and enforcement, doing so, necessarily, with male representation or other intervention.

Women's Actions on Their Own Behalf: Extracting Marital Freedom

Premarital agreements in which male kin in premodern Jewish communities acted to protect the marriage and divorce interests of their (remarrying) mothers, and those of their daughters, sisters, or other dependent female kin, were normal and ubiquitous practice across the Jewish world. We have noted the self-interest of such kin and of the male-administered, premodern community as a whole in such agreements and the fact that concerns about women in marital jeopardy were not just familial but communal. Women assertively also took matters into their own hands regarding marriage and divorce and other issues at the intersection of their lives and rabbinic law.

Assertive Women

Sixteenth-century Egyptian Jewish women used Nile tributaries for ritual immersion even when these were not filled with water throughout the year, a stipulation for their halakhic use as ritual baths (mikvaot; sing., mikva). Indeed, they violated repeated, vehement prohibitions of this behavior by Rabbi David ben Zimra (Radbaz, 1479, Spain–1573, Safed), a leading decisor in Safed, to whom their behavior was referred. In one sixteenth-century Jewish community, possibly Damascus, local authorities forbade the use of mikvaot on festivals and the Sabbath (which begins at sundown on Friday; women's ritual immersion is to take place after nightfall). This delayed women's immersion by a day or more, without which the couple's resumption of sexual relations after the rabbinically calculated time a wife was deemed a menstruant, already a minimum of twelve days a month, was forbidden. "Some women" refused to wait and began to immerse before nightfall on

Friday—meaning the immersions were halakhically invalid. It turned out that the women knew that in other communities, immersion in the mikva was permitted on the Sabbath and holidays and used that fact—and transgressive behavior with serious implications for husbands (invalid immersion meant that sexual relations remained forbidden)—to pressure their rabbis to open the mikvaot on these days.[24] These women were not rejecting or even defying rabbinic law; they were demanding a say in the terms of its application, using pressure tactics in an area in which men had a compelling, common interest with them.

We have much other evidence of women's assertiveness. Halakha forbids a nursing widow or divorcee from remarrying for twenty-four months, in order to protect a new husband from being made to serve the interest of his predecessor (the support of a new husband for children of a previous marriage had to be negotiated). Remaining unmarried for two years, however, without the economic partnership of a husband defied the interests of such widows and of their kin, on whom they were likely to fall dependent. We hear of the case of one widow who gave birth four months after her husband's death, whose female relatives raised a racket at the moment of birth so that the woman would not hear the child's cries and begin to nurse him. They immediately engaged a wet nurse so that the widow would not fall into the rabbinic category of "nursing his fellow's offspring" (*meneket havero*) and could, therefore, remarry without delay, permission she in fact received.[25] Clearly, this woman's female kin knew and were "working" the strictures of patriarchal, rabbinic law preemptively and successfully on their kin's behalf. Did they act in coordination with male kin? Probably. Nor was this the only recorded instance of preventing this disability falling on a woman widowed while pregnant. Another source notes one such woman herself engaging two wet nurses before the birth in order to evade it.[26]

Women who got conditional divorces from husbands away on lengthy business trips often used these to effect divorce even when the men returned within the specified time before the divorce took effect, hiding and waiting out the clock until after the date on which the get took effect. When such women could not be located and the couple reunited—a prerequisite for the marriage to be deemed resumed—rabbinic authorities were forced by their own rules to recognize the divorces as having taken effect. Rabbinic sources quote one such sixteenth-century woman, from Damascus, who waited out the term of her conditional divorce, given not because her husband was traveling but because of severe marital breakdown (if he did not succeed in placating her within thirty consecutive days, it would take effect), declaring, "The get is a kosher get! It was conditional on my being reconciled and reunited [with my husband] but I did not reunite with him because I did not wish to reconcile and I hid in order to flee [the marriage]! I have received my get, now give me my ketubbah [monetary divorce settlement]!" In one case, from Jerusalem, rabbis even colluded with a woman known to be abused in her marriage to extract a conditional get from her husband, knowing she would use it to escape the marriage.[27] Such behavior was common, Rabbi David ben Zimra (Radbaz) calling it "an everyday occurrence," and the means by which women attained the "privilege to be freed from their husbands."[28]

Another woman, from Istanbul, fearing, rightly, that a slew of failings and offenses by her husband that met technical grounds for a court-mandated divorce would not deliver one, announced her intention to move to the Land of Israel, which, she clearly knew, was even stronger grounds for a court-forced divorce when the husband refused to move there.[29] The rabbinic decisor was consistently unsympathetic to the woman and we do not know if her quest for divorce succeeded. We certainly know that she tried.

We see such resourcefulness emerging under the threat of iggun and its impact on halakhic ruling in the case of twenty-one agunot in 1540s Safed, whose husbands had gone down in the same shipwreck, with no bodies to prove death. The eminent kabbalist and halakhist Rabbi Joseph Karo (1488–1575) argued against lenient dispensation that would allow the women to remarry. But one of these women took matters into her own hands and remarried without such dispensation. Other rabbinic decisors argued against Karo's position, citing the fear that, without rabbinic accommodation in a lenient ruling, *just as one widow in this group married without asking rabbinic permission (as clearly her partner also did, with the necessary participation of two witnesses and an officiant— that is, five transgressive Jews in this one case), the other women in this situation would do likewise.*[30] Thus, we see that rabbinic awareness that women facing iggun would act assertively, even transgressively on their own behalf, led to arguments for leniency in a cluster of agunah cases.

These rabbis also expressed fear that, if denied means to remarry—
that is, to engage in licit sex—agunot would engage in the illicit kind,
with male partners, of course; they worried that rabbinic stringency,
particularly in cases of young women tied in marital captivity to dead
men or, in another subset of cases, to converted levirs in Iberia, would
lead to licentious behavior and the subversion of rabbinic authority and
social control altogether. As one decisor in Istanbul explained a rabbinic colleague's desire to rule leniently about a case discussed in 1503,
"he saw . . . the future outcome [of the woman remaining an agunah],
since women have frivolous minds, first they are outside the house and
next they are in the streets": stringent ruling might cause a breach in
sexual norms. Rabbis in Candia (Crete) voiced this same fear about a
woman left stranded there by a husband in Istanbul: if not freed by divorce (which they beseeched the Istanbul authorities to arrange), she
would "go astray."[31] Authorities in Safed several times issued rulings that
released agunot in halakhically dubious cases because of expressed fear
that failure to do so would result in the women pursuing "evil ways."[32]
Assertive action by women and rabbinic fear of such behavior, not martyred compliance or pleading, led to the agunah who remarried without
rabbinic release from iggun reclaiming her life, and *to broader rabbinic
arguments for leniency*. Minna Rozen probed the circumstances of lenient and stringent rulings when there were precedents in both directions and found that decisors in Istanbul tended to leniency in cases of
agunot whose husbands were feared but not proven dead, as opposed to
cases of agunot in that state for other reasons. The negative economic
consequences to the community were the same regardless of circumstances, but decisors had a specific fear of young women with no hope of
being released, as opposed to women who could still hope that a living
husband would relent, becoming sexually transgressive.[33]

Sixteenth-century rabbinic authorities in Istanbul, a city to which
many refugees from the forced conversions in Spain and Portugal and
the expulsion from Spain (1492) migrated, argued in favor of dispensing with the requirement of release from levirate marriage by converted
levirs who remained in Iberia for fear that the agunot not thus freed
would themselves convert.[34] Women clearly knew of rabbinic debates
and disagreements about release of such agunot, as well as about the
rabbinic distinction between acts done ab initio (*lehat'hila*) and post

facto (*bediavad*), the latter of which could be ruled acceptable. Some women bound to levirate marriages acted on this knowledge and remarried without having received either halitsa or rabbinic release from its requirement, confident that rabbis would not invalidate their remarriages. Rabbis were well aware of this behavior and considered it in making halakhic rulings. Thus, we learn from rabbinic sources of a childless widow whose converted levir remained in Portugal where, freed of anti-Jewish discrimination, he had amassed substantial assets and was not going to leave. This agunah "heard that there are rabbinic sages who say that if she proceeds and remarries, they will not separate her [from her second husband], and she acted and remarried!"[35] Rabbinic decisors in Ottoman Palestine, to which many Iberian refugees also immigrated, expressed similar fear about the actions agunot denied relief might take, citing the case of an agunah from Corfu: denied release from iggun, she converted.[36]

No less than a daughter-in-law of Rabbi Joseph Karo, widowed from a childless marriage, took matters into her own hands in 1580 with strong backing from "her family," surely a reference to rabbinically knowledgeable male relatives. She and the levir—another of Karo's sons—had been feuding bitterly ("a burning fire") for two years in the context of a dispute between their respective families—meaning she had been in marital limbo at least for this amount of time. Finally, "someone advised her relatives" to instruct her to go to the synagogue during Monday-morning Torah reading—that is, in very public Jewish space and in the presence of not just kosher witnesses but rabbis, likely Karo himself—and spit at the levir three times, each time proclaiming, "This is the levir who wishes to take me in levirate marriage. I do not want you, I do not want you, I do not want you!"—which she did.[37] The bold action of this woman, unnamed in the sources, triggered learned debate among the sages first of Safed, then of Jerusalem (to whom the case was referred by those in Safed who wished a negative ruling). The question was the efficacy of the woman's act in forcing the levir to enact normative, that is, male-initiated halitsa (clearly, the woman's act was not deemed sufficient to free her, yet neither was it deemed ineffectual, since, according to some authorities, it necessitated the levir giving her halitsa, against his will).

Some decisors, incensed by the woman's assertiveness and female presumption on halakhic processes, favored punishing her, arguing that there should be no "coercion of [the levir] doing halitsa; *rather may she sit and her hair grow white [as an agunah], seeing that she behaved incorrectly*" (my emphasis). Rabbinic authority—patriarchal authority—was paramount, in whose protection the use of iggun as a punishment for women was an always-available tool. This consideration, and it would appear, rabbinic power struggles were such that all the Ashkenazi authorities in Safed (Karo, and surely his daughter-in-law, followed Sephardi halakhic custom) who pronounced on this case ruled against forcing the man to enact halitsa. In the end, however, the majority of the rabbinic decisors of Safed ruled that he should enact it. *And he did*: the handwritten *shtar*, the legal document attesting to the halitsa of "the daughter-in-law of our teacher, the great Rabbi Joseph Karo, may his memory be blessed," is preserved among a collection of such documents, including divorce documents, from Jerusalem.[38] None of these documents names the woman; she was of interest solely as the embodiment of a halakhic problem.

In this instance, as in others we have seen, men intervened against a patriarchal privilege exercised by other men in order to protect their own interests. Such latitude did not contradict traditional Jewish patriarchy; it was an inherent part of it, of patriarchal privilege. Elevated social status and wealth were surely necessary elements to such dynamics operating on women's behalf, in this era as in others we have seen. In fact, we find that there was ancient precedent for what Karo's daughter-in-law did—and why she was able to do it. Rabbi Simhah ben Samuel of Speyer (eleventh to twelfth century) advised a widow who did not wish to marry her brother-in-law—who was threatening to rape her, intending for this to enact marriage—to "spit in the face of the levir in front of witnesses and thus initiate the Halizah process."[39] The widow in this case is described as being "of distinguished lineage and wealthy," the former term indicating rabbinic descent. Lineage and wealth gave this woman access to a ranking rabbinic decisor and a call on his consideration. The upshot was powerful support in evading a levirate marriage she did not wish and retaining marital liberty, which her status and wealth positioned her to exercise advantageously in a marriage of her own arrangement. We hear, too, of a sixteenth-century woman, in Istanbul, who also attempted to force halitsa by having the levir ambushed by non-Jewish thugs her family hired, brought to a house before

Figure 3.2 Halitsa document of the daughter-in-law of Joseph Karo. From Porgos, *She'elot u'teshuvot*.

three Jewish men (constituting a rabbinic court), and spitting in his face. The decisor tasked with deciding if this act meant the levir had to enact halitsa, coerced by rabbinic action if necessary, ruled against this. Whatever eventuated in this case, assertiveness on the woman's part, with the active support of male kin, is amply attested. We see this, too, in the behavior of another widow in a levirate situation, also in Istanbul, who feared that the levir (who did not want to marry her) was maneuvering to deny her the settlement due her as a widow, and began selling off marital assets to ensure she got the settlement's value. She failed to get rabbinic support, which went to the levir, as Rozen says it always did in the rulings of Istanbul rabbis in disputes between levirs and widows, but she certainly attempted to protect her interests. Women in such actions evidenced clear understanding of the workings of rabbinic law in their situations. One widow, whose two husbands predeceased her (there were no children from the second husband), was so desperate to avoid being forced into a levirate marriage that she sought stigmatized halakhic classification as a "fatal/murderous wife" (*isha katlanit*), which status barred her from remarriage to anyone! This woman, too, lost her case but showed audacious and informed inventiveness in pressing it.[40]

That families—women and men kin—coached women is clear. Decisors certainly thought they did: the rabbi adjudicating one woman's (unsuccessful) suit for divorce dismissed one of her ironclad claims (her abusive husband had withheld sex) on the grounds that her relatives had advised her to make it.[41] Rabbis knew that women shared strategies for liberating themselves from marriage. Rabbi David ben Zimra (Radbaz) went so far as to say that even the conversion of some women to Islam when denied divorce upon the claim of a husband's impotence was preferable to women as a whole learning that such a claim could deliver a court-enforced divorce.[42]

Levirate marriage (*yibbum*) and release from it (halitsa) are both biblically mandated, opposing acts, leading to theoretical rabbinic disputes about which should take precedence, as well as deliberations in actual cases. The woman's preference in case of dispute between her and the levir was decidedly secondary, if that. Since the levir took possession of the deceased man's assets, levirs had incentive to declare, truthfully or not, a desire for *yibbum*, in order to demand compensation for forgoing its benefits, compensation rabbinic rulings deemed self-evidently reasonable. The system favored the levir's position and prioritized levirate marriage over releasing the widow to marry as she determined—with her prospects for remarriage improved by having received her widow's settlement, as well as return of her dowry. As Minna Rozen puts it about decisors in sixteenth-century Istanbul, who all ruled in favor of men in cases of conflict between men wishing and women refusing levirate marriage, they were resolved that "money that found its way to the paternal line should not find its way out."[43]

Ruth Lamdan shows that rabbinic decisors in sixteenth-century Palestine and Egypt also overwhelmingly privileged *yibbum* over halitsa and almost never favored even trying to force a man to give halitsa—that is, ruling in favor of the agunah wishing release. Rabbi David ben Zimra, in Safed, was a champion of levirate marriage. He ruled that in the case of a married levir and also in a case when the levir was seeking the marriage explicitly for monetary benefit—gaining control of the deceased's assets, rather than for the act's biblically stated purpose (using the widow to give postmortem life to a deceased, childless man)— *yibbum* rather than halitsa was preferred. Other decisors ruled *in principle* that levirate marriage was to take precedence over release in case of conflict between a resisting widow and the levir. Kabbalists prioritized similarly, citing mystical reasons: the *pleasure that the levirate marriage would give the dead man*.[44] Two authorities cited the doctrine of the transmigration of souls in this regard, saying that "the soul of the dead brother temporarily resided in his surviving brother's body until it was released by his brother into his widow to produce a child."[45] Howard Adelman shows that rabbinic authorities in sixteenth-century Italy also privileged *yibbum* over halitsa and were loath even to try to force a refusing levir to enact halitsa and free his sister-in-law, at most *encouraging halitsa extortion* as a means for the woman to buy her freedom to marry someone else.[46] If she lacked such means, that outcome was on her.

There are recorded instances of rabbinic "leniency" in favor of the widow. One was the case of a forty-year-old widow whose levir was a four-year-old boy who, according to the Safed *posek* Rabbi Moshe Mitrani (Hamabit), was to be encouraged to enact halitsa so that the woman would not be reduced to abject poverty (or, in the case of a wealthy woman, unused to doing menial work, to caring for a child-husband who, obviously, was incapable of fathering a child with her). In another instance of leniency, Mitrani said that a man who all knew was abusive to the widow with whom he sought to enter a levirate marriage against her will, seeking this for financial benefit and in order to torment her, should be coerced to give her halitsa.[47]

Revenge and vindictiveness of the levir, abetted by rabbinic actions, certainly operated in cases of women caught in the halitsa trap.[48] Lamdan describes a case of halitsa extortion in sixteenth-century Palestine and disagreements between decisors in Safed about whether to enact coercive measures to induce the levir to free the widow, which he was refusing to do, while also demanding a payoff he knew she could not give. Against the opinion of some decisors, including Joseph Karo, that pressure (the threat of social excision, herem) should be put on the levir to enact halitsa, another decisor, Rabbi Levi ibn Habib (Ralbach) (ca.1480, Spain–1545, Safed, whose rulings we will encounter elsewhere, in each case against women), argued otherwise. Ibn Habib held that even if the levir was married (as in this case), and the widow past childbearing age, rabbis should not pressure the levir to enact halitsa. Rabbi David ben Zimra (Radbaz) strongly supported ibn Habib's position, the upshot of which would be that the woman remained an agunah. Since previous decisors (*rishonim*)—"the eminent authorities [geonim] of the past," he argued, had not reached consensus in favor of pressuring a levir to enact halitsa, the current generation of decisors had no such authority. Rabbi Moshe Mitrani accepted the argument privileging levirate marriage over release from it as definitive, *and argued that the woman should pay the brother-in-law for halitsa to the full extent of her means (or their exhaustion)*—explicit rabbinic endorsement of extortion. In this case, however, it was not a question of the woman's ability to pay, and thus, even an extortive path to freedom, since the levir had said explicitly that he was acting vindictively, punitively, in order to inflict iggun on the widow. Nevertheless, Mitrani wrote that if it was truly money the levir was seeking (which, again, was not the case), "he [that is, his lust for revenge and vanquishment of the woman] should *be satisfied and appeased in knowing that the woman had offered him all she had*" (my emphasis). Astoundingly (or perhaps not), Mitrani closed his halakhic responsum by stating, "And may God . . . protect the daughters of Israel who are agunot and open for them the gates of light, amen." After ruling in ways that condemned this woman and others to iggun, Mitrani throws the ball to God to save agunot from actions like his own.[49]

Minna Rozen found that decisors in sixteenth-century Istanbul "never" coerced a man to give a get, no matter what or how well attested the circumstances. This included two cases that came before Rabbi Tam ibn Yahya involving wives seeking divorces from men who lacked full sexual organs. Ibn Yahya treated the men with "maximum leniency" and forbade their being excommunicated socially to pressure them for divorce (as apparently the women's kin had sought), or forced by the rabbinic court to divorce their wives (obviously, the problem had not been disclosed before the marriages; it would seem that marriage, including the always-available option of chained wives, could have been an attempted social "cover" by these men for their condition). These decisors also denied requests by women claiming that the husband was sexually repulsive (*ma'is alai*), one of the permissible grounds for women to ask for divorce, but accepted such claims from men who, of course, already possessed decisive halakhic advantage in divorce.[50]

From fifteenth- and sixteenth-century Italy, home to multiple Jewish ethnicities following different halakhic customs, Howard Adelman offers much evidence of rabbinic collusion with halitsa extortion as entirely normal and self-evident. As rabbis ruled it normal that women seeking gittin compensate husbands to receive the get, they ruled similarly about women seeking halitsa, finding this situation no different from that of any financial transaction where one party seeks something the other possesses.[51] The major decisor Rabbi Joseph ben Solomon Colon (Maharik, ca. 1420–1480) ruled that the widow's release was not just to

be enacted but "forced [a policy rabbis were otherwise loath to sanc-
tion] *if the woman had no assets* . . . but if she were rich, a financial compromise should be worked out" (my emphasis)—explicit instruction to
extort the widow for her freedom, and clear indication that decisors saw
women's release from marriage not as a matter of ethics or justice but as
men's business opportunity. "Yibbum and the threat of being trapped as
an aguna," writes Adelman, "served as a vehicle for her late husband's
side of the family to recoup some of the assets they contributed to the
[supplemental ketubbah payment, the *tosefet*] ketubbah." This was no
"tragedy," but a deliberate and normal rabbinic policy serving male interests, literally at women's expense.

About this situation, Adelman asks:

> As with so many other similar matters involving marriage, a central ques-
> tion was [the means a woman had to extricate] herself from a difficult
> position. . . . Could a [levir] be forced to release his [sister-in-law]? If a
> woman claimed that her [levir] disgusted her [as the reason she sought
> halitsa], could she be punished as a rebellious woman? Could halitza be
> forced for this reason?

Rabbis of this time and place, Adelman found, were "very unsympathetic" to women made agunot for want of halitsa. Despite a general
position favoring communal control, even capital punishment when he
felt that rabbinic authority was being challenged, Rabbi Leon Modena
(1571–1648), head of the Italian and German Jewish communities of
Venice, "was remarkably reluctant to force halitsa."

In the face of such realities, women became inventive. In one case
Adelman describes, a woman demanded that her future brother-in-law
sign a prenuptial agreement obliging him to give her halitsa, should she
fall into need of it. When he refused, the wedding was postponed.[52]

Did this premodern, entirely traditional Jewish woman succeed in
getting that prenuptial agreement? We know that she refused to marry
on the scheduled date and that any postponement throws the wedding
into doubt—that she used the pressure at her disposal to try to protect herself. Since marriage was a financial institution, presumably her
groom wanted the marriage he had contracted, on terms he found at

least satisfactory, perhaps even compelling, to proceed. Given her behavior, he may have wanted, needed, the match more than she did. This
bride had leverage, knew that, and used it.

Women in marital jeopardy or actual iggun sought and could get
help from family, in particular from male kin, but women also sought
help from unrelated men. Noa Shashar published the great rarity of a
letter written by an agunah in Frankfurt an der Oder, in 1792, which
she addressed to "my dear friend" Yakev. Frida, the daughter of Mechel,
had visited Yakev's parents and there learned that Yakev "wished to do
a mitzvah and help me regarding my evil husband, whom you yourself
see to be an evil man, since he told you that his wife [Frida] was dead
and that he was not married." Not only was this a lie, which is what
prompted Yakev to wish to "do a mitzvah and help" Frida. Her husband
had ruined Frida financially and had not returned a loan of funds from
Frida's son from a previous marriage, when she had lent these to her
husband on condition that he repay them when her son needed them
for his own business. Frida asked Yakev's help in obtaining a get and a
written commitment from her husband to pay her ketubbah settlement
and the sum due her son, and gave Yakev power of attorney to those
ends. "My very dear friend," she wrote, "upon receipt of this letter, take
it to Rabbi [Shteg]" and have him detain her husband, lest he flee. The
husband was to be directed to come to her to give her the get or appoint
a messenger, at his own expense, to deliver it; she was poor and could
not afford to travel to her husband's location. We do not know the outcome of Frida's efforts but they show not just wealthy but also financially
distressed agunot acting on their own behalf.[53]

Concluding

The evidence shows that Jewish women in traditional societies across
the Jewish world behaved not just economically but politically in their
own interest—that is, with awareness of power dynamics and of their
own positioning in them, and armed themselves with the requisite
knowledge of the workings of Jewish and non-Jewish legal and communal systems to do battle on their own behalf. They acted as self-evident
participants in the halakhic legal system—as its constituents and entitled
claimants. Halakha in the pre- and early modern worlds of Ashkenaz,

Italy, the Mediterranean, and the Middle East was dynamic, influenced by its constituents, very much including women, who did not hesitate to engage its categories and to violate them *as part of the functioning of the system*. Jews, women and men, who exceeded or violated Talmudic norms in private agreements within and between families in pursuit of their interests and who also used Muslim or nonecclesiastical Christian courts, as well as rabbinic courts to that end, continued to live as Jews under rabbinic law, within tight Jewish communities. In such communities, such behavior was both known and normal, in the common and sociological uses of that term. Their behavior was incorporated into Jewish life and became part of that life and its systems of governance. Halakhic authorities knew that if they did not adjudicate appropriately in various situations in family law—about property, inheritance, the terms of marriage and divorce—the Jews involved, prominently women, would neither acquiesce nor confine themselves to pleading but would seek recourse outside of rabbinic norms or authority. This knowledge factored into halakhic decision-making. Jewish behavior created a de facto realm of "norm" that included formally transgressive actions that fed back into the officially normative Jewish legal system (halakha), changing it.

There is effort today in some Orthodox circles to promote the claim, derived from Evangelical Christian preaching to women in those communities about dutiful, Christian women's submissiveness to patriarchal authority, that such behavior is properly, historically, traditionally, Jewish. It isn't.[54]

Despite strong strictures, beginning in the Talmud, forbidding taking intra-Jewish disputes to non-Jewish courts, medieval Jews, prominently women in divorce disputes, made extensive use of such courts, both Christian and Islamic, to which subject we now turn.[55]

4

Using Non-Jewish Courts, and Rabbinic Courts

Women and Justice Systems

Studies based on the Cairo Geniza and the responsa of Moses and Abraham Maimonides show that women from both "socially weak" and "well-placed" backgrounds in Egypt and Palestine under Fatimid rule (969–1171) took inheritance and other property cases and marriage and divorce cases to Muslim courts for better terms than they would get in rabbinic ones, or to exert pressure for better outcomes in the latter. The evidence indicates that women in particular used this expedient. "The old scholarly consensus that Jews adhered faithfully to their courts and made use of Muslim courts only in exceptional cases," writes Oded Zinger, "is no longer tenable. . . . Jewish use of Muslim courts was pervasive."[1]

Indeed, a tenth-century source from the head of the Talmudic academy of Pumpedita (in today's Iraq), Sherira Gaon (906–1006), asserts that the practice of Jewish women going to Muslim courts in order to pressure or force their husbands to give them a divorce occurred as early as 651 CE, that is, shortly after the Muslim conquest of Iraq (636 CE). The practice was so pronounced that rabbinic authorities instituted a takkanah, a rabbinic ordinance, known as *takkanat hamoredet*, concerning the "rebellious wife" who refuses to perform rabbinically prescribed domestic functions for a husband, including sex, and who seeks divorce, overturning the Talmudic ruling on this subject. This ruling states that, in order to force "rebellious" wives into submission, divorce should be delayed for a year with subsistence needs vouchsafed in the ketubbah withheld and the value of the ketubbah settlement progressively diminished until its exhaustion. But social reality compelled a very different policy. In order to prevent Muslim courts from playing a role in Jewish family law—and encouraging Jewish women to convert, since a woman who converted to Islam when her husband did not could obtain a divorce in sharia courts—the "ordinance of the rebellious wife" ruled that such wives were to be divorced immediately, with restitution of their dowries (goods they brought into the marriage or their value) as well as full payment of their ketubbah settlement. About this Sherira Gaon stated: "And afterwards, the Rabbanan Sabborai [successors of the sages of the Babylonian Talmud, redacted ca. 700 CE], saw that Jewish *women were becoming dependent upon the Gentiles to get divorces from their husbands by force* . . . from which ruin emanates" (my emphasis).[2] Sherira stated that the "ordinance of the rebellious wife" was in force in his time in Babylonia (Iraq) and had been for some three hundred years already, and urged that it be enforced in North African communities as well. Two centuries later, Rav Samuel ben Ali Gaon confirmed that the ruling was enforced in Babylonia, and sources from Franco-Germany show that it was enforced there in the eleventh century as well.[3] Rabbi Asher ben Yehiel (the Rosh), a major thirteenth-century Ashkenazic decisor, wrote some of his works in Spain, where he was appalled to see this ordinance applied, allowing "rebellious" wives to get swift divorces with favorable settlements; such was the fear of Jewish women going to Gentile authorities to force such settlements.[4]

As we have seen, there were several overlapping legal and political institutions to which Jews in Geniza society were subject and had access: rabbinic and Islamic religious courts and those of the Islamic state, and the controls of Jewish communal officials. For women, the most important institution was the rabbinic court, for it was primarily here, says Eve Krakowski, so long as she remained Jewish, "that a woman could hope to escape a ruinous marriage or achieve any other basic social and economic goal: receive an inheritance, contract or renegotiate a marriage, or pass on her property after she died."

Yet, Krakowski shows that Jewish women seeking divorce appealed to Muslim courts when they failed to obtain relief in rabbinic ones. In such circumstances, women could "circumvent the Jewish leadership entirely, or try to force its hands, by turning to an Islamic qādi [religious judge] or to state officials," a point women emphasized in petitions to Jewish authorities. "I appeal to my lord . . . and to the community," says a typical (undated) letter narrated by a woman seeking divorce, "to grant me justice from (my husband). Otherwise I will be forced to go to the nations of the world"—meaning to an Islamic court—"that they may save me."[5]

This is the situation Sherira Gaon referenced with alarm regarding the ordinance concerning the rebellious wife, which sought to meet the demands of such women lest they press them in sharia and Islamicate offices. Citing the findings of Jessica Goldberg about Mediterranean Jewish merchants' (men's) use of rabbinic courts before resorting to alternatives, Krakowski notes that the ever-present threat of a legal opponent taking his case to a qadi's court or to a state tribunal pressured both parties to a dispute to reach agreement before one of them took such action.[6] We see this dynamic in a case Krakowski cites, when concessions were made in a commercial case on condition that the case be dropped from an Islamic court and adjudicated in a rabbinic one.[7] This dynamic clearly also operated in the behavior of women plaintiffs in rabbinic courts and in the handling of the cases they brought there, with the possibility of women's appeal to non-Jewish authorities ever present. This reality, the difference, in Krakowski's terms, between "rabbinic law on the page and on the ground," testifies both to "the far-reaching social impact of prescriptive rabbinic law in Fatimid and Ayyubid Egypt [909–1249], and . . . its . . . limits."[8]

Ashkenazi women also appealed to non-Jewish—nonecclesiastical Christian—courts, and used threats of such recourse to better the terms they would receive in rabbinic courts in marital and divorce and associated property disputes.[9] We see evidence of such behavior in communal ordinances, prohibiting, on pain of social, economic, and religious excision, the initiation by Jews of proceedings in non-Jewish courts, particularly in divorce cases. The Spanish/North African decisor Shimon ben Tsemah Duran (Rashbats, 1361–1444) explained the reasons for such ordinances as follows: "Since, as is well known, the husband holds the wife in his power [under rabbinic law], it happens at times that the wife will cast her fate in the hands of idolators, preferring to litigate in their courts—that is why this ordinance has come to prevent them from doing so on pain of . . . herem." A similar ordinance, derived from the rulings of Rabbi Jacob ben Meir (Rabbenu Tam), enacted in Ashkenazic communities, decreed such excision from the community on "any man or woman . . . who shall sue his fellow [Jew] in the courts of the idolatrous gentiles."[10] If there had not been significant use of non-Jewish courts by Jews, prominently by women, specifically about divorce, there would not have been such communal responses.

We see a later expression of this dynamic in sixteenth-century Prato, Italy, in the case of a prominent widow, Judita da Pisa, whom Rabbi Azriel Diena sanctioned severely for turning to Catholic authorities to administer her directives about her extensive assets. Diena was particularly concerned, Howard Adelman writes, that members of such a distinguished family had turned to the secular authorities. He put Judita, her brother Jehiel Nissim, and their supporters in herem and ordered the children and their property removed from the authority of the non-Jewish court, that the Jewish court was to appoint a guardian for the children, and that Judita and her children were to take their case to a rabbinic court. Diena threatened that if these conditions were not met, Judita would be penalized with loss of her dowry.[11] This was a particularly extreme sanction since, under halakha, the dowry remains the wife's possession.

Confirmation of the common recourse of women to non-Jewish courts and of rabbinic desire to eradicate this behavior comes from an interesting source: rabbinic textual formulas for herem codified in the medieval period. Ada Rapoport-Albert shows that such formulas refer explicitly only to men, with women neither named as individuals nor denounced as a distinct category—with one exception: use of the phrase "man or woman" is found in "rabbinic ordinances . . . prohibiting, on pain of herem, the initiation by Jews of legal proceedings in non-Jewish courts, particularly in divorce cases."[12]

On the one hand, halakha, adjudicated by rabbis, was the primary, if not the only legal system by which premodern Jews lived under both Christian and Muslim rule. The premodern Jewish community, the kehilla, was a self-governing, legally recognized, corporate entity, and Jewish identity, like all premodern identity, was collective.[13] Legally, the kehilla had authority—political legitimacy, as well as power—and means to implement decisions. It had state-sanctioned mechanisms of enforcement because a governing elite empowered to enforce the demands of rulers on Jews, particularly fiscal exactions, served the interests of those authorities. The power of the kehilla to enforce demands on Jews internally was a concomitant benefit to the kehilla leadership, rabbinic and lay. This made the kehilla, and halakha, the first and primary address for internal pressure for reforms.

But we have seen the limits of the powers of the kehilla and of rabbinic courts, and the de facto means by which reforms benefiting women, then recognized as normative, came into existence. The enactment of communal ordinances prescribing herem for women turning to Gentile courts in divorce cases attests to the reality and efficacy of women's tactics to effect improved conditions for themselves as they continued living traditional Jewish lives—there was nothing else—within the kehilla. The use of Gentile courts for intra-Jewish disputes despite formal strictures forbidding this, and acceptance and application of the verdicts of those courts within the community, constitutes powerful evidence of de facto realities.[14]

The record of the behavior of premodern Jewish women regarding halakha as it affected the most critical circumstances of their lives exemplifies the fluid, dynamic, active state of engagement, the "loop" system of Jewish law. Because there was no "neutral" or "semineutral" civil sphere in premodern societies that Jews could inhabit, to use Jacob Katz's terminology for an essential characteristic of European Jewish modernity, Jewish behavior necessarily fed back into the larger social folds of Jewish communities.[15]

Jews—women—who turned to non-Jewish courts in divorce disputes were not enacting separation from, much less desertion of, their Jewish communities or rabbinic law. One example, albeit unusual, proves the case. Jewish women in late medieval, Venetian-controlled Crete did not go outside the halakhic system when they took marriage disputes to the ducal court, Venetian Crete's supreme judiciary, since the authorities there, as everywhere in the premodern world, recognized rabbinic law as that which governed Jews in internal Jewish affairs. Under Venetian rule, this understanding was the more pronounced, since there was no divorce for Catholics: use of a Venetian ducal court in Jewish divorce disputes meant an appeal to halakhic adjudication there, administered by non-Jewish authorities. But the point in going outside the community, in taking a dispute out of the rabbinic court to the ducal authorities, was to better the settlement terms *under halakhic rubrics and in traditional communities*—since nothing else was then possible for Jews short of conversion.[16] This was not aberrant but traditional Jewish behavior.

The transmission of the Jewish, religious sphere into the state sphere in Venetian Crete, Rena Lauer argues, was not just facilitated by women, but by women's "double disenfranchisement as Jews and women," a disability that, in this instance, "did not limit them, but rather empowered them" to exercise assertive expedients on their own behalf.[17] We should see this behavior as a premodern expression of what Iris Parush terms the benefits of women's marginality.[18] We can appropriate for these women Lauer's conclusion about communal leaders in Candia, Venetian-controlled Crete. As both women and Jews, the women who took their cases to courts there "saw the Venetian judiciary as a legitimate venue" for adjudicating their cases, "a venue whose use did not undermine dedication to and observance of halakha."[19]

Jewish women in divorce disputes also used rabbinic courts, and their husbands Gentile ones, when each party perceived advantage in those routes. Sometimes women used both legal systems in support of their claims in the same case. Thus, in fourteenth-century Catalonia, Spain, in a case documented unusually thoroughly, a wealthy and highly literate Jewish businesswoman pursued her son-in-law aggressively, first to force his giving his wife, her daughter, a get; and then again, after he had done so, on terms she had set, when he attempted to invalidate the divorce, having arranged a deceitful system whereby he obtained his divorce settlement but left his wife an agunah. The tactics and argumentation this woman used, both inside the rabbinic system and outside of it, and that she deployed against her son-in-law's use of Gentile authorities, seeking to force the case back into rabbinic court, where she felt (rightly) that the odds were in her favor, were extremely informed and sophisticated—and appear to have been successful.[20] Notably, in this case, the mother cited Catalonian royal privilege to Jews authorizing rabbinic courts as the legal system governing Catalonian Jews—reminding us that, whatever rabbis claimed about their authority, ultimately its force derived from Gentile warrant.

Concluding: Why Were Reforms Benefiting Women Implemented in the Medieval Era?

Women and Politically Engaged Economics

Avraham Grossman, whose book treats the entire medieval Jewish world—Ashkenaz, Sepharad, Provence, Italy, and the Middle East—concludes, in answer to the question of why reforms benefiting women emerged in the medieval period, that "the important role played by [women] in supporting the family had a decisive impact upon the improvement of [their] status . . . no other factor exerted such a decisive influence upon the status of the woman during [this] period."[21]

I am saying several other things in addition: first, that women's economic contributions supported not just their individual families but the Jewish community as a whole and contributed significantly to its welfare, economic and existential—and that community authorities understood this at the time and acted on that perception. And second, that it was not women's economic contributions per se that led to the reforms, but their political behavior in translating those contributions into leverage on the community (kehilla) and on rabbinic jurisprudence that led to reforms. Kehilla authorities acted on the perception of women's economic importance, treating women as political players because women acted as such. It was the readiness of women to use their economic clout to press the kehilla or, failing to obtain relief within, to seek relief outside of it or pressure by non-Jewish authorities on the community, that caused rabbis and the community to respond to their needs. This pattern of consciousness and behavior I call "politically engaged economics."

Grossman's characterization of medieval Jewish women as both pious and rebellious is apt and instructive, though he appears to distinguish between these types, identifying rebellious women with those labeled in halakhic discourse as such, as *mor'dot* (plural of *moredet*). I am saying the terms should be ascribed to the same women and actions; that to act assertively on their own behalf within the halakhic system was simultaneously "rebellious" and pious. Simha Goldin, on the other hand, attributes the emergence of reforms that benefited medieval Ashkenazic women to their piety, or more precisely, to rabbinic awareness and appreciation of that piety and its importance, given existential threats to the communities of Ashkenaz.[22] There is much evidence, however, that it was not women's piety but their appreciation of their economic significance to the kehilla and astute, determined application of that power—political behavior—that prompted the reforms. Major reforms that not only exceeded Talmudic prescriptions but violated them were not the result of good behavior on the part either of women or the male kin who helped them, or of rabbis and heads of Jewish communities, but of realpolitik.

Although the halakhic—that is, the legal, not merely the descriptive—category *ishah hashuva*, an "important woman," is Talmudic (Pesahim

108a), referring to women who enact ritual obligations normally incumbent only on men, it is significant that medieval and early modern halakhic decisors—Rabbi Eleazar ben Judah of Worms (the Rokeah, 1160–1238), Rabbi Samuel ben Meir (Rashbam, ca. 1085–1158), and Rabbi Manoah of Narbonne (late thirteenth to fourteenth century, Provence)—expanded on it. They defined *ishah hashuva* (among other identifiers) as a woman who was independent of her husband, either because he allotted her freedom, because she was widowed or divorced, or "because of her economic status, including her production of an independent source of income from 'the fruits of her own labor.'" Commenting on the above-cited Talmudic passage and the commentary on it in the Tosefta (mishnaic material not included in the Mishna), Rabbi Mordechai ben Hillel (thirteenth century, Germany) asserted that "in our times, all women are to be considered *nashim hashuvot* [important women]."[23] That pronouncement by jurists reflected lived reality, the assertive behavior of women.

5

Socioeconomic and Halakhic Realities
in Early Modernity

Ottoman Turkey, Greece, Palestine, Syria, Egypt

The socioeconomic–halakhic realities we have seen in the medieval period (roughly from the advent of Jewish life under Christian and Islamic rule, respectively, through the thirteenth century), in multiple Jewish spheres, marked Jewries in the Ottoman period (late thirteenth to early twentieth century) as well.

Despite rabbinic pronouncements demeaning or denying women's intelligence and business acumen and seeking to bar them from economic activity, Jewish women in Middle Eastern communities during the Ottoman era were economically active, with some enjoying economic independence, possessing money or property through wills, gifts, or from their own financial or commercial activities.[1] Women were moneylenders and traders, selling in markets a range of handicrafts they made or bought from Muslim women, something Muslim women did not do:[2] a Jewish women's niche. Ruth Lamdan cites a sixteenth-century non-Jewish traveler's account which notes that Jewish women in Turkey went about "with revealed faces," unlike Muslim women, which facilitated their presence in markets. Women from across the mixed ethnic spectrum of Ottoman Jewries—Sephardi, North African and Middle Eastern, Western (Ashkenazi), and Romaniot (Greek-speaking)—held and managed property, in particular apartments, houses, or portions of houses, for rent. Such women generally were not wealthy but belonged to the middle classes or were economically marginal, using rents as means of sustenance.[3]

But not all women were economically marginal. In the Ottoman capital, Istanbul, throughout the sixteenth century to at least the beginning of the seventeenth, there was a circle of powerful Jewish women known as Kiera or Kira/Kyra (Greek, "Lady") who served the royal palace as exclusive providers of goods and services to the enclosed women of the harem, who were forbidden direct contact with the outside world—an elite Jewish women's niche. The Kyra supplied the harem with jewelry and clothing, forming friendships with the sultan's wives and mothers. They enjoyed substantial economic returns and even attained positions of influence, which they sometimes used to advance the interests of the Jewish community, acting as *shtadlaniot*—intercessors with the non-Jewish world—and sometimes falling victim to court intrigues.[4] One wonders if such women ever interceded on behalf of any agunot.

Jewish women in sixteenth-century Safed went into the surrounding countryside to purchase fruit and vegetables, which they sold in town. A rabbinic court approved a widow's guardianship of her children on the basis of her demonstrated economic prowess—her ability to provide for them, rather than this burden falling on the community. Thus, a consideration we have seen operating in Geniza society on behalf of women's expanded rights continued to do so. Another widow was known to manage her late husband's business so successfully that she sent her son abroad as her agent with a consignment of goods to sell. We know of a Jewish woman who rented a shop in Jerusalem's markets and that Jewish businesswomen sued men in business disputes. Women secured loans, which they could not have done if they did not own and know how to leverage property. The latter behavior was sufficiently widespread that opposition and attempts to rein it in arose in Jerusalem, which communal authorities resisted because the impoverished community required the women's activities.[5]

Mothers gave sons money through wills, gifts from their property, or from their ketubbot. Mothers also used their financial and commercial expertise to help sons in distress; one such mother took control of all the property of a son forced to flee from his hometown and even ran his business. Mothers loaned money to sons and guaranteed their loans, becoming their business partners.[6] Women used their economic clout to settle their sons' marriage matches, including against the wishes of the sons or husbands,[7] and intervened when their sons were levirs, advising for or against marrying the widow. In one case, the mother and grandmother of a thirteen-year-old levir argued, accurately, that the boy was a juridical adult under halakha and thus legally competent to release his sister-in-law through halitsa to marry someone else.[8]

When mothers and sons had business disputes, both took them to rabbinic as well as to Muslim courts for resolution. One son sued his mother in the sharia court in Jerusalem over an oath she had made to give him money, which she did not honor.[9] Other cases also show Jewish women appealing to Muslim qadis, who ruled on Jewish property and family disputes, from child guardianship to child-support arrangements in cases of divorce or paternal death.[10]

Communal sources attest husbands and other male kin taking measures beyond and conflicting with Talmudic law, including, as we have seen for the medieval era, using the Muslim institution of the waqf, the religious charitable trust, as a mechanism through which wives, sisters, and mothers could inherit or enjoy perpetual use of property.[11] Such arrangements were also written into prenuptial and other agreements in communities in sixteenth-century Palestine, Egypt, Syria, and in Istanbul, Salonika, and Larissa, Greece.[12] Women in Palestine and Egypt from North African, Middle Eastern, and Romaniot communities had clauses written into their ketubbot stating that any profit they earned from their efforts belonged to them, while the obligation to cover their living expenses, a husband's obligation in the ketubbah, remained on the husband—a custom the sixteenth-century decisor Radbaz upheld against claims by husbands who, he noted, had accepted these terms at the time of their marriages. Radbaz even specified that the terms were binding whether written or not, since this arrangement was known local custom in Egypt—in his words, "even when this contravenes halakha."[13]

In Romaniot communities, women had marked economic power that translated into beneficial halakhic rulings at stark variance both with Talmudic law and established Jewish practice elsewhere. The thirteenth-century rabbi Isaiah di Trani the Elder (1180–1250) noted that, whereas "in most lands a husband inherited his wife after her death (unless she had no offspring) [in which case half of the dowry would revert to her heirs from her parental house, since that was the asset's source], in lands where Romaniot tradition was followed, a husband did *not* inherit his wife's property upon her death, unless a specific stipulation to this effect had been made at the time of the marriage" (emphasis in the original).[14] A responsum of the sixteenth-century Spanish refugee Rabbi Jacob ben Solomon ibn Habib (?1445-1515/16), written from Istanbul, records encountering a marriage custom that Romaniot Jews observed strictly:

no matter the size of the woman's dowry, the husband had no rights to it and he could only do business with it (the usual arrangement) if it was kept by his wife. Ibn Habib noted the upshot of this arrangement, comments Talya Fishman: the woman always kept an eye on her property.[15] It would seem that such women would equally have had their eyes on their husbands and their economic doings. Ibn Habib deeply disapproved of this practice and wished to curtail it lest it serve as a model in other communities, including his hometown, Salonika. Rather than a wife's economic dependence on a husband, which the ketubbah assumes, this situation depicts the opposite—the husband's economic dependence on his wife—and was intolerable on that account.

We grasp the normality of women's economic activity, assertiveness, and efficacy in all regions and eras of Jewish life from Ruth Lamdan's comment that: "Throughout the sixteenth century, both married and unmarried women [in Ottoman realms] were active not only in *traditional 'feminine' occupations, such as money-lending and real estate transactions,* but also in other professions and crafts, practiced both in the home and in the markets" (my emphasis).[16]

Women and Marriage in Early Modern Italy

Howard Adelman provides extensive insight into how Jewish marriage operated in early modern Italy, probing the interplay between lay behavior and halakhic ruling through dynamics we have observed in other places and periods.

Adelman brings the following example among many to illustrate women's male kin working to protect them when doing so was in their own interest. This example also illustrates women acting assertively on their own behalf and entirely normal Jewish recourse, prominently by women, to non-Jewish courts, in this instance those of Catholic Italy, in that quest.

He shows that women and "their families" required that engagement contracts include pledges that the husband not take an additional wife, lest their kin be entrapped in a polygynous situation, abandoned without being divorced or receiving the payouts due upon divorce, thus becoming agunot. According to Italian prenuptial agreements, he writes, should a husband nonetheless take a second wife, the first was to receive her ketubbah settlement and her dowry, with her relatives inheriting her remaining assets. Though not a prohibition of polygynous relationships, such provisions, if enforced, were serious disincentives to entering one. One example of how such provisions played out in actual relationships is that of Chiara, daughter of Abram Salom, in the early seventeenth century. She and Jacob Bueno contracted a prenuptial agreement before a Venetian Christian notary, according to which Jacob would have to pay Chiara a significant sum and give her a divorce (presumably, with her divorce settlement and return of her dowry) if he took a second wife. On a trip to Cairo, Jacob married another woman. Chiara then sued him in a Venetian court, which seized Jacob's assets and gave them to Chiara, who bequeathed them, in 1663, to her daughters and son. Adelman also documents extensive agreements and court cases to prevent women becoming trapped in a levirate obligation or subject to a levir's extortion in order to obtain release from such, and to collect substantial sums if such agreements were violated.[17]

We see the nature and vitality of women's economic activities in the case of one Rosa Romanina, the widow of Moses Guastalla, who in 1643, in Verona, dictated her last will and testament before Jews who recorded it. Though "illiterate," Romanina had extensive property consisting "of her own dowry and inheritances that she had received from her father and others, as well as the proceeds from her many business activities, including moneylending, rights to property, and ownership of a ritual bath."[18] In her testament before a Christian notary, she "referred to her illness, to a sense of impending death, and to her clarity of mind as she departed from traditional lines of succession and bequeathed property along female lines, especially those of her maternal family and not those of her paternal side"—her husband's line.[19]

In sum, in early modern Jewish modernity in multiple regions, as in other eras and locations we have explored, women were vital economic agents at all levels and used non-Jewish courts as well as rabbinic ones, and modalities like prenuptial negotiations and contracts, trusts, and wills, to advance their interests in actions that sidestepped, exceeded, or violated Talmudic rulings. All this was part of traditional Jewish life. Not only were women economically vital; they understood the clout this gave them to better their legal and actual circumstances. Like their medieval forebears, they became participants in halakhic processes on their own behalf with the same inventiveness and assertiveness they manifested in their business lives, advocating for themselves in both spheres as a self-evident matter of course.

In the critical area of family law, women's real status in Jewish societies—a function of their economic importance, political behavior, and the complicated patriarchal dynamics we have explored—made for Jewish law that improved women's options under the still operative, inescapable rubrics of androcentric, patriarchal, rabbinic law. For all the differences in places and periods of Jewish life, these striking facts typified premodern Jewish societies across the Jewish world.

6

Backlash

Medieval Jewish women's assertive actions to better their rights in marriage and divorce and the reforms that expanded those rights met opposition, expressions of which we have already encountered. In Ashkenaz such reaction received concerted expression, with demonstrable effects. Avraham Grossman, Simha Goldin, Martha Keil, Rachel Furst, and Elisheva Baumgarten all document rabbinic reaction in Ashkenaz against the power of women, which most date as beginning in the middle of the twelfth century (some date it somewhat later). Rabbis expressed this backlash in both statements and acts of omission, such as accounts by Rabbi Ephraim of Bonn (1132–ca. 1200) that omit mention of women's prominence in acts of martyrdom during persecution, despite this behavior being attested in many contemporaneous sources. In one work he went so far as to blame a woman for the massacre of the Jews of Blois, France, in 1171, after a blood libel there, calling her a *gevartanit*, a "masculine-like, tough female" whose "arrogant, strong-willed personality" he held responsible for the community's destruction.[1]

The antiwoman hostility of a major decisor of the time, Rabbi Asher ben Yehiel (the Rosh, 1250–1328), is expressed in responsa "where he stresses that the reforms made for the benefit of the woman [in particular those attributed to Rabbenu Gershom, prohibiting polygyny and divorce of a woman against her will] created an intolerable situation in which 'the power of the woman is greater than that of the man.'" Accordingly, he ruled against pressuring men to give a get; against women in levirate cases; against women petitioning for divorce on grounds that their husbands were mentally ill or had repellent physical conditions; and against immediate divorce of a "rebellious wife," contravening the geonic ordinance concerning the rebellious wife, which ordained immediate divorce with full payment of settlements due the wife. He asserted that, whereas women in earlier periods had been "modest" and thus merited the consideration of the geonim, "in our times, the women of Israel are immodest and boastful,"[2] their power needing to be curbed. He ruled against compelling a mentally ill, extremely violent husband to give his wife a get, against the pleadings of the wife that this be done while the man was still legally competent, fearing that his condition would deteriorate to the point that he would not be competent, leaving her an agunah "forever."[3]

The "significant" rabbinic "retreat" from the ordinance of the rebellious wife, in Avraham Grossman's characterization, even in cases of violence and the husband's violation of rabbinic law, is also seen centuries later in sixteenth-century Italy, in a case adjudicated in Ferrara by Yehiel ben Azriel Trabot of Ascoli (ca. 1512–1590).

A woman, reports Howard Adelman,

> described as enlightened and pious, declared that her husband was repulsive to her (*ma-is alai*) because he . . . physically and verbally abused her, squandered his assets, including giving them to charity instead of supporting the family, vowed to give his possessions to the state treasury, and forced her to have intercourse with him during her menstrual period. She asked the rabbis to force him to divorce her. . . . Trabot listed the medieval rabbinic authorities, most of whom were from Muslim lands, in favor of forcing divorce for reasons of repulsion. Against these rabbis, Trabot presented other rabbis, mostly from Catholic Europe, who opposed forcing divorce on the grounds of repulsion. Their main reason, not explicitly stated by him but present in the texts he mentioned, was their fear of women acting on their own and seeking support to dissolve marriages. Trabot stated that "even though her husband abused her and wasted his money, these were not good grounds [to force divorce]." He also ruled out forcing divorce when a woman claimed her husband compelled her to have intercourse with him during menstruation because witnesses could not substantiate her charge [!]. Trabot then cited a common maxim meant to reassure women of the merits of marriage—any marriage: "It is better to dwell in grief with a burden than to dwell in widowhood."[4]

The rabbinic retreat from the ordinance of the rebellious wife in both Christian Europe and in some Muslim countries manifested in a backlash specifically against the core features of the ordinance: immediate, rather than delayed, divorce of the woman seeking a get, and her retention of ketubbah and other divorce settlements. The main architects of the backlash against this ordinance were the major French and German sages of the twelfth century: Rabbi Eliezer ben Nathan (Raban) in Germany; Rabbenu Tam in France; Rabbi Zerahiah Halevi in Provence; and in Egypt, Maimonides. Subsequent decisors, like Asher ben Yehiel and then his disciples, reiterated and amplified rulings against the ordinance, effectively nullifying it.[5]

Given his preeminence, Rabbenu Tam's position on this issue, says Grossman, was decisive with the sages of Ashkenaz and France in subsequent generations. Tam "strongly attacked the ordinance of the moredet [rebellious wife], in a manner unprecedented by any other sage before or since. In his words, the Geonim did not have the right to make [this] regulation . . . forcing a husband to give a get." He challenged the validity of such a forced get with the ultimate patriarchal taboo and abusive cudgel: the threat that children born in any subsequent marriage to a woman divorced according to the ordinance would be mamzerot/im. Obviously, no such concern about the legitimacy of such divorces had led decisors in the Middle East, North Africa, and Ashkenaz, prior to Rabbenu Tam, during his lifetime, or shortly after it—the geonim Rabbi Isaac ben Jacob Alfasi, Rabbenu Gershom Me'or Hagolah, Rabbi Shmuel ben Meir (Rashbam), Rabbi Simhah ben Samuel of Speyer—to terminate the ordinance, which had been enacted in Jewish communities for some five centuries and which they enforced.[6] Rabbi Simhah of Speyer even addressed the legitimacy of progeny explicitly, saying in the case of a woman who had been badly beaten and humiliated by her husband that a get by coercion—meaning a get imposed by the coercive actions of non-Jewish authorities—must be given, with no concern that such a get, "granted against the husband's wishes, might lead to the birth of a mamzer in the future."[7]

Rabbenu Tam, however, elevated the taboo of *mamzerut*—victimizing children—in the service of ending a significant power of women to terminate their marriages with financial security. In Goldin's characterization, "the fear of mamzerut (of creating mamzerim), was an essential and central element in his thinking."[8] Tam's elevation of this fear was such that, arguing against implementation of the geonic ordinance in the cases of women who sought divorce by declaring "He is repulsive to me," he stated: "It is better to let her remain an agunah rather than entering a situation in which her children *might be considered* mamzerim" (my emphasis).[9] This formulation, using the passive tense about the children of a woman released from marriage by rabbinic coercion of the husband, obscures the fact that it is rabbinic ruling that deems children mamzerot/im or not. As we have seen from the statement of Rabbi Simhah of Speyer above, any such ruling is not automatic but a decision. A finding of—or for—mamzerut, as evident in the backlash, is inseparable from broader considerations and other goals, and is neither inevitable nor necessary. The argument against the ordinance of the rebellious wife on grounds that it "will cause" mamzerut is circular, tautological. Goldin accepts at face value Tam's horror of mamzerut, neglecting the potency of asserting such a threat in achieving his aims in eviscerating the geonic ordinance. Presenting *mimzur*—a rabbinic ruling causing someone to be classed a "mamzer/a"—as if this were automatic and autonomous served (and continues to serve) to control women and deny them marital and physical freedom. Moreover, it was only the assumed, normal existence of agunot in Jewish society—agunot as an accepted fact of Jewish life—that made (and makes) ready recourse to *mimzur* possible, weaponizing iggun as a preferred social policy to contain and subdue women's control over their own marital status and rights by threatening dire consequences to their children. The cumulative "harsh words" of Rabbenu Tam, "the greatest of all the Tosaphists, written around the middle of the twelfth century," says Grossman,

> made a powerful impression. Anyone examining the position of the German and French sages in the 12th and 13th centuries can see this clearly. Many of them were taken aback by his firm position and by the fear of illegitimacy of the children who would be born in the wake of such an imposed get and retreated from the Geonic ordinance.[10] One can also observe a certain withdrawal from the Geonic taqqanah [ordinance] among the [sages of Provence]. Thus, R' Zerahiah Halevi (Raza"h) argued that the ordinance of the moredet was from the outset intended to be . . . temporary.[11]

Halevi asserted this though neither the authors of the ordinance nor the decisors who implemented it for centuries in communities across the Jewish map had expressed any such temporality about it.

In one ruling, Maimonides accepted the ordinance of the rebellious wife in part, in the case of a woman who says she refuses sexual relations because her husband is physically revolting to her; an exception most other medieval decisors rejected. Even in such a case, however, Maimonides ruled that, while a rabbinic court must force the husband to give an immediate (rather than a delayed) get, the woman is to be denied her ketubbah settlement, incurring a significant financial penalty in order to discourage other women from using this claim to end a marriage via the ordinance. He ruled thus despite saying in sympathetic-sounding language that such a marriage must end because a woman repelled by her husband "is not like a captive, to be subjected to intercourse with one who is hateful to her";[12] nonetheless, such women were to pay for their freedom and be made a chilling example to other wives.[13] In another pronouncement, however, Maimonides rejected the geonic ordinance altogether, claiming that the ruling had not established itself in "most of Israel" (the Jewish world), that great rabbis did not accept it—despite the facts that, in the late tenth century, Sherira Gaon had ordered enforcement of the ordinance in the communities of North Africa and that it had been enforced in multiple communities for hundreds of years.[14] If that had not been the case, and known to be the case, there would have been no need to overturn it.

Other decisors, even a minority who ruled for divorce without delay, also reinstituted the financial penalty on women seeking divorce on grounds of some sexual nature. Rabbi Isaac ben Avraham (Rizba), in the late twelfth century, ruled that a woman who asks for a get because her husband is impotent is to be believed and divorced but not given her ketubbah settlement. "Although Rabbi Isaac ben Abraham's judgment releases the wife from her impotent husband," notes Goldin, "it leaves the major portion of the property owed her, the ketubah settlement, in her husband's hands. . . . His opinions are an indication of his general tendency to be uneasy about the power of women and their economic strength."[15] Minna Rozen shows that this position was standard in the rulings of later decisors in Ottoman lands: proof of the woman's claim was required through her readiness to depart her marriage impoverished or with severe financial loss.[16]

Grossman pinpoints a crucial element in understanding the rabbinic backlash against women's marital rights: the reason for divorce most frequently cited in medieval halakhic literature was the wife's "rebellion" against having sexual relations with her husband and/or performing servile duties rabbinically deemed incumbent on a wife and intrinsic to marriage. The ordinance of the rebellious wife upended Talmudic penalties on such a "rebel"—divorce delayed for a year, with the value of the ketubbah progressively reduced until its exhaustion, at which point the woman could get her divorce—instead mandating immediate, unpenalized divorce. Women clearly grasped, and it would appear likely, communicated to one another the opportunity the ordinance presented. As Grossman notes, they would "rebel" in order to force a divorce on favorable terms.[17]

The benefits to women of this ordinance are obvious, but its importance in Ashkenaz was amplified after institution of Rabbenu Gershom's ordinance prohibiting a wife's divorce against her will. Taken together, the two ordinances meant that a woman could force a husband to divorce her swiftly and without financial penalty, while a husband could not compel a woman to accept a divorce.

As Grossman states:

> The sources indicate that the [ordinance of the rebellious wife] was observed by Jewish society in both the Muslim world and Christian Europe for . . . nearly five hundred years. . . . [T]his ordinance gave great power to the Jewish woman. *It would be a mistake to see the issue of the [rebellious wife] only through the narrow halakhic prism of grounds for divorce. It also had important implications for the status of women, both in the home and in society generally.* If, during the period of the Mishnah and the Talmud, the husband was able to threaten his wife . . . explicitly or indirectly, that he would divorce her . . . *similar power was now given to the woman* whose position vis-à-vis her husband . . . changed in a fundamental way. (my emphases)[18]

In fact, a threat to the superior status of men in marriage and divorce had already been created through both ordinances attributed to Rabbenu Gershom, that which prohibited polygyny as well as that which prohibited divorce of a woman without her consent. Various rabbinic voices began to protest the combined effect of these ordinances as a subversion of the proper subordination of women to men.[19] As Asher ben

Yehiel (the Rosh) put this perception at the end of the thirteenth century, "The status of the woman is liable to compete with and prevail over the status of the man." The fear of women and their power was such that, in Goldin's characterization, men began to see women "as a 'political' threat." [20] Over the course of several centuries, German decisors debated weaponizing levirate marriage against women (beyond the disabilities inherent in this institution) in order "tip the scales" in [men's economic] favor in cases when the widow refused such a marriage. "The stronger the woman's status became, the more eager the men became to restore to themselves the property that was being taken, as they perceived it, from their families" when the widow in a levirate situation got release from the obligation to marry the levir and her late husband's means did not pass to his brother via such a marriage, but to her.[21] Traces of the fear of women's economic power were seen in Ashkenaz as early as the eleventh century—that is, around the time that Rabbenu Gershom's ordinances were enacted.[22]

It is against the equalizing of power of women in the critical area of marital freedom that we should see the full rabbinic backlash that began in the mid-to-late twelfth century. The reforms that had benefited Jewish women overwhelmingly concerned marriage and divorce, so the backlash when it came was also in this area, though not confined to it. As Baumgarten establishes, a finding supported by Martha Keil, this is also when rabbinic decisors began gendering the wearing of prayer shawls and fringed ritual garments and other positive, time-bound rituals, like those of the Sukkot holiday, as exclusively male—a major new demarcation of Jewish gender.[23] Limiting the latitude of Jewish women to exit marriage with their entitled resources intact and reestablishing clear male privilege about this became critical, and that is what rabbinic decisors began to do.

The scattered nature of the sources, says Grossman, prevented previous scholars from discerning the marked increase in the number of "rebellious" women in thirteenth-century Germany seeking to divorce their husbands. He collects these sources and synthesizes their cumulative significance.

Rabbi Meir of Rothenburg (Maharam, 1215–1293) ruled against a woman who had demanded a divorce, responding to the appeal of a scholar from Regensburg, who implored him to take action to reduce the large number of women who had "rebelled against their husbands" and sought divorce at their own initiative. The interlocutor referred to these women as having "elevated [*higbihu*] themselves above [become arrogant toward] their husbands," insisting that "the women of Regensburg have always" behaved thus, "and even more so in these times. Therefore, you (R. Meir) must stand in their way."[24] He suggested to Rothenburg that in cases "where the 'rebellious' woman refused to have sexual relations with her husband and wished to divorce him without real justification, the ban of Rabbenu Gershom Me'or Hagolah be waived and the husband be allowed to marry a second wife," an action he felt would "stem the increase in 'rebellious' wives."[25] Rabbi Meir responded to this plea, says Baumgarten, "by employing similar vocabulary to affirm that women in his times were not as 'modest' as women had been in the past and ruled"—citing what one might think a strange prooftext, the advice of the advisers of the Persian King Ahashverosh (book of Esther 1:20)— "that women should 'treat their husbands with respect." Some of Rabbi Meir's students repeated this ruling "in an effort to limit women's ability to divorce their husbands and especially to exercise their financial rights after divorce, by claiming, 'In our generation of immoral women, they should not be believed'" regarding claims of a husband's repulsiveness, impotence, or other grounds for asking divorce, to be forced, if necessary, by a rabbinic court.[26]

Baumgarten, and Grossman at length, cite a pattern of hostile speech in these discussions—claims that women are no longer "modest," as they allegedly were in earlier generations; that they are "loose," "brazen," and no longer worthy of being believed when they claim their husbands are sexually repulsive. Rabbi Meir's student, Asher ben Yehiel, "described the women of his generation as '*shahtzaniot* (haughty).'"[27] Grossman rightly notes that, of course, these adjectives were all applied by men, and "were we to [be] privy to even some of the voices of the women, the picture received would certainly be different."[28] When it comes to judging "real justification" when women sought divorce, we have the judgments not just exclusively of men, but of the men who made the judicial decisions about women's status and rights, including property rights; men who increasingly perceived their own status and standing— including, of course, as husbands themselves vis-à-vis women—as endangered by women achieving equal or even superior options to men in divorce. They were the most interested—prejudiced—of parties.

Rabbinic actions followed rabbinic words. Grossman cites another source from these "scattered" expressions: the words of another disciple of Rabbi Meir of Rothenburg, Rabbi Hayyim ben Yitzhak Or Zaru'a, stating that Rabbi Meir, in concert with other sages, had ruled contra the geonic ordinance that a "rebellious" woman wishing a divorce is not to receive her ketubbah settlement; and further, contravening not just that ordinance but Talmudic law and long-established Jewish practice that such a woman is also to be deprived of assets she brought from her parental house into the marriage as a dowry or gift. About all this, Grossman concludes, "the fact that leading figures proposed such an edict, opposed not only to Talmudic halakhah but to what had long been accepted [custom] both in the Ashkenazic communities and outside of them, clearly indicates the *great social crisis underway and the panic felt by the leadership*" (my emphasis) about women's ability to liberate themselves from marriage and retain important assets in doing so.[29]

Finally, Grossman cites yet another measure, preserved in the thirteenth-century halakhic writings of Rabbi Mordekhai ben Hillel, another of Rabbi Meir of Rothenburg's disciples, that would have echoes in the Jewish future: every couple wishing to be divorced, even if they had the agreement of the local rabbinic authority, could not proceed unless they obtained the consent of rabbis of other communities as well—and paid them for their assent.[30] The multiplication of levels of rabbinic involvement in divorce complicated and impeded access to it while inventing new layers of rabbinic function, control, and remuneration for newly mandated services. Without the benefits afforded to them by the reforms of the prior era, the new impediments to divorce affected women far more than they did men, who enjoyed structural advantage in divorce to begin with.

As noted, Grossman sees the background to these regressive measures in a very high rate of divorce in Ashkenazic society in the thirteenth century, "often at the initiative of women," a rate he estimates as higher than 20 percent and increasing in subsequent centuries. The prevalence of divorce in the twelfth and thirteenth centuries, he notes, also explains the exhortations in *Sefer Hasidim* (The Book of the Pious) against men divorcing their wives except in cases of infidelity (in which case the woman was to lose her ketubbah settlement—an inducement for men to level this accusation, the mere leveling of which had consequences for the wife but not the husband). There was a high rate of divorce initiated by wives in Spanish and Mediterranean Jewries in this period as well.[31]

Why the high rate of divorce in medieval Ashkenaz, specifically? Grossman cites several factors but foremost among them was the improved economic status of women there beginning in the eleventh century and attested particularly in the thirteenth and fourteenth centuries, deriving heavily from women's prominence in moneylending to non-Jews. Women also received substantial dowries and inheritances from their parents, which were in effect their private property. With increasing economic independence from a husband, "divorce did not affect [the woman's] economic situation" adversely, which is why Maharam (Rabbi Meir ben Barukh of Rothenburg) and his colleagues used economic sanctions against women[32] when they sought to limit women's initiation of divorce.

Goldin characterizes rabbinic decisors at the end of the thirteenth century as flummoxed by the problem of rebellious wives, a query from one judge (*dayan*) from the community of Regensburg depicting his fellow rabbis as "orphans and the sons of orphans," perplexed and floundering about how to deal with such cases. "Nonetheless," says Goldin, "all of their questions related to the attempt to curb the financial powers of the 'rebellious wife' and sought to clarify how and to what extent it would be possible to restore to the husband the property that the wife was entitled to take with her, or how to fine her on account of the amounts connected with her estate or her inalienable assets." The writers were restrained from completely undoing the ruling of Rabbenu Gershom Me'or Hagolah concerning enforcement of the ordinance of the rebellious wife, says Goldin, only by the women's threat "to turn to the Christians. The sources did not make clear whether women were simply intending to seek assistance from the Christian authorities against their husbands or were considering converting to Christianity. What is certain is that, whatever their intention, *it deterred the men*" (my emphasis)—a dynamic we have seen operating in other situations.[33]

Rabbinic discourse on this issue continued to be troubled. Halakhic decisors were clearly concerned about women having too much power. But they were also concerned that too hard a crackdown—revoking the Ashkenazi ban on polygyny, as some proposed, so that a man whose wife refused a get could simply marry another woman, leaving the first married against her will—would encourage vindictive behavior by husbands having nothing to do with just teaching women their proper place. Such a crackdown, they feared, would encourage women treated in this way "to embark on a path of sin"—conversion or prostitution.[34] The proposed solution was to leave the ban on polygyny in force but to impose financial penalties on a wife being divorced under the ordinance of the rebellious wife—gutting one of the ordinance's chief provisions. In his opinion and ruling in response to the legal query (she'elah) put to him by the abovementioned "orphans and sons of orphans," the rabbinic judges of Regensburg, Rabbi Meir ben Barukh of Rothenburg argued that the "rebellious" woman in such cases "should be punished in some way in order to teach all women a lesson," and for this reason—and not on alleged grounds of preventing mamzerot/im—he opposed a rabbinic court compelling the husband to give her a get. Rather, he said, the woman should be given a get ("should"—and if the husband refused?)—but not immediately, and be penalized financially when she got it, in Goldin's paraphrase, "so that other women would learn a lesson . . . appreciate their husbands, and not rebel against them." Rabbi Meir also took a very dim view of a wife's relatives giving "her advice on how to break up the family unit while retaining her husband's property"—more evidence that women's kin shared knowledge and experience of halakhic workings to help one another, and that rabbis were aware of and threatened by this behavior. In the last decade of the thirteenth century, Rabbi Meir fought the increased incidence of "rebellious" wives through rulings against their property claims, including even assets from the dowries they had brought from their parents' home, which, he ruled, contrary to Talmudic law, were to remain with the husbands, "a severe [and at that time], almost unprecedented punishment." He also applied this ruling to women's kin who were helping one another, one of his students attested, ruling that if it were discovered that a woman's mother convinced her to "rebel," "*the mother was to be punished* by having *her* possessions ceded to *her* husband, and having a get, without the ketubbah payment, 'throw[n] in her face'" (my emphasis).[35]

The backlash against the economic power and advances achieved by women began to be expressed in the late twelfth century and gained momentum thereafter.[36] Goldin says that, however influential Asher ben Yehiel was (and "he was a forceful halakhic leader known for his widespread

influence"), until the end of the fourteenth century his restrictive rulings in this area were not adopted by the majority of halakhic decisors.
Thereafter, however, because of profound changes in Ashkenazic Jewish
society, especially migration to Eastern Europe, where economic conditions, Jewish–Christian relations, and the nature of Jewish education fundamentally differed from those in medieval Franco-Germany, there was
a "shift in the status of women, and . . . beginning with the 16ᵗʰ century,
the women of Ashkenaz would lose some of the achievements they had
gained in the previous era."[37] In fact, however, as Goldin himself shows
and other scholars establish, the regression in women's rights began far
earlier than this. It well predated "the tumultuous events of the 14ᵗʰ century"[38] in Ashkenazic history (referring to severe anti-Jewish persecutions), which Goldin sees as a turning point. Nor was the regression in
women's status and rights a mere side effect of anti-Jewish persecution,
Jewish migration, or other shifts in Ashkenazic culture and society. It
was a specific, explicit, patriarchal-rabbinic backlash against women and
their perceived attainment of intolerable power, specifically the power of
marital self-determination, against the rightful privilege of men.

Dating and tracing the regression in Jewish women's actual status
in marital rights merits full study. However, it is clear that, if the early
medieval period presents a primer in dynamics that produced positive
change for women's actual marital rights across the Jewish world, dynamics shifted dramatically for the worse because of a conscious, articulated rabbinic backlash against the power of women altogether, and
against their ability to obtain divorces while retaining financial assets
in particular. That backlash reasserted and enhanced the power of men
to impose marital captivity on women. Once articulated by the most
authoritative medieval decisors and their disciples and students across
Jewish ethnic lines, rulings against women's rights in divorce became
embedded halakhic precedent, applied in subsequent eras, as we have
seen regarding the Ottoman era. They are enacted to this day.

We see one instance of the backlash against women's options in divorce playing out in mid-sixteenth-century Salonika, when a young Jewish woman named Reina,

> married to a man named Avraham, became entangled in a family
> drama. . . . Her widowed mother wanted to remarry and Avraham's

father opposed the match [surely because of inheritance disadvantage to Avraham and, therefore, to him in such a remarriage]. From the writings of . . . Rabbi Samuel ben Moses de Medina [the Maharashdam, b. 1505, d. Salonika, 1589], we learn that Reina, either in solidarity with her mother or because she had her own issues with her husband [got involved in the dispute and sought] a divorce from Avraham.

. . . Reina [citing various details about the wedding night] claimed that her husband was impotent . . . wrote the Mahardashdam in his . . . response. Reina wanted a chance to remarry and have a son who would say kaddish for her [after her death]. Avraham, however, did not want to give Reina a get. Should he be compelled?

This question was posed to de Medina (Maharashdam), a revered authority who established an important Talmudic academy and rabbinic court in Salonika.[39]

He acknowledged that earlier scholars were flexible about compelling the granting of a get when there was just cause. He noted that the earlier rabbis even held that a wife's mere assertion that her husband was "disgusting" to her was sufficient grounds.

Still, the Maharashdam declared that a man may not be compelled to give a get in every instance. He was skeptical of Reina's charges and wrote that the young woman may have *been influenced by a circle of "bad women."* (my emphases)[40]

Israeli rabbinic courts today rely on this and other rulings of the Maharashdam to refuse to "compel a husband to divorce his wife—even if she is able to establish grounds that they might accept for doing so—if the husband agrees in principle to divorce but insists, in exchange for a get, that his wife meet what the judges deem to be his 'easily fulfilled' demands."[41] The same is true about the rulings of a major decisor in late fifteenth-century Italy, Rabbi Joseph ben Solomon Colon (Maharik, ca. 1420–80). His rulings were sought from as far as Ulm, Nuremberg, and Regensburg in Germany, as well as Istanbul, and he acted as a decisor with authority also to overrule decisions of other decisors (an appellate court). Colon also ruled that a wife is required to meet her husband's "reasonable" demands in exchange for a get.[42] This is get extortion, sanctioned explicitly by authoritative, early modern decisors in rulings that continued and solidified the late medieval regression in halakhic decision-making about women and their right to divorce without being extorted for it or made agunot. "Rarely, if ever," write Susan Weiss and Netty Gross-Horowitz, "will rabbis [in Israeli rabbinic courts] decide that a husband's terms are unreasonable or not easy to comply with . . . for all intents and purposes, the Mahardasham–Maharik rule places full negotiating power in the hands of the husband and absolves the court of having to take any responsibility for determining conditions of divorce, even in the most heinous of circumstances."[43]

In the case of Colon/Maharik, there is reason to believe that he had a particular tendency to stringency and denial in cases of agunot: while he rarely asked other decisors for supportive rulings, in cases of divorce and agunot he did,[44] a tactic structurally injurious to women. This behavior fit a larger pattern of negative rulings by Colon on women, for example, that women could not be agents for large dealings (he excluded small ones or else women would not have been able to buy groceries). Colon's ruling overturned that of the medieval decisor Raban, noted above, on this very question, "in the context of [Colon's] attempt to establish a husband's control over family finances and protect him from financial collusion between his wife and son."[45] We have seen, of course, that medieval women regularly engaged in the types and scale of business and financial activities that Colon now sought to prohibit, with the sanction and encouragement of rabbinic colleagues. Colon's ruling was an explicit, patriarchal action, expanding on the regressive momentum begun centuries earlier and taking aim at the economic dynamism of women, which had so underlain their ability to promote the reforms of earlier eras.

Agunot from Spain and Portugal after the Mass Conversions and Spanish Expulsion

There is other evidence coming from the early modern Sephardi sphere documenting concerted rabbinic action against women's ability to terminate marriage or the obligation to levirate marriage. It comes from rabbinic handling of circumstances that became pronounced in the fourteenth and fifteenth centuries after the mass, forced conversions of the Jews of Spain and Portugal and the expulsion of the Jews from Spain in 1492.[46] Wives of converted men who wished to remain Jewish and live in openly Jewish communities fled Iberia, becoming part of a large Sephardi diaspora in Ottoman realms. There, they sought rabbinic acceptance of divorces they had obtained from their husbands or, if they were widows in childless marriages, release from the obligation to marry, or obtain halitsa from converted levirs in Iberia.[47] In this situation, rather different from what we saw in medieval Jewish conditions, it was not men but women who moved to distant locations, migration that left even converted husbands and levirs in control of their marriages and lives since under halakha, converts remained Jews. Halakhic literature from eleventh-century Ashkenaz documents Jewish women separating from converted husbands, thereby becoming agunot.[48] But the difficulty in early modern Sephardi modernity was vastly compounded by the scale and circumstances of the Expulsion, with the termination of openly functioning rabbinic communities in Spain and Portugal and the dispersion of Iberian Jewish exiles to distant lands.

The Jewish faithfulness of these women worked against them. The circumstances meant an increased need for gittin and halitsa while simultaneously heightening the incentive and market for get and halitsa extortion, with converts demanding payoffs.[49] When women succeeded in obtaining divorces, they faced another ordeal in the communities of their migration when they sought to remarry and rabbis challenged the validity of their gittin. Salonika, destination of large numbers of Spanish and Portuguese exiles, became a very important city on the Jewish map in the sixteenth century, a vital trading and textile center and home of important yeshivas and decisors, like de Medina (Maharashdam).[50] Here, things went beyond the already dire situation for women of some fault found (or alleged) in a get. In this cohort, with converted husbands or levirs in distant lands, such a finding or allegation meant certain and permanent iggun.[51] Under the traumatic circumstances of the mass flight from Iberia, with panic, family separation, and fatalities en route, factors other than the familiarly patriarchal-legal entered halakhic decision-making about the status of women needing halitsa or a get. Such women became the fulcrum on which questions of shaken postexpulsion Sephardi group identity and coherence were decided. One decisor, Rabbi Jacob ben Solomon ibn Habib, whom we have encountered previously ruling negatively on women's rights, was himself born in Castile and a refugee after 1492, first to Portugal, and then, after the mass, forced conversion there, in 1497 to Salonika.[52] Ibn Habib ruled against release of refugee women needing halitsa out of sympathy for the converted levirs back in Iberia. To him and some other decisors, to dismiss the levirate claim of the latter, thereby releasing their sisters-in-law to remarry, would be to accept the permanence of the men's severance from the Jewish fold.[53] Ibn Habib—whose son, Levi ibn Habib, himself had converted in the mass, forced conversion in Portugal, reverting to Judaism in Salonika, where he joined his father's yeshiva and himself became a *posek*—argued vehemently, emotionally, against this, insisting that the conversions were forced. The Hebrew terms for "forced convert" and "raped"—*anuss*—are the same, and ibn Habib emphatically pronounced the men "*anussim gemurim*," totally coerced victims—and the widows, obligated to them in levirate marriage and needing halitsa in order to marry someone else. Better, he maintained, to hope that the converted men would leave Iberia and return to fully Jewish lives than to acknowledge their permanent loss to the Jewish people by freeing the women.[54] The means of the men's continued connection to the Jewish people—the chains binding them to such association—would be their wives or sisters-in-law, chained in marriage or obligation to marriage to them, a literal double bind. Women were not just chained. They *were* chains, the people's adhesive.

Even had the return to the Jewish fold of converts that ibn Habib and other decisors wished for actually transpired, this would not, of course, necessarily or even likely have meant that such men would release their sisters-in-law through halitsa, with or without payoffs. Moreover, as always, it would first be on the women to locate the men, who could be anywhere in the far-flung Sephardi diaspora that encompassed North Africa, Palestine, and the rest of the Ottoman Empire, Italy, the Netherlands, and the New World, and obtain their agreement to enact halitsa—in recognized rabbinic courts.

Ibn Habib's stance went beyond halakhic rulings by the medieval tosaphists of France and Germany, who had upheld the halakhic status of male converts specifically to contract marriage and give gittin.[55] It went beyond the ruling of the "rabbinical triumvirate of Salonika," who, in 1514—that is, very close in time to the mass, forced conversions—issued a "special haskama [understanding] regarding the Marranos [male converts in Iberia] as Jews as far as marriage and divorce were concerned, i.e., they practically regarded the Marranos as Jews in every respect"[56]—a ruling that made women very likely to fall into permanent iggun. Ibn Habib's stance, based on explicitly extrahalakhic criteria—keeping converted men within the Jewish fold—is another instance of regression in the marital rights of women through intentional rabbinic action, in this case instrumentalizing women through their marital vulnerability under rabbinic law in the service of perceived larger, group goals, gendered male.

As is the case generally in halakhic, academic, and popular writing, to ibn Habib and other decisors ruling like him, "Jews" meant (and means) men, with no recognition of women as half of "the Jews," including in this situation of group trauma, which, of course, women and men bore equally.[57] In the rulings just cited, the first of which upheld the Jewishness of conversos (men) regarding halakhic marriage and divorce, and the second, which went beyond this, ruling stringently (le'humra), a priori, against release of agunot bound to conversos, women were victimized. The first of these rulings clarified and solidified prior halakhic practice upholding the validity of the marriages entered into and divorce decrees given by converted men. The second ruling innovated in explicitly positing a larger social "good" for which the lives of agunot were to be sacrificed. The readiness to sacrifice Jews who were women—in Salonika, the best of Jews as the rabbinic value system itself defined this, in contrast to its defined worst of Jews—converts—on the altar of ostensibly "group" values—the welfare of "the community"—can only be attributed to two related things. It is attributable, first, to the unconscious, pervasively assumed Otherness of Jewish women. Second, it is attributable to the associated normality with which rabbinic decisors saw agunot as an accepted fact of Jewish life, their presence in Jewish society a given, so normal that iggun could be applied as a policy option on behalf of "group" needs, the "group" defined as constituted of men, at the women's expense. Freed to remarry, agunot, of course, could participate at least in the demographic rebuilding of decimated Spanish–Portuguese Jewry, then the subject of grave demographic concern.[58] This community had experienced recurrent assaults across Spain beginning in countrywide pogroms in 1391 and culminating in the catastrophes of the expulsion from Spain in 1492 and the sudden, forced, mass conversion of Portuguese Jewry, including Spanish Jews who had fled there to escape conversion, in 1497.[59] There were particular catastrophes involving children in the latter event.[60]

Birthrate aside, we might think that benefit might also have been seen in the sheer presence in the communities of the traumatized Sephardi diaspora of these best of Jews.[61] Women fleeing the lands of mass apostasy for openly Jewish lives could have been elevated as models, celebrated, and halakhic priority given them, if only to reward heroic fidelity to Judaism in a time of mass defection and demoralization: mass conversion was unprecedented and Jewish society as a whole, across ethnic lines, was reeling.[62] But this was not how this rabbinic gaze perceived the situation. The "people" were men. Social policy regarding them could be and obviously was flexible—the Jewish status of converted men was to be honored with full exercise of their patriarchal privilege to determine marriage and divorce, that is, control the lives of women. Agunot, on the other hand, were—agunot, a given, nothing new. They were wholly expendable in this situation, as they were altogether. Their trauma was both normal and female—Other. Gendered assumptions operate in the policy expressions of group trauma, too, in this instance enacted in policy that privileged (converted) men and further victimized women, agunot.

In fact, this shocking double standard had precedent among earlier Sephardi decisors. Rabbi Shimon ben Tsemah Duran (Rashbats, 1361–1444), the leader of North African Jewry in his time (North Africa being another prime destination for the Iberian refugees), frequently handled halakhic questions arising from the new reality of converted Jews as a mass feature of Jewish life.[63] Many of the questions concerned the ritual fitness (kashrut) of wine handled by converted men, the wine trade being central to internal Jewish economics, given the ritual status of wine in Jewish practice and the halakhic requirement that Jews handle wine meant for Jewish consumption.[64] But questions of the property and wealth of such men as a consideration in their deciding whether to remain in or leave Iberia (including the island of Majorca) also arose. In a case he adjudicated immediately after the anti-Jewish riots and mass conversions in Spain of 1391, Duran expressed support for "a continued life of religious coercion [i.e., continued life as an ostensible Christian convert] in spite of the real possibility to escape Spain and return to Judaism, all in order to protect one's property."[65] In Duran's words, "even if the anusim [forced converts] were themselves [as opposed to their critics] to say that the main reason for them to stay [in Majorca] is none other but that their property will not be taken from them, they are not to be called intentional worshippers of another god,"[66] idol worship being a fundamental prohibition in Judaism, for which the Talmud (Sanhedrin 74) prescribes that a Jew choose martyred death (kiddush hashem, sanctification of God's name) over compromise, one of only three such situations.

In contrast to this remarkable understanding shown for the material considerations of converted men and the losses they would incur in emigrating in order to return to open Jewish life, in another case, Duran ruled against a woman who had done precisely this. A Jewish man escaped from Majorca "in fear for his life while his wife was forced to convert . . . later the woman herself fled to North Africa in order to escape Christian coercion and return to Judaism"[67] (and to her husband), behavior one might expect a rabbi to deem exemplary and reward accordingly.

Not, however, Duran, who wrote the following in ruling about *the penalty the woman was to pay* for incurring financial loss to her husband, who, apparently, was seeking to divorce her—and not pay her ketubbah sum:

> And to his losing all that he owned in his taverns because of her rush to leave [!] . . . she is responsible for his loss, because it was not in the conditions of the marriage contract (ketubah) that she would sanctify the name of the Lord by leaving Majorca [!], and if she did sanctify the name of the Lord and lost [her husband's] property by her sanctification, we did not find that the woman will be exempted from [being found to have caused this loss to her husband] . . . so it is simple that the husband is released from [the financial stipulations of] her marriage contract [her ketubbah settlement] since the kingdom took it [confiscated the man's property]. (my emphases)[68]

About this case and Duran's remarkable position, Ram Ben-Shalom says, "Duran *justified the claim of the husband against his wife for rushing too quickly to escape religious persecution* [!] in Majorca and sacrificing the family's considerable property there in order to do so. It would seem that he thought she should have first made responsible arrangements for the property *while living as a convert* and only then should she have returned to Judaism" (my emphases).[69] "Living as a convert," of course, meant violating on a daily basis the fundamental imperatives of halakha—Sabbath, holiday, and kashrut observance, while outwardly, at least, also committing the cardinal offense of idol worship—worshipping the Christian god, as Duran himself phrased this, employing a standard rabbinic and popular Jewish reference. An astounding position, it would appear to us, for a rabbinic authority to take, privileging property over fidelity to Judaism and refusing idol worship—the behavior the Talmud demands. That a *posek* would severely penalize a pious Jew for behaving as this woman did and actually recommend that she should have remained a convert, violating Torah laws and a fundamental Jewish theological imperative on a daily basis, is truly mind-boggling. The only possible explanation is the assumed, fundamental—essential—Otherness of women that was part of rabbinic mentality, and unconscious patriarchal, male solidarity of the rabbi with the husband.

Yet another prominent Jewish leader in Castile at the end of the fifteenth century, Don Isaac Abravanel (b.1437, Lisbon–d.1508, Venice), also expressed notable empathy for converted Jewish men and offered them recompense for the pain of violating Torah commandments as conversos. He promised them that in the messianic era, all that would be made right, assuring them that, however difficult such repentance would be, in that time "the Blessed One will let them [have] the fruit of their womb [sic; their children born of their Christian wives] and the fruit of their animals and land, and all their handiwork. . . . Let them not think that [having returned to the Jewish fold] they will have to leave their capital and depart from wife and children and *dwell in lonely poverty, want, and physical asceticism*" (my emphasis).[70] The distinction between this concern for the sensibilities of converted men and empathy for an *imagined future* in which, the rabbi fantasizes, these conversos would fear experiencing loss and loneliness—and all the other actual anguish routinely imposed on agunot—is striking.

A distinction began to be expressed in sixteenth-century rabbinic responsa about women needing halitsa or gittin from converted men who remained in Iberia: between marriages contracted before and after the mass conversions at the end of the fifteenth century. In the first case, the halakhic validity of witnesses to the act of kiddushin—their strict Sabbath and kashrut observance is required for the marriage ceremony to be valid—was assumed, and the need for a get or halitsa, therefore, clear. In the second case, though both parties to the marriage remained Jewish under halakha, conversion having no effect on this status, there was no way, postconversion, that the witnesses were halakhically observant and therefore "kosher," and their witnessing of kiddushin valid. Since the marriages they witnessed were not valid, the women involved did not need gittin or halitsa, some decisors in Salonika ruled.

Yet, in the latter cases, when the decisors are quite pronounced, even vehement, that the women are entirely free to marry, it is very clear from the language of their responsa that this ruling was, foremost, an expression of anger and punitiveness toward the converted men and an occasion to express those sentiments, rather than being primarily directed to or about the agunot involved. The decisors excoriate these men for remaining in the "lands of *shmad*" (apostasy) rather than leaving, and choosing, specifically, open openly Jewish communities in Ottoman lands, where they would revert to full Jewish lives, rather than heading for the explicitly named (Protestant) Netherlands simply to evade the Inquisition.[71] Men are clearly the focus; women, whose predicament or choices receive no such elaboration, merely the occasion for the pronouncement. For all the critical practical difference for the women involved in rulings that they were absolutely bound, or absolutely not bound, to divorce or halitsa, respectively, by converted husbands or levirs, the common ground between these opposing positions was the instrumentality of chained women in the service of other goals. In the first instance, the women were treated, and sacrificed, as instruments of communal continuity. In the second, women were used as instruments to inflict punishment for perceived deliberate and ongoing male disloyalty to Judaism through the loss of the men's privilege to decide their marital status and freedom.[72]

There can be no disregarding the personal, family experiences of decisors in this era as a potent factor in their decision-making about the status and privileges of male converts, whether in sympathetic identification with them, as appears to have been the case for Rabbi Jacob ben

Solomon ibn Habib, and his son, Levi, or fury against them, expressed by other decisors. Both subjectivities were manifested in rulings about agunot—using agunot and their predicament in the furtherance of the *posek*'s preferred communal policies.

The regression in rabbinic policy toward women seeking divorce and marital freedom continued between the mid-seventeenth and nineteenth centuries and thereafter, to which history we now turn.

7

"Agunot, Halakhic Decisors, and Suffering"[1] in Mid-Seventeenth- to Mid-Nineteenth-Century Europe

Noa Shashar's study, focusing on the Ashkenazi world from 1648 to 1850, is the first comprehensive historical account of agunot and their actual treatment by halakhic authorities.[2]

Her book is based on examination of a vast number of rabbinic materials, including works of rabbinic law, from the earliest through those produced during the era she studies, including responsá (*shutim*) by halakhic decisors to questions posed to them about cases, in which they state their opinions about what should be done. But—and in this her work is pathbreaking—she also studies the rulings of rabbinic courts on actual cases of agunot, showing not just what a decisor ruled should be done in a certain situation, theoretical or actual, but what rabbinic courts actually did in cases of women who came before them seeking release from iggun.[3]

Shashar reminds us that there were several ways that women could become agunot, including being widowed in a childless marriage and requiring halitsa, release from her husband's brother(s) in order to marry someone other than the levir. She shows that halitsa extortion was common in this period and region, as it was in earlier periods and parts of the Jewish world we have explored.[4] An agunah of this type had to pay the costs of her travel to a levir, or of his travel to her location, including the costs of lodging and food for such trips, and rabbinic court fees. Sometimes such agunot had to buy off multiple brothers of the deceased husband, who saw the entire affair as a business opportunity—and would refuse to do so, preferring to remain agunot with a wife's claim on a deceased husband's assets, if such existed, over untenable costs in sequential halitsa extortion.[5] Two hundred years of records yielded not one case when a rabbinic court imposed sanctions on a levir for refusing to perform halitsa, even when the deceased husband had left explicit instructions that his kin do so, and without a payoff. Some husbands even specified in their wills an amount the levir could demand in a payoff, so normal was the expectation of such payment.[6] Sometimes a *rabbinic court itself held such an agunah hostage, refusing to proceed with a halitsa to which the levir agreed* until a male relative of the agunah acceded to the court's demands on another matter entirely.[7] As we saw in the cases of Iberian agunot, here too the predicament of agunot was useful in advancing other goals—an opportunity.

Yet another route to iggun, in this period as in others, was conversion by men, whose wives could escape becoming agunot only if their now-Christian husbands (still Jews under halakha) came to a rabbinic court and not only participated in the get ritual but, as the only party actually giving the divorce, activated the proceedings, an absurdity some such men noted.[8] Awareness of the business opportunity in holding the power of the get survived baptism; converted husbands demanded payoffs. Some flatly refused to cooperate and, unsurprisingly, enjoyed support from the non-Jewish authorities in this stance. Some, in this period and region as in others, gave the get.[9]

This situation posed an obvious ethical "moment" to halakhic adjudication, to which the response was, almost without exception, wanting. The eminent halakhic decisor Yehezkel Landau (1713–1793), described as enlightened and "renowned for his bold and often lenient decisions, especially on matters involving the welfare of the community,"[10] rejected the request of the rabbi of Aszod, Hungary, to release a woman whose husband converted and took all the couple's possessions, decreeing that "so long as [the woman] does not obtain a get from the convert, she shall remain an agunah."[11] The phenomenon of decisors insisting on rabbinic divorces from converted men and ruling that their wives remain agunot until and unless that happened was so common that Yosef Perl (1773–1839), a leading figure in the Jewish enlightenment movement, scored it (among a host of other critiques of rabbis) in his writings.[12] In this Ashkenazi realm, as we saw in early modern Sephardic ones, rabbinic protection of patriarchal privilege in marriage extended to the worst of Jews in rabbinic ranking, trumping even the supposedly worst of Jewish sins: *shmad*, conversion (the Hebrew term derives from the word for "destruction"). Male converts—the term for them, *meshumadim*, among the worst terms of opprobrium in Hebrew or Yiddish—ranked above pious Jewish women who sought not to subvert or abandon rabbinic law but to uphold it.

The period that Shashar studies opens with a time of mass violence against Jews in Polish lands, an era known in Jewish parlance as *gezerot takh va'tat* ("the evil decrees of 1648–49"; in Ukrainian and Polish historiography, as the Chmielnicki rebellion).[13] Jews were killed, taken captive, raped; some converted, many fled—all of which had a catastrophic effect on families and created a huge upsurge in the numbers of agunot, as attested by multiple sources, Jewish and non-Jewish.[14] Shashar examines how the agunot of this time, most of whose husbands had disappeared in some way, actually fared in rabbinic courts when they sought release from iggun. She shows that even those who eventually obtained release, having met extensive criteria in cases of a husband's disappearance and suspected demise to establish his death, had first to travel a long and costly path of appeals and other processes. The difficulties meant that the majority of agunot could not pursue even the possibility of release.[15] But even women who could pursue the long, arduous, stressful, and financially costly effort to try to obtain release found that the rabbinic authorities who adjudicated their cases did not make things easier but multiplied difficulties.

Shashar documents a practice not mandated by halakha, in which a halakhic decisor would require the concurrence of two or more additional decisors in cases *where he deemed release of an agunah justified*—even when the decisor had incontestable proof, by multiple standards, of a man's death in cases of a husband's disappearance.[16] Of necessity, this requirement meant delays and added costs—and that is when the approbation of all the other halakhic decisors eventuated. One such an additional decisor did not handle a request for his supportive ruling promptly and lost track of the letter, finding it by chance only during the search for leaven on the eve of Passover.[17] Obviously, the agunah and her situation had not registered as pressing, let alone urgent.

As we have seen, even when a get was given, its validity could be challenged after the fact as a further method of extortion by a husband or just to torment the woman. In one such instance, the decisor, Rabbi Gershon Ashkenazi, required *three* other *poskim*, in addition to himself, to certify that *a get already given* was valid.[18] In the meantime, the woman was in halakhic purgatory. She was forbidden to remarry or, if already remarried, forbidden to her second husband, as well as to her first, with any children of the second marriage labeled potential or actual mamzerot/im, with the weightiest of stigma and other social and economic costs affixed to her and them. Of course, if the get was deemed invalid in the end or even if there was continued, unresolved doubt about its validity, the woman was an agunah.

The requirement of additional halakhic authorities to support a decisor's judgment that release was warranted turned a woman's life and anguish into a halakhic event, the occasion for a joust of demonstrated rabbinic erudition about previous cases and rulings, precedents, and reasoning—what the Yiddish writer Chaim Grade would call "the display of codifiers"—with the women the mere pretext for displays of Talmudic virtuosity.[19] This stringent standard applied to cases of agunot defied an explicit ruling by a decisor mentioned above, Joseph ben Solomon Colon (the Maharik), the foremost halakhist of late fifteenth-century Italy, albeit not regarding cases of agunot. One of the most important of Colon's responsa—listed first in his published edition of queries and responses (she'elot u'teshuvot)—stated that "no one could be forced to take a case to an outside court when there was a court in the place where the defendant was living; *for it often happened that rich people took their cases to foreign rabbis in order to make the poor surrender*" (my emphasis).[20] This was admirable protection for structurally disadvantaged litigants who were not agunot. When such litigants *were* agunot, no such rule applied, no concern to assure that the disadvantaged party was protected in the formal processes of adjudicating the case, like deciding its location, when this is often critical to, or even determinative of, case outcomes. Colon's rulings that profoundly disadvantaged women in divorce, however, were deemed sacrosanct and remain so in contemporary rabbinic courts.

We know from this period as from earlier ones that agunah cases were often also used as occasions for rabbinic power struggles and contests of halakhic supremacy among some of the biggest names in halakhic history. We have discussed the rabbinic controversy in Safed in the 1540s about one such case of iggun. That dispute was between Rabbis Joseph Karo and his slightly younger colleague, Moshe Mitrani, head of a yeshiva and major decisor, who would serve as the rabbinic head of Safed after Karo's death.[21] The case involved an agunah whose husband was below deck when the ship he was on sank: there would be no meeting halakhic criteria to establish his or any of the other men's deaths.

Karo and a good number of other rabbis refused to give the woman dispensation to remarry; Mitrani and another rabbi argued that a rabbinic court is not required to rule stringently (le'humra) in the case of an agunah (on the contrary; the Talmud twice enjoins lenient rulings in cases of agunot). He held that if the woman was ignorant (or I would say, the opposite, informed and aware), and had not asked rabbinic permission but had already remarried, she should not be told to separate from her (second) husband, a position (about not contesting an ex post facto marriage) even one of Karo's supporters in this case upheld.

The woman indeed remarried, but, *under pressure from Karo*—her husband divorced her. The rabbinic deliberations about the case went on for more than three years, matters being more complicated by the fact that the husbands of twenty other Jewish women went down with the same ship. Karo justified his stringency by arguing its need *in order to prevent the twenty other women from also remarrying*—and he chastised Mitrani *for "trespassing" on his, Karo's, turf and involving himself in the matters of people who were not in Mitrani's congregation.* The matter came down not to a question of the legal ruling per se, but of rabbinic turf, a "personal power struggle between two veteran" rabbinic authorities vying for supremacy in the same prestige-laden town in Ottoman Palestine.[22]

Rabbinic power disputes over the status of agunot were not confined to the biggest names in the halakhic pantheon. Claiming that there was a defect (p'gam) in the get or its delivery was an established form of abuse by vindictive husbands against wives. Rabbis in authority disputes with one another could also wreak havoc on women's lives with claims that the divorces or annulments of marriages arranged by rabbinic competitors were invalid. We hear, for example, of a case about a girl, Yekuta, from sixteenth-century Tripoli, North Africa, who was married at the age of nine—and shortly thereafter thrown into iggun for fifteen years. Her family moved to Egypt, where she asked a rabbinic court for release from her marriage; her family argued that her marriage had been conducted against her father's will (while she was a minor, lacking legal authority to consent) and that a rabbinic court had annulled it. Yekuta remarried and had children but, in a contest of rabbinic wills and authority, *nine years later* several rabbis contested the validity of the annulment and ruled her forbidden to her second husband and her children, mamzerim. After many more proceedings that went all the way to a rabbinic court in Jerusalem—meaning time, money, and anguish—Yekuta's claim was upheld.[23] We don't know how long she lived, but it is safe to say that she spent much and perhaps most of her life in marital limbo and fighting for legitimate marital status. During all this time, she and her children would have suffered the severe emotional and social consequences of sexually related stigmatization in traditional societies, and she and her family, the economic consequences of her dependence as a married-yet-not-married woman with children. It is important to note the weighty consequence of such stigmatizing of women and children in such cases, the latter with the stain of mamzerut. Fear of such stigmatization, as we have seen, was so potent that it was weaponized effectively in the rabbinic backlash against women's marital freedom that began in the late twelfth century.

There is much other evidence of agunot becoming ensnared in rabbinic power struggles that resulted in them remaining agunot. Ruth Lamdan describes a case about an agunah from Corfu that went to rabbis in Palestine, Egypt, Crete, Istanbul, and Venice (meaning much money and time expended).[24] Women of little or no means, who were the vast majority of this or any Jewish population, had no hope of even pursuing such cases, meaning that most women made agunot, stayed agunot.[25]

The problem of rabbinic jousting over women's marital status compounding iggun, then, was nothing new, but Shashar says it typified the period and region she examined and suggests that its extent there was greater than in previous eras. What led to the stringency by the decisors Shashar studies, their requiring the approbation of additional decisors in order to free agunot whose cases they themselves felt warranted release? It was fear that freeing agunot would give them a reputation for leniency—in halakhic terminology, for being a *mekel*—*which designation would damage their reputations.* The rabbis' primary, operative consideration was not the women involved, the ruin or redemption of their lives, but their own reputation and standing with other decisors. Ruling stringently in response to those considerations clearly indicates that, not only was there no rabbinic consensus in favor of freeing agunot, but the opposite was true: *the rabbinic expectation, the norm, was not to use every halakhic means to free agunot* but to multiply obstacles to such release, building on a precedent of rabbinic stringency established in previous cases of agunot. Shashar cites the ruling of the young Yehezkel Landau, eminent even in his youth, against an agunah *even when two other decisors had approved her release*, because he feared being considered lenient *would hurt his developing reputation*.[26] Referencing Landau and the halakhic genius of the late eighteenth century, the Vilna Gaon, Haym Soloveitchik has argued that, until the post–World War II era, ritual stringencies (*humrot*) were the practice only of halakhic decisors, the pinnacle of the rabbinic elite, in their own personal practice.[27] But enacting stringencies in the cases of agunot for fear of being labeled "lenient" grossly crossed from the personal to the social. Decisors who multiplied obstacles to the release of agunot were not enacting extreme personal piety for themselves but stringencies with the most dire impact on the lives of others—of women and their children, *while simultaneously benefiting themselves*.

Thus far we have discussed two periods when there was a documented upsurge in the incidence of agunot.[28] Those instances occurred in the sixteenth century, during and following the catastrophe of Iberian Jewry, and as a result of the Chmielnicki persecutions in Poland/Ukraine in the seventeenth century. Regarding the former period, among the refugees in the Ottoman Empire, we have seen instances of rabbinic leniency, if only de facto, in cases of women whose husbands were converts, when some of these women remarried without rabbinic permission and rabbis chose not to try to force dissolution of those marriages. How common was such behavior, quietly absorbed by rabbinic acquiescence? How much happened "under the radar," not even brought to rabbinic attention? The current state of research does not provide an answer, but as we have seen, rabbinic sources clearly attest that some such cases occurred.

We have certainly seen instances where the greatest halakhic authorities of the time, such as Joseph Karo, ruled severely about a "regular," common case of iggun—of group iggun—caused by the disappearance of over twenty husbands in a shipwreck. And we have seen Yehezkel Landau's ruling that left an agunah chained in marriage to a convert because he insisted that the convert give a get, and similar rulings by ibn Habib in Salonika.

One of Shashar's most important contributions is her documenting a marked disparity between leniency expressed in rabbinic responsa and highly restrictive, administrative, and "bureaucratic" practices of decisors who rendered actual judgments in cases of agunot—deciding if they were to be released from their marriages or not. She notes a twice-stated Talmudic formula directing leniency in agunah cases—"*mishum igguna akilu bah rabbanan*"—"About agunah cases, the rabbis ruled leniently" (Gittin 3a; Yevamot 85a)—the only time the Talmud enjoins leniency in ruling—and asks what actually happened when agunah cases reached rabbinic courts for adjudication in the extensive geographic range—from eastern France to Ukraine—and period that she studies.

It is important to clarify the difference between opinions expressed in rabbinic responsa and rulings of rabbinic courts. The former are responses to questions asking the decisor's opinion about how a posed case, actual or theoretical, should be handled and what ruling should be given. They are not records of rabbinic rulings in actual cases. Judicial application of an opinion stated in a responsum is an entirely different matter.

Shashar shows that scholars who discussed iggun but were not historians have treated responsa as if they were rulings applied in actual cases and, on the basis of the leniency often expressed in theoretical language—leniency in accordance with the above-cited exhortation in the Talmud—concluded that rabbis "left no stone unturned" to free actual agunot.[29] In fact, two noted historians also make this assertion, with no cited evidence.[30] As Shashar shows, the opposite was the case, with difficulties multiplied, making it rare for agunot to achieve release from captivity, a finding she confirms by scouring the protocols (*pinkassim*) of rabbinic courts, which show very few releases (*heterim*) of agunot. There is no evidence to support repeated claims that rabbis showed leniency to agunot from the Chmielnicki pogroms. The evidence supports the opposite conclusion.[31]

Even confining the discussion to responsa, however, does not yield a picture of leniency, since these frequently discuss cases that dragged on for years, even decades. Shashar notes that it was not unusual to find cases of agunot extending over twenty years. She cites one case documented in a responsum extending over thirty years.[32] The long duration of these cases aroused no comment, much less consternation on the part of the rabbis involved. Nor did it evoke any expressed determination even to speed the handling of cases of agunot (irrespective of the outcomes). The duration of cases was reported simply as fact. Agunot were a normal, inevitably occurring halakhic problem, like forbidden leaven discovered as having been in one's possession during Passover, or the status of an egg laid on the Sabbath.

While extant records of rabbinic court rulings from the period and region Shashar studies are not plentiful, the court records she has—including from Frankfurt am Main, Altona-Hamburg-Wandsbeck, Krakow, Prague, and Metz—are from some of the largest and most important Ashkenazi communities of this time, whose courts were also regional, serving surrounding, smaller communities.[33] These records show some releases of agunot, so there is no explaining the paucity of such rulings in speculation that somehow, only rulings on agunah cases were omitted from them.

We have noted one of Shashar's central findings, that decisors required the assent of two or three or more additional authorities before they would act on their own finding to release an agunah. But Shashar also documents a general reluctance by decisors even to consider agunah cases, which meant condemning the women to perpetual iggun.[34] Whether handled or denied consideration, stringency, not leniency, was the rabbinic norm in cases of agunot.

There were also cases where a decisor would accept release of an agunah de facto (*bediavad*) but not ab initio (*lehat'hila*)—that is, the decisor would not try to force dissolution of a marriage of an agunah who had not obtained formal release,[35] behavior we have encountered in other eras and places. This means that women who brought their cases for rulings up front—who enacted normative, "good" behavior and did not act on their own—were disadvantaged, and those who acted on their own, benefited: freed themselves.

There was no systematic way that women could inform one another of such realities; individual women either figured this out and, with willing men, acted on it, or not. Norms of proper marriage and dissolution of it, on the other hand, along with the rest of what constituted the education of girls, were conveyed to girls and women in multiple ways. This information was largely about prohibitions—the "Do nots" of halakhic observance, regarding holidays, the ritual diet, sexual abstinence in marriage during the rabbinically calculated duration of menstrual status, and norms of dress and other behaviors. Such education and socialization was done within the home and in other female spheres by mothers and other women. In the first volume of her memoirs, depicting the 1830s and 1840s in Russian Poland, Pauline Wengeroff (1833–1916) gives a rich account of traditional women's sphere and the education and socialization of girls within it.[36] Girls could also have tutors (melamdim), whether privately engaged or in young girls' schools (heders) or both. There were written sources—distilled halakhic guides, piety literature, and petitionary prayers (tkhines) directed at women.[37] The norms of halakhic marriage and its dissolution and the fear of stigma for their violation were certainly conveyed, formally, informally, and in lived experience.

We have seen evidence of women's informal means of conveying critical information to one another about marriage and how women might work the system to escape marital captivity, the obligation to levirate marriage, and/or halitsa extortion, and other disabilities under halakha. These means of communication were necessarily limited to immediate contacts, in family (which, given realities of Jewish life, could be far-flung) and community, since means of systematic dissemination were under communal control, to which women were denied access. Such information was more likely to circulate among women of the rabbinic, scholarly elite; the aforementioned, self-halitsa-enacting daughter-in-law of Joseph Karo surely had such connections, though we should not discount how such information in elite households could pass to servants and tradespeople, the latter very much including women, and from there, more broadly.

In whatever ways and to what extent women got information about how to work rabbinic and communal systems to their best advantage, they lacked the means for, or even access to, broad or systematic means for its transmission. Such means were pivotal to constructing and conveying both established and new traditions, such as Lurianic kabbalah and the liturgical innovations of sixteenth-century Safed, as well as Karo's major new halakhic works. They undergirded the dissemination of Sabbatianism and Hasidism in the following centuries and, as Chava Weissler has shown, enabled the emergence and spread of the new genre of Yiddish-language petitionary prayers for women (tkhines), most of which were composed by men.[38] Not just the physical means of dissemination—the printing press—but access to it, a political decision, determined what got transmitted. This access women were denied.

The lessons they learned, the tactics they developed to evade or escape marital captivity, could not be transmitted systematically, meaning that when it came to rabbinic law and their lives, generation after generation of Jewish women were left to reinvent the wheel or to be broken on it, one ruined life at a time.

Shashar concludes that two crucial variables operated in the outcome of agunah cases in the region and time she studies: the geographic location of the decisor relative to the agunah, and his location on the rabbinic status scale. The decisor being local to the agunah tended to operate in her favor, if for no other reason than that there were no travel costs in appealing to him. But this variable declined in significance or was obviated when decisors required the assent of multiple other authorities of similar or greater stature (*geonim mefursamim*), whom they sometimes designated specifically and who almost always lived elsewhere, negating the geographic benefit and privileging the hierarchical principle.[39] The requirement of assent from additional authorities in order to free an agunah is a stringency (*humra*) that contravenes the Talmudic directive to leniency in agunah cases. Yet that stringency found expression in Joseph Karo's *Shulhan Arukh*, the code of rabbinic law that became authoritative in this period,[40] a status it retains among the halakhically observant—as normative an expression as conceivable.

The demand for particular expertise in cases of agunot and indications of a power struggle about this, in fact, began earlier than the period Shashar studies. Already in the sixteenth century, Rabbi Meir Katzenelenbogen (the Maharam of Padua, 1482–1565) said, "An even greater evil I have seen: that one young rabbi who has just received ordination will praise himself loudly . . . and begin ruling on the laws of divorce, without seeking the advice of other older halachic authorities in the community. They should leave such rulings to those older men who are more experienced, and they should observe and learn until they are older."[41] We hear similarly, in a lengthy responsum by the abovementioned Rabbi Samuel de Medina (Maharashdam) of sixteenth-century Salonika, about the need for women refugees from Iberia to obtain gittin or halitsa from converted husbands who remained there, in cases where the (converted) witnesses to their marriages were not halakhically valid, which meant that their marriages were invalid—which meant that gittin and halitsa were not necessary. In his long discussion of the question, de Medina shows great reluctance to rule leniently unless backed by nine!—other decisors: a quorum (minyan) of decisors! He eventually settled for the backing of other authorities in Salonika to rule "leniently"—about cases *in which the marriages were not valid to begin with.*[42] Minna Rozen and Ruth Lamdan show that such demands were not unusual in sixteenth-century Istanbul and Safed, Lamdan citing "the inclination to stringency by sages" of that period and egregious examples of severity in cases of agunot.[43] We have also noted the demand expressed in the thirteenth century for multiple rabbinic approvals for divorce, an innovation that would create difficulties particularly for women given their preexisting disadvantage in rabbinic divorce. The trend to heightened demands and stringencies in agunah cases seems only to have increased with time, beginning earlier than Shashar says, but possibly with new demands and/or rationalizations for stringency in the era and region she studies.

Was the traumatized sixteenth century a time when rabbinic stringency against ruling for release of agunot increased? Did national trauma—Esther Benbassa and Aron Rodrigue rightly compare the trauma in the post–Spanish expulsion era to that after the Shoah[44]—translate into reactionary rabbinic rulings about women? We have, indeed, seen precisely such a connection in the stringent ruling of Jacob ben Solomon ibn Habib, discussed above. Did acute national trauma and anxiety translate, in the hands of post-Expulsion rabbinic decisors, Sephardi and Ashkenazi alike, into increased repression in one sure area of life that Jewish men could control—women, through restriction of their marital freedom and correspondingly increased male power?

Why did the Ashkenazic authorities whose records Shashar studies multiply the difficulties for women seeking release from iggun? We have discussed rabbinic fear of being labeled "lenient" (*mekel*), a devastating norm of self-imposed paralysis. But Shashar also offers a historical explanation for this behavior, citing several factors that emerged in the time and place she studies.

One factor was a decline in rabbinic authority and a shift of power within communities from rabbis to *parnassim*—the wealthy lay leadership who made rabbinic appointments and even began to designate candidates for rabbinic ordination.[45] This shift triggered compensatory, inflated rabbinic claims of status, an insistence on unique and exclusive rabbinic authority, within which there was to be a hierarchy of more authoritative rabbis over others deemed inferior in knowledge and lacking credentials to rule on difficult cases. Shashar illustrates this dynamic exhaustively in the rulings of one of the ranking halakhic authorities of his time, Menachem Mendel Krochmal (the Tzemach Tzedek), and those who cited him in their own rulings.[46]

It would appear that the demand for heightened professionalization and credentialing was a new element in the rabbinic regression we have traced regarding women in marriage and divorce, making for increasingly restrictive rulings. Severe rulings restricting permitted behavior were treated as a more telling statement of authority than granting it. This dynamic found particular expression in cases of agunot from the second half of the seventeenth century on. Shashar shows how it manifested in claims not just for a monopoly by rabbinic authority over marriage and divorce law, but for the jurisdiction of only the greatest of halakhic masters—*gedolei hador*—in this area.[47] The aforementioned Yehezkel Landau was particularly emphatic in the demand for many years of learning in other areas of halakha before a rabbi should presume to handle an agunah case (in addition, of course, to expertise in the laws of marriage and divorce).[48] Claims of decisors about the scant learning of rabbis of lesser rank and their disqualification to rule, particularly on marital law, were widespread in this period and that which followed, as Mordechai Zalkin's exhaustive social history of community rabbis in the Pale of Settlement in the nineteenth and early twentieth centuries documents.

These developments predated modernity and cannot be ascribed to its upheavals, let alone to defensive traditionalist responses to heterodox religious movements (especially what came to be known as the Reform movement), which only emerged in the mid-to-late-nineteenth century, and then in Protestant German states, not Eastern Europe. These were indigenous developments within rabbinic culture and society, with medieval precedent on which they enlarged.

But external forces in the era Shashar studies, the era of enlightened absolutism in Europe, also made for increasing demands for extreme degrees of competence before a rabbi should handle marriage and divorce cases. Yehezkel Landau composed what became a very influential halakhic tract, *Sefer Hukkei Ha'ishut*—The Book of Marital Laws—in response to the request of Emperor Joseph II of Austria (1741–1790) for clarifications about rabbinic marriage law. Joseph II made this inquiry in the context of his Edict of Toleration of 1782, which, among other goals, sought to erode the Jewish autonomy—Jews living by rule of rabbinic law—that had defined Jewish status throughout the medieval period. Responding to a threat to rabbinic control of marriage through the expanding ambitions of the absolute state claiming civil jurisdiction in matters of personal status, Landau replied that only rabbis with rarefied halakhic expertise could pronounce on cases of agunot, and even then, he said, only in consonance with "the opinion of [other] renowned rabbinic experts." As Shashar notes, "The discourse directed to the outside [in Landau's book] was intended to make clear to the [state] authorities that the state did not have the competence to execute the functions that rabbis discharge."[49] Such a claim, directed to the outside, compounded difficulties "inside" for women seeking release from marital captivity.

In contrast to the situation today, when most agunot are in marital captivity because of a husband's refusal to give a get and/or his extortion to give one, with such demands supported by rabbinic courts, in previous eras most agunot were in this status because a husband had disappeared. The primary concern of rabbinic law was the purity of patriarchal lineage within legitimate, that is, patriarchal marriage. In this context, an oft-cited fear was that, if an agunah were released and remarried and her first husband subsequently returned, as very rarely did happen, rabbinic authorities and traditional communities would deem her an adulteress, meaning forbidden to both husbands, who would both be required to divorce her. Any children born to the subsequent marriage would be deemed mamzerot/im. As Shashar notes, however, this fear was based on an exceedingly remote, overwhelmingly theoretical possibility of suffering, while failing to free agunot inflicted certain suffering.[50]

The precedent of restrictive rulings leading to very few agunot being freed in the two hundred years that Shashar studied has been passed on to and become part of current halakhic practice.

8

Agunot vs. Iggun

Strategies

What strategies did agunot in this era employ on their own behalf?

With sufficient means, they could "*posek*-shop"—denied by one decisor, they could try to seek another, hoping for a better outcome. This hope had limits, however. Added to the difficulties we have discussed, a second decisor often would refuse a case on which another rabbi had ruled negatively, or would rule as had the first rabbi, fearing being seen as upstaging the latter, or being sullied with the dreaded label *mekel* (lenient)[1]—with such self-concerns, rather than the welfare of the agunah, paramount.

Without the benefit of knowing the precedent of their medieval and early modern forebears—behavior the keepers of Jewish group memory did not highlight or memorialize, unlike stylized reports of women's martyrdom during the Crusades—early modern agunot perpetually reinvented strategies against iggun. As in earlier eras, this included turning to non-Jewish authorities for disposition of property disputes with heirs or would-be heirs of their husbands in order to better the terms of settlements, whether or not they could obtain release from iggun.

Such disputes were common and women's recourse to non-Jewish courts was an established behavior in Eastern Europe and in other European spheres in this period, as it was in previous eras elsewhere.[2] Use of such courts did not necessarily mean a better outcome for the Jewish (or the Christian) women plaintiffs.[3] What is significant is Jewish women's ongoing use of whatever means available in attempts on their own behalf. The fact that women could not have been relying on a systematically relayed women's tradition of educating one another about this tactic means that each generation discovered it anew and showed fresh initiative in applying it, even if, from a historical perspective, the behavior was of ancient lineage. Determination to escape marital captivity, not any acceptance of it as pious, martyred behavior, characterized Jewish women in this period as in the others we have examined.

Responsa of this period show frequent, intentional use by men of iggun as a tactic in marital disputes, as well as iggun arising from economic difficulties, or opportunities, including men leaving home to serve as religious teachers or tutors (melamdim) in a community school or private setting in distant locations. Since divorce in rabbinic court normatively entails payouts to the wife specified in the ketubbah and any other prenuptial agreements (if the husband had any means), as well as returning her dowry (if this had not been lost in the husband's business or was unavailable because it was in use securing a loan),[4] deserting a wife freed the husband from such payments and had always been an incentive to abandonment. Whereas, however, in earlier eras there was organized pushback against such behavior, there is no record in early modernity and modernity of rabbinic or communal efforts to impose consequences or disincentives to husbands for desertion. On the contrary, the incentive to desertion, facilitated by the way the male-led community (kehilla) operated in this place and time, increased.[5] As we saw in Geniza and Ottoman Jewish society, men also wielded the threat of desertion and making the wife an agunah to extort concessions in marital disputes.[6]

The rabbinic and communal materials that Shashar studies document the, often desperate, economic straits of agunot. For all the differences in time and place, what was true in Geniza society and early modern Ottoman Jewries typified the Ashkenazi world Shashar studies as well: iggun entailed extreme poverty, with depictions of an agunah's household as "devoid of everything," agunot and her children "lacking bread."[7] It also entailed social discrimination. Poverty-stricken agunot sought work on the bottom of the work scale, as servants or nannies, but faced reluctance to hire them for fear that children might be born to them from "doings" in the households of their employers. Any such children of agunot—who would be deemed mamzerot/im—were not just pariahs because of that stigma but were likely to become a financial burden on the community, with the onus of this policy put on impoverished women rather than on the males of the household responsible for the pregnancies. Agunot were treated as a threat to social order and community morals and so suffered secondary victimization. In the communal ordinances of the community of Altona-Hamburg-Wandsbeck in northwest Germany, agunot are among those listed as *forbidden to be hired* as maids.[8] How were these already-victimized women to support themselves, their children? Where was the traditional Jewish "communal paradigm" that Simha Goldin perceived in medieval Ashkenaz, or in Polin—"Gentle Polin [Poland]" as Rabbi Moshe Katz Geral, "head of the Beth Din of the Holy Congregation of Metz," characterized it in a penitential prayer for the Days of Awe and Repentance?[9]

The Tales of Two Memoirs

We can get a sense of how common iggun was in early modern Ashkenaz and about strategies agunot employed there to escape it from the two surviving full memoirs of this period. One is that of the ethicist and businesswoman Glikl Hamel (1646–1719) from northwest Germany. The other is that of the Talmud prodigy Salomon Maimon (1754–1800), who left Poland for German lands in search of enlightenment.[10]

We learn not just from the particulars these very different memoirs convey about marital captives and captivity but from the very fact that the only two surviving full memoirs from this period and region both testify to this abuse. Glikl informs us that other women of her station, time, and place also wrote ethical wills, of which genre her memoir is a (partial) type, and that such other writing did not survive.[11] It is something of a miracle that Glikl's did, that it was preserved, hand-copied by generations of her descendants and published almost two hundred years after her death, and that it has become famous. Her memoir is the only reason we know of her. Maimon, on the other hand, became a philosopher acknowledged by non-Jewish contemporaries, his genius and writing recognized in his own time and the latter, therefore, preserved. For all their differences, two memoirs from roughly the same period and against the odds of Glikl's surviving, both testify to the reality of iggun from personal, if highly divergent, gendered experience.

Glikl writes as a woman, herself, we would note, vulnerable to iggun on several counts. Her husband, Chaim, of frail health, was often away on long business trips; illness, accident, and/or criminal incident were all possible routes to her becoming an agunah. She tells the story of a relative of hers, Sarah, who lived in Altona and whose husband, a money changer, disappeared. People gossiped that he had deserted her because of marital quarrels over his financial difficulties (if this circumstance was assumed, it was not a rarity). He was gone for more than three years, during which "Sarah lived as a living widow [agunah] with her fatherless children, forced to suffer people saying and judging [her and her husband and the cause of her circumstances] as they wished."[12] His fate—as a murder victim—only came to light after that of yet another murdered Jewish man was revealed. That wife, too, was an agunah until her husband's death was confirmed.

Glikl's detailed account of how both murders came to light—and how two agunot were finally declared widows and freed of iggun—illustrates how difficult and fraught such discoveries were and how critical to that end was both the existence of competent Gentile authorities in an urban setting and their willingness to cooperate with Jews (if also threatening them) in interrogating witnesses and the perpetrator and in digging up gravesites. Such circumstances did not obtain in most locations in which the predominantly village and small-town Jewish population lived. Sarah reported identifying marks that would be found on her husband's body, which indeed were found—because the corpse had not yet disintegrated and the investigation proceeded quickly, also not common circumstances. She was then "in truth a widow . . . and . . . became lawfully free to marry again," as was the other "living widow."[13]

Maimon's autobiography gives quite different testimony to iggun, from the perspective of a perpetrator. He deserted his wife and children in Poland while he went to Germany in search of "enlightenment," eventually joining the circle of enlighteners (maskilim) around Moses Mendelssohn[14] (this after many times, while still in Poland, departing for far-off tutoring positions, a known circumstance for iggun). After several years of his absence in German lands, Maimon's wife tried to locate him, hiring and sending a Jewish man from Poland who found him in Hamburg—in northwest Germany, very distant from Poland. "He had been commissioned by my wife," Maimon writes of the messenger, to demand "that I should either return home without delay or send through him a bill of divorce." Maimon refused the first option on the grounds that he had "not the slightest prospect of getting on in the world or of leading a rational life" in Poland. He refused the second on the grounds that he was "not inclined to divorce my wife *without cause*" (my emphasis). There could be no more glaring expression of male privilege underlying self-absorbed cluelessness, even (or the more so) in a brilliant intellectual, than this. His wife was not asking him to cease his quest for enlightenment in Germany, only that if that was his priority, that he give her a get. To Maimon, this was divorce without cause. Clearly, a woman's "cause"—to be free of a dead marriage and able to remarry did not count as one, and was his prerogative to decide.

Maimon's wife's messenger appealed to the rabbi of the community, who summoned Maimon to appear before him, which summons Maimon refused. In a later conversation that did transpire, the rabbi focused not on Maimon's chained wife but on his lapsed religious observance. Maimon continued on his path of seeking secular education and compatible intellectual company; his wife remained an agunah. She and their eldest son later came to Germany themselves, finding Maimon, now in Breslau. How much time, how many years, had elapsed between Maimon's departure for Germany or his wife's request for a get and this point, we do not know but the interval had to have been substantial. Maimon "credits" his wife with "the courage of an Amazon" in taking this initiative, but with no understanding that the man he had become could not return to the Jewish life of his upbringing, to his "former barbarous and miserable condition" in Poland, depriving himself "of all the advantages [he] had gained" as a member of the illuminati.

Maimon's wife refused further delay and demanded a get. He finally consented to appear before a rabbinic court, with whose rabbi Maimon jousted (he was after all a genius in Talmud and this was an opportunity to best his interlocutor, who apparently equally relished the opportunity to go halakhic rounds with him), an encounter that ended without a get being given. His wife—Maimon never refers to her by name, only as "my wife"; we learn her name, Sarah, from his report about his marriage decades earlier—then resorted to entreaty, to which Maimon finally yielded.[15] He gave the get and sent her off with "a sufficient sum of money for household purposes"—surely a reference to her ketubbah settlement—which he, aggrieved, termed her "booty." After years of abandonment, physical travail, and financial cost in tracking Maimon down over great distances and poor and dangerous roads— Glikl's account gives a vivid sense of how treacherous travel in this time was—while pursuing halakhic recourse in several far-flung German

Jewish communities and rabbinic courts, this agunah got a get. And her "booty."[16]

Concluding: On the Change for Worse for Agunot

A major finding of Noa Shashar speaks for itself: Ashkenazic halakhic decisors in the period 1648–1850 systematically required the assent of several, even numerous, other decisors before they would release a woman from marital captivity, even in cases they themselves found warranted release. As she shows, this practice greatly lessened the already poor odds of an agunah obtaining release. In fact, the overwhelming majority of cases Shashar studied did not end in the agunot being freed.[17] And we know only about the cases that reached high rabbinic courts, when the financial and other costs of such litigation prevented the vast majority of agunot from even pursuing release. There is no way, therefore, to extrapolate from the sources the number of agunot in the period and locations she studies. What Shashar shows, however, is a clear pattern of rabbinic behavior that prevented release of agunot from marital captivity when cases did reach adjudication—a rabbinic policy, and a social, communal, and religious norm of agunot remaining captive. Jewish society, habituated to the presence of agunot as normal and to such women being—or becoming—a halakhic "problem," perpetuated that reality.

We have seen Shashar's historical explanation for the difficulties that decisors in this period added to an agunah securing a get. Still, questions remain about the regression in women's legal status and actual rights from what we saw for the early medieval era. As the reforms that benefited women occurred in real historical time and require historical explanation, so does the regression.

I have argued that, during long periods of Jewish history and throughout the Jewish world, particularly during the medieval era, women's awareness of their economic importance and their assertiveness in exerting it resulted in reforms that bettered not just their formal legal status but their ability to effect actual protections for themselves. I have called this women's pattern "politically engaged economics." The success of this behavior, however, clearly depended on a rabbinic orientation and communal environment that was malleable and pragmatic. The

nexus between effective behavior by women within a pragmatic communal mentality and reforms benefiting women broke down, gradually but
surely, in the context of an ideologically driven rabbinic backlash against
women's rights in marriage and divorce. While women at all levels—in
Ashkenaz, this included high-level banking—remained economically
active and critical to the livelihoods of their families and communities,
as Jay Berkowitz shows was true in late eighteenth-century Metz, France,
this importance ceased to translate into protections for women in actualized family law.[18] What was true of Jews as a whole in Christian
Europe—an inability to translate economic importance into political
power, something that made Jews politically "safe" for rulers and played
a role in the dialectics of Jewish toleration—now marked women within
Jewish society, where this had not previously been the case. Women's
inability to translate economic heft into political power meant that they
no longer posed an active threat to the patriarchal foundations of Jewish
society, a threat rabbinic authorities of the late medieval backlash had
perceived and acted explicitly to crush. New reforms were not created
and the medieval ones were vitiated. The "community paradigm" that
Simha Goldin cites for medieval Ashkenaz and that I believe is substantiated by the evidence for that period and place and others, which saw
the benefit of the community in that of women, not out of benevolence
but pragmatism, ceased to exist. From Shashar's findings and in much
other evidence, we learn that agunot were on their own, abandoned,
barred as social pariahs even from the most marginal employment, their
poverty and desperation an individual misfortune, entirely their own
to bear. That latter situation remains the case to this day, yielding the
"poor agunot" in Jonathan Sarna's phrase,[19] and the incessantly cited
"wretched," women, the "*dalot*" whose cry never elicits effective action.

The dynamic, interactive loop mechanism in halakha regarding family law, a fluidity between de facto and de jure that operated in earlier
eras, in which women's actualized rights increased, atrophied. These
shifts long predated the demise of the traditional kehilla in modernity
and the emergence of movements of modern Judaism, which posed a
threat to traditional rabbinic authority that both scholars and apologists see as responsible for modern halakhic intransigence in general,
and regarding women's rights in particular. The two shifts I cite—the
worsening of women's rights and the end of women's ability to translate

economic importance into enhanced rights because of explicit rabbinic actions—occurred entirely within traditional, premodern Jewish societies. In such communities, both communal and rabbinic weakness was pronounced Numerous scholars of Jewries East and West, medieval and early modern—of Geniza society (Cohen, Krakowski), Ottoman Jewries (Rozen; Rodrigue and Benbassa), Ashkenaz (Fram), Italy and the Mediterranean (Adelman, Furst, Woolf)—document this weakness. The supposedly determinative power of premodern rabbis and communities was not responsible for reforms that benefited women, nor was modernity, with the demise of premodern rabbinic power, responsible for the regression in women's actualized rights. To attribute that regression to the demise of such alleged power is to shift responsibility for conscious, specific actions by rabbinic authorities from themselves onto anonymous historical forces and to make these authorities victims, in place of those they victimized, and victimize.

Jacob Katz, Michael Silber, and other historians emphasize the ideological challenge from heterodox religious movements that emerged in European Jewish modernity as a factor triggering a correspondingly ideological Orthodoxy, itself a modern phenomenon, and increasing halakhic rigidity.[20] But the late medieval and early modern rabbinic backlash against women's power and enhanced rights also took self-conscious, ideological expression if, of course, not in the form possible for Orthodoxy after the invention of industrialized mass communication in newspapers and ideological journals. The backlash against women's rights that began in the late medieval era was articulate and explicit—ideological. And it was communicated effectively and authoritatively through established means of communication by the rabbinic elite in subsequent responsa and other halakhic works, like the sixteenth-century *Shulhan Arukh*, second only to the Talmud in its authority, and in the hugely influential commentaries on that work; as well as in Yehezkel Landau's *Book of Marital Laws*—all of which became and remain the stuff of halakhic ruling and precedent about marriage and divorce, enacted in rabbinic courts to this day.

This regressive change is a tremendously important, underresearched chapter in Jewish history. Based on what scholars have said, breakdown of the nexus that led to meaningful reforms for women—politically engaged economics and the loop mechanism in halakha—appears attributable to patriarchal backlash against early medieval reforms that had benefited women and against the power of women that both drove those reforms and was furthered by them. That backlash began in the second half of the twelfth century, and was reinforced and expanded in subsequent centuries. It was expressed in halakhic pronouncements and rulings and in communal practice, in an openly misogynistic mentality that sought to keep women "in their place," a "place" undergoing concerted and specific halakhic definition in this period beyond anything in previous rabbinic pronouncements.

It is relevant in this connection to cite Martha Keil, who discusses not the decline in the nexus between economics and women's rights in family law but the related, developing disparity between women's economic importance and their declining status in "socio-religious life," which became manifest at this same time. She notes: "Excluding women from . . . socio-religious public life was an attempt to oust them from the last bastions of public honour because they had become so important and influential in business and hence also in the running of the community. The main argument behind this exclusion was that the reputation of the men was defined by the modesty of women." Keil argues that regression in women's rights correspondingly received physical expression in sacred space, the synagogue. "Banishment," she writes, "soon became manifest in architecture," in the creation of separate "women's shuln" (women's synagogues). These were simultaneously part of the main synagogue, that is, male space, and apart from it, from which women were now "absolutely prohibited," "because they had their own room now . . . something which had not been the case in the eleventh and twelfth centuries." Women's exclusion from the synagogue interior did not occur suddenly, in a single act, but depending on the community, proceeded over decades and in stages. Subtle changes began "during the Late Middle Ages,"[21] dating that aligns with what Elisheva Baumgarten established about the beginning of a gendered regression in the status of women in rabbinic law and ritual practice in Ashkenazic realms. These various expressions were related, each part of the backlash against women's power and status in premodern Ashkenazic societies.

Although the demand for heightened professionalization of rabbis dealing with divorce may be datable to the period and region Shashar studies, the evidence strongly suggests that the rabbinic tendency to

severity in agunah rulings that she documents was not a new development, originating when modern ideological currents and the weakening
of the traditional kehilla were beginning to be manifested in Europe, or,
by 1850, had advanced in certain settings. The tendency to such rulings
in agunah cases cannot be attributed to a politicized rabbinic reaction
against modernity. Rather, it was the continuation and augmentation
of a pattern that began in late medieval Ashkenaz with articulate assertion of misogyny and patriarchal privilege by ranking halakhic decisors,
then solidified by their disciples and successors. We have suggested that
this tendency may have become more pronounced in the traumatized
aftermath of the catastrophe of Spanish–Portuguese Jewry, taking expression in rabbinic rulings in Ottoman settings that instrumentalized
women in the service of group needs defined as male, responding to a
heightened sense of Jewish helplessness then gripping Jewish societies
across geographic and ethnic boundaries in expanded male control over
women. Trauma and responses to it, including group trauma, are gendered. When a patriarchal elite—some, perhaps many of whose members had personal traumas and perceived failures to compensate for
(such as conversion within the family)—controls expression of national
trauma, crafting official narrative and law in response to it, that expression will take, and took, misogynist form.

This schema suggests that roughly concurrent—and possibly
interacting—processes of regression in the rights and status of women
occurred in both Ashkenazi and Sephardi spheres. Whether there was
cross-influence (major decisors were well aware of and highly sensitive
to their colleagues' rulings) and not only concurrence merits study.

It was these developments within traditional, premodern Jewish society, long predating the emergence of the denominations of modern
Judaism, including Orthodoxy, that overrode women's ability to translate economic heft into political power and meaningful protections for
themselves. These were indigenous developments within traditional,
premodern Jewish societies and rabbinic culture and not a reaction to
external challenges posed by modernity.

9

Iggun in Modernity

The problem of iggun has not diminished in modernity, whose onset in Europe I date roughly from the late eighteenth century with the erosion and demise of the self-governing, corporate kehilla and the establishment of new centers of Jewish life that lacked a proximate (the UK) or any medieval past (the United States), and where Jewish life was established on entirely voluntary foundations.[1] Arguably the problem has worsened, for several reasons.

As we have seen, a husband's incentive to abandonment was inherent in the mandate of the ketubbah settlement as administered in its patriarchal context, that is, dependent on enforcement by a patriarchal system—and was nothing new; we have seen reference to men abandoning wives explicitly in order to evade its payment. But the Industrial Revolution produced mechanized mass transit—railroads, steamships—that enabled migration on a scale previously inconceivable. Some 2.3 million Jews left the Russian Empire between 1875 and 1914 in the largest migration in Jewish history.[2] Massive migration itself undermined communal coherence. Internal Jewish migration, from Eastern European to German states, Austria, France, Belgium, Holland, and England, and external migration, to Ottoman Palestine, Argentina, South Africa, Australia, and the United States, were accompanied by a huge increase in abandoned wives. Husbands often failed to divorce wives and in far-off locations, where they were unknown and where effective communal controls had ceased to exist, or, in the United States, had never existed, or, in England, where no medieval-style kehilla was reestablished when Jewish resettlement occurred under Cromwell, simply married anew.[3] While men departing for distant locations, causing wives to fall into iggun, was also nothing new in Jewish history, the dimensions of this migration, combined with the demise of communal controls, vastly exacerbated the problem.

Haim Sperber has identified 5,399 cases of agunot in or originating in Eastern Europe in the second half of the nineteenth century and 3,652 in the early twentieth century, with desertion the chief cause.[4] In 1867 the Hebrew-language newspaper *Hamagid*, first published in Lyck, East Prussia, began featuring a dedicated page on which it printed appeals from agunot seeking disappeared husbands. The paper's editor himself wrote and published articles about agunot.[5] Fathers of agunot and rabbis who, aside from seeking to help desperate women, feared the unraveling of traditional norms and their authority when men failed to divorce wives and simply married anew, also placed ads on behalf of agunot seeking missing husbands.

Margalit Shilo calls such pages a "Wailing Wall" for the cries of agunot.[6] As we have seen in other eras and places, desertion contributed mightily to already high levels of Jewish poverty in Eastern Europe and among new immigrant communities, increasing the calls of destitute women and children for community assistance. In 1905 the National Council of Hebrew Charities in New York created the National Desertion Bureau because of this growing problem; financial aid for agunot constituted the second largest item in the United Hebrew Charity's budget in 1905.[7] In Kyiv 13 percent of applicants for communal welfare in 1913 were deserted wives—and this was just one category of agunot in the community's records.[8] Unlike the situation in the medieval period, when at least the financial cost of women's marital captivity figured as a communal issue, such considerations lapsed in modernity.

"For our many sins," begins an undated letter of Rabbi Moshe Nahum Yerusalimsky, sent from somewhere in the Russian Pale of Settlement to Western rabbis,

> there are some who have breached the bounds of decency and have cast off the obligation to support their families. . . . Among them are men who . . . have taken themselves other wives in place of those they betrothed according to the law of Moses and Israel. . . . An outcry has reached us from many towns and cities from living widows [agunot] left without support from their husbands and without anyone to hear the wailing of . . . children asking for food. . . .[9]

Similar announcements, pleading for information to locate husbands, appeared in Yiddish newspapers in the United States and other places of mass Jewish immigration. The major Yiddish newspaper in New York, *Forverts*, published a "Gallery of Abandoning Husbands"—a list of deserters with their details and photographs.[10]

War is always the occasion for the undocumented disappearance of husbands and the creation of agunot. Jewish men were combatants in the armies of all the countries that fought in World War I, whose Eastern Front was Congress Poland and the Jewish Pale of Settlement, major Jewish population centers. There were many Jewish casualties, military and otherwise, documented and not. Abandoned, impoverished, desperate women who became agunot could become prostitutes, lured through deception or desperation.[11] Yiddish novels of the period excoriated procurement through deception and criticized traditional customs that abetted traffickers—matchmaking, "and the orthodox law of divorce," for creating agunot.[12] Conversion of men also resulted in wives becoming agunot. Of course, such men were outside any controls of the Jewish community and churches in Imperial Russia encouraged their swift remarriage to Christians in order to lessen the chances of family pressure against the conversion or to give the wife a get (in the doing of which, of course, a convert would recognize rabbinic law and act as a Jew, behavior hardly acceptable to church authorities or advisable for a new convert needing to demonstrate sincerity). Thus, as ChaeRan Freeze notes, "Rabbinical authorities could not, and gentile authorities would not, act to formalize the end of Jewish marriage and [free] agunot."[13]

Freeze's encyclopedic study of Jewish marriage and divorce in Imperial Russia shows that there was extensive marital breakdown there, deriving from multiple causes and expressed in various ways and that, contrary to what is often asserted, women's marital captivity was exacerbated but hardly caused by the era's mass emigration.[14] Haim Sperber confirms this, finding that "most agunot cases between 1901 and 1914 [in the United States] were not the result of international migration [only 20 percent being attributable to it]. Most deserted women were either born in America or had been living [there] long before they were deserted."[15]

Desertion as a cause of iggun, then, was not simply occasioned by long-distance migration, or by modernity, that is, by anonymous, accidental circumstances. Refusal of a levir, Jewish or converted, to release his sister-in-law from the obligation to marry him was in modernity, as in previous periods, another source of iggun, as well as the occasion for extortion. Many men refused to divorce wives simply to avoid having to repay the wife's dowry and pay the ketubbah settlement. Unsafe conditions led to the demise of many Jewish men whose "corpses were found in the forest. Given the weakness of the Russian police and the difficulties in identifying victims [of crime] (who were normally stripped of their papers as well as their money), many women never learned about the fate of their husbands,"[16] and without halakhically valid witnesses, they became agunot without hope of release.[17]

Get and halitsa blackmail existed, too. A rabbi in Russia wrote to his counterpart in New York about a man who had departed for America and failed to send support for his family and was also demanding the huge sum of a thousand rubles to divorce his wife, Miriam Devorah of Kielce. "'I have spoken to the woman's father, who is a poor man,'" the aforementioned Rabbi Yerusalimsky wrote. "Nevertheless, he told me that to secure her release . . . he would sell everything he has and would give the man 100 rubles. If that is not enough, he will try to obtain help from his relatives, perhaps another 200 rubles."[18] In 1893 Roza Vershavskaia, childless and widowed after a year of marriage to a simple merchant, at age twenty-one found herself extorted for halitsa by her brother-in-law, who demanded an exorbitant five hundred rubles to release her. The rabbinic authorities to whom she and her father appealed to force the man to give her halitsa advised her "to turn to the rabbi in the hometown of the brother-in-law with a petition for an amicable settlement of their mutual claims [there was also a financial dispute between them, in which the brother-in-law was clearly using halitsa extortion to extract a favorable settlement], *and an inducement for the levir* to fulfill the divorce" (my emphasis).[19] We also hear of cases in tsarist-ruled lands of rabbinic dispensation releasing men from the prohibition of polygyny in order to help husbands whose wives refused a divorce because of disadvantageous terms attached to it. Such settlements required that the wives abandon their own claims or be deemed "rebellious," with the financial penalties that entailed. In the case of David Khaim Geller vs. his wife, Khaia Yudis Geller, from Warsaw and Koidanovo (in the Minsk province), respectively, in 1904, the rabbis involved expressed sympathy for the plight of the husband, whom they wished to "free . . . from the onus of celibacy . . . and to spare him the loneliness that he does not deserve. We hereby permit him, notwithstanding his present wife, to marry another [woman]. . . ." About Kahia Yudis, however, they hastened to emphasize that she "did not have the right to marry" until she accepted a get on her husband's terms.[20]

References to agunot appear in memoirs and letters of this time. In her memoirs, Pauline Wengeroff (1833–1916) recalls a childhood skit she put on in her wealthy home in 1830s Brest-Litovsk during her family's lavish Purim *suda* (holiday feast), in which she disguised herself as an agunah begging for food. Wengeroff's father, she reports, failing to recognize her, was not pleased at the intrusion and wanted the intruder ejected. Her reminiscence illustrates both the poverty of agunot and the social discrimination they faced. It also testifies to the prevalence of agunot as a social reality, to have impressed itself already on the mind of a child.[21] The adult Wengeroff had a personal connection to the issue, too: her brother, Ephraim, departed Russian Poland for the United States (at some point converting to Christianity), leaving his wife and child behind. Only years later, in the context of a return trip to Europe to claim his inheritance from his paternal grandfather, did he give his wife a get, apparently under family pressure: she was a paternal cousin so her fate was quite relevant to his father.[22]

Ita Kalish (1903–1994), member of a prominent Hasidic family, recalls a sainted family member who would help "Jews in distress," including an agunah attempting to locate her husband.[23] Anna Babaeva, a sixteen-year-old girl pressured, she testified in a letter in 1909 to the tsarist authorities, to marry a man who subsequently disappeared, thus became an agunah.[24] She herself had earned a permit to reside outside the Pale of Settlement, a precious privilege that opened wider economic opportunities. Her husband, however, lacked one—marriage caused a woman's residency status to be subsumed in that of her husband—and if she did not obtain a get, that is, get divorced, and show such documentation to the tsarist authorities, she faced expulsion to the Pale. Babaeva's inability to secure a get indeed lost her the right to reside and do business outside the Pale.

References to agunah cases abound in the responsa of the renowned decisor Rabbi Yitzhak Elhanan Spektor (1817–1896) of Kovno, in which a rabbinic biographer cites one hundred and fifty-eight responsa concerning agunot.[25] References abound, too, in the responsa of other major halakhic authorities of the time, such as, Naphtali Tzvi Yehuda Berlin (the Netziv), head of the prestigious Volozhin yeshiva; Shlomo Kluger; Shaul Natanson.[26] Mention of agunot thrust into poverty and loneliness comes in a variety of sources, often incidentally, as in a memoir that mentions a nanny: "Roiza, a middle aged woman, an agunah whose husband's whereabouts were unknown . . ." She performed all manner of domestic menial work—cooking; washing; sewing; live-in, round-the-clock childcare. "Lonely and childless . . . [she] poured all her . . . love" on the child in her charge, singing folk songs and telling melancholy tales through which "she expressed her own aspirations and wept copious tears over her own grief."[27] Aside from the economic consequences of iggun, the loss of (unstigmatized) children of one's own was another grief it imposed. The absence of Jewish men was so common in Kopyl, hometown of the memoirist Avraham Paperno (aka Paperna, 1840–1919), that he notes that it was "the order of things" "for wives to be left behind by their husbands . . . so that ten months of the year" Kopyl "appeared to be partly a town of Amazonki [Amazons], or rather young female traders waging a desperate struggle for existence without the help of the male sex."[28] Haim Sperber has given us a sense of the number of women made agunot through desertion or the death of husbands without timely news of either event or witness testimony meeting halakhic standards in the case of death. The Jewish family of the Pale of Settlement, a vast area stretching from the Baltic Sea to the Black Sea and then home to the world's largest Jewish population, like that of medieval Ashkenaz and Geniza society, was highly unstable, as ChaeRan Freeze amply demonstrates. Halakhic norms added iggun to other consequences of marital breakdown for women.

Agunot figured prominently in Jewish literature of or about this era, in both Eastern Europe and among the Jewish population (Yishuv) in Palestine. The poet laureate of the nineteenth-century Eastern European Haskalah, Judah Leib Gordon, wrote the iconic poem "The Tip of the Yud" in which he excoriated rabbis for indifference to the plight of women altogether and to those made agunot because of rabbinic pedantry and callousness in particular.[29] Shmuel Yosef Agnon, later winner of a Nobel Prize in Literature, penned "Agunot," the first of his works produced in Palestine, in 1907, and changed his last name, Czaczkes, to Agnon, derived from that word. He used the term to convey "a condition of tragic suspension that cannot be unilaterally dissolved," referring to the unresolved state of his religious conflicts. The fact that "iggun" could be applied to signify existential limbo—a use also employed by the pioneering writer Devorah Baron in Palestine—and could convey this meaning to the reading public speaks volumes about the familiarity of marital captivity in Jewish society.[30] The great Yiddish writer Chaim Grade wrote a sympathetic novel, *The Agunah*, about a woman in Vilna, a town renowned for rabbinic scholarship, whose husband was a soldier in World War I in a unit that was wiped out and who was an agunah for more than fifteen years; there was much circumstantial evidence of his death but no halakhic witnesses to it. The novel focuses on rabbinic pedantry and rivalries about her case, which ended in further tragedy for her and others, including the one rabbi who ruled her free to remarry.[31] It is significant that the agunah in this novel is not, in her own eyes, "religious," yet societal norms and taboos about "adultery" and mamzerut were such that, despite her certainty that her husband was dead, remarriage without rabbinic dispensation when a suitor appeared was inconceivable to her. I call this stance "tradition-friendly," which characterizes many in contemporary Israeli society.

Iggun in the Prestate Yishuv

Since halakha governed Jewish life across the Diaspora, including North Africa, Syria, Lebanon, Iraq, Iran, Yemen, Turkey, Kurdistan, Afghanistan, as well as in the Old (pre-Zionist) Palestinian Yishuv, iggun existed across the Jewish world. Male abandonment was so common that a source cited by Margalit Shilo relates that, "there was an ancient custom in Jerusalem. When the bride and groom stood under the marriage canopy . . . the groom would [affirm] to the rabbi . . . conducting the ceremony that he would not leave the country without the permission and agreement of . . . his wife."[32]

Such agreements notwithstanding, Shilo reports that the "high incidence of agunot became an oppressive problem in Jerusalem and in general through the Land of Israel" in the prestate era. This was attested in letters, responsa, and the pages of local newspapers, including, as in Eastern Europe and the United States, hundreds of classified advertisements from agunot and their parents from all strata of society, including the wealthy and status-laden, seeking absent husbands in order to obtain divorces. Although there was an important difference between religiously motivated Jewish migration to Palestine and economically motivated migration to other places, with direct implications for at least one major cause of iggun—Jews coming to Palestine tended to come *en famille*—this did not prevent homegrown iggun in the Holy Land arising for the same reasons that caused it in the lands of Jewish Exile. Shilo recounts, "One journalist portrayed Jerusalem as a city of mourning, not because of the destroyed Temple, but rather because of the ruined households within its confines. Among the tales of desertion and privation that he published were those of a young woman, with a babe in arms, whose husband abandoned her and went off to Africa . . . and of an agunah with five children whose husband set sail for Australia."[33]

Payoffs to obtain gittin were an expedient there and then, too. The wife of Nathan Halevi of Safed told local rabbis in 1903 that she would forgo the alimony and other obligations of her ketubbah in order to be released from marital captivity—that is, pay for it. A wealthy Sephardic agunah from Jerusalem whose Ashkenazic husband had deserted, managed to buy herself a writ of divorce " 'by wasting large amounts of money and bribes.' "[34] In the encounter between traditional Eastern and Westernizing Jewries in the modern period, we also hear of efforts to address iggun, the tropes of which are distressingly familiar.[35]

Then and Now

Iggun not only continues today but has worsened in the last eighty or so years in both scope and nature, for several reasons.

One cause is grounded in the fundamental geographic remaking of the world Jewish population since World War II. The destruction of two-thirds of European Jewry and virtually all of Eastern European Jewry and that of the Balkans (e.g., the community of Salonika) in the Shoah, and, since 1948, the demise of Middle Eastern and North African Jewries, resulted in a shift of the centers of Jewish life to the United States and Israel, where very different conditions of Jewish life obtained compared to those in the traditional Jewish centers.[36] We have no information on which to judge trends in the communities of North Africa and the Middle East in this period, but there is reason to say that the situation has worsened among Jews in Western Europe, the UK, South America, and Australia, where the rise in overall Jewish wealth in the post–World War II era has made for previously inconceivable sums demanded by husbands in get extortion, a practice that continues to be abetted and enabled by rabbinic courts. The expansion of extortive behavior by men and the dimensions of demands made on women in return for a get, however, must be seen as symptom rather than cause.

Half of all Jews today live in Israel, where there is no civil marriage or divorce, only religiously enacted proceedings for citizens by their respective religious authorities. "Personal status" issues—birth, death, marriage, divorce, and listing on citizenship papers (unless someone requests the designation "no religion")—are determined by religion. In the "start-up nation" of technological innovation, the self-assigned, individual nature of religious identity, which historians identify as a major signpost of Jewish modernity, does not exist. Religious identity on the basis of assumed group affiliation incurred at birth is wholly premodern, as is the type of the religious identity assigned: for Israeli Jews, this is not just Jewish but Orthodox, no other form of Jewish expression being officially recognized. For the past several decades, with the Chief Rabbinate headed by two ultra-Orthodox rabbis, one Sephardi, the other Ashkenazi, that identity has been personified as not just Orthodox but ultra-Orthodox, meaning, among other things, lacking in secular education and rejecting values like the civil equality of women.

Israel's policy perpetuates the Ottoman Empire's millet system (subjects categorized by religion), which the founders of the state retained as part of political deals with the ultra-Orthodox establishment.[37] By law, personal status for Jews is under the control of the state's Chief Rabbinate, regardless of the religious orientation of the parties involved. Chief Rabbinate courts have a poor, indeed notorious, record in handling divorce. Orthodox rabbinic courts and the Orthodox rabbinic establishment in the United States have equally dismal records. Despite—or because of—the emergence in the last century of organized efforts on behalf of agunot, the record not only has not improved but has worsened, as a defensive Orthodox establishment's strident resistance to feminism has targeted agunah advocacy as part of that resistance. This stance has pitted women's self-protection in marriage and divorce against loyalty to Orthodoxy, which is depicted as synonymous with Judaism, which is portrayed as under mortal threat from modernity altogether and from feminism in particular.[38] The methods of agunah-advocacy organizations have failed to prevent iggun or to offer a systemic means of freeing agunot—that is, to end the problem. Instead, these methods aim at managing iggun, accepting it as an inevitable malady, an unavoidable "tragedy," whose incidence can be limited but not ended.

Identifying Iggun as a Communal Problem: Marital Captivity Enters the Jewish Public Sphere

As noted, agunot began to be treated as a problem of Jewish society, not just as a halakhic issue for rabbinic decisors, with the attention of newly founded Jewish newspapers to the issue in the second half of the nineteenth century. In 1865 the editor of *HaMagid*, Eliezer Lipman Zilberman, published a long editorial labeling iggun one of the most important problems for the nascent Jewish press to address and promising that his Hebrew-language weekly would pressure rabbis to address it.[39] Ads naming missing husbands and seeking information to locate them followed, as did similar actions in other Hebrew-language papers, *HaMelitz*, *HaCarmel*, and *HaZefira*, beginning in the 1860s.[40] *HaMelitz* and *HaZefira* became dailies in the 1880s and made agunot a prime subject of reporting. We get a sense of the importance that traditionalist elements ascribed to this attention in the response of the Orthodox press, in particular *HaLevanon* and its editor Yehiel Brill. Brill accused Zilberman of exaggerating the problem of agunot and published editorials arguing that the matter should be left to rabbis. Other Orthodox papers, *Mahazikei HaDat* and *Kol Mahazikei HaDat*, indicated their editorial positions by publishing few ads about missing husbands. The politicization of "the agunah problem" in Jewish public space had begun.

It was largely the Hebrew-language, rather than the Yiddish-language press, that put agunot on their pages' agenda.[41] There were far fewer readers of Hebrew than Yiddish and by language choice alone, such readers were expressing "modern" inclinations. Taking the issue of agunot out of purely rabbinic, legal discourse and into the Jewish public sphere was a significant act of secularization. Haim Sperber shows that prominent rabbinic figures—Rabbis David Friedman, Naftali Zvi Yehuda Berlin, Hayim Berlin—were not only aware of media attention to the problem but responded to it, themselves citing articles, a sure sign that change was infiltrating even traditional circles opposed to the media encroaching on rabbinic turf.[42] Other rabbis used information about missing husbands published in newspapers, seeing such papers not as a threat to their control of this issue but a resource.[43] Based on meticulous reconstructions of the published data, Sperber estimates that there were at least forty thousand agunot in Eastern Europe during the second half of the nineteenth century.[44]

Jewish marital captivity was debated publicly in France and Algeria, annexed to France in 1834, in the late nineteenth and early twentieth centuries after the reinstitution of civil divorce during France's Third Republic. Jews began getting civil divorces, and men thus divorced would often deny their wives a get or extort for it; levirs also refused to enact halitsa for sisters-in-law, demanding payoffs to free them for remarriage. While all this was nothing new, what was new was the weakening of the rabbinic legal system as any kind of recourse for women once there was civil law regulating marriage; men could simply ignore rabbinic law and courts since their marital status was established by civil law. Women who abided by rabbinic law, however, were victimized. They were stranded between legal systems, divorced under one but not the other, or widowed, yet not free to marry without halitsa. They and their families began appealing to communal authorities for help. In Algeria in particular, where Jews became naturalized French citizens in 1870, parents often paid husbands large sums to free their daughters and wanted relief from extortion.[45]

All this sparked a transnational debate among European and North African Jewries, publicized in 1907 in French Jewry's two communal newspapers *Archives Israélites* and *Univers Israélite*. The papers reported about French and Algerian rabbis who proposed and opposed reforms and about the disagreement on the issue between French rabbis and eminent authorities from Eastern Europe, including Rabbis Yitzhak Elhanan Spector and Naftali Berlin. The debate spread elsewhere and included England's chief rabbi Hermann Adler, Holland's chief rabbi

Joseph Hirsch Dunner, and Rabbi David Zvi Hoffman, rector of the (Orthodox) Rabbinical Seminary of Berlin.

The French rabbinate proposed two measures to address get refusal: conditional marriage (*kiddushin al tnai*) and rabbinic annulment of the Jewish marriage (*hafka'at kiddushin*) when the couple got a civil divorce but the husband refused the wife a get.[46] Both proposals were swiftly vetoed by Eastern European *poskim* who threatened to put French Jewry under religious ban (herem) if they were implemented. Other Jews—in particular immigrants from Eastern Europe at a time of substantial and increasing Jewish migration from there—would, and should, they warned, refuse to marry French Jews or their offspring if the reforms proceeded.[47] Rabbinic action to ameliorate iggun and help agunot would, and should, according to these elements, cause schism, a threat repeated many times since in other settings.

The problem of women needing halitsa reached the office of the French Ministry of Interior after two Algerian widows from childless marriages sought help there when their brothers-in-law refused to enact halitsa. That office referred the problem to the Ministry of Religion, which, in turn, contacted the Consistory, the state-authorized-and-supervised Jewish community (which, since Napoleon, was defined as a purely confessional entity with no juridical powers).[48] This made the issue overtly political between French Jewry and the French state and posed a potential threat to Jewish civil status: the Revolution had made marriage a civil function, with religious ceremonies optional and legal only after a civil marriage had been performed; levirate marriage had been outlawed since 1804. Algerian Jews, as French citizens, were subject to French law.

The Consistorial grand rabbi of the time, Lazare Isidor, responded to the Ministry of Interior's potentially ominous query by claiming that, with the French abolition of "tribunals" (meaning the premodern kehilla's rabbinic courts) in Algeria and the application of French law to matters of personal status, the Jewish community had no means to force levirs to give halitsa as, he claimed, it had done previously. He thus skirted the dangerous implication of Jewish "tribalism" and "orientalism" in conflict with French Jews' mandatory, preeminent subservience to French law. Isidor, however, went beyond this with an extraordinary argument. He distinguished between the ruling of the Napoleonic

Sanhedrin (1807), which exempted Jewish soldiers in the French Army from observing rabbinic law that conflicted with their service—the dietary laws, Sabbath and festival observance—and the situation of widows needing halitsa.[49] Whereas, he said, men serving in the military were under positive obligation to obey French law requiring military service, there was no French law mandating marriage, so women needing halitsa in order to remarry were on their own, with no call on the assistance of the state. Because the refusal to perform halitsa did not conflict with French law, Isidor dutifully maintained, "the rabbinate"— the same one that had authorized violation of core halakhic practice in the service of the state—"did not have the halakhic authority to abolish" halitsa.[50] Observant women—good, pious Jews obeying the dictates of halakha—would get no help from the official state rabbinate.[51] Here too, as we have seen in other contexts, the operating assumption of rabbis, whether premodern or, as in this case, quite modernizing, was the Otherness of women and a self-evident double standard regarding women's claim to protection or service from the community, conceived of as constituted of males. In this instance, as in that of Iberian agunot, women would be sacrificed on the altar of communal priorities deemed more compelling than those of women loyal to halakha.

Iggun made a major leap onto the modern communal radar as a problem for European Jewish society—that is, demanding communal and supracommunal, transnational organization and response—in the early twentieth century. The Jüdische Frauenbund (JFB), the League of Jewish Women, founded in Germany in 1904, called public attention to Jewish white-slaving feeding on impoverished Jewish women in Galicia, Poland, Romania, and Russia.[52] Preying on their poverty and naivete and the ease of enacting halakhic marriage, which requires only two (male) witnesses and a (male) officiant, not necessarily a rabbi, traffickers lured women into phony marriages. Such marriages, however fraudulent, were binding under halakha unless a rabbinic court invalidated them; the contrast with what is entailed in women obtaining rabbinic divorce and the ease of entrapping women into halakhic marriage is impressive. Of course, such cases would never reach rabbinic courts. Sold to brothels, shipped far from families and anything familiar—Germany, Austria, the Balkans, and South America were common destinations— these women became agunot as well as sex slaves. Pimps also targeted already-existing agunot with promises of gittin, offering liberation to desperate women then sold into slavery.[53]

The problems were vastly exacerbated by World War I, whose Eastern Front was Congress Poland and the Pale of Settlement, home to several million Jews. Along with the rest of the larger and Jewish populations there, women were direct casualties of the war and the hunger and disease in its wake but many were further victimized when husbands disappeared and they became agunot. Vast pogroms raged in Poland during the war, perpetrated by tsarist soldiers, and then in Ukraine from 1918 to 1921, in the latter of which an estimated one hundred thousand Jews were murdered. Hundreds of Jewish communities were attacked and destroyed and hundreds of thousands made homeless. Large numbers of women were made agunot from the depradations.[54]

Accordingly, agunot were a central topic at conferences organized by women's organizations in the 1920s: Bnos Agudath Israel, in Lodz; the Vienna Women's Conference (part of the second World Congress of Agudath Israel); the World Conference of Jewish Women, in Hamburg; and the Women's International Zionist Organization (WIZO), meeting in Zurich.[55] Many at the time recognized that the problem was situated in rabbinic marriage and divorce, if apparently conceived of as confined to the disasters then occurring in Eastern Europe. Dr. Ada Reichenstein, a delegate from Lemberg, Poland, to the World Congress of Jewish Women in Vienna in 1923, described the "question of Jewish marriage and divorce [as] an *ostjüdische* [Eastern European Jewish] catastrophe."[56] There were some twenty-five thousand women in Congress Poland alone whose husbands had disappeared during World War I and who could not remarry because the deaths had not been confirmed by halakhic criteria.[57]

Many called for recognized rabbinic authorities to reform halakhic marriage and divorce, in much the same language that veteran agunah advocates Susan Aranoff and Rivka Haut would use in 2015, saying:

> We believe that halakhic solutions to this problem exist. Over the ages, wise rabbis have devised ways of easing difficulties caused by halakhic strictures. In the area of finance, for example, the clear Torah [biblical] prohibition against Jews taking interest on loans to other Jews has been creatively circumvented. . . . Banks in Israel and even some in the United

States that serve Orthodox clientele make use of "*heter iska*," a rabbinically created document which structures forbidden interest as profit from an investment.[58]

It would not cheer Haut and Aranoff, or agunah activists who have followed them since, to learn that such words—in particular, the comparison of nonaction on iggun with the creative solution of *heter iska*—were pronounced almost verbatim a century ago in several locations in Europe.

Bertha Pappenheim, Orthodox founder of the JFB, petitioned rabbis to modernize marriage, divorce, and inheritance laws for the sake of the approximately twenty thousand agunot in Eastern Europe, who "were living in misery, in danger of being . . . tricked into false marriages and . . . prostitution."[59]

At the 1927 International Conference for the Protection of Jewish Girls and Women in London, writes Naomi Seidman, "Pappenheim spoke bitterly and forcefully about the failure of the rabbinate to address this issue":

> We have at this meeting several rabbis from Eastern Europe, and I had hoped that they would listen to us, and do something to improve the difficult position of so many Jewish women. It is not only a question of "agunoth," [an apparent reference to women whose husbands had disappeared] but also of facilitating divorce [altogether]. I had hoped that a Sanhedrin of Rabbis would come together and that they would introduce the needed ritual reforms and re-organize Jewish ceremonial dealing with this matter. That is what I had hoped, but I have been told that we must not expect it, for the rabbis do not have the power to introduce the changes asked for. In that case we must continue to flounder within this "golus" [exile], but it is a "golus" within a "golus" [that is, women's predicament was its own "exile," in addition to general, Jewish exile].

Seidman continues:

> As other writings make even clearer, Pappenheim was not persuaded that the rabbis were truly powerless to address the problem of the agunah; she was particularly offended that rabbis seemed willing to reform Jewish law

to make business dealings easier [a reference to *heter iska*], while claiming that the same could not be done . . . for women.[60]

In September 1929, Pappenheim, who envisioned a possible solution to iggun coming only from Orthodox decisors and was convinced that halakhic means to this end existed, sent a carefully worded but clear letter to the Great Assembly of rabbis of Agudath Israel (Agudah for short), then meeting in Vienna. Agudah was an ultra-Orthodox political party founded in Poland in 1912. One of its central tenets and radical innovations, which began to be articulated in the late nineteenth and early twentieth centuries, was the concept of *da'at/da'as Torah*, a dogmatic belief in and deference to rabbinic decision-making by Agudah rabbis as infallible, even about matters outside of halakha, like politics. Marriage and divorce, of course, were core areas of rabbinic jurisprudence. Agudah's council of sages was "the main forum for deciding . . . policy for the party and its followers," and it met regularly.[61] The assertion of such supreme rabbinic authority, operating in so highly organized a structure, seems to have encouraged Pappenheim to expect decisive action for agunot.

Pappenheim's letter to Agudah's Great Assembly of rabbis came after the Second World Congress of Jewish Women, meeting in Hamburg in June 1929, had passed a resolution calling for a convention of Orthodox rabbis that would craft "a comprehensive approach to the problem" of iggun.[62] The JFB sent the letter in its name, clearly aware of the role an organization could play that individual victims could not. Pappenheim, like agunah advocates today, stressed the lives wasted when women were trapped as agunot and pleaded for this to be taken seriously as a Jewish and rabbinic concern. Head of a resolutely middle-class organization that championed marriage and child-rearing for Jewish women, Pappenheim lamented the forced celibacy and childlessness of agunot because they lost their fertile years in iggun and decried the path to prostitution through desperate poverty caused or exacerbated by their captivity.

Her letter read:

To the honorable Assembly of Rabbis of the "Great Assembly" in Vienna,
We wish to put before the conclave of rabbis and scholars in Vienna one
of our concerns about the fate of the Jewish community, whose welfare
and hardships lie at the doorsteps of women.

Every member of the assembly knows that Judaism the world over is in a state of alarming retreat, both in terms of numbers and quality, in terms of the resources and will to serve the supreme goal; and that women, even if they are the majority in quantitative terms, are not powerful as they were in the past and cannot discharge their material or spiritual obligations effectively.

If we are to protect our communal existence, we must today more than ever relate to the born and the unborn as links in a chain. But we are losing countless members of our tribe, partners in fate, blood kin—and in particular, the youngest, the best, those with the greatest in joy of life, the healthiest, and the ones most suited to raise our next generation, because some of these people consciously distance themselves from Judaism. [They do this] because Jewish leaders don't understand how to keep their flock within the camp and lose influence over them, because they fail to understand the nature of these times and people's real situation.

Aside from the spiritual malaise that affects the majority of Jews, there exists a small group of women with whom fate has dealt cruelly and who have not yet found the desperate courage to seek help for themselves outside of their family circle; who have not found the strength to build new lives for themselves, good or bad, pure or sullied. I refer to agunot.

Agunot—women left in the lurch by halakha and its judges and legal interpreters, women who are healthy and young and pulsing with desire for life, women who are loyal to the House of Israel and to its ethical demands—until they realize that they are alone and abandoned; that for them, ethics do not exist, because what is demanded of them is asceticism, denial of life-desire, prostitution, and unnatural behavior, rather than joyful and vibrant hope.

Therefore, we ask the assembly of rabbis and scholars, in the spirit of deep Jewish compassion that demands love for all creatures, whoever they may be, to turn its attention to the fate of these women, whom interpretations of Jewish law out of tune with this time threaten with ruin, so that, to the number of Jewish men in all the countries who fell victim to the world war shall not be added a large number of women—in Eastern Europe they speak of 20,000—who will be buried alive as widows or sink into un-Jewish living.

The approach the Orthodox have taken in this matter until now has already lowered the esteem of the rabbis and weakened the authority of Orthodox rabbis.

We women serve those [other] women who don't know how to organize collectively, coming from the same sad, common fate that unites them, to appear before your assembly! Since justice must be one of the pillars of the Jewish world, in the name of these weak, humiliated, powerless women, we appeal most earnestly to your great assembly's sense of justice, to seek ethical means to free the agunot of the war from their captivity.

Isenbüerg, 29 July 1929[63]

Polish Jewish women also took up the cause of agunot. Leah (Levin-Epstein) Proshansky published about the problem for the Warsaw-based Yiddish-language monthly *Froyen Shtim* (*Women's Voice*), whose inaugural issue in 1925 called attention to the problem, scoring in particular rabbinic inaction regarding abandoned wives left undivorced by emigrating men.

Seidman notes:

Proshansky's article . . . excoriated such husbands . . . but reserved its harshest criticism for the rabbinic leadership that treated the problem with indifference. While rabbis were quick to criticize women for succumbing to immodest fashion trends, they were silent in the face of abandonment. . . . In her essay, Proshansky directly takes on the notion that the Polish rabbinate sympathized with abandoned women but was unable to help them. . . . In Proshansky's words, rabbinic literature is full of halakhic accommodations to urgent circumstances. She mentions as an example *heter iska*, the rabbinic ruling rendering it permissible to lend money with interest despite a biblical prohibition. . . . For men saddled with mentally ill wives, rabbis found a way to allow the husband to divorce his wife without her consent. The general [halakhic] principle which states that in a life-and-death situation even the Sabbath may be desecrated, should also apply to these women, whose situation is one of equally extreme need.[64]

Finally, Proshansky wrote, the principle of *et la'asot* (literally "It is time to act," a halakhic principle that allows violation of halakha in extreme circumstances) might also prod rabbis, if they deigned to concern themselves with women's lives, to find a solution that would allow agunot to remarry.

Indeed, what would those pleading for rabbinic action a century ago say to those of today—and vice versa—about this pronouncement by the Australian advocacy group Unchain My Heart?

> Thankfully there are loopholes available to solve pressing issues in halacha.
> Can't charge interest? Heter iska.
> Can't work the land on Shmita? Heter mechira.
> Can't carry on shabbos? Eruv chatzeiros.
> Can't walk far on shabbat? Eruv Tchumin.
> Can't enforce a loan after Shmita? Pruzbol.
> Can't own chametz on pesach? Mechirat Chamets (with a bonus Bitul).
> Can't cook on Yom Tov for Shabbat? Eruv Tavshilin.
> Promised to do something? Hatarat Nedarim.
> First born that has to fast on erev pesach? Siyum.
> Want to eat meat during the 9 days? Siyum.
> A woman won't agree to divorce her husband? Heter Meya Rabonim.
> A man won't give his wife a get? Sorry, there's nothing we can do. Halacha is halacha.[65]

Blu Greenberg, in the first book by an Orthodox feminist on women and halakha, a work both of critique and apology, devoted a chapter to divorce and halakhic solutions to iggun—in 1981. Applying her signature pronouncement about women and halakha, she concludes, regarding the failure of Orthodox rabbinic authorities to end iggun: "It bespeaks a lack of rabbinic will to find a halakhic way."[66]

Organized attempts to rouse attention and ire about Jewish women's marital captivity go back over 150 years. So do proposed halakhic actions to at least ameliorate, if not end, the abuse. Both men (rabbis) and women entirely within the traditional fold have pressed for rabbinic action and proposed specifics, to no avail. There is nothing new about this, though the record appears unknown to agunah advocates and, certainly, to victims and potential victims.

As we have seen, weakness of rabbinic court enforcement long pre-dates modernity and the dissolution of the traditional kehilla: it marked the medieval kehillot of both Ashkenaz and the Middle East—in the heyday of Jewish self-government. The problem of men abandoning wives and children, leaving women agunot, and families often desti-tute and desperate, was endemic in all premodern and early modern Jewish communities. Attempts to ascribe rabbinic court weakness and family breakdown and abuse to modernity do not withstand historical scrutiny. Modern conditions—meaning, in all Jewish settings (until to-day's Israel), abolition of the powers of rabbinic and Jewish communal government—sealed this weakness but did not create it.

In late nineteenth- and early twentieth-century Tunisia, we see both traditional and modern types of marital abuse of women playing out. Tunisia was an Ottoman province but also came under French colonial rule—as had Algeria, though without annexation to France. Most Tuni-sian Jews were Ottoman subjects, meaning subject to rabbinic law for marriage, divorce, and inheritance. Some Tunisian Jews had French citi-zenship, making them subject to French law for these matters—unless they voluntarily also sought rabbinic marriage and divorce, which most did—while being able to escape halakhic strictures at will: the definition of the modern Jewish condition.

Based on records of the rabbinic court in Tunis about Jews who were Ottoman subjects, Yuval Haruvi found frequent failure of husbands to pay ketubbah settlements and frequent abandonment of wives and children— marital abuse of the old, traditional type.[67] Among Jews with French citi-zenship who, in addition to mandatory civil marriage, also married under rabbinic law and then divorced, he found ample evidence of husbands refusing to give gittin or extorting for it, with no recourse for wives or the community because the men's actions had no standing under French law, which had abolished rabbinic authority—abuse of both the traditional and modern kinds. Haruvi ascribes both types of abuse to "deterioration of the norm of family life among Jews of Tunisia in the modern era," but as we know, such behavior was of ancient provenance; family instability was a Jewish norm across time and Jewish ethnicities. The "modern" in this be-havior was entirely tactical, using new methods—evasion of the premod-ern community's means of pressure—but hardly innovative in substance.

PART TWO

The Present

10

The Present State of Jewish Marital Captivity

Agunah-Advocacy Organizations; Halakha Then and Now

A variety of Orthodox organizations exist in multiple countries with the proclaimed aim of helping captive women obtain gittin.[1] The affiliations and political and financial backing of these organizations vary, but all abide by halakha as defined by Orthodox or ultra-Orthodox *poskim* (halakhic decisors) and work under the aegis and by permission of halakhic courts. All these courts are adjudicated and administered by men—Orthodox or ultra-Orthodox rabbis.[2] In order to understand and assess the tactics of these organizations, we must understand the constraints within which they operate and the nature and function of Orthodox halakhic adjudication today.

Halakha as a system of law today is nothing like that which operated in premodern kehillot. In contrast to any medieval state, absolutist states emerging in early European modernity and fully modernizing ones, as well as tsarist Russia, viewed the autonomous kehilla as an intolerable affront to their internal coherence and emerging national ego and sovereignty and abolished or seriously weakened it (or, in the United States or modern Britain, never authorized it). This made halakha and obedience to it voluntary. As the title of one book puts it, this is when "Judaism [in its Western variants, we note] became a religion" rather than a system of governance.[3]

There is no overstating the impact or significance of the end of Jewish theocracy—governance by religious authority enforcing halakha with coercive measures. Most Jews in settings where the autonomous kehilla was abolished or where it had never existed stopped observing halakha strictly or at all. From Divine imperatives made normative and enforceable in real life by the power of state-authorized rabbinic and communal bodies, laws were transformed into inconsistent, nostalgic, or guilt-ridden traditions. Orthodoxy in any of its variants, as all the other movements of modern Judaism, arose in response to these unprecedented conditions, with a sense of urgency to save Judaism from feared oblivion, which the newly named "Orthodox," or "Torah-true," and those who would come to be known as ultra-Orthodox (haredi), were certain would result from the demise of the traditional kehilla.[4]

Orthodox Jews, who claim that they, unlike Jews in any of the progressive denominations, continue an unbroken tradition going back to Moses at Sinai, are nothing like premodern Jews in the voluntary nature of their obedience to halakha, with the option of dropping it while remaining Jewish ever-present if, for profound reasons, not simple to exercise. Not only is that subservience voluntary; it clashes with the nature of modern societies. However anomalous Jews were as the only tolerated non-Christian group in Europe, the premodern kehilla was harmonious within the larger premodern social and political structure in which religion was established and there was no religion-neutral, civil space for anyone. This structural harmony was true for Islamic realms as well.

The element of choice in halakhic observance fundamentally alters not only the nature of the adherent's relationship to the system but the system itself, which was constructed as mandatory governance (theocracy), not merely a set of teachings. As Aranoff and Haut describe the situation in the United States, the Orthodox Jewish community is a "subculture" that "persists in complying with its own legal system though its laws deny women and children rights that are theirs under the civil legal system"—rights that Orthodox Jews claim; Haym Soloveitchik depicts Orthodox choice as "a conscious preference of the enclave over the host society"—a choice no premodern Jew had, Jewish identity being corporate and acquired at birth.[5] Since modernity, those who choose to adhere to halakha as a mandatory system—the contradiction is glaring—are at fundamental variance with the larger world, even if they also inhabit and benefit from that world in other aspects of their lives, a split unknown in premodernity.

The Situation in Israel

The situation in Israel is different in some fundamental ways from that in the rest of the Jewish world and similar in others. There, as we have seen, law puts personal status matters in the hands of the country's respective religious authorities. In the absence of civil marriage or divorce, even atheists must use religious authorities.

It has become increasingly common for Israeli Jews to flout the religious authorities for marriage. Jewish couples fly to Cyprus or elsewhere to marry, or have ceremonies in Israel conducted by friends, or Conservative (in Israel called Masorti) and Reform rabbis, and then register as married with the Ministry of Interior, having gotten requisite documents for legal purposes (health insurance, loans, property, the status of children) from lawyers.[6] Modern Orthodox alternatives outside the state's Chief Rabbinate have also arisen and are being used increasingly. Such marriages are conducted by the Chuppot organization and by independent rabbis.[7]

Rabbis conducting such marriages can incur a penalty of two years' imprisonment for it. The Chief Rabbinate has fulminated against such marriages and those conducting them but has not, thus far, pursued criminal sanctions, surely because the ultra-Orthodox establishment, which does not recognize the state, has never been sanctioned for operating its own rabbinic courts for personal status issues. Any case against modern Orthodox or Masorti rabbis for doing the same would likely not withstand the scrutiny of an independently functioning Supreme Court. But any marriage by Jews, however and wherever it is conducted, that is registered with the Ministry of Interior, except those conducted within the haredi world, will end up in a Chief Rabbinate court for divorce and for the change in the parties' marital status to be registered officially, something needed for subsequent marriage and other legal requirements. There is no other way for Jews in Israel to get divorced legally except through Chief Rabbinate or haredi rabbinic courts.

Women who live by Orthodox-administered halakha or who, in Israel, have no choice, cannot obtain a divorce unless their husbands grant it. Orthodox rabbinic courts, of whatever variant, are staffed entirely by men. There are in Israel women rabbinic pleaders, *to'anot rabbaniot*, who assist women in Chief Rabbinate courts but they have no power and make no decisions. Rabbinic courts, Israeli and Diaspora alike, operate by male rule, that of the husband, who has the prerogative to grant or withhold a get, and that of the rabbinic tribunal adjudicating cases. While women in the Diaspora, unlike those in Israel, have theoretical choice to disregard the halakhic system if denied a get, that choice is often theoretical only, as we will discuss.

Get Extortion

Given the law establishing religious jurisdiction over personal status, the state of Israel refuses to get involved in cases in which a woman's freedom is withheld under that system. That recusal enables get extortion, to which the state not only turns a blind eye but which it endorses.

Rabbinic courts in Israel and elsewhere not only condone such extortion but encourage it, in the words of Susan Weiss, founder and director of the Center for Women's Justice, "as a valid, efficient, and religiously acceptable method of divorce resolution. Blackmail does not invalidate a Jewish divorce"—unless exercised by the wife, because this would impinge on the husband's free will to end a marriage.[8]

"In a similar vein," Weiss continues,

> the Supreme Court [of Israel] has upheld the validity of contracts [written in rabbinic divorce courts], in which women have waived . . . property and legal interests in return for a . . . divorce, *refusing to find that such divorce agreements were signed under duress. The civil court has deemed a get sufficient "consideration" in exchange for the relinquishing of those interests.* [Supreme Court] Justice Haim Cohen wrote: "*A divorce agreement is no different from any other kind of agreement. One who wishes to obtain something, gives up that which is rightfully his* [sic], *or offers additional payment, in order to secure the object of his desire.*" (my emphasis)[9]

The gendered-class nature of get extortion escapes Justice Cohen, as does the bizarre analogy between the preset contract that is halakhic marriage and fluid contracts negotiated between individuals, both of whom then reasonably share responsibility for the contract's terms, including choice of the jurisdiction and manner of adjudicating any dispute about it. Women, in Justice Cohen's sophistic egalitarian reasoning, are bound by the same laws as "everyone else," when women as a class suffer systematic discrimination in rabbinic divorce and, in Israel, lack of alternatives to it. Applying equal standards in a situation of systemic discrimination against one of the parties to a contract is shockingly obtuse.

In another case, in 2016, a state court ruled entirely legitimate a demand for 500,000 shekels (then $131,000) in return for a get and faulted the woman for refusing the deal, constructed by a rabbinic court. As *Haaretz* related:

> In September, the man told judges at the Haifa Rabbinical Court he would "free" his wife in exchange for 800,000 shekels compensation, and was persuaded to reduce that sum to 500,000 shekels. The woman's father told the rabbis they could not afford the terms, and the judges decided to free the man from prison [where he was held for get refusal after being told to give one], while the woman filed an appeal.
>
> The religious judges . . . said the [husband] can no longer be regarded as recalcitrant, *or the woman an "agunah,"* because her husband has agreed in principle to the divorce. In response to her father's offer to pay 50,000 shekels for the divorce the rabbis said that had he really been interested in freeing his daughter *he would have given the requested amount.* (my emphasis)[10]

This is the judgment a secular court upheld.

Outside of Israel, the ability of secular courts to intervene depends on the legal status of religion and state and marriage and divorce law in each location.[11] In recent years, US agunah advocate Esther Macner has applied a legal tactic relying on secular legislation that criminalizes "coercive control" by spouses, clearly directed against get-withholding men. It defines "a pattern of behavior that interferes with the spouse's personal liberty as a kind of domestic violence," and applies this to get refusal. As of this writing, Macner, founder of Get Jewish Divorce Justice, a nonprofit that advocated passage of such a statute in California, has succeeded in applying this definition in one case, with the agunah receiving a get as well as custody of her children and a restraining order against her abusive ex-husband, setting what Macner believes is an important precedent. As of April 2022, Macner had alerted more than a dozen agunot in the state of California of the possible applicability of this law to their cases.[12]

Rabbinic prerogative, however, can override any such action by deeming gittin given under threat of civil consequences "coerced," hence invalid under halakha, as has already occurred in Israel and elsewhere.

Rabbi Jonathan Hool, a rabbinic judge in the United Kingdom, advised a man who said he was going to give his wife a get rather than face civil sanctions under the country's Domestic Abuse Act of 2021 not to do so because Hool would rule such a get "coerced"—invalid.[13]

However much premodern precedent there is for pressure on husbands by non-Jewish authorities at the behest of wives, their families, and communities in divorce cases, of rabbinic courts coercing husbands to give gittin as a result of such pressure, and of rabbinic ruling upholding the validity of such divorces, contemporary rabbinic practice prefers restrictive innovation to invalidate such divorces over application of emancipatory precedent. In Israel, Susan Weiss and other attorneys have sued get-refusing husbands for civil damages in Israel's family court system, the same tactic employed by Macner and the UK's Domestic Abuse Act.

These suits, Weiss writes,

> claim that withholding a get is not a man's religious right but a civil wrong and that women are entitled to compensation for emotional distress and for the infringement of their basic right to dignity and liberty [vouschafed under Israel's Basic Law on Human Dignity and Liberty]. The family courts have agreed and about a dozen judgments have awarded significant damages. . . . These suits have been greatly beneficial to women, who in almost all . . . cases have either received their gets in exchange for a waiver of their material claims or been awarded damages. But rabbinic courts view these judgments as an invasion of their jurisdictional turf, a challenge to the rule against "forced" divorce, and an implicit criticism of the way rabbinic courts drag out contested divorces.[14]

Israeli rabbinic judges have stated, with the same reasoning as Dayan Hool's in the UK, that they will invalidate any get given because of civil measures against the withholding husband, meaning that wives freed in such cases remain agunot—reinstituted into iggun by rabbinic action.

As long as rabbis retain control of women's marital status, applying androcentric, patriarchal laws to maintain control of marriage and to protect and perpetuate their own financial and other interests in this system, they can and will find ways to obviate any civil action to free agunot or lift the stigma of "mamzer/a" from any actual or future children of a freed woman.

To appropriate Blu Greenberg's classic pronouncement, "Where there is a halakhic will, there is a halakhic way"—not to end iggun but to maintain it.

Institutionalizing Get Extortion

Susan Aranoff and Rivka Haut cite case after case in the United States of rabbinic courts abetting get extortion, a phenomenon they call "the open institutionalization of extortion." "The idea," they note, "that it is acceptable for men to put a price tag on the get was so widely accepted that Rabbi Yehuda Levin, director of Get Free . . . unabashedly described himself as a 'negotiator' whose mission was to obtain a get for a woman at the lowest possible price" (including, presumably, his own fee). Get extortion, they report, "is so widely accepted by rabbis that they actually solicit 'charitable' donations for that purpose," thereby normalizing and encouraging the blackmail of women and the commodification of divorce—for women.[15] That this formalized abuse continues is apparent in a paid ad ("sponsored content"), running on Facebook in March 2021, in which a profusely bearded Rabbi Yacov Barber of New York advertised his services, for a fee, offering chained women to be "your advocate and guide in navigating the very challenging journey of divorce."[16] Barber is not alone in offering such services.[17]

One case of get extortion perpetrated by a rabbinic court reached the justice system of New York State in 1992 (Golding v. Golding). In that case, an appellate court ruled invalid a settlement the woman had signed accepting all her husband's demands about the terms of their divorce in exchange for a get. The settlement, written in Hebrew, which the woman could not understand on her own, was drawn up by the rabbinic court, whose rabbis told her that signing it was the only way she would receive a get.[18]

Other egregious cases of get extortion have reached public attention. In one, a husband refused his wife, a Shoah survivor, a get unless she signed over to him her reparations payments from Germany. In another, a woman whose husband withheld a get finally received it after she paid him $15,000 and agreed not to file assault charges after he dragged her for a block as she held onto the open door of his car, breaking her leg.[19] Although it is impossible to determine the number of get-extortion cases that do not reach public attention, it is safe to say the publicized ones are a minority.

The Ketubbah: Useless as a Legal Document; Nonrecognition of Violence against the Wife or the Father's Sexual Abuse of Children as Cause for Divorce; Outs for Men

For all the differences between the legal standing of rabbinic law in Israel, where it has state recognition, and in the United States, where it doesn't, rabbinic courts in both countries, indeed everywhere, use the same system and operate similarly in divorce cases.[20] It is this consistency, rather than dissertations about religion–state differences, used to deflect attention from systematic abuse of women in rabbinic courts, that warrants our attention.

Whatever its importance as an actionable legal instrument in Jewish premodernity, the ketubbah today is entirely symbolic. In decades of agunah advocacy in Orthodox rabbinic courts in the United States, Aranoff and Haut encountered but one instance in which a woman received the divorce payment the ketubbah mandated, or when the rabbinic court had even inquired into the monetary value of the ketubbah in question, so clear was its irrelevance. As a legal document (as opposed to an often adorned, framed piece of calligraphy), the ketubbah was wholly irrelevant. And in the one exceptional case that Aranoff and Haut encountered, the woman had given up far more in other assets before she was awarded the value of her ketubbah: its meaning had become symbolic even in that case.[21] Nitzan Caspi Shiloni of the Center for Women's Justice in Jerusalem confirms this reality for Israel as well: "In the vast majority of cases, perhaps more than 99 percent, women don't receive the [monetary value of the] ketubbah."[22]

Violence by a husband does not constitute even grounds for divorce in rabbinic courts of either country, let alone actions beyond such a finding to force a get or dissolve the marriage through annulment. Aranoff and Haut detail the case, widely reported in the US press, of Blima Zitrenbaum, who was found unconscious, bludgeoned and bloody, in her apartment in Monsey, New York (an ultra-Orthodox neighborhood) one Sabbath morning in 1996.

> Police suspected Blima's estranged husband, Joseph, was the assailant. [They] were not unfamiliar with the family because Blima had previously obtained an order of protection against Joseph, and the police had been at the Zitrenbaum home numerous times [because of] disturbances. Joseph, a known drug addict, was sought by the police in connection with other crimes as well.... Joseph was apprehended.... Blima remained in critical condition for weeks ... [before] she emerged from a coma.[23]

Aranoff and Haut, too, already knew of Blima Zitrenbaum because she had sought a get and appealed to several rabbis for help to obtain one. They, however, said that her husband retained the right to grant or withhold divorce. Even after Joseph was convicted of the attempted murder of Blima, they held "that Blima must remain married to him until he agreed, of his own free will, to give her a get."[24]

Violence against women is not considered grounds for a rabbinic court to issue even an order for a husband to give a get (*hiyuv get*), much less order sanctions meant to force him to give one (*kfiyat get*).[25] The level of violence involved is irrelevant. Of course, a murdered woman no longer needs a divorce. And if she is brain-damaged, in a coma, she is incapable of receiving one. But in the latter case, if the husband is Ashkenazi, he can get rabbinic dispensation from the ordinance prohibiting polygyny to marry bigynously without giving a get. If he follows Sephardi or Mizrahi halakhic custom, recourse is even easier. There was never a rabbinic ordinance in these Jewries banning polygyny, and if a rabbinic court authorizes a second marriage for a man without the first dissolved, the state of Israel will waive the ban in criminal law against polygyny for him.[26] One such highly publicized instance occurred in November 2021 when the well-known, married, ultra-Orthodox Israeli actor and singer Shuli Rand, embroiled in a long divorce dispute with his wife (not involving violence), got rabbinic dispensation and married an additional wife, the TV celebrity Tsofit Granat. The ceremony was conducted by a Chief Rabbinate rabbi; video clips of the happy couple and wedding festivities were broadcast on evening news. The first woman to whom Rand was, and is still married has refused to accept a get that comes with financial terms she rejects.[27] Obviously, his ability to marry another woman while she cannot marry another man gives him the upper hand in their dispute, an advantage, as we have seen, defended by both rabbinic and Israeli civil law. The ongoing Kin case in the United States is another instance of a get-withholding man marrying polygynously through rabbinic agency in the context of a prolonged divorce dispute.

Extreme violence, criminal conviction, and ongoing criminal behavior by a husband do not deprive him of the right to withhold or grant a get in Israel, any more than they did in Blima Zitrenbaum's case in New York. Thus, despite the husband of Shira Isakov being convicted and sentenced to twenty-three years' imprisonment for attempting to murder her in front of their toddler through beating with a rolling pin and multiple stabbings, leaving her hospitalized for weeks in a coma, and despite having contracted from prison to have her murdered by a fellow prisoner's contacts outside, a miraculously recovered Ms. Isakov (given a 10 percent chance of survival upon admission to the hospital) still had to petition this husband for a get. And he refused to give one until relenting in hope that this might lead to consideration in his sentencing.[28]

A husband's violence is not basis for a rabbinic court even to say that a get is warranted, much less order one to be given. Thus, for just one example, of which she says there are too many to recall, Nitzan Caspi Shiloni cites a case in which a husband had pursued his wife with a knife and the rabbinic court to which she turned, asking for a court-forced get, refused on grounds that the husband had not been duly warned, twice, in the presence of witnesses, against murdering her. Furthermore, the court stated, it was not established that the husband meant to murder the wife.[29] In another case, a man who had been violent to his wife for years came into her house after she left him and tried to strangle her, an attack one of their children thwarted. She sought a get and heard this from the rabbinic court: "While on the one hand, there is no justification for violence by a man against his wife . . . *on the other hand*, there is no doubt that the husband's *outburst was the result of the difficult situation he found himself in as a result of his wife's filing for divorce.* There is no doubt that if she had only agreed to his request to return to live with him normally, this would never have happened" (my emphases).[30]

Sexual abuse of the couple's children by the husband has also been ruled irrelevant in divorce cases in which rabbinic courts adjudicated child custody (custody can be adjudicated in Israeli family court if one member of the couple files a divorce action there before the other does in a rabbinic court). Rabbinic courts have told women in such cases either to agree to the father's access to, and even custody of children—even when a civil court had ordered no contact—or be denied a get or any financial settlement.[31]

How Bigyny Became Legal in Israel

Bigyny became legal in Israel after political machinations during an extended, bitter dispute in the 1970s between the two chief rabbis, the Ashkenazi Shlomo Goren and the Sephardi Ovadia Yosef.[32]

The latter succeeded, first, in overlaying the halakhic disagreement between the two with claims of ethic discrimination (Goren was acting like an Ashkenazi "imperialist" in refusing to approve a Sephardi man's petition to marry bigynously); and then in getting a law passed by the Knesset that removed the requirement that both chief rabbis approve such petitions. Henceforth, only the approval by a rabbinic court was needed. It is clear from Goren's pronouncements against a husband living with two wives simultaneously (he did not oppose all bigynous marriages) that he was influenced by anticipated negative public opinion in Israel should bigyny (at least in the case being deliberated) be legalized. In short, he understood that the issue was political, as Yosef himself had made it.

Goren was not alone in that sensitivity. When asked if he would ever approve a man's request to marry bigynously, the revered leader of US modern Orthodoxy, Rabbi Joseph B. Soloveitchik, "said that he never signed [such] a marriage permit, even when its halakhic basis was sound, *because an American Jew would not be willing to accept a distinction between the ability of the husband to take a second wife, and that of the wife, who in a similar situation remains 'chained' (agunah)*" (my emphasis).[33]

As we see in this instance and did regarding proposals from the nineteenth century on to prevent or limit iggun, there is no halakhic decision-making devoid of politics, be these inter- or intradenominational, personal, interpersonal, or a combination of those. There can be no simple, pious acceding by agunot to "halakhic authority" as if that authority operates, has ever operated, or can operate apolitically, in the absence of turf and authority battles, however unrecognized, unconscious, or vehemently denied these may be. We recall the jurisdiction battle over agunot between Rabbis Karo and Mitrani in sixteenth-century Safed, and how the fear by European decisors of being labeled "lenient" in the seventeenth to nineteenth centuries factored in their restrictive practices toward agunot. Recorded disputes about who can exercise legitimate authority to rule and efforts to claim and control this power go back as far as recorded rabbinic discourse.[34] They were rife among sages referred to reverentially as "the *rishonim*" ("the first") during the medieval era.[35]

Any party to this problem who rejects astute political thinking and action to end women's marital captivity, and in the case of agunot, their own captivity, robs themselves of any effective action. They also perpetuate the problem for others by modeling ineffective and delusional behavior—the delusion that "good" conduct will elicit rabbinic action to end their marital captivity. Ineffective behavior enables the abuse and contributes to the self-perpetuating assumption that iggun is a problem that can only be managed but not ended.

Data

It is impossible to obtain a full, accurate count of the number of agunot, past or present, for several reasons.

There is not now nor has there ever been a central authority that keeps such records. Rabbinic courts were independent, each conducting its own affairs. That remains the case in the United States; Israel and Britain, which have state-recognized rabbinates; and in France, which has a centralized communal structure, the Consistory. More significant, no rabbinic court opens any records it keeps to outsiders. In Israel, where Knesset committees sometimes request statistics about iggun, the Chief Rabbinate plays semantic games to deny the problem and, despite being a state-authorized entity, does not open its records to independent assessment, even to the Knesset, nor does the Knesset demand this.

About the United States, Aranoff and Haut cite a figure of two thousand agunot whom they attempted to help over the course of thirty years beginning in 1985. They report receiving an average of sixty to seventy calls from agunot annually, most from the United States but also from Latin America, Israel, and Europe.[36] The Organization for Resolution of Agunot (ORA), based in New York, reported in 2014 that it received 150 calls a year from agunot seeking assistance. A survey of Jewish social service organizations in the United States and Canada reported that these organizations had been contacted by 462 agunot in 2011 alone. In 2006 the largest rabbinic association in the United States, the Orthodox Rabbinical Council of America (RCA), in a statement about prenuptial agreements, referenced "a significant agunah problem in America and throughout the Jewish world," without, however, stating numbers of cases even its own court handled.[37] Of course, the number of women seeking help from organizations is but an unknown fraction of women in marital captivity.

A survey conducted in Israel in 2013 cited evidence of get extortion in thousands of cases.[38] The agunah-advocacy organization Mavoi Satum, whose lawyers regularly handle divorce cases in rabbinic and state family courts, cites 1,700 women a year refused a get in Israel, reporting in 2023 that "one out of five women in Israel is unable to freely exit her marriage."[39]

Because there is no transparency of rabbinic-court records or access to them by outsiders, whether researchers or potential clients, not only are there no full, vetted statistics from the United States or Israel but no systematic way to assess the record of these courts in adjudicating divorce and get refusal. There is no basis on which a consumer can make an informed judgment about which courts to use or avoid, nor any accountability to the Jewish public. The basics of good governance—transparency, accountability—are wholly lacking.

Rabbinic authorities also deliberately obfuscate terminology in order to deny the problem, manipulating application of the term "agunah" to women seeking and refused gittin. Until a case is fully adjudicated and perhaps not even then, rabbinic courts do not assign the term "agunah" to such women. But extending the length and associated costs of get proceedings is a common tactic of extortion as well as a means of financial gain for the court. Even a defender of rabbinic-court handling of iggun, Rabbi Leib Landesman, states that "lawyers and to'anim (client representatives before a beit din) often have no desire to expedite their cases, since the more time is spent, the greater is their fee."[40] While justice is delayed, the system asserts that the woman who has sought a get and whose case is being stonewalled in order to harass and pressure her to accept a bad deal is not an agunah.

Attorney Batya Kahana Dror, until 2022 director of Mavoi Satum, decries

> a fundamental error in the way in which the rabbinical courts determine recalcitrance by a husband. The . . . the courts only consider [him] . . . recalcitrant after a rabbinical court has ruled that a divorce must be issued or accepted, but . . . it may take many years after a divorce suit is filed for the court to issue such a ruling. . . . In many cases, the rabbinical court will [accede to] a man's request to try reconciliation, thereby delaying a decision requiring him to grant a divorce [without which courts do not label the woman an agunah].

But, says Kahana Dror, "rabbinical courts treat men leniently and . . . often fail to issue rulings requiring them to give a divorce, thereby reducing the chance that they will refuse to grant the divorce and be considered recalcitrant [and their wives, agunot]." It was Mavoi Satum that handled the case, cited above, in which the Jerusalem Rabbinical Court, an arm of the Chief Rabbinate, refused to order a serially violent husband to give his wife the divorce she sought because, in the judges' reasoning, the man had beaten her only because she had sought a divorce.[41]

Professor Ruth Halperin-Kaddari, chair of the Rackman Center for the Advancement of Women at Bar-Ilan University, also cites manipulation of terms and the processes that produce them to deny the number of women denied a get in Israel. "The data," she states, "is not only misleading, it . . . camouflage[s] . . . divorce-abuse against women." Halperin-Kaddari notes yet another way that rabbinic courts manipulate agunah statistics downward, citing frequent cases "in which a woman files a suit for divorce in the civil court—allowing it to rule on financial, custodial, and property matters—but in which the husband demands the matter be heard only by the rabbinical court. . . . Rabbinical courts frequently consider [such] a woman . . . recalcitrant if she refuses this demand," meaning that not only is she not an "agunah," but herself becomes a target for rabbinic sanctions.[42]

Nitzan Caspi Shiloni of Jerusalem's Center for Women's Justice also documents this abuse.[43] On October 6, 2021, the center posted on its Facebook page this report on the Chief Rabbinate's manipulation and falsification of agunah statistics:

Remember the old joke about the persecuted Jew who likes to read antisemitic newspapers, because all they talk about is how rich, successful and powerful the Jews are?

This morning, during a meeting of the Knesset's Constitution, Law and Justice Committee, Israel's state rabbinic court presented outrageous statistics claiming that there are only 25 get refusers in the entire country, and that rabbinic court's special agunah department is currently handling a grand total of 5 cases.

... These "statistics," a masterclass in ... manipulation, don't reflect the number of women who are unable to get divorced; they reflect the number of women who have been deemed "deserving" of a get according to the ... rabbinic court. This distinction matters: Only in a tiny fraction of cases—51 out of 4,158 cases ... did the rabbinic court rule that the woman has grounds for a get. That's 1.2%.

The rabbinic court's statistics don't include ... women whose requests for a get were denied because they did not have sufficient grounds for divorce [including] domestic violence ... ; they don't include the thousands of women who have been waiting for years for the rabbinic court to issue a decision on their case; they don't count the women whose husbands have fled the country. ...

When committee chair, MK Rabbi Gilad Kariv, pressed the representative of the rabbinic court who was presenting these statistics, the representative admitted that there were between *2,000 to 3,000 cases that had been opened two or more years ago and for which the rabbinic court had yet to issue any decision* [meaning that] none of these women are considered cases of get refusal. (my emphasis)[44]

Another insidious tactic by rabbinic courts in Israel and the United States alike to obfuscate the nature and dimensions of women's marital captivity and gaslight the public is flipping the designation "get refuser" from the husband to the get-seeking wife. Rabbinic courts label a woman refused a get (*mesorevet get*), who rejects an extortionist get deal to obtain it, not as an agunah but as herself a "get refuser" (*mesarevet get*). Claims then follow of equal numbers of men supposedly held in marriages against their will as women held captive, as if men do not have and exercise halakhic options to marry polygynously if an impaired wife cannot, or an extorted wife will not accept a get with the conditions attached (as is the case with Shuli Rand's first wife), while women have no halakhic, or in Israel, state-recognized legal option for remarriage aside from the get.

Thus, we get the following. The editors of the New York–based *Jewish Week* reported in 2011 that "in Israel, estimates of 10,000 agunot have been reported by the *Wall Street Journal* and the *Jerusalem Post*, in contrast to claims by [the ultra-Orthodox] Agudath Israel, that there are 180 in the Jewish state, and remarkably!—an equal number of men who are being refused divorces by their recalcitrant wives."[45] The *Jerusalem Post* reported in 2017 that the Rabbinical Courts Administration of the Chief Rabbinate published statistics seemingly showing that, over the previous five years, more women had refused to accept a divorce than men had refused to grant one.[46]

The purpose of withholding and distorting information about get refusal and extortion is to distract and deflect effective action against the abuse. The relatively new distinction between an agunah and a "*mesorevet get*," for a woman who has been refused a get by a husband as opposed to a woman whose husband has disappeared, is also misleading. The halakhic status of the women in these instances, as well as in cases of halitsa refusal or conversion or incapacitation of a husband, is identical. All are agunot. The now common phrase "agunot and *mesoravot get*," as if there is a difference, is distortive. No such case-sensitive terminology and false distinctions were used in eras when the main cause of women's marital captivity was the husband's disappearance, as get refusal is now. Introducing this pseudo-distinction suggests that women being extorted for a get have recourse—paying ransom, whereas women whose husbands disappeared or were incapacitated did not (as one interlocutor, justifying the distinction, stated to me). The distinction serves get extortion, iggun denial, and victim blaming. Given systematic, deliberate obfuscation of get abuse by iggun-deniers through terminological manipulation, this neologism should be dropped by any agunah advocates.

The word "tragedy," from the Greek, means something fated, inevitable, unavoidable. Iggun is nothing of the sort. It is literally a man-made problem and the only inevitable thing about it is that it results necessarily from kinyan and kiddushin—from rabbinic marriage. Its "management" as an ongoing, necessarily occurring problem ensures production of the secondary and tertiary abuses we have seen.

11

Divorce in the Conservative/Masorti and Other Movements

Evasions and Illusions

The Role of Interdenominational Politics in Aborting Solutions

Our discussions have focused on classical rabbinic halakha as adjudicated in modernity by Orthodox rabbinic authorities because this is where the purely legal aspect of marital captivity overwhelmingly resides. As this work has argued, however, iggun is not solely or even primarily a halakhic issue, nor is it to be written off as an Orthodox, sectoral issue because the women involved accept halakhic authority, or don't realize they are doing so, or, in Israel, have no choice when they seek divorce.

The Conservative movement, called Masorti in Israel, also rules by halakha and has taken a more expansive approach toward preventing iggun than any version of Orthodoxy. The first such effort was proposed by Rabbi Louis M. Epstein in 1935. Epstein had studied in one of the foremost Lithuanian (haredi, non-Hasidic) yeshivas of Eastern Europe, Slobodka, and was an acknowledged scholar of rabbinic family law.[1] He proposed adding a codicil to the ketubbah that would, under specified circumstances, empower a woman to write her own get.[2] His proposal, in Jonathan Sarna's words, "set off a firestorm of criticism aimed less at its content, which involved complex issues of textual interpretation, than at the 'great insolence' of those (Conservative) rabbis who sought to advance it without . . . approval from the foremost Orthodox sages of the day." As in the Algerian episode, here too authorities opposed to the proposal threatened schism if it was enacted: the Orthodox "Agudath ha Rabbanim . . . unanimously agreed to 'excommunicate' anyone involved in a Jewish wedding" using such a ketubbah.[3]

Women's rights being sidelined to power struggles between competing rabbinic authorities, which we have traced into early Jewish modernity in the Middle East, thus migrated to the United States. "While the agunah controversy helped to define the distinctive features of the Conservative movement," notes Sarna, "it did little . . . to resolve the plight of . . . anchored women."[4] On the contrary, women were not the issue in battles over iggun; the issue was, and remains, lines of denominational definition—male power struggles.

A similar effort to Epstein's, in 1953, by the eminent, equally Orthodox, Talmudic scholar Saul Lieberman, who headed the Talmud faculty of the Jewish Theological Seminary of America, met the same fate. Lieberman proposed that a clause be added to the ketubbah that would obligate a divorcing couple to bring their dispute to a specified rabbinic court for arbitration, citing but not specifying financial consequences for the husband if he did not cooperate in giving a get. This omission has been cited by some as a halakhic reason for the refusal of Orthodox authorities to accept the Lieberman clause, which initially had the agreement of the leader of modern Orthodoxy, Rabbi Joseph B. Soloveitchik.[5] But there is no doubt that the refusal was political: the need to withhold what could be taken as Orthodox imprimatur for a proposal emanating from a rabbinic scholar associated with the seminary that ordains rabbis for the (competing) Conservative movement. Neither Lieberman's scholarly renown nor the fact that the Conservative movement was seeking to apply established halakha, ostensibly the demand of Orthodoxy, determined the outcome. Soloveitchik withdrew his endorsement of the Lieberman clause under pressure by the Orthodox Rabbinical Council of America (RCA).[6]

The Conservative movement adopted the Lieberman clause, which also posed the problem of the involvement of civil courts in enforcing monetary fines a rabbinic court would assess for noncompliance with its rulings, a legal problem even if the ketubbah was presented as a civil contract rather than a religious document.[7]

Basing itself on an expedient, *tnai bekiddushin* (conditional kiddushin), as developed by Rabbi Eliezer Berkovits (though with earlier, French precedent), an Orthodox authority largely shunned in Orthodoxy for his liberal position on women's rights, the Conservative movement has adopted retroactive annulment of marriages, *hafka'at kiddushin*, in cases of get withholding by the husband or refusal by the wife. Berkovits's condition states that if the marriage ends in civil divorce, within six months of which the husband gives a get, the marriage will be considered to have been valid. But if no such get has been given within six months, the marriage will be deemed to have been null and void (annulment has no effect on the status of children born of the marriage as long as the parents were valid marriage partners at the time of the marriage).[8]

The Orthodox establishment vehemently rejected this method, too.[9]

Get in the Reform and Reconstructionist Movements

The Reform movement gives primacy to individual conscience rather than halakhic authority in religious decision-making and, from its origins, recognized civil divorce as ending religious marriage enacted under its or any rabbinic auspices.[10] Problems with this approach include the emotional and ritual imbalance created when a marriage enacted through religious ceremonies is terminated without such ritual, and, on the practical level, the issue of get-refusing men going to Reform rabbis for a second, religiously performed marriage without first being required to give wives wishing this a get.[11] The expectation of the early Reform movement was that traditional halakha would disappear. Given not just the persistence of Orthodoxy and ultra-Orthodoxy but their resurgence after the Shoah, and in Israel their official recognition, this stance enables get refusal. Effectively, and ironically, given Reform's core criticism of Orthodoxy, the Reform position privileges a rigid, legal, and denominational stance over the welfare of women. That position is a perfect example of egalitarianism gone awry in the absence of a feminist—woman-centered—approach. In any case, we see that the problem of Jewish divorce and of women's marital captivity, even outside of Israel, is not confined to Orthodoxy or to adherents of Orthodox practice.

The Reconstructionist movement offers egalitarian gittin and prefers that couples get divorced in a ceremony using such a get, in addition to civil divorce. If one party is unwilling or unable to participate in these proceedings, the movement will recognize civil divorce alone, though individual Reconstructionist rabbis differ in their willingness to conduct subsequent nuptials if a previous marriage has not been terminated with a get. A Reconstructionist get can also be given unilaterally in cases in which either party refuses or is unable to participate.[12]

Managing the Problem rather than Ending It

Halakhic Prenuptial Agreements: "The Dangerous Illusion"[13]

The modern Orthodox world in the United States began elaborating prenuptial agreements in 1983 when Rabbi Joseph B. Soloveitchik approved a version for use by the Rabbinical Council of America. This version stated that if a husband refused to give a get after the couple had divorced civilly, fines in the amount of $250 a day, indexed to inflation, would accrue to him. In 2006 the RCA passed a nonbinding resolution stating: "Since there is a significant agunah problem in America and throughout the Jewish world, no rabbi should officiate at a wedding where a proper prenuptial agreement on get has not been executed." The RCA did not make this suggestion binding, however, nor did it even actively promote its own prenup until 2023. Despite this and considerable resistance to prenups by some, the RCA prenup made some headway within modern Orthodox families,[14] without awareness of the document's significant drawbacks.

The RCA prenup does not provide for automatic termination of a marriage under any circumstances, including the husband's violence or criminal conviction, and gives complete control over the terms of the get agreement to its rabbinic court. That specification allows for prolonged and costly get proceedings, themselves commonly used to pressure the woman to agree to disadvantageous terms in order to be free of the marriage, and the divorce proceedings. It allows for get extortion and for the court itself to operate to enact extortive agreements. According to the director of the RCA's rabbinic court, the Beth Din of America, the financial penalties this prenup imposes on the get-refusing husband "are almost always waived in exchange for the get itself. . . . The Beth Din of America exercises absolute control over [these] payments and may waive them at its discretion."[15] In short, the RCA prenup *uses divorce abuse—get withholding—to empower its rabbinic court, making that court the pivotal, decisive party to a divorce and giving it an interest in maintaining such a role.* One wonders if the RCA's declaration in 2006 of the existence of a substantial number of agunot was not made in the service of this institution-building goal.

It does not take much imagination to see how a get-refusing husband, having signed the RCA prenup, could engage the process with this court, incur fines he knows will not be enforced, and, when it suited him, offer a get in return for them being waived and receiving whatever other concessions he demands, having all the while inflicted the irreparable harm of lost life-time and costs on his wife through the RCA's process. The RCA court, after all, like all outside of Israel, has no enforcement power; a get-withholding husband can simply walk if he doesn't like its terms. The wife, on the other hand, needs the get. The deck is stacked for women to accept whatever terms the court sets as the price for their freedom and an end to the hemorrhage of life-time and finances.[16]

But there is additional and, I believe, pivotal meaning behind the obvious in this assertion of rabbinical-court primacy in dissolution of a couple's marriage and in the terms of that dissolution. Marriage and divorce is the only area of halakha in which Orthodox authorities in Israel can compel compliance, and elsewhere, can reliably depend on compliance with rabbinic rulings. Jews use secular lawyers and courts in all other areas of law—torts, business agreements, criminal matters— areas that, in premodern kehillot, were in the communal and rabbinic preserve as much as the laws of ritual observance. Since the demise of the traditional kehilla, those areas are not adjudicated in rabbinic courts, even in Israel (with minuscule exceptions, on a voluntary basis).[17] Of all rabbinic law, divorce is the only area that remains in rabbinic hands on the premodern model, that is, with determinative (if not tangible) enforcement power. The RCA prenup makes this power explicit. A halakhic prenup marketed, as is this one, as the solution to iggun and as the explicitly posed alternative to sweeping solutions proposed by Rabbis Emanuel Rackman and Moshe Morgenstern,[18] discussed below, which the RCA vehemently rejected, is a singular opportunity to assert rabbinic efficacy to actually enact halakha in a court, not just teach it as theory. The RCA constructs its prenup to enshrine hugely shrunken rabbinic power in the one area rabbis can still control—women and their marital freedom. We can readily see that these and other Orthodox rabbinic authorities need agunot and for the agunah "tragedy" to continue: with its demise would come the loss of the last assertion of rabbinic power over a segment of the community that has no other recourse—halakhically observant women or, in Israel, all Jewish women seeking divorce. To fundamental patriarchal values is wedded the last gasp of rabbinic power to adjudicate halakha in the real world.

The ultra-Orthodox Agudath Israel of America does not use any prenuptial agreement, claiming, in the words of its spokesperson Rabbi Avi Shafran, a "concern that introducing and focusing on the possible dissolution of the marriage when it is just beginning is not conducive to the health of the marriage," and that a prenup could lead to divorce "when a marriage might, with effort and determination, have been saved." Apparently, Rabbi Shafran is unfamiliar with the text of the traditional ketubbah.[19]

The Israeli organization Mavoi Satum ("Dead End," a seemingly strange name for an agunah-advocacy organization) operates under modern Orthodox rabbinic auspices and advocates halakhic marriage done by its affiliated rabbis, not those of the haredi-staffed Chief Rabbinate. It promotes a prenup that specifies financial penalties for get refusal and conditional marriage, meaning that if the stated condition—the husband giving a get—is not met, the marriage "should" be automatically annulled (it specifies no agent or context for such action).[20] Of course, what should and what does happen are very different things. None of the above-stated actions obligates an outcome, since rabbinic authorities can and do rule as they wish and can find objections, including alleged lack of respect for the rabbinic court, to override agreements that limit a husband's—or the court's—authority in divorce. They can argue, citing the Talmudic principle *anan sahadei* ("We are witnesses"), that if a woman and man lived together in a sustained, open manner, the relationship constitutes marriage and a get is required to dissolve the union, even if the couple *never had any marriage ceremony*.[21] Rabbinic authorities can always declare dissolution of a marriage, however this occurred, invalid and label the freed woman an adulteress and any children from a new relationship mamzerot/im. They rely on women, having internalized the fear of these stigma, to accede to such intimidation and to condition moving on with their lives on the permission of such authorities. Without such internalization, the invalidations and threats would have no force. As Sylvie-Anne Goldberg notes, "In a traditional society, control of women works through the women themselves"[22] (in the words of one extreme spokesman, "Dear girls, our salvation lies in . . . your hands"). That dynamic is even more operative now than in the past.

The Jewish Orthodox Feminist Alliance (JOFA), based in New York, champions a range of Orthodox feminist causes, including agunah advocacy. It promotes use of halakhic prenuptial agreements and features this advice prominently on its website as its "strongly" recommended action in the interest of "agunah prevention." Simultaneously, it notes, if obliquely, the limited efficacy of prenups, stating, "A well-written and properly executed prenuptial agreement is a *possible means* to ensuring fair and lawful proceedings in the event of a divorce." Enigmatically, it states further that "while a prenuptial agreement is not a guarantee, it can prevent *other women* from becoming agunot in the future" (my emphases). There is no explanation of the meaning of this latter phrase, though it is at least some acknowledgment that even the best prenup cannot ensure protection to a woman seeking this for herself before her own wedding. On the right side of a split opening page, alongside the recommendation of a halakhic prenup, JOFA's site features, in a bolded box, a "Tefillah [prayer] for Agunot" in Hebrew and in English. This prayer appeals to God "to free the captive wives . . . the faithful daughters of Israel, from their anguish," and to "grant wisdom to the judges of Israel to recognize oppression and rule against it."[23] Women are left with the recommendation of a prenup acknowledged as no guarantee and hope for Divine intervention with the rabbis who would control their fate if they became agunot.

Trusting any rabbinic court or individual rabbi to act as any prenup directs is ill-advised. Such documents—as they were throughout Jewish history, as we have seen—can be and are violated. A husband can recant any agreement he signed and assert his rights under halakha to withhold a get and/or extort for one, and is sure to find some rabbinic court eager to assert itself into the case. This is especially so if the prenup had an automatic-annulment clause dispensing with a court role in case of divorce—meaning, that its terms threaten rabbinic court authority. Rabbinic bodies, not least in power struggles with one another, can and do contest prenups and the actions based on them (the divorced woman dating or remarrying) after the fact. Conditioning the lived outcome of a divorce or annulment on rabbinic approval additional to that of the rabbi involved in the divorce or annulment itself guarantees the continuation of iggun. Such deference empowers intimidation tactics aimed at keeping control of divorce in the hands of whichever rabbi or rabbinic establishment is asked, including by third parties, for an opinion, or who insinuates himself or itself into a case, unasked.

The actions that Mavoi Satum advocates are no guarantee of preventing women's marital captivity or freeing agunot. On the contrary, the organization explicitly enshrines acquisition and sexual sanctification (kinyan and kiddushin) as the means to enact marriage when these are the cause of iggun, as well as inherently degrading to women. It lionizes kinyan and kiddushin as the traditional Jewish way to marry for *non-Orthodox* couples who just want to avoid the Chief Rabbinate, and for couples, secular or religious, who want a more personal ceremony than those Chief Rabbinate rabbis typically perform, with no explanation of what kinyan and kiddushin mean in the moment or their future consequences. Modern Orthodox Mavoi Satum openly opposes the ultra-Orthodox Chief Rabbinate, but the latter establishment is a symptom, not a cause of iggun. Substituting modern Orthodox rabbis for the haredi ones who dominate the Chief Rabbinate in an organization that maintains a state-authorized monopoly on Jewish marriage and divorce enacted by traditional halakhic methods is no solution to iggun.[24] Promoting this goal as if it were such a solution misleads the ignorant and, however unintentionally, perpetuates marital abuse. It is a prime example of agunah-advocacy organizations managing, and thereby enabling, that abuse rather than ending it by targeting its cause with effective action.

Asserting, as does Kylie Eisman-Lifschitz, since 2022 chair of Mavoi Satum, that the solution to ultra-Orthodox men (rabbis) detached from social reality deciding get cases is the appointment of women "representatives" "in the rabbinic courts" defies comprehension.[25] Halakhic precedent in divorce cases includes the "Maharik–Maharashdam rule," according to which a woman is not entitled to rabbinic-court action to promote the giving of a get if the husband claims that, in exchange for it, "the wife meet what the rabbinic judges deem . . . his 'easily fulfilled' . . . and 'reasonable' demands,"[26] that is, accept get extortion. As long as decision-making is in the hands of men adjudicating divorce cases according to such criteria, what possible difference could the presence of female "representatives" on such courts make?[27] Surely, a "kinder, gentler" environment for adjudication of prejudiced, misogynistic rulings is no solution. Women's "representation" on rabbinic courts as currently constituted would provide such women paid employment while appropriating them in the service of the agunah industry and a new, noxious fiction that rabbinic courts offer agunot fair treatment and relief.

We see another instance of misplaced effort, reflective of the state of agunah advocacy, compounded by misleading reporting, in the action of the Yad La'isha organization in yet another chapter in the ongoing Kin get-refusal case. In September 2022 that organization, which operates under the auspices of Rabbi Shlomo Riskin (a known critic of the Chief Rabbinate), petitioned the Supreme Court of Israel to order the Chief Rabbinate to refuse burial of family members whom Mr. Kin, at some point, might seek to have interred in Israel. It won the ruling it sought, which some hailed as precedent-setting and momentous.[28] Those characterizations are very hard to fathom. In a practice well familiar to us, not only has the Chief Rabbinate said that it will condition any action it might take on a supportive ruling from other rabbinic authorities, but there is a very small subset of cases in which such action might apply. Most important, even if all the above conditions were met, the agunah involved would remain an agunah, as indeed Lonna Ralbag, the agunah in this case, does after this "momentous ruling," decades after seeking a get, much of her life having been spent in iggun.[29] Maneuvers like this, which are a cat-and-mouse game between get refusers and whichever rabbinic group engages them in a struggle, evade and divert attention from the real issue—a woman's ability to end her own marriage and rabbinic refusal to annul marriages when there is get refusal or extortion. Reporting that deludes the public, especially women, into imagining that effective efforts are being made to free agunot is part of the complex of behaviors that perpetuate iggun.[30]

The Center for Women's Justice (CWJ) in Jerusalem has devised the best prenup available, developed by the rabbinic scholar and Israel Prize laureate Professor Rabbi Daniel Sperber. It combines monetary fines for nonissuance of a get (which, as noted, is subject to enforcement, meaning litigation) with the crucial and distinctive feature of automatic annulment of a marriage if the couple has not resided together for eighteen months. It also obligates the couple to take all matters but the get itself to Israeli Family (that is, civil) Court for adjudication, in order to keep financial and child custody questions out of rabbinic courts. In theory, at least, this lessens the possibility of get extortion; this clause, of course, is also subject to enforcement, that is, litigation, should the husband renege.[31] Even should a court eventually rule against the husband, the wife would have lost irrecoverable life-time, as well as money and emotional health in the process of pursuing it—no different from regular get extortion.

In fact, we know that such clauses do not necessarily operate as they have been constructed to do. Susan Weiss and Netty Gross-Horowitz detail cases in which rabbinic courts have refused to proceed with a get that the man, after many hearings in rabbinic courts and financial pressures brought by civil actions, is willing to give—until and unless any civil rulings against the husband about damages for get withholding or for property or child support are voided irrevocably and decisions on all such matters are transferred to the rabbinic court for adjudication.

They report the rabbinic-court scribe recording in one such case:

HUSBAND: Yes, I want to divorce. But I do not want to go to family court [in which the Center for Women's Justice had filed and won a tort claim for the woman because of the husband's get refusal]. . . .

COURT: If there is a damages claim against the husband for . . . get refusal . . . even if the husband were to plead before us that he wants to give the get, *we will not allow the ceremony to take place. And even if we were to allow it, the get would be invalid* according to all opinions [because the rabbis would rule it "coerced"] *and if the wife would remarry any child born to her would be a mamzer.*

JUDGMENT: Only after it has been proven to this court that the tort claim against the husband has been dismissed with prejudice and cannot be re-opened, will this court hear a request to arrange a divorce.—Rabbi Haim Shlomo Shaanan, Head of Tribunal. (my emphasis)[32]

This is not about women's marital freedom but about the institutional interests of the rabbinic-court enterprise.

Any prenup, including the best, is a contract and, as such, can be violated and contested.[33] Attempted enforcement of prenups entails litigation, expensive and possibly prolonged, the sheer threat of which, in particular by a husband of means, can be used as a tool of get extortion, no different from primary get extortion.[34] To men of means, the monetary fine, even if enforced, let alone if only partially enforced, is not a deterrent.[35] To men without means, such a fine is also meaningless. Moreover, the problem remains of states (outside of Israel) recognizing the standing of a religiously contextualized contract and acting as its enforcement mechanism, any contest about which entails litigation.

Prenuptial agreements, of course, do nothing for couples already married by kinyan and kiddushin, marriages in which every wife is a potential agunah, an agunah in waiting.[36] In order for the first part of the CWJ prenup to provide any protection for already-married couples, they need to sign the center's postnup, and there is no ready-set occasion, like the wedding, for this. Such action takes special commitment and effort, occasions for which the CWJ has tried to create but that reach only a minority of the already-married. The second, most important part of the CWJ prenup, establishing conditional marriage with automatic, retroactive annulment in case of get withholding, is of course inapplicable in a postnup.[37]

Ultimately, in the case of a divorce or annulment obtained in whichever rabbinic court or, as in the CWJ prenup, enacted automatically under specified conditions, the decision that the marriage is over, and behavior according with that decision, rests with the couple. It rests in particular with the woman, should the husband renege or any rabbi or group claim that the prenup, get, or annulment is invalid. No agreement, however constructed or supported by halakhic rulings, can compel social acceptance. It is up to the parties to the marriage who have signed a prenup or engaged other protective legal action, and in particular to the women, to enact these agreements in behavior that accords with the marriage having terminated.

In the best of a bad situation, that is, when acquisition and sexual sanctification of the woman (kinyan and kiddushin) are used to enact marriage, the officiating rabbi, implementing rabbinic organizational policy, will require use of the CWJ prenup. The only organization that now follows this policy is Chuppot, which operates independently of, and in opposition to, the Chief Rabbinate. Chuppot weddings use kinyan and kiddushin and are for Jews recognized as Jewish according to

(Orthodox) halakhic criteria, per this organization's definition (Chuppot disputes the Chief Rabbinate's conversion criteria, claiming they are needlessly stringent).[38] Chuppot's halakhic adviser, Rabbi Kalman Pesach (Chuck) Davidson, stresses that it is critical for officiating rabbis of weddings to require use of the CWJ prenup, it being unreasonable to expect a young, inexperienced couple in the throes of engagement excitement or, I would argue, older, previously married women to require this. Nor is it good policy to leave its requirement to the respective parents of the couple, who may disagree about it, causing strife and pressure on the party desiring the prenup (likely the bride's parents), who are acting against the norm and thus at a disadvantage, to relent. (The fact that the traditional ketubbah is a one-sided prenup on the woman's behalf does not register on anyone's consciousness because the document is a ritual formality, having long ago lost legal force.) The matter, Davison urges, should be removed from individual decision-making and made policy, as his organization does.[39]

"Agunah Day"

In 1990 ICAR, the International Coalition for Agunah Rights, declared the Fast of Esther—the eve of the holiday of Purim—"International Agunah Day." Since then other organizations, such as ORA, as well as individual communities (all Orthodox, I believe), have promoted observance of this day. ORA calls for recitation of Psalms, typically recited for the severely ill or injured. ICAR promotes the following activities:

- Declaring the Fast of Esther International Agunah Day and advocating legislation to that effect;
- Initiating and promoting events, presentations, demonstrations, rallies and exhibitions in the public sphere;
- Initiating a special event or meeting in the Knesset;
- Mobilizing a media campaign;
- Distributing pamphlets containing special prayers at synagogues and during demonstrations;
- Promoting a nation-wide study day;
- Organizing protests in front of the Knesset and/or the homes or work place of get-refusing husbands.[40]

With the possible exception of the last item, in selected cases and even then in very limited application—none of these actions would free a single agunah, much less end iggun. A nationwide study day—of what? The same sources that could lead to solutions but don't, because the vast majority of rabbinic courts don't apply them and persecute the few who have? The same sources that enshrine a husband's privilege and power over the wife, make his free will in divorce sacrosanct, and women supplicants in a system stacked against them? A "meeting" in the Knesset—with whom, to what end, and with what tools to effect results, when marriage and divorce by law no imaginable Knesset is about to change are in the hands of the Chief Rabbinate? Such a proposal has no political "legs," and to suggest otherwise is to mislead and endanger the ignorant.

Tzviya Gorodetsky was an agunah in Israel for twenty-six years. Her violent, marginally employed husband was in jail for nineteen of them for defying a rabbinic court order to give her a get, steadfastly maintaining that refusal while receiving a bed, three meals a day, and medical care on the public tab. In the summer of 2017, Gorodetsky declared a hunger strike in front of the Knesset in the hope of rousing the Israeli parliament to take action to free her. She got a sunburn and lost weight for her effort.

Gorodetsky was finally freed because Nitzan Caspi Shiloni of the Center for Women's Justice enlisted Rabbi Daniel Sperber, who, after studying her case, convened his own rabbinic court (the other rabbinic participants have not disclosed their identity for fear of retribution by the Chief Rabbinate), which annulled her marriage after finding gross halakhic irregularities in its enactment.[41] Some of those irregularities were automatically disqualifying under halakha, not least that Tzviya bought the ring used in the ceremony—it was not her husband's possession, as required in order for him to "acquire" her in rabbinic marriage. Furthermore, were there kosher (halakhically valid) witnesses to the ceremony, conducted in the Soviet Union, meaning not just male and halakhically Jewish but observant of the Sabbath and kashrut? Without such witnesses, the ceremony is also invalid, and if so, does not require a get. All these, of course, were facts throughout Gorodetsky's long ordeal. *Yet no Chief Rabbinate rabbi had bothered to inquire into the details of her wedding ceremony, though it could have ended her ordeal summarily and freed her decades earlier* (and saved taxpayers millions of shekels in care

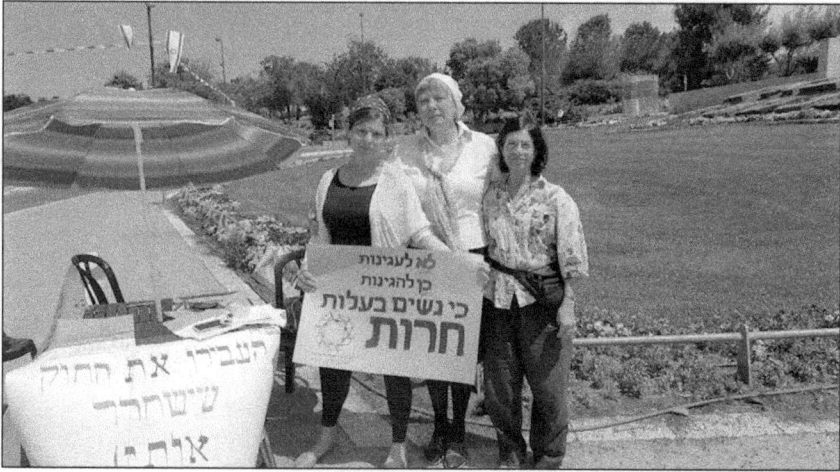

Figure 11.1 Nitzan Caspi Shiloni, Tzviya Gorodetsky, and Shulamit Magnus, hunger-strike vigil at the Knesset, summer 2017: "Pass the law that will free me!" Credit: Nitzan Caspi Shiloni.

Figure 11.2 Annulment of Tzviya Gorodetsky's marriage in the court of Rabbi Professor Daniel Sperber (seen from behind), with Attorney Nitzan Caspi Shiloni and court recorders. Credit: Nurit Jacobs-Yinon.

Figure 11.3 Tzviya Gorodetsky testifying in Rabbi Sperber's court in the hearing for annulment of her marriage. Credit: Nurit Jacobs-Yinon.

Figure 11.4 Tzviya Gorodetsky with Attorney Nitzan Caspi Shiloni, with the document certifying annulment of her marriage and her marital freedom. Credit: Nurit Jacobs-Yinon.

for her deadbeat husband). Instead, the Chief Rabbinate rabbis handling Gorodetsky's case preferred to engage in a yearslong power struggle with Mr. Gorodetsky.[42] Not halakhic leniency but stringency—or even the most basic competence—would have released this woman, swiftly. But even basic halakhic competence was lacking in Chief Rabbinate courts.

Prayers for agunot and "Agunah Days" enshrine the problem, enabling it. Giving the abuse of women in marital captivity fixed, ritual expression—meaning that it is repeated reliably—normalizes it as a feature of religious life and the religious calendar. What is the use of formulaic attention to this problem, raising awareness of it, without effective steps to end it? The best prenup is better than none and some are worse than none, but this is not how to end iggun. Doing a prenup before enacting marriage through kinyan and kiddushin is like having an antidote on hand after taking poison—and hoping it works. Clearly, it is better not to take poison in the first place. Prenups are a tool to manage, that is, to perpetuate, not end, iggun, and can themselves factor in marital abuse.

Even the best of them do nothing for agunot denied freedom, extorted for it, abused in rabbinic courts, now. To focus on prenups is to distract attention from agunot and to mislead about the whole problem of Jewish marital captivity.

About "Agunah Days," we can only cite Miroslav Volf (speaking of mass shootings in the United States in the absence of serious gun regulation): "There is something deeply hypocritical about praying for a problem you are unwilling to resolve."[43]

12

Intradenominational Politics and Rivalries Abort Solutions within Orthodoxy

The Courts of Rabbis Morgenstern and Rackman and Their Undoing

We have seen how the problem of women's marital captivity was used to erect denominational boundaries between the newly established Orthodox and Conservative movements of the United States in the early twentieth century. It has been put to the same use between competing groups within Orthodoxy as well.

Several Orthodox rabbis, aside from the aforementioned Louis Epstein, Saul Lieberman, and Eliezer Berkovits, have proposed solutions to free agunot and end iggun. In 1997 Rabbi Meir Simcha Feldblum of Yeshiva University published a proposed alternative to kinyan and kiddushin that would obviate the linked problems of iggun and mamzerut. It was subjected to halakhic objections and Feldblum to intense personal attacks, and achieved no practical results.[1]

In the same year, Rabbi Moshe Morgenstern of New York, who was ordained by the eminent halakhic decisor Rabbi Moshe Feinstein, initiated his own rabbinic court headed by Rabbi Emanuel Rackman, a prominent figure in modern Orthodoxy. The agunah-advocacy group Agunah, Inc., worked with this court (the Beit Din Tsedek Le'Ba'ayot Agunot, Court of Justice for the Problems of Agunot) and referred dozens of cases to it that, using a variety of halakhic methods, freed nearly all of the agunot involved. Susan Aranoff, who worked with Agunah, Inc., cites more than one hundred women who applied to this beit din for help to end their marriages in just the first year after the court's founding, and hundreds freed during the short course of its existence.[2]

Rackman and Morgenstern applied the established halakhic principle of *mekah ta'ut*—"a mistaken transaction"—to annul a marriage the bride entered on the basis of incomplete or inaccurate information, on the assumption that, had she had full information, she would have refused the marriage. Their innovation lay in recognizing and acting upon three types of *mekah ta'ut* in the established category of "serious defect" in the groom and in expanding the situations covered by this principle, including cruelty and physical and emotional violence that only became manifest after the marriage.

They also recognized as grounds for annulment a husband's extramarital sex, whether hetero- or homosexual (as we recall, under halakha such intercourse is adulterous only if the woman involved is the wife of another Jewish man), arguing that, in the era of AIDS, this constituted a threat to the wife's life; the bride's ignorance of the fact that rabbinic courts in the United States lack the power to force a man to give a get; and her ignorance of the nature and consequences of kiddushin.[3] Rabbi Morgenstern also used another expedient, *get zikui*, to free agunot, utilizing the halakhic principle that actions done on another's behalf are acceptable even without the beneficiary's consent. The beneficiary, in this case, is the recalcitrant husband, who is relieved of the offense of defying rabbinic authority in refusing his wife a get after being instructed to do so by the rabbinic court, which then issues the get on his behalf.

Rabbis Morgenstern and Rackman encountered a "tsunami of criticism" from the Orthodox establishment, including from Rabbi Mordechai Tendler, grandson of Rabbi Moshe Feinstein, and Rabbi Joseph B. Soloveitchik.[4] Morgenstern was disowned by his community and attacked physically by ultra-Orthodox vigilantes. The elderly Rackman was subjected to a campaign of slander about his allegedly failing mental capacities and to publicly enacted shunning in venues that had long been his turf.[5] The RCA's rabbinic court, the Beth Din of America (affiliated with the Orthodox Union), issued a lengthy letter rejecting the position of the Rackman–Morgenstern court that cruelty (including violence) or drug addiction discovered after the marriage were grounds for annulment.[6] The ultra-Orthodox Agudath Israel of America and the modern Orthodox National Council of Young Israel denounced the Rackman–Morgenstern beit din and declared its actions invalid, the women it freed, still married—that is, agunot—and any children born to them from new relationships, mamzerot/im.

At Rabbi Rackman's request, Susan Aranoff published an annotated statement of the court's halakhic procedures and precedents. The document, "Principles and Procedures for Freeing Agunot," presented the three categories of "error" (*ta'ut*) that the court accepted as grounds for annulment of a marriage and their halakhic bases and justification.[7]

The critical import of the Rackman–Morgenstern court was that it offered a route both to freeing current agunot and to ending iggun altogether since, if its practices were adopted widely, or even if the court itself just continued to function, men would know that get withholding would be cause for annulment of the marriage on grounds of mental cruelty presumed to have been present, if not manifest, at the time of the wedding. This was supported by the argument that no bride knowingly intends to deliver herself into a form of subjugation. In Aranoff's words, "Even without proving pre-existence [of a groom's defect] the second and third forms of *ta'ut* postulated that . . . a woman would not knowingly agree to a marriage that is a form of bondage."[8]

Critics of these "Principles" objected to them on the grounds that the Rackman beit din was "defining halakhic marriage out of existence" as they "might allow any agunah who was a victim of domestic violence to attain her freedom[!] To the court's critics, declaring domestic violence in itself grounds for invalidating a marriage undermined the legal structure of Jewish marriage" (my emphasis).[9] As we have seen, one such prominent critic, Rabbi J. David Bleich, put the matter with bracing honesty, asserting that halakhic marriage is, precisely, "an exclusive conjugal servitude" of the bride to the groom.[10] Iggun, in this view, is a perfectly legitimate outcome of marriage. The damning problem, then, was not the validity of the halakhic methods that Rackman and Morgenstern were applying but their outcome—success in freeing current agunot, *with the clear potential of ending women's marital captivity altogether*. Critics of the Rackman court, Aranoff writes, "faulted [it] for [its] 100% record of freeing agunot" as "prima facie evidence against the validity of the beit din's decisions."[11] Perpetuation of iggun, not success in ending it, was and remains the goal.

Nothing could better illustrate the futility of appealing to halakhic methods to free agunot and end iggun when the problem, fundamentally, is not halakhic, the absence of remedies, but political, the refusal to apply them, and social—acquiescence to such behavior.

Rabbi Morgenstern eventually left Rabbi Rackman's court (which continued to function and added new members—significantly, Sephardi rabbis) and started his own. The Israeli Chief Rabbinate denounced him. Jonathan Sacks, then chief rabbi of Britain, celebrated as a spokesman for Jewish ethics and an eloquent, urbane representative of and apologist for moderate Orthodoxy, lent his name and office to the denunciations.[12]

Other major figures in modern Orthodoxy—Rabbis Shlomo Riskin and Saul Berman (the latter then head of EDAH, a modern Orthodox think tank)—also rejected that court. While Riskin had extensive dealings with iggun and wrote a book about rabbinic divorce,[13] Berman was so sure that agunot were not a significant problem in modern Orthodoxy that he confidently asked an audience of two thousand, gathered at the Second International Conference on Feminism and Orthodoxy organized by JOFA in 1998, how many of them knew an agunah. He was very taken aback when one-third to one-half of the attendees raised their hands. Nonetheless, Berman maintained his criticism of the Rackman–Morgenstern court and did not retract his statement denying the existence of the problem of iggun in modern Orthodoxy.[14]

Other prominent rabbis—in the ultra-Orthodox world, notably Rabbi Mordechai Tendler—freed agunot in their courts, including on grounds of *mekah ta'ut* because of mental or physical illness, such as the groom's drug addiction or criminal record, information about which was not shared with the bride before the wedding. Tendler at one point put the number of agunot he had freed at thirty, but he *had not made his actions known*, preventing agunah activists from sending agunot to his court and possibly being freed. Tendler and others claimed that his revered grandfather, Moshe Feinstein, *similarly had freed agunot but not made this known or even recorded those cases in his authoritative, precedent-setting, published responsa*, preventing the signal assistance that such recording and publication would have given agunot and injuring the cause even of limiting iggun: if men knew that marriages were being annulled by authorities of such stature on the basis of *mekah taut*, they would have far less incentive to engage in get refusal. Crucially, other rabbis and rabbinic establishments running rabbinic courts would have gotten a clear message about how to handle cases of get refusal. At the very least, public knowledge of such rulings by ranking *poskim* would have signaled authoritative disapproval of get abuse, causing the bull market in get extortion to lose some of its sizzling value and social acceptance. But such considerations clearly were not operative. Tendler's court ceased functioning in 2005 after he was accused of sexual improprieties with congregants and agunot.[15] He, too, had publicly rejected the Rackman–Morgenstern court.[16]

In 2004 Professor Aviad Hacohen, on the Law Faculty of Bar-Ilan University (where Rackman was chancellor), published a volume, *The Tears of the Oppressed*, that detailed halakhic sources for solutions to iggun. The book, in Aranoff's words, "had no discernable impact on the agunah situation nor on the embattled status of the Rackman beit din," nor did a similar collection produced by another Orthodox scholar, Professor Bernard Jackson of England, one of five learned volumes that the Agunah Research Unit at Manchester University has published on this subject.[17] Another such learned tome, *Za'akat Dalot*, produced by the Masorti movement's Schechter Institute of Jewish Studies, has met a similar fate.

The problem is not lack of halakhic methods to free agunot and end iggun but explicit defense and perpetuation of traditional halakhic marriage, including its inevitable consequence of women's marital captivity; infighting; and, with a few exceptions, lack of will and even minimally responsible communal behavior.

Sadly, discord about solutions to iggun also surfaced among women engaged in agunah advocacy. Veteran advocates Susan Aranoff and Rivka Haut parted ways over the Morgenstern–Rackman court, whose methods Haut and her husband, Irwin—an Orthodox rabbi who himself served for a time on that court—originally supported but came to reject. Rivka Haut became an outspoken critic of that court, citing fear that its rulings would not be widely recognized within Orthodoxy. Aranoff acknowledged the grounds for Haut's concern but argued that if even 15 percent of Orthodox society accepted the court, that would provide sufficient community for freed agunot to find new spouses, a possibility foreclosed to them as agunot.[18] One might also argue that persistence and effective public education and support for women freed through the means that the Rackman and Morgenstern courts used would have increased the percentage within Orthodoxy who accepted those methods and the agunot freed by them, creating a new social reality. This, in turn, would have upended acceptance of iggun as inevitable and inescapable, "tragic" but normal. Persistence could have created new norms, just as these are created continuously within Orthodoxy about many issues, though we concede that control of women and protection of male power and prerogative in marriage and divorce is in its own class as the third rail of traditional Jewish patriarchy. Certainly, not persisting has yielded only the persistence of iggun.

Significantly, JOFA did not issue a statement of support for either the Morgenstern–Rackman or the Morgenstern court and continues to use traditional methods of agunah advocacy, which manifestly fail to end iggun. Aranoff concedes that JOFA's support "would not [itself] have carried the day for the Rackman beit din," but maintains that the absence of such support for that court even from an openly feminist Orthodox organization hurt the court's credibility.[19] The failure of support from this quarter surely was demoralizing to those behind Rackman's efforts and contributed to the perception of iggun as unsolvable.

Intra-Orthodox Power Struggles Stymie Even Prenuptial Agreements

Intra-Orthodox political struggles also mark disagreements even over prenuptial agreements. These disagreements function to delineate intragroup borders and legitimacy, or lack thereof, just as they have functioned in interdenominational disputes. As we have seen, ultra-Orthodox authorities and organizations do not use prenups; modern Orthodox ones are willing to, while, with a few exceptions, not requiring their use. In Israel this issue has served the contest over legitimacy between these wings of Orthodoxy, with the ultra-Orthodox (obviously having no acquaintance with Jewish history or even, it would appear, with the traditional ketubbah) claiming that prenups per se are illegitimate because they preempt sacrosanct male control of marriage and its dissolution. Organizations that use them, in the words of head of the haredi Shas Party, member of Knesset, several-times minister, convicted, jailed, and reindicted for financial crimes, Rabbi Aryeh Deri, seek to "destroy" the rabbinate and are "borderline Reform. They [do] everything for free, [are] welcoming, lenient and all that," he said. "But we all know the truth."[20]

In these remarks, Deri was referencing the Israeli modern Orthodox organization Tzohar, which endorses (while not requiring) a prenuptial agreement that imposes financial penalties on a get-refusing man, without requiring that this be adjudicated in a rabbinic court in the event of divorce. That this latter condition—rabbinic involvement and recognition in the get business—is the crux of the matter is seen from a case in 2017.

In that case, a Jerusalem Regional Rabbinical Court (an arm of Israel's Chief Rabbinate, which is staffed by haredi rabbis) *refused to process a get for a couple in agreement about getting divorced*—there was no get refusal or other impediment—*until the clause in their prenuptial agreement, written by a lawyer, that imposed financial penalties on the husband in the event of get refusal was voided.* Forty-four haredi rabbis in the state system signed a rabbinic injunction against halakhic prenups, with Avigdor Nebenzahl, chief rabbi of Jerusalem's Old City, writing, "A person who signs such an agreement is not an Orthodox rabbi and his halachic rulings cannot be relied upon."[21]

Crucially, Nebenzahl noted that, while opposed in principle to all prenuptial agreements, he could abide by that of the Rabbinical Council of America, *which, as we have seen, gives the rabbinic court total control over the get settlement, including the right to void any financial penalties on the husband*, but not that of the Tzohar organization, which levies financial penalties on a get-refusing husband but does not require the couple to take that matter to a rabbinic court. Of this, Rabbi David Stav, head of Tzohar—*who leads that organization's fight to wrest control of the haredi-staffed Chief Rabbinate and replace it with Tzohar rabbis*—stated, "Our agreement and the RCA agreement rely on the same [halakhic] principles. But we do not require the couple to go to the rabbinic court *nor is there any halachic requirement for this.* This proves that Rav Nebenzahl's opposition is purely political" (my emphasis).[22]

This case reinforces what we have already seen: women's marital captivity or freedom is instrumentalized to draw boundary lines between competing male groups. Women's lives are not just sacrificed *in* these disputes; their lives serve the interests of these disputes themselves. This dynamic is not confined to Orthodox vs. Conservative denominationalism; it functions equally in intra-Orthodox power struggles.

Such power struggles, essentially turf and ego battles, need iggun. Iggun and its *irresolution*—jousts about legitimate and illegitimate actions, properly authorized or not, by whom—are essential to Orthodox power struggles and battles for supremacy. Moreover, they are essential to exceedingly brittle, fragile Orthodox identity. This means that the system in any of its parts will never end iggun but offer only continued administration—management—and expansion (as in the attempt of the Chief Rabbinate in the case of "the agunah from Safed," as will be discussed), and exploitation of it. It will continue to practice measures, above all, enacting marriage via kinyan and kiddushin that cause iggun, doubling down on the use of these degrading rituals as the only "authentic" Jewish way to marry.

Women are not and have never been the focus of rabbinic deliberations about iggun. Women are a side issue, serving the purposes we have seen. Women are an abstraction in halakhic legal theory, a category for administration, like other categories in halakha but of a particularly sensitive nature given the patriarchal anxieties and obsessions we have discussed. Women's disabilities under the halakhic system provide the grounds for lucrative legal processes requiring entire administrative apparatuses and for assertions of personal and organizational ego.

Such a system is not and will never be a—let alone *the*—remedy for Jewish marital captivity. The Jewish historical record points us to the route for meaningful change: unapologetic assertion and initiative by women on their own behalf, as agents, not objects, of Jewish practice, in the context of concerted communal support.

Tactics of a Threatened Chief Rabbinate

Since Rabbi Daniel Sperber has several times convened his own rabbinic court, which freed agunot long stymied in the Chief Rabbinate system, he has become a particular target of Chief Rabbinate ire and, remarkably, given his eminence as a scholar far outstripping that of his critics, attempts to impugn his competence.[23] Thus, he and Nitzan Caspi Shiloni of the Center for Women's Justice, who refers cases to him and works closely with him on them, were targeted in a press release issued by the Chief Rabbinate court's spokesperson Shai Doron on November 8, 2021. In its statement, this court alleged that Rabbi Sperber's court, which had freed an agunah through annulment of her marriage, had been guilty of the supreme offense of marrying a woman to two men simultaneously (since, in freeing the agunah, he had made her eligible to remarry, which she had done).

The Chief Rabbinate court, its statement asserted, rushed to the rescue in obtaining a get from the woman's first husband—only then, after the woman had been an agunah for almost ten years and only after Rabbi Sperber's court had nullified her marriage, her husband having long refused to give a get; how they only then, suddenly, achieved this feat remains a mystery. The statement of the Chief Rabbinate court repeatedly accuses Rabbi Sperber and his court of lack of competence, both legal, reiterating several times the Chief Rabbinate's legal monopoly on divorce for Israeli Jews, and halakhic, citing its own alleged superior competence.[24] It notes, goadingly, that the other rabbis on Rabbi Sperber's court remain anonymous, although anyone familiar with the tactics used in such situations understands why these rabbis would condition their participation in this court on their continued anonymity.

The statement belittles the woman (she is ignorant of halakha, which is what allowed her to fall victim to Rabbi Sperber's ignorance and incompetence). It violates her privacy with irrelevant, demeaning gossip about her allegedly advanced age and use of (repeatedly unsuccessful, it deems it necessary to say) fertility treatments in her second marriage. This marriage, the Chief Rabbinate court claims, also ended in divorce, arranged through its auspices, supposedly because the second husband had been surprised (by "a friend") to learn that his wife had not been divorced from her first husband (which, technically, is true, since Rabbi Sperber annulled that marriage, sidestepping her husband's long-standing get refusal).

Sound like a cheap gossip sheet? Petty, mean politics? Professional jealousy? Patronizing, malevolent, and misogynistic revenge against a woman who, failed utterly by the ever so competent—and legitimate!—state rabbinic court (the very same court that had so botched Tzviya Gorodetsky's case), finally got relief from another rabbinic court? That is who is in charge of marriage and divorce in Israel, officially at least; as we know, haredi courts operate in this arena unhindered and unslandered by the Chief Rabbinate.

To this extraordinary public offensive by the Chief Rabbinate court, Caspi Shiloni responded with a statement on her Facebook page about the particulars of this case. Pasted over a copy of the Chief Rabbinate's statement, Caspi Shiloni wrote in red, "FAKE NEWS." She also posted a statement from Rabbi Sperber about it.[25]

The woman in question had never been married to two men simultaneously, she said. Her first husband was violent in a previous marriage, for which he had served prison time—information he withheld from his second wife before they married, to whom he was also violent. He refused her a get and demanded a payoff to give one (his right to which claim the Chief Rabbinate statement defends). The woman is not divorced from her second husband; that statement too, said Caspi Shiloni, was false.

Rabbi Sperber's statement reads:

> From what I have heard, the judges of the rabbinic courts are doing a great evil to a woman who suffered much for long years, to whom they are currently adding more suffering and anguish and impugning her family life. The astounding thing is that for almost ten years they did not manage to do anything for her, and now, when she has found some tranquility for her soul, they saw fit to sabotage her life. We would also note that the injunction "Keep distant from falsehood" applies to judges and their assistants, too. Would that they were capable of seeing the value of compassion.[26]

Deception, Disinformation, Cluelessness

Iggun continues for a number of reasons. High among them is the lack of public understanding of the nature of the problem—its origin in kinyan and kiddushin—and its history, as well as the actions of multiple interested parties in perpetuating it.

Such actions very much include misrepresentation by rabbinic organizations and their defenders, which, first, minimizes and denies the existence and scope of the problem through various manipulations, and second, conveys the (mis)impression of heroic rabbinic action to free agunot when husbands refuse them gittin and, far worse, commit the actionable offense of defying rabbinic orders to do so in the rare instances that rabbinic courts issue such orders. Against these evildoers, apologists pose rabbis and their allies—to quote Caspi Shiloni, as "supermen," riding to the rescue.[27]

Caspi Shiloni cites the publicity generated by Member of Knesset Bezalel Smotrich in April 2021 when he spent a few hours in a Chief

Rabbinate court in a case of an agunah who had spent years in one seeking a get. "Smotrich signed as a guarantor for the woman's financial commitment to the husband, to the tune of NIS 650,000 [then about $250,000], in return for him granting the get—for get extortion, in short. Thus, as reported, Smotrich 'freed the agunah.'" In other words, collusion with and enablement of get extortion was presented as rescue. The message conveyed in the publicity about Smotrich's action, replete with the triumphant faces of the three rabbinic judges and of Smotrich (his was even refracted a second time in the Plexiglas—not, however, that of the agunah, because, of course, she is just incidental to this event)—is the legitimacy and normality, the self-evident necessity, of get extortion. We also get the fantasy that some prominent benefactor will materialize to—*guarantee payment by the agunah*—to the get-extorting husband. Smotrich and many others in Israel are on record as opposing ransom deals with terrorists. With get-extorting husbands holding women hostage, however, ransom is not just legitimate but heroic. The fact that this was get extortion is lost in distortive statements and images claiming that an agunah was "freed."

This was no isolated case of such distortion about iggun and agunot by rabbinic courts and the media organs that support them. In an article published in January 2022, Caspi Shiloni critiqued the Chief Rabbinate court's narrative about two cases (real names withheld) of one woman, "Naama," captive for thirty-three years, and another, "Hadas," an agunah for fourteen years whose husband escaped from the court during proceedings about the case.[28] The court described Hadas's case as "a success" and "an accomplishment for the beit din headed by Rav David Lau" (the Ashkenazi chief rabbi). *Behadrei Hadarim*, a haredi newspaper, announced Naama's case with the headline "A Stormy and Moving Drama in the Rabbinical Beit Din, Which Reached Salvation through a [female] Employee of the Beit Din." The story was illustrated with the photo of a beaming haredi man striding triumphantly before the doorway of the Chief Rabbinate court.

Yitzhak Tessler's article in Jerusalem.mynet on January 6, 2022, was another celebratory piece about this case, hailing the "happy ending, with three-way conciliation" that supposedly occurred, the heading proclaiming breathlessly, "All in the Same Case and the Same Hearing Room in the District Rabbinical Court of Jerusalem."[29]

Here are the particulars of these cases, provided by the rabbinic court and reported, regarding the first case, by Caspi Shiloni, and about the second case, by Tessler.

Hadas's husband had refused a get, repeatedly demanding an exorbitant payoff for it, after also asking the court to order *shalom bayit* (reconciliation) counseling, a known delaying tactic by get-refusing men, abetted by rabbinic courts.[30] *After six years of rabbinic-court proceedings*, the man left the room during one hearing and disappeared. *Only at this point did the rabbinic court recognize Hadas's status as a mesorevet get*, a woman denied a get—an agunah—and her husband as a get refuser (*mesarev get*)—the conferring of neither of which title obligates the court to any action to end the woman's captivity.

Allegedly, the court made efforts to locate the husband. In the end, a donation made to the organization Yad La'isha secured the services of a private detective, who quickly located the man—in Tel Aviv—*seven years after he had disappeared and nearly fourteen years after Hadas asked for a get.* He was brought before the rabbinic court, which had him incarcerated, after several months of which he gave the get.

Does this story accord with the headline proclaiming "success," much less one attributable to the court over which Chief Rabbi Lau was presiding? Why, Caspi Shiloni asks, did it take a donation to a private organization to hire a detective to locate the get refuser when taxpayers fund an entire "Agunah Unit" under the aegis of the Chief Rabbinate's court? What of the six years it took for that court even to assign the status "agunah" to Hadas?

The lack of transparency of this and all rabbinic-court functions makes an accounting of the financial cost to Hadas and to all agunot caught in that system impossible to obtain. Clearly, there is financial benefit to these courts in multiple hearings, for each of which fees are charged, and in associated functions like "domestic peace" (*shalom bayit*) counseling, which the courts routinely mandate using affiliated counselors, even when there has been violence against the wife and police action against the husband. There is certainly no financial incentive for rabbinical courts to resolve cases expeditiously.

In the second case, Naama suffered extreme violence from a husband who beat her, restrained her physically, almost threw her out a window, and refused to give a get. Terrified by his threats on her life, Naama fled to a battered women's shelter and eventually closed her divorce case out of terror of being in her husband's presence in unending rabbinic-court proceedings. Naama remained an agunah, raising the couple's daughter on her own. *Thirty-three years later,* when the husband needed to establish his marital status as "separated" in order to secure financing for a kidney transplant, he turned to the rabbinic court for this certification. It was then that a female legal clerk in the court—the "hero" of Tessler's article—searched the court's archives and saw that a divorce file involving the man had been opened thirty-five years earlier, that he was extremely violent, had refused a get for over thirty-three years, and that the case, in Tessler's telling, "surprisingly" had been closed at the wife's request.

The case was reopened and the man, because he now needed it himself, actively sought to give a get. The rabbinic court contacted Naama, who adamantly refused to restart get hearings because this would entail proximity to this husband. The court told her that she need be present only for the end of the ritual, when the wife receives the get physically into her hands. In fact, that is untrue and an outrageous claim. The woman's presence absolutely is *not* required under halakha for this act, and in cases where there has been violence or other abuse, the wife's presence should be dispensed with, categorically and automatically. The court could and should have ordered the husband to appoint a messenger to deliver the get to Naama in his stead. This is a well-established halakhic option for men, obviating their presence at get proceedings, and done routinely, even just for the man's convenience. It should be standard practice in all cases of violence against wives, and clearly, in this pervasively androcentric system, isn't.[31]

According to Tessler's report of the court's narrative, in the encounter that ensued the man "fell on his knees and begged forgiveness" from Naama, who "nobly" gave it, and the get proceeded, with all three, including the adult daughter—a lawyer who represented her mother in the proceedings and *whom the father had never before met, much less supported*—leaving "content." In the court's telling, a "happy ending," with a photo of the daughter in the beit din illustrating the "moving" event.

Really? Caspi Shiloni asks. Who would return to Hadas the *thirty-three* years of life and freedom, the possibility of another relationship, other children, that she lost in marital captivity to this man, to the knowledge during all those years that she remained married to him? Who would return to Naama the fourteen years she lost to her captor and his rabbinic enablers?

In what universe, we might ask, was either of these cases a "success," or were the fitting terms to describe the ending in Hadas's case "emotional" and "moving"? Only in an androcentric universe in which iggun never happens—because it can never happen—to the men in charge of the rabbinic courts—or of reporting about them. Such reporting feeds the public false information and impressions that rabbinic courts work to end women's captivity, that happy endings mark get proceedings, that the women who are victims of the system are "content" if and when egregious, years- and decades-long abuse inflicted on them ends.

We recall Avraham Grossman's cautionary comment that the term "rebellious wife" never came from women about themselves but is the terminology of men with the power of reporting, of shaping norms and public "knowledge," as well as deciding the outcomes of women's quests for marital freedom. So, too, the terminology we see in the reporting about these cases. No woman, certainly no agunah, would apply these terms to what she experienced in rabbinic courts. It is long since time that terminology reflect the experience of the victims, not the perpetrators and enablers of this abuse.

Rabbinic Apathy, Incompetence, Malevolence

In the case we have discussed of multiyear get refuser Israel Meir Kin, a resident of California, his long spurning of rabbinic-court orders to give his wife a get led the court to issue an injunction against Jewish burial of his family (obviously, in the United States), the most severe of traditional sanctions. When Kin's mother died in 2019 and he shipped her body to Israel for burial, Israel's Ashkenazi chief rabbi hearkened to the California court's ruling and ordered the woman's body denied burial until Kin complied with the court's directives and gave his wife a get.

Supposedly, Kin agreed to this; he denies it. On someone's word that he had agreed, without taking the obvious step of requiring delivery by certified messenger of an actual get to Kin's wife, Lonna Ralbag, before the burial proceeded, Kin's mother was buried and with her, any leverage on him to release his wife. Ralbag remains an agunah while Kin has remarried, having obtained from another rabbinic court (which, obviously, did not recognize the authority of the first) dispensation from the Ashkenazic prohibition of polygyny. The rabbinic incompetence and negligence in this case, across multiple jurisdictions and levels of rabbinic jurisprudence in several countries, including Israel's Chief Rabbinate, are breathtaking.[32]

The problem of iggun remains androcentric, even as women, even dead ones, are victimized. At the time of the fiasco involving Kin's mother, I conjectured that the rabbis in this case would never have delayed, recommended, or threatened burial of a male rabbi or major donor. But there was no need for conjecture. On December 3, 2020, Ynet reported live from the funeral in Jerusalem of the grandfather of another longtime get refuser who had been ordered by a rabbinic court to give a get, which directive the man, who fled to Gibraltar, ignored. His wife, Esty Sompo, referencing the Kin case and the tactic she mistakenly thought had been enforced of withholding burial in order to extract a get, petitioned the head of the Jerusalem rabbinic court to withhold burial of her husband's grandfather until her husband gave her a get. *The head of that beit din refused the agunah's request, saying it "had no grounds" to be honored: the grandfather in question was a leading rabbi in the prestigious Mir yeshiva.* The women in both the Kin and Sompo cases remain agunot.[33]

We see rabbinic malevolence regarding iggun clearly in the postscript to the already egregious case of Tzviya Gorodetsky.

Once her marriage was annulled by Rabbi Daniel Sperber's court, Gorodetsky withdrew her request to the Chief Rabbinate court for a get, closing her file. This meant there were no longer grounds to keep her ex-husband in jail for get refusal, a situation in which she had no interest and sought to end, her freedom, not his incarceration, having been her goal. The Chief Rabbinate, however, incensed that an independent rabbinic court had done what it had not—freed her—rejected the annulment by Rabbi Sperber's court—*and sought to keep the man in jail*. It pursued, in the words of the Center for Women's Justice, "*a historically unprecedented criminal case against Meir [Gorodetsky and sought] to cement Tzviya's status as an agunah*" (my emphasis): that is, *to reinstate* her as an agunah—and restart the futile, decades-long power struggle between itself and this man, at her expense.[34] Who and what were to benefit from such action, had it succeeded? As is asked in any criminal case: Cui bono?

There have been other reported recent attempts by rabbinic authorities to reinstate freed agunot into iggun. In two cases of such power struggles involving an agunah (the second of which resulted in such reinstatement), the joust was not between a state-authorized court and an independent one, but between two courts of the same establishment, the Chief Rabbinate.

The "Agunah of Safed"

The first of such cases occurred in 2016 and became known as that of the "agunah of Safed."[35] It concerned a young woman whose husband was in a persistent vegetative state after a motorcycle accident. Seven years after she became an agunah, in a highly unusual action, the local Chief Rabbinate court in Safed, in 2014, enacted a *get zikui*, a divorce it issued on her husband's behalf. The halakhic grounds for this were that the husband, were he able, would wish to grant the get, since he could not fulfill the marital obligations he undertook at the time of the marriage; in acting on his behalf, the court was benefiting him, a halakhic option even without the recipient's consent. The Safed court cited its reliance on two of the ranking decisors of the last century, Rabbi Avraham Yeshaya Karelitz (the Hazon Ish) and Rabbi Tzvi Pesach Frank.[36]

Two years later, after vocal criticism by Aharon Leib Steinman, the senior-most non-Hasidic haredi rabbi, another such authority, Rabbi Haim Kanievsky, and the Sephardi chief rabbi, Yitzhak Yosef, the Supreme Rabbinical Court of Israel, that is, the Chief Rabbinate's superior division, challenged the Safed court's ruling and sought to have the woman's get voided through a petition filed before it by a third party— that is, filed neither by the husband, obviously, nor, of course, the agunah. The upshot of this action would be to return the woman to a state of iggun as permanent as that of her comatose husband.[37]

Batya Kahana Dror, then director of Mavoi Satum, who represented the woman in her original case to gain release, filed suit on her behalf before the Supreme Court of Israel. In a rare action—the court loathes involvement in cases concerning the religious establishment, given the latter's authorization to run a parallel legal system deciding personal status for Jewish citizens—the court ruled the attempted intervention of the Supreme Rabbinical Court invalid because of lack of standing and on other technical grounds, thereby sustaining the action of the Safed rabbinic court.[38] Although this woman's freedom was upheld in the end, the Chief Rabbinate's action added years of proceedings and anguish to her already long state of limbo, which began in her twenties and extended into her mid-thirties. Its action was invalidated only because of technicalities and because an agunah-advocacy organization with the means to do so—Kahana Dror's ability to argue a Supreme Court case—intervened at the highest legal level, hardly a normal set of circumstances other agunot could hope for. This agunah got "lucky."

The takeaway from this case alone is that in no construction of reality can the Israeli state rabbinate be deemed agunah-friendly. Moreover, *as Kahana Dror argued before the Supreme Court and the court's ruling noted, if the Supreme Rabbinical Court's action had been sustained, every get could be challenged post facto by third parties—and there would never be certainty that any marriage that ended in divorce was in fact terminated. The very term "divorce" would lose meaning. This is what the Chief Rabbinate sought to do—create a ceaseless stream of court actions for itself fueled by the creation of new agunot.*

It is important to note that, though the Safed court acted to free the agunah in this case, the rarity of its action was attested by the shock with which it was greeted by both rabbinic jurists and the media.[39] That court, moreover, for months refused to publish its *nimukim*, the halakhic grounds for its action,[40] *lest these be applied in other cases.* It did so only after its action and authority to take it had come under withering criticism and moves to overrule it. This behavior accords with that of Rabbis Moshe Feinstein and Mordechai Tendler in the United States, who also did not publicize rulings that freed agunot. The same happened in the case of Israeli get refuser Oded Guez, who, despite having his name and photo publicized on the internet, being excommunicated socially, fired from his job at Bar-Ilan University, pursued by Interpol, arrested in Belgium (for using a false passport), and extradited to Israel, continued to refuse to give his wife a get. She was finally freed in 2019—five years after seeking to divorce—only when a Chief Rabbinate court, in a very rare move, declared her marriage null.[41] That court, too, has refused to publish the grounds on which it annulled the marriage, *lest they be applied in other cases.*

The refusal of Chief Rabbinate courts to release the grounds on which they free agunot on the rare occasions they do so is a known problem. Rabbi David Golinkin, halakhic expert of the Masorti movement, and its Center for Women in Jewish Law have responded by publishing case studies, based on actual cases in Chief Rabbinate courts (identifying information of the principals withheld), in which they cite halakhic expedients and responsa of decisors that could be applied to free the agunot involved. The stated aim of doing this is "to pressure the rabbinical courts to publish their decisions in a timely and orderly fashion, much as civil court decisions are published, and to encourage rabbinical courts to use the halakhic tools . . . at their disposal . . . to free . . . agunot."[42] A most worthy goal, but the odds of these courts listening to anything emanating from the Masorti movement, however substantiated by halakhic rulings of decisors revered in Orthodoxy, are nil. As we have seen, the Orthodox establishment (in Israel, the Chief Rabbinate and haredi authorities; in the United States, the Rabbinical Council of America, Agudath Israel; in Britain, the chief rabbi) anathematizes even card-carrying Orthodox rabbis, like Rabbis Meir Simcha Feldblum, Eliezer Brekovits, Emanuel Rackman, Moshe Morgenstern, or Rabbi Daniel Sperber, who are halakhically assertive in this area, rejecting vehemently every effort to establish prevention of iggun or release of agunot as a halakhic norm. Proffered assistance is only relevant when the potential recipient wishes to solve, not perpetuate, a problem.

The Problem of Authority

In any of its variants, Orthodox Judaism—that is, the modern construction of traditional practice labeled with this or other terms (modern, haredi, ultra-Orthodox)—is an extremely hierarchical authority system based on acceptance of the binding authority of rabbis, past and (legitimate ones, in the respective judgments of Orthodoxy's various segments) present.[43] If anything, modern variants are more authoritarian than premodern traditionalism, with ultra-Orthodoxy having innovated a doctrine of infallibility for certain of their rabbinic authorities.[44] If we were to mark the defining line between any version of Orthodoxy and other forms of modern Judaism, and within Orthodoxy itself, it is the question of rabbinic authority.[45] Understanding this is critical to grasping why women's marital captivity has continued but also theoretically, at least, how it could be ended—if rabbis enjoying authoritative status used it to that end, as Bertha Pappenheim implored a century ago. That has not been the case nor, it is clear, will it be the case, notwithstanding a possible few, outlier, invariably persecuted exceptions.

Rabbis who apply halakhic methods to free agunot or are sympathetic to such action, as well as scholars of Orthodoxy, cite unwarranted and exaggerated halakhic "stringency and conservatism" and withholding regarding women's marital captivity and other halakhic issues.[46] Rabbi Professor Daniel Sperber speaks of a "dread of ruling" by decisors.[47] Rabbi Moshe Chigier cites "diffidence and hesitation" by Israeli rabbinic courts, which could issue compulsion orders to get-refusing husbands but rarely do.[48] Professor Tamar Ross notes "the sharply fundamentalist turn that Orthodox Judaism has taken since the nineteenth century in response to the shift from traditionalism to modernity [that] has served as a strong deterrent of [halakhic] change."[49] Rabbi Nathan Lopes Cardozo published a book of essays whose unifying theme is the argument that traditional halakhic behavior, as opposed to that manifested now, is creative and responsive to ethical demands, not rigidly technical or conservative; behavior that Rabbi Sperber calls the "over-codification of Halacha, a sort of pietistic OCD syndrome, which stifles the true spirit of Judaism."[50] Professor Lawrence Kaplan, rejecting the historically quite recent assertion of infallible haredi rabbinic pronouncement, describes the latter's purpose as "to suppress discussion by demanding an akedah [binding for sacrifice] of the intellect in which one submits to the superior wisdom of the 'great one.'"[51]

Clearly, the lack of centralized rabbinic leadership resolved to end iggun facilitates its perpetuation. But decentralization would seem to offer at least as much chance for resolution since independent authorities, one would think, can rule as they deem right, as some, albeit a tiny minority, have sometimes done. Theoretically, decentralization should create a "free market," with women able to choose the rabbinic courts that offered remedy. Of course, this assumes the existence of such courts and transparency about how all the courts operate.

Forthright rabbinic behavior to free agunot and end iggun, however, requires not only halakhic audacity and resolve but structural and financial independence. We have noted the perceived calumny in being labeled a *mekel*, a rabbi who rules "leniently" on cases of iggun. Fear of being labeled (tarred) as "Reform" or "Conservative/Masorti"—movements demonized in Orthodox and ultra-Orthodox circles, where the very terms are epithets—and extreme Orthodox fragility and sensitivity about approval impede not only action to free agunot but, as we have seen, even publicizing rulings when agunot are freed. Even so pedigreed an authority as Rabbi Mordechai Tendler cited fear of criticism by "powerful, entrenched forces"[52] as the reason he kept secret the occasions when he freed agunot. Difficult as it is to imagine that his grandfather, Rabbi Moshe Feinstein, whose halakhic authority was (and is) supreme in all sectors of Orthodoxy and among any who observe halakha, felt similar fear and therefore did not publish his rulings freeing agunot, that appears to be the case.[53] The case of the "Agunah of Safed" alone clearly illustrates that the system operates on intimidation, with knee-jerk, panicked reaction to criticism from "higher" authorities—with the jerking, invariably to the detriment of women. I know of no case where the opposite momentum operated: when decisors criticized other authorities for *not* releasing a woman from iggun, let alone for not using every means available to free agunot altogether and establishing a norm of release rather than captivity.

The authorities who have acted forthrightly to free agunot—Rabbis Morgenstern, Rackman, Sperber, and Simcha Krauss—are or were independent, not "establishment" rabbis. They did/do not earn their livings from rabbinic organizations or affiliated institutions, or were or are retired. This frees them from fear of denunciation, defamation, shunning, and financial consequences. Financial independence enables at least the possibility of halakhic independence.[54]

The failure of recognized authorities even to publicize when they free agunot perpetuates iggun as a social norm and its perception as an intractable problem, an inalterable fact of life, and an inevitable tragedy of women as a class subject to victimization rather than a solvable problem of Jewish society. Rabbinic courts that free agunot and make this known upend this circular, self-fulfilling behavior and make women's marital captivity a solvable problem.

The lack of determined leadership, unified or decentralized, concerning women's marital captivity, on the one hand, and the continued compliance of women and the community as a whole with the system as it is, on the other, guarantee its continuation. Only other methods, and different behavior, will yield different results.

Aranoff cites hundreds of women who "vote[d] with their feet" to accept remedies from the Morgenstern court during its short tenure. Clearly, more such courts, operating openly, would be a pivotal step in reducing the scope of the problem, and ending it.

The record does not make hope for such behavior realistic.

"Metahistorical Halakha" and Agunot

There is some indication that independent (as opposed to Chief Rabbinate) haredi rabbinic courts are more forthcoming in cases of agunot than are modern Orthodox ones.[55] Without exaggerating any such possible disparity, having seen the clear limits of any possibly more forthcoming policy from that quarter (e.g., the failure of eminent haredi decisors to publicize when they freed agunot, or the grounds on which they did so), it is important to consider the possibility that the peculiar (in all senses of that word) philosophical approach of the revered doyen of modern Orthodoxy, Rabbi Joseph B. Soloveitchik ("the Rav"), to halakha is responsible for even greater rigidity in this branch of Orthodoxy than in its more right-wing variants. The latter reject secular study, in particular, subjects like history and philosophy that affect values and modes of thinking. Soloveitchik, by contrast, earned a PhD in philosophy at Friedrich Wilhelm University in Berlin in 1932, writing his thesis on the epistemology and metaphysics of the neo-Kantian philosopher Hermann Cohen. He retained a lifelong interest in neo-Kantianism.[56]

Soloveitchik makes the remarkable claim that halakha, like the rules of mathematics, is "metahistorical." It is literally not a human endeavor, let alone a male one, influenced by or reflecting any historical or cultural circumstance, whether cultural, economic, political, or, needless to say, gendered. While circumstances may affect the halakhist's "soul," halakha itself is impervious to them, he claims. Notably, and I believe not coincidentally, Soloveitchik uses the case of the agunah to exemplify the utter divorce between contingent circumstances and halakha operating in its own impervious realm. Having made the argument for halakha as metahistorical, he writes: "For example, we always participated in the distress of the poor agunah," citing the Talmud's injunction to rabbis to exercise leniency in cases of iggun. "But when a rabbi sits and rules on the question of an agunah, he decides on this problem not pressured by feelings of sympathy, despite the fact that his mercy is aroused for this wretched woman, but based on the principles of close halakhic scrutiny. A critical, precise explanation alone determines his ruling." Soloveitchik compares this imperviousness to the immovable trajectory of a satellite that, once launched, follows its necessary path, which no change to the force that originally propelled it can alter.[57]

Soloveitchik applied his fundamental claim about halakha, in the specific instance with which he saw best to exemplify it, when he opposed Rabbi Rackman's court and its actions to free agunot. As reported by Rabbi Nathan Lopes Cardozo,

Rav Soloveitchik's famous argument with Rabbi Emanuel Rackman . . . is another example of the former's sometimes extreme halachic conservatism. In several places, the Talmud introduces a rule that states: *Tav lemeitav tan du mi-lemeitav armelu—It is better to live as two than to live alone*, which refers to the fact that a woman would prefer to marry almost any man rather than remain alone.

Rav Soloveitchik sees this as a "permanent ontological principle," which is beyond historical conditions, and that even in our day needs to be applied and cannot be changed. This principle operates under the assumption that even today's women prefer to stay in a marriage, no matter how unfortunate the circumstances. . . . *This means that a woman cannot claim that had she known what kind of person her husband is, she never would have married him* [my emphasis]. If she *could* make this claim [emphasis in the original], her marriage would be a "mistaken marriage," which would not even require a *get* . . . since the marriage took place on a false premise and the woman would never have agreed to it had she known. In that case, she was never considered lawfully married and could leave her partner without receiving a *get*. Since this obviously has enormous repercussions . . . it could help thousands of women. Rav Soloveitchik was not prepared to take that approach and thus blocked the possibility. . . .

Rabbi Rackman . . . strongly disagreed and claimed that a Talmudic presumption such as this depends on historical circumstances, as in the days of the Talmud when women had no option to live a normal life if they were not married . . . but none of this is true in modern times when women have great freedom and are able to take care of themselves, both financially and physically. If so, there would be good reason for a woman to claim that had she known her husband's true nature, she would never have married him and she would be able to leave her husband without the need for a *get*.[58]

In their disagreement about halakhic means to free agunot, Rabbi Soloveitchik said to Rabbi Rackman, "Rackman, you may be right and I may be wrong. You see Halacha historically and I see it metahistorically—" meaning operating outside human realities.[59] This assertion is the more remarkable given Soloveitchik's explicitly sociopolitical reason, cited above, for never granting a man's petition for a bigynous marriage using the dispensation of *heter meah rabbanim*—*in the United States, he specifies*, where this would encounter fierce criticism—clearly indicating that, in a different setting where such reaction would not be anticipated, he would so grant: social and historical contingencies clearly do operate in his halakhic rulings. In any case, according to this thinking, rabbis would/should dismiss even a million women saying, "I want a divorce," because, "ontologically," no woman wants a divorce. And men, of course, or at least some of them, know better than women what women want.[60]

One wonders how Soloveitchik came to privilege the Talmud's pronouncement about women preferring to stay in any marriage over being alone over its pronouncement that rabbis should rule leniently in cases of agunot. It is a strange assumption, since, of course, the Mishna (Ketubbot 7:10) states grounds on which women can petition for divorce and a husband is even forced to give it. Rabbenu Gershom's ordinance prohibiting divorce of a woman against her will also testifies to women who wished divorce. And then there is the mountain of halakhic rulings in cases where women not just sought but fought for divorce, the huge literature about "rebellious" women, and about women hiding and waiting out conditional divorces in order to force them to come into effect, and about women who acted aggressively to force halitsa. Perhaps

Soloveitchik privileged the assertion about women preferring to be in any marriage because this "ontologizes"—essentializes—women, while privileging the injunction for leniency in cases of agunot would ontologize and essentialize rabbis as liberators rather than captors.

Orthodox Despair

In *The Wed-Locked Agunot*, Aranoff and Haut conclude that "we . . . say to women, loud and clear, 'Stay away from Orthodox batei din [rabbinic courts].'" They articulate no alternative, however.

Summing up the work of decades, they admonish agunah-advocacy organizations and activists:

> We have done all that we can in this three-decades-long struggle. When we began, we thought that raising the awareness of the dimensions and severity of the agunah problem would spur [rabbis] to action. When we realized this was hopeless, we thought that mobilizing community pressure on the rabbis would bring change. That, too, we discovered, was a misconception. We did succeed in putting agunah [sic] on the Orthodox community's agenda. We believe our agunah advocacy deserves credit for the adoption of religious prenuptial agreements. . . . Though of limited value, these prenuptials are better than nothing. The marketing of these prenuptials as a . . . solution, however, deludes the community into thinking that agunah problem [sic] is solved, which, sadly, is untrue.[61]

Haut concludes a piece, published in 1994, with this searing indictment:

> As a student of Talmud, I know that if the ancient Rabbis were alive today they would never permit this injustice to continue. They would find, or create, halakhic solutions to this problem as they did with other problems. They found a way to free a non-Jewish slave who was only half-free, arguing that he must be free to marry and procreate, for that is God's will. Jewish women are as deserving of rabbinic compassion as were those half-enslaved Canaanites. Clearly, we are living in an era of unworthy rabbinic authorities. We should not abdicate the tradition we love because of their weakness.[62]

We hear a more recent expression, albeit far more muted, of defeat and retreat from agunah activism in the words of the Israeli halakhic pleader (*toenet*) Dr. Ayelet Segal, who "wanted to study Talmud and Halacha on a high level, and . . . to help people." Having served in the IDF as an officer responsible for soldiers' conditions and well-being, she chose to study "the laws of divorce and property laws pertaining to couples." Segal was one of the few in her all-women's class to pass the Chief Rabbinate "pleader" exams. But working in that role in Chief Rabbinate courts was demoralizing, she said. "In contrast to the IDF, where I felt that I could accomplish some good and justice would be done, in the [rabbinic] court system, I did not feel it to the same degree. Divorce proceedings do not always end quickly, and some of the courts don't act with enough determination and speed against get refusers."[63]

Segal left the Chief Rabbinate court system to teach Talmud to women.

Other Efforts and Expedients to Free Agunot

More recently than the efforts of Rabbis Rackman and Morgenstern, Rabbi Daniel Sperber, in Israel, and Rabbi Simcha Krauss, in the United States, have applied halakhic expedients to free agunot.[64] Methods include annulment of the marriage (*hafka'at kiddushin*) because of a technical flaw in the conduct of the ceremony (inadmissible witness; "acquisition" that was not unilateral by the husband; use of a ring for kiddushin that was not his property); and *get zikui*. Although *get zikui* was developed to give husbands an option against wives who refused divorce, Rabbi Moshe Antelman, of New York and then Israel, has applied it to free agunot.[65]

Rabbi Sperber, who has acted decisively in several highly publicized cases to free agunot, does not use the broader categories of *mekah ta'ut* that Rabbi Morgenstern employed.[66]

Widely and normally applied, this measure, as well as *get zikui*, would end iggun. Such application would mean confronting patriarchy's core assertion of male ownership and control of women's bodies and lives. It would mean male rabbis acting as deracinated rabbis and not as men. This has never happened, and won't. The closest we get to testing even the possibility of such positioning is seen in statements of the modern Orthodox Rabbi Yoel Bin-Nun in Israel. Responding to charges by Orthodox feminists that "rabbinic authorities . . . forbid them from . . . assuming certain halakhic practices simply out of the wish to delineate . . . differences between Orthodoxy and other denominations," Bin-Nun expressed readiness to consider such women in a new "category of *bnot horin* (independent women) to whom the traditional concept of 'woman' . . . does not apply" (yes, there would be "women" and "independent women"). However, Bin-Nun "*specifically exclude[d] the status of women in marriage*" *from this possible new category*, and does "not envisage the possibility . . . whereby the husband acquir[ing] exclusive right to [his wife's] sexual services [sic!], can be annulled" (my emphasis).[67] For all their differences, Bin-Nun and J. David Bleich both uphold the latter's identification of rabbinic marriage as the wife's conjugal servitude, a definition the Conservative rabbi and Talmud scholar Gail Labovitz, finds accurate. Rare agreement across ideological and denominational lines!

Deception and False Hope: Shaming as a "Solution"

Some agunah-advocacy organizations promote shaming as a tactic against get-refusing men. They publicize the names, photos, and whereabouts of certain get refusers—those who defy the rarely applied rabbinic-court directive to a husband to give a get (*hiyuv*), and—a crucial additional condition—to whose defiance the court has also formally applied the term *seruv*, "refusal," meaning "contempt of court." Only in such instances, that is, after lengthy, involved, and costly court processes, and with the permission of the rabbis involved, do agunah advocates picket the designated man's home or workplace, post notices with his photo about his get denial on social media, and pressure his community to deny him synagogue or other honors. This is the tactic that the American organization ORA authorizes, and that Israel's Chief Rabbinate has on rare occasions also employed.[68]

It is crucial, however, to emphasize that *seruv* is a rare action and that years or decades of get refusal and hearings elapse before a court even considers issuing the required prior order, a *hiyuv*, to a husband to give his wife a get.

An article in March 2021 in *The Jewish Voice*, a Brooklyn, New York–based newspaper voicing conservative religious positions, hailed a purportedly successful case in which a get refuser was arrested by New York City police for abusing a second wife—second, not sequentially but cumulatively—he had remarried bigynously while she remained captive. Under arrest, he finally gave his first wife a get, seventeen years after she sought it. The paper applauds another case in which a man freed his wife after nearly fourteen years of captivity; both releases occurred following such authorized shaming.[69] But organizations such as ORA, which works under the direction of the Beth Din of America, only take such actions in cases of *seruv*—that is, not when or because the man has refused his wife a get, but *because he has defied the rabbinic court*—that is the actionable offense—and with the rabbinic court's permission.

It is worth reading ORA's policy in the organization's own words and those of *The Jewish Voice* regarding these cases, reported with the headline "Brooklyn Man Finally Gives Wife Get After 17 Years":

> According to a web site named Ora [sic], other men have also been served with a *seruv* for a get but have not complied.
>
> Ora, however, follows the advice of leading and nationally recognized Poskim [decisors], according to the VIN [acronym for *Vos is Nayes*, an ultra-Orthodox newspaper] report.
>
> There is a debate among the Poskim regarding the parameters of what defines an improper get me'usa [forced, invalid get]. "Ora only publicizes the seruvim issued by the Beis Din [rabbinic court] and with their authorization to publicize it," explained Rabbi Yonatan Klayman, Director of Advocacy for Ora. . . . "Ora works closely with the Batei Dinim [rabbinic courts]. . . . The Beis Din generally authorizes publicizing a seruv when, in their view, it would be impossible to obtain [a get] otherwise," remarked Keshet Star, CEO of Ora.[70]

Picketing in front of a highly selected get refuser's home or office may offer dramatic, sensationalist, and self-promoting opportunities for activists to vent outrage and pose heroically—consider the hyped presentation in the *Jewish Voice* article—but is no solution to get abuse, much less iggun:

Commenting on the Hafif get, Rabbi Dr. *Noam Weinberg tweeted: BREAKING IN FLATBUSH: Jeff Hafif Gives Wife A Get After SEVEN-TEEN YEARS As Movement Grows To Pressure Husbands!!! Let's keep the pressure on and get these women the freedom they deserve! Who is next? @ RStomel @skjask.* (text bolded in the original)[71]

To suggest that shaming tactics, undertaken only after years of get refusal and rabbinic- court proceedings, including a court finally approving a specific shaming, are a solution to iggun insults intelligence and reality. It feeds the falsehood that rabbinic courts act swiftly or decisively on behalf of agunot, when even the few women freed after such publicity have lost irrecoverable years of their lives in captivity and untold sums in the struggle. Get refusers, as in the Kin, Sompo, and Guez cases, often relocate, leaving state or country in the rare event that rabbinic courts pressure them to give a get, much less order that they do so (*hiyuv get*), or still less, apply the term *seruv* to them. All this makes the already questionable efficacy of groups that condition shaming actions on rabbinic permission the more questionable, and the deception that such tactics are either systematic or broadly effective itself worthy of shame. Do rabbinic courts open their records, or the agunah-advocacy organizations that herald shaming of selective get abusers give verified statistics for the number of women freed through this tactic—and in particular, the percentage of cases resolved in this way—with which to measure the tactic's effectiveness? Of course not.

Scenes in front of get abusers' homes or places of work are as much about burnishing the image of rabbinic divorce courts and the agunah organizations that work with and for them as they are about any agunah. Such scenes present these systems as justice-affirming and effective when any such assertion defies reality, misleading the ignorant and leading them to harm, and perpetuating iggun.[72]

Shaming tactics under the control of the same rabbinic establishments that create and perpetuate iggun, targeting the end product of the system and its necessary and inevitable symptom, the abusive husband, rather than the root cause of the abuse, are part of managing Jewish marital captivity rather than ending it. Stating, as does ORA, that halakhic prenuptial agreements are the means for women "never [being] placed in this position again"[73] is a shockingly misleading claim.

"Sheer Chaos, Total Disregard for the Rule of Law" in Rabbinic Courts

To misogyny and abuse in the behavior of Israeli rabbinic courts, Susan Weiss and Netty Gross-Horowitz add documentation of utter professional failure: "sheer chaos . . . a Kafkaesque turmoil"; disorder, they write, that goes beyond the problem of rabbis not coming on time to hearings or the lack of clear and accurate protocols, or even the right to a "fair and public trial."

> What lies at the heart of this chaos is total disregard for the rule of law . . . and the right to a fair hearing and an impartial tribunal. . . . The rule of law means that law . . . cannot be vague, confusing, or arbitrary. . . . [But] not only do Israel's rabbinic courts deny principles of democracy, justice, equality, dignity, and human rights, they also deny those rights erratically, arbitrarily and capriciously. So while the argument can be made . . . that states should accommodate and allow for the self-governance of (or even joint governance with) "identity groups" like rabbinic courts run by Orthodox Jews . . . it cannot, we argue, turn a blind eye to unclear rules, arbitrarily imposed.
>
> The confusion that reigns in Israeli rabbinic courts is such that even a veteran divorce advocate, if asked on what grounds a rabbinic tribunal will order a husband to give a get, will . . . search for an answer. . . . Is adultery grounds? Domestic violence? How much violence? If there are grounds, what is the necessary burden of proof?[74]

The rule of law, argue Weiss and Gross-Horowitz, "is a check on the potentially unbridled and coercive power of . . . governmental bodies. Rabbinic judges . . . should not be allowed to do anything they want." But in Israel, they note, such judges do not pledge allegiance to "*the laws* of the State of Israel [but] only to 'the State of Israel.' . . . Rabbinic judges . . . do not pay even lip service to laws enacted by the Knesset" (emphasis in the original), including Israel's Basic Law on Human Dignity and

Liberty, which "recognizes the value of the human being, the sanctity of his [sic] life and being a free person."[75]

The rabbinic regime is a theocracy functioning within Israeli democracy—a parallel legal system to which all Jewish citizens are subject, forcing them into rabbinic courts about the most personal matters and for women, their very freedom. This includes not only women who marry in religious ceremonies but women who go abroad to marry and get caught in rabbinic courts when they seek divorce and to establish their marital status as "single."[76]

Weiss and Gross-Horowitz's book is the Israeli equivalent of Aranoff and Haut's on the situation in the United States. Both detail case after case of egregious rabbinic-court handling of women seeking divorce. Weiss and Gross-Horowitz address failure to enact rational, let alone just, handling of cases in the state-recognized-and-authorized rabbinic courts; Aranoff and Haut document this same failure in rabbinic courts lacking state recognition. Despite the vast difference in legal underpinnings, the respective rabbinic courts in these countries, in which, between them, 85 percent of the world's Jews live, share an abysmal record of dysfunction and obtuseness, abuse of power, wanton cruelty, political machinations, and rank misogyny, including active participation in get extortion of women, which, as we have seen, they deem an entirely reasonable and even self-evident course of action.[77] It is noteworthy that an account of the practices in Israeli rabbinic courts in divorce cases, published in 1995, describes administrative sloppiness and overall chaos, and arbitrariness and abuse in rulings, in terms no different than those in Weiss and Gross-Horowitz, published in 2013.[78]

An Absurd and Telling Afterword: The "Last Jew of Afghanistan" Is a Get Refuser

On August 29, 2021, as the last US troops were leaving Afghanistan and the country fell to the Taliban, the Jewish Telegraphic Agency (JTA) reported the following, as published in *The Times of Israel*:[79]

> JTA—Zebulon Simantov, Afghanistan's last Jew, has not left Kabul, despite the best efforts of some Jewish figures and organizations.

One of them was Moshe Margaretten, a US ultra-Orthodox fixer whose passion is bringing Jews out of danger.

Margaretten paid Moti Kahana, an Israeli-American businessman . . . to be a middleman and get Simantov out—but Kahana told Margaretten what many others had heard: Simantov was not leaving because of his long-standing refusal to grant his Israeli wife a "get." . . . Simantov feared facing Israel's legal system, which penalizes such a refusal.

But Kahana hatched another idea. The team that he sent into Kabul to extract Simantov learned that there were . . . women in danger of being targeted by the Taliban as they assumed . . . control of Afghanistan— among them members of the country's national women's soccer team. . . .

Was Margaretten interested in paying for their extraction?

"Absolutely," Margaretten said. "Give me 10 hours."

Within a day, Margaretten, who is based in Williamsburg, Brooklyn, had drummed up $80,000 from his ultra-Orthodox community. He wired the funds to Kahana's consultancy . . . and by Wednesday, Kahana was . . . coordinating the extraction of . . . 23 people. Margaretten said that the money would also assist the refugees after their departure.

. . . Margaretten was bemused by the trajectory of the week: a failed bid to persuade a recalcitrant husband to flee danger resulted in the *successful rescue of women from a repressive society.*

"He didn't give a get, a divorce, to his wife. She lives in Israel. And, because of that, he's scared to go to Israel," he said. "That's a very fun story." (my emphasis)

We may be forgiven for failing to see the "fun" in this story. The last Jew in Afghanistan, a get refuser: What are the odds? How much iggun flies under the radar, unreported, unknown to most, until some circumstance brings it to light—or never does, the captive woman, like this man's wife, bearing her plight on her own? And on the other hand, here was this get refuser, with so many options! He refuses extraordinary assistance marshaled to extricate him from Afghanistan because he fears that in Israel, where not only his chained wife but his five siblings and two daughters live, his get refusal might ("would," the reports erroneously said) mean legal consequences. Having refused his wife a get for twenty years, he exercised free choice to remain in Afghanistan while continuing to deny her freedom, enjoying the male privilege of ownership of a woman's liberty, aligning him well with his country's new rulers. All this, enabled and abetted by the halakhic system and Jewish charity.

Ultra-Orthodox men raise a huge sum to rescue Afghani women, but neither they nor the reporters who write the story see any irony, much less anything amiss, in the abject failure of such saviors to do anything to free agunot in their own society.

Simantov eventually was brought out of Afghanistan to Israel and, after extraordinary publicity to his story, gave his wife a get. The reporting about this case overwhelmingly focused on the man and his traditional behavior—his koshering of chickens, tearful visits to the graves of his family—with his long-standing marital abuse a "bemused" "fun" side note. (" 'I am very eager to travel to Israel and see lots of people there,' Simantov told the [Israeli] Kan public broadcaster last month.") The article about this carried the shocking, trivializing byline, "Simantov mazal tov."[80] This man's threatened captivity in Taliban Afghanistan was a deadly serious matter calling for urgent intervention; his wife's captivity in iggun, the occasion for jokes.

Of course, koshering chickens, visiting family graves, and chaining wives are all part of traditional Jewish male behavior, so it makes sense that the reporting about this man portrays him as a good, if eccentric, Jew ("Jew," of course, means male; we do not hear this designation about his chained wife). Note, too, how both the article about the man's refusal to leave Afghanistan and the one about his arrival in Israel say that Simantov had refused to leave Afghanistan for Israel "in order to avoid dealing with his divorce and with [Israeli] rabbinic authorities, who sanction those who do not grant a Jewish divorce . . . because Israel's legal system . . . penalizes such a refusal." If only these statements reflected reality.

Would that we had reporting about the last agunah of Afghanistan— and the rest of the world.[81]

PART THREE

Denying Iggun a Future

13

Thinking outside the Chains to End Jewish Marital Captivity

This book has distinguished between, on the one hand, managing Jewish marital captivity with policies based on the circular understanding that iggun is ineradicable and that, intentionally or not, perpetuate iggun, and on the other, ending it. We turn now to strategy and tactics to end this abuse.

Choice: Not Simple, but Assisted

We have emphasized the element of choice in modern halakhic life, which distinguishes it fundamentally from premodern Jewish life. The obvious question is why any contemporary women with a choice—certainly, Jews outside of the state of Israel—would subject themselves to a system that denies women's basic human rights and is blatantly abusive: why any woman with choice would consent to remain captive when she could "just" walk away.

The question makes logical sense, but this is about life, not logic. The question, and in particular, the "just" adverb commonly attached to it, disregards profound emotional, social, and material realities: the impact of family, of formal and informal education, of socialization—of lived lives. To say to halakhically observant agunot, "Why don't you just leave?"—is to be wholly out of touch with the ties that bind women in any variant of traditional observance. It is to disregard connection to traditions many cherish, to core memories, associations, and identities. Failing to appreciate that aspects of Orthodox life satisfy many women, including women not born into it who choose it, and posing what is not really a question but a demand—"Why don't they just leave?"—is unfair and unproductive.[1]

Such a demand overlooks the crisis that occurs when a woman's marital life is in conflict with belief in the authority of halakha as adjudicated by a venerated entity called "the rabbis," whose authority derives from Divine Revelation to Moses on Sinai. That authority governs all aspects of daily life, from what and how one eats, to how one dresses and speaks, and certainly, the supremely sensitive, taboo-laden areas of marriage and divorce.

"Orthodoxy" does not mean belief in God but rather belief in and acceptance of the authority of the rabbis, past and (Orthodox) present. Even when individual rabbis prove wanting, even very wanting, the fault is understood to be individual and aberrant, not systemic and normal. An entire edifice of belief and meaning and a way of life are threatened by any suggestion that halakhic marriage and divorce are androcentric, patriarchal, and misogynistic.

Women who know no life outside of Orthodoxy have formal choice to leave, but that choice is often theoretical only. To disavow the authority of halakha in the most fraught area of human and Jewish taboo—regarding gender (women's "proper" "character" and roles) and sex—has tremendous emotional and material consequences. It means being stigmatized as an "adulteress" and one's children and even children's off-spring being stigmatized as "mamzerot/im"—and quite possibly, seeing oneself, and them, as such. It is to risk alienation from parents, children, siblings, friends, and community; from the synagogue one has prayed in, the schools one has attended and those one's children attend and from which they will be expelled, shunned by erstwhile friends. It is to risk alienation from one's neighborhood, job, and livelihood. This is not a decision about a law or a set of them but about one's entire life and sense of self, everything one has been taught, believed, lived, and for many, loved, and about serious, devastating consequences. I know of no study of agunot, specifically, who have left the system to free themselves, but memoirs of Orthodox women and men who have left that world for any reason illustrate the catastrophic price, emotional, familial, legal, and financial, such people regularly pay, including loss of custody and even visitation with their children.[2]

To posit an option that Orthodox women have to "just" depart from the requirement of a get is effectively to blame the victims rather than to appreciate, as with other situations of abuse, women's complex imbrication with the world in which they were raised or that they joined, and to provide means that enable exercise of real choice. That includes the choice to remain traditionally observant while rejecting victimization as agunot. Posing a "choice" for agunot to "just leave" is the equivalent of get extortion, saying, "Want freedom? Pay for it." Traditionally observant women are as entitled to freedom of religious conscience and choice as anyone else and should not be confronted with a choice of ceasing to be who they are as the price of freedom from dead marriages and get abuse.[3]

This same holds for women who are not Orthodox or even consistently religiously observant but who see traditional marriage and divorce rituals as "authentic" and anything else as invalid or ineffective; or who have an emotional connection to traditional rituals—people I call "tradition-friendly." They, too, are not free to simply walk away from such practices. They have internalized these from family and the larger culture as the only ones possessing ritual efficacy—the power to effect status change—from single to married and married to divorced. Such Jews are also vulnerable to social stigmatization, of which "adulteress" and "mamzer/a," in Israel, also have serious consequences under civil law. "Tradition-friendly" attitudes are particularly pronounced in Israel, given official recognition and funding of Orthodoxy and the suppression and demonization of other forms of Jewish religious expression precisely as inauthentic and illegitimate. This stance is well expressed in the behavior of the agunah in Chaim Grade's novel by that name, discussed above. Despite not considering herself "religious," and her certainty that her husband had been killed along with the rest of his army unit in World War I, remarriage when a suitor appeared was inconceivable to her without rabbinic sanction. Grade's agunah lived in Vilna, whose culture was suffused with traditional Jewish norms, as is that of contemporary Israel.

On the other hand, neither women of any Orthodox variant, nor tradition-friendly women, nor the vast majority of any Jewish women know the truth about halakhic marriage and its consequences. To take the first group: in a video that the Israeli organization Chochmat Nashim produced in 2021, entitled "No More Sacrificing Women on the Altar of Agunah" (sic), several Orthodox agunot in the United States describe their situations. One, Chaya, was married for five years and had waited nearly half that amount of time for a get at the time the video was made. In it, she says she called "rav" (rabbi) after rav, one of whom explained to her, "You are an agunah." To which she responded, "OK, so what do I do? *I don't know halakha.* Can you please explain to me what the steps are, what do I do about it?" To which the rabbi responded, "I don't know. You're stuck. This may never end" (my emphasis). Not one agunah interviewed in this video had any idea to begin with of what she was facing, let alone that the problem originated not with a bad husband but with her wedding—with any halakhic wedding.[4] If this is not *mekah ta'ut*—an agreement made on the basis of incomplete or deceptive information that would have led the bride to reject the marriage had she known of it, and that is grounds for annulling the marriage without need of a get—nothing is. And it describes the reality of the vast majority of women who marry via kinyan and kiddushin—that is, in ceremonies using traditional language—in whatever kind of ceremony they have. As Joseph Turow of the University of Pennsylvania's Annenberg School for Communication says, "You can't really consent to something unless you understand it."[5]

Even women who do "know halakha," in the words of Professor Ilana M. Blumberg about herself, who "have had an outstanding education, both religious and secular," and are even professionals who "know how to speak for" themselves, do not know what dehumanizing objectification transpires routinely in rabbinic divorce courts, nor the fundamental reason that women are abused there. In a detailed account in *Haaretz* in August 2023, Blumberg described her experience in her agreed divorce from her husband in a Chief Rabbinate court.[6] She expresses shock at the crass, crude behavior of the officiating rabbi who, despite the most perfunctory contact with them, admonished her and her husband to reconcile; behavior, she later learned, that is his standard practice in the more than a thousand divorce cases he handles yearly. Moreover, the rabbi reminded her husband repeatedly of his right to withhold a get from her, exhorting him, "You don't have to give a get." Her husband could, indeed was being openly invited to force Blumberg to remain married to him against her will, to activate that privilege right there in the court, with its help. Blumberg wonders about the impersonality of the divorce ritual, about three men—"rabbis? employed witnesses?"— who, per halakhic mandate, witnessed her staged, passive receipt of the get document (the woman is not allowed to *take* it but must only *receive* it, dropped into her cupped hands by her husband)—her final wifely act as the receiving vessel of her husband's actions, closing the circle with which the marriage began. She quotes the disgusted remark the just-divorced husband of another couple emits as he exits his proceedings, discarding the male head covering he has been required to don— "Ridiculous ceremony"—and comments that if only the rabbinic court had bothered to explain the rituals involved, they would have been—less offensive? Inoffensive? And she concludes, regarding the statement on the website of a rabbinic divorce court in Chicago that proceedings there are handled sensitively, that such professed treatment develops because of the element of choice in the United States, "where religious divorce is optional," as opposed to the situation in Israel, where it is the only legal possibility for Jewish citizens. In this account, the problem is a matter of more consumer-friendly, personal handling and explanation—a kinder, gentler patriarchy, a toned-down misogyny. Blumberg speaks of her former husband and herself filing complaints about their experience. To whom? To the same entity, accountable to no one, that operates these courts?

A bride whose remarks perfectly express "tradition-friendly" thinking is quoted on Mavoi Satum's website:

> My partner opposed the Chief Rabbinate's involvement in the process, due to a combination of ideological gaps and jarring encounters with the rabbinate in the past. I am secular (agnostic, not an atheist) . . . but I have *a warm place in my heart for religion due to a close connection with my grandfather who was religious. From an emotional point of view, I am less attached to the postmodern alternatives of the institution of marriage even though they are not inappropriate in my eyes. For me there is added value to a wedding insofar as it reflects its original content, i.e. the religious content.* . . . So we were religiously married by an Orthodox rabbi at a private wedding. (my emphasis)

This woman, and many like her, will not have a Chief Rabbinate rabbi officiate at her wedding, in her case because of her partner's bad experience. She is not religious but also not antireligious; she has positive emotions about "religion," meaning something she associates with a beloved grandfather, who will not be present physically at the ceremony but *will be part of it for her through her enacting his tradition there.* Intellectually, she has no objection to "postmodern" wedding ceremonies but these don't carry emotional resonance for her. She wants the traditional ceremony, just in ways that fit her and her partner's taste. She obviously has no idea what kinyan and kiddushin mean, in the moment of enactment or in case of desired divorce.

Tradition-friendly and Orthodox women alike have no simple choice to "just" leave an abusive system. Positing such a choice assumes that they somehow know and grasp all this book has presented—that marital captivity is not an individual misfortune that befalls the unlucky but a necessary and inevitable outcome of marriage *kedat moshe ve'yisrael*—"according to the law of Moses and Israel," in the words of the traditional rabbinic marriage formula. They do not know that marrying in that way makes every woman an agunah-in-waiting. They do not know that, should they wish to divorce and their husbands refuse to give them a get, they will not find swift or even rational justice in rabbinic courts but will be subjected to the abuse detailed in this book and in those of Aranoff and Haut, and Weiss and Gross-Horowitz; documented on the websites of ORA, JOFA, Mavoi Satum, and the Center for Women's Justice and in the latter's podcasts by Rivka Lubitch and Nitzan Caspi Shiloni;[7] publicized on the Facebook pages of Flatbush Girl and Unchain My Heart; and available abundantly through a search of the word "agunah."

Women do not know that the problem of iggun is not personal but political, not individual but systemic. While reports of egregious agunah cases make it into the news regularly, *this news is not absorbed as knowledge that women as a group possess about women as a group.* Each victim falls into iggun individually, or so she thinks. The problem is lack of understanding that the problem is systemic in nature, and that its solution therefore lies in systemic, organized remedies.

Whatever some may know about this issue, especially from agunah-advocacy organizations, they do not know that the system will not, cannot cease being patriarchal, androcentric, misogynistic, and abusive, or deliver results other than those it delivers. They do not know that the system needs this issue and, under all foreseeable conditions, whether state-authorized in Israel or independent elsewhere, will not end it. On the contrary, the abuse worsens, with extravagant measures to restore to captivity women who had managed to escape it, after years or in some cases decades of efforts, and then only after potent outside intervention which, by definition, is exceptional. Two such cases are those of "the agunah from Safed" and Tzviya Gorodetsky, both of whose freedom the Chief Rabbinate sought to revoke. When no extraordinary intervention materializes, rabbinic efforts to return freed agunot to captivity succeed.

The failure of rabbinic courts in both the United States and Israel to publicize, much less promote, the grounds on which they have freed agunot on the rare occasions they do so shows that the goal is perpetuating iggun. Nor is such behavior confined to courts in these two countries. We have noted British rabbinic judge Jonathan Hool's advice to a get refuser against giving a get when the man said he would do so rather than face penalties under the country's Domestic Abuse Act. Hool advised this, he said, because such a get would "be" (that is, some rabbi would deem it) "coerced," hence, invalid.[8] According to this perverse logic, this man (or any man and all men) would be doing his wife/their wives a favor to withhold a get, given the threat of rabbinic action that would damn the freed women as adulteresses and any future children of theirs, mamzerot/im. Of course, such advice, which leaves women only the alternatives of marital captivity and get extortion, or stigmatization, serves get extortion. The clear message: under no circumstances is marital captivity to end. The supposedly petrified rabbinic system will spring to life at the prospect of means to end iggun.

Respecting the Difficulty: Other Impediments

Keeping Agunot in Iggun: The Mamzer Threat; the "House of Cards, It's All Dominoes" Lie

Halakha defines mamzerot/im as Jews born of illicit unions, one of which is that of a married woman with a man other than her husband. Their status more resembles that of Dalits, "untouchables," in India than that of people once called "illegitimate" or "bastards" in Western discourse. They and their offspring are barred from marrying any Jew but another mamzer/a or a Jew by Choice. Israel's Chief Rabbinate keeps actual "mamzer" lists and bars anyone on them from state-enacted marriage. It also enforces other, civil disabilities on people to whom it affixes this label. The Chief Rabbinate ascribes paternity of a child born three hundred days—ten months—after a divorce to the divorced husband, regardless of whether the couple had intercourse since the divorce and in defiance, of course, of the biology of human gestation. The stated rationale for this policy is prevention of the child being labeled a mamzer/a—by this same establishment. The result is ascription of paternity to a man who wants nothing to do with the child, does not give child support, and is not involved in the child's schooling or health, while denying the child's biological father any paternal rights or obligations in these matters. Should the biological father wish such involvement, he has no legal right to it or to any records or decisions about it. This situation victimizes children and their mothers, who are left in unsupported single parenthood.

The abuse that is "mamzerut" is inherently and inseparably part of the abuse that is iggun. The threat of *mimzur*—of labeling a child a mamzer/a—operates intentionally to prevent new relationships by women unable to obtain gittin. Some such agunot have had abortions of pregnancies they otherwise desired, for fear of the child's being abused as a mamzer/a.[9] The threat of having one's children stigmatized and, in Israel, burdened with onerous civil consequences keeps agunot chained to rabbinic courts that collude with get withholding and extortion. This fear and threat factored in the split of Rivka Haut and Susan Aranoff over the Morgenstern beit din, which offered the most serious prospect of ending iggun ever to manifest within Orthodoxy.

Iggun will only end when people cease treating "mamzerut" as an objectively existing state and recognize it for what it is: as a created social condition that abuses women and children in the service of iggun. There have been attempts to abolish mamzerut through halakhic means. Rabbi Meir Simcha Feldblum's alternative to kinyan and kiddushin was one. Currently, an effort to that end is underway by a group led by rabbinic pleader Rivka Lubitch of the Center for Women's Justice in Jerusalem. She has amassed abundant information about the abuses suffered by those labeled mamzer/a/ot/im, and about halakhic approaches to terminating the term's credibility and social application.[10]

There is no overstating the power of this social stigma in keeping women, including non-Orthodox Israeli women, in marital captivity. Agunah advocates refer in terrified language to the consequence of *mimzur* should women be freed in ways rabbis or "the community" reject. I have encountered this reaction many times when I have said that iggun will only end when a critical mass of women act to liberate themselves: insist that their marriages be ended swiftly and without extortion by whichever halakhic method is applicable, or else they will walk and enact an end to their marriages themselves. "Yes," I hear, "iggun is a tragedy, but it will be compounded (note the passive tense) if the woman goes on with her life without (the right) rabbinic-court authorization, is labeled (passive tense) an adulteress, and children of another relationship 'are' mamzerot/im." Such speech treats mamzerut as if it were an objectively occurring condition rather than a literally man-made and adjudicated category,[11] dependent on the collaboration of acquiescing communities for its credibility and social force.

Mamzerut is not the question. *Mimzur*—the action of labeling someone a mamzer/a, and then acting on this stigmatization, reifying it in social and communal behavior, is. When we treat this category as an action, requiring communal collusion for social credibility and force, we see how to end it.

This goes to the heart of observant women's beliefs, lifestyle, memories, family ties, and identities, to which fraught subject we now turn.

What if One Is Orthodox or "Traditional," Fears the Stigmas "Adulteress" and "Mamzer/a," and Perhaps Even Holds Stigmatized Beliefs Herself?

There is no minimizing the dilemma, anguish, and fear that women, whether Orthodox or "tradition-friendly," can feel at the prospect of defying taboo-laden norms about marriage and divorce, which necessarily also means a break with rabbinic authority seen as inviolate, or at least, as authoritative and "authentic." That was the nature of authority I realized I was rejecting in my own early-adult experience, described in the preface to this book. I do not claim that my experience speaks for anyone else. I can say that I know the fears entailed in such rejection and very much respect the difficulty. Ultimately, I decided that what I had been taught—that traditional observance is all a "house of cards," a "line of dominoes," and that if you reject any piece of "it," "it" all falls—was not true. Or, more accurately, that it would be true only if I acquiesced in that pronouncement. If I did not wish to lose traditional Sabbath observance, I would not. So *shabbes* as I had always known it and other traditional observance stayed, if larger understandings necessarily changed as I transitioned from an assumed Orthodoxy and an uninformed fear of and hostility to other forms of committed Jewish religious life, to observance in which feminism and other values I learned in new contexts informed my life and practice. The deeply thoughtful and dedicated fellow travelers in my quest, whom I found in West Mount Airy, Philadelphia, Palo Alto, California, Cleveland Heights, Ohio, and Jerusalem, immeasurably enriched me and enabled me to make my Jewish self, woman and Jew, whole. But all this was far from a simple or straight path and I am the last person to understate the difficulties.

Much had to shift and it was not at all clear how to navigate that transition. In stark contrast to Orthodoxy, nothing was *charted*, and that is very frightening when one's identity and daily behavior were previously very charted, and in that sense if not others, safe. That is, to say the least, a challenging path, while continued Orthodoxy or nonideological, conventional adherence to established norms ("tradition-friendliness"), or a combination of both, is the opposite: one follows what authoritative others decree and is the social norm, and is spared ambiguity, internal conflict, and, above all, decision-making, once the decision to cede control of decisions to others is made, or left unchallenged. About myself, I knew that I had to proceed because no other option was livable.

I am saying that choice of this kind is a real, if not a simple, option. And that the alternative to something wrong is not an unrecognizable life and chasmic loss—unless we allow that or allow others to impose it on us. We can choose otherwise. I say, with my dear friend, Rivka Haut, z"l, when she spoke of unworthy rabbinic authorities, "We should not abdicate the tradition we love because of their weakness."

While there is no "simply" walking away from the system as it now operates, there can and I believe, must be an assisted ability of women to turn away from it when the alternative is marital captivity and associated abuses extending even to unborn children. Turn away, not at the cost of their lived lives but in order to go on with their lives as they choose to live them. The task that lies before women is complex and difficult in every sense, cultural, religious, and familial; psychological, communal, legal, and financial. But women engaging that task, not alone and individually but with systematic communal support, is the only way that Jewish marital captivity will cease and captive women will be freed.

Corrupt, abusive systems rely on ignorance and intimidation. It is up to those who wish to see abuse end to counter ignorance and deception with full and honest information to give the needed help for people to transform information into knowledge;[12] and to provide systematic, effective help to agunot so that they have real alternatives to captivity and not the engineered, abusive "options" that enablers of the current system construct.

Two elements are necessary for iggun to end and agunot to be freed.

The first is clear understanding that *revah* and *hatsala*, "relief and deliverance,"[13] from iggun will only come from women, with systematic, communal support. Here, the historical record provides critical lessons. Premodern, entirely traditional women acted resolutely, forthrightly, creatively, and transgressively to protect themselves in marriage and divorce. They did this as good Jews and members of their communities, supported and facilitated by female and male kin, including members of rabbinic families. These women did not ask permission. They did not supplicate. They did not cede decision-making over their own lives to anyone. They did not accept a sacrificial "fate" on the altar of purported fealty to a system or a community but saw themselves as rightful consumers in that system, with rights to their own lives, all of which was not a betrayal of Jewishly lived life but fulfillment of it. All this was—and is—traditional Jewish behavior.

The second necessary element is systematic and effective communal support.

The Community Paradigm

In order for iggun to end and agunot to be freed, there must be an understanding that the community as a whole has a vital interest coinciding with that of women who, though half of the Jewish people, are a class subject to marital captivity and extortion for their freedom; that marital captivity is a Jewish problem—not an Orthodox, or an Israeli problem, or a problem of "the poor, wretched, tragedy-struck agunot," a class of Othered victims, but of Jewish society, which has tolerated this abuse and must now see to its end.

These understandings, enacted through concrete deeds, are necessary so that women who wish to end their marriages will not be faced with the "choice" of divorcing themselves from the rest of Jewish life as they wish to know it, if they do not get swift, unextorted relief when they seek divorce—which we know is not the case now nor likely to be the case in any foreseeable future. That posited choice, in fact, the threat—stay in marital captivity or lose the rest of your lived life—is meant to keep women compliant with marital captivity and today, it succeeds. The only way to actualize the same right of Jewish women to religious and cultural conscience that Jews overwhelmingly define as a fundamental human right is to give women the means truly to make a choice to exit iggun: one that does not tell them to do this at the cost of the rest of their lived lives and other severe punishment.

Petitioning, pleading for rabbinic action regarding iggun demeans the petitioners and empowers anew those who keep the chains on, reminding them of their authority and power and reifying it with each petition from women, who signal their vulnerability and dependence thereby. Abusive individuals and systems feed off signals of vulnerability and dependence. Sending them perpetuates iggun. This means a very different approach than agunah-advocacy organizations pursue.

A comprehensive, communal initiative to end iggun and free agunot requires, first, systematic dissemination of full and honest information about iggun, its origins and ongoing perpetuation, and its systematic nature, intended for the public. This requires professional construction and maintenance of a dedicated website with such information, that is, a "passive" source, available to those who seek it. But there must also be "active" outreach with this information, directed by professionals expert in the use of social media modalities to seek and reach audiences. Materials can be in English, Hebrew, and Yiddish to start but must also be available in other languages.

A communal approach to end iggun and free agunot means support services staffed by social workers trained about this issue, who assist agunot in processing their situations and determining their options, with professional counseling for their children and other family members as well. Such support offers rabbinic services to help agunot process any religious crisis they may be experiencing and help them to navigate leaving captivity but not Jewish life as they wish to live it—to help women see that these issues are separable, and that packaging them as inseparable is part of the abuse that keeps the chains on.

A communal approach to ending iggun provides legal services, free or scaled to means, and in particular, expert help when women are threatened with loss of custody of their children; when communal and, in Israel, state resources are brought to bear against captive women in custody suits, or against them or their children because of "mamzer" regulations.[14] It provides employment, career, and financial counseling; free or subsidized housing so that women who need to leave their homes have decent housing while they work out their lives; and relocation help for women who need that. Isolation—agunot experiencing their situation individually—is one of the most devastating and crippling realities of the current situation and a potent engine of its continuation. Professionally organized support groups connecting agunot with one another could be one of the most effective tools the communal initiative offers. All these efforts, working synergistically, create the conditions for true choice for women in marital captivity, as well as the means to cease the ongoing creation of iggun and agunot.

Implementing such organized, comprehensive help might be possible through existing Jewish women's organizations. But the project to free agunot and end iggun must be a specific, dedicated effort, given the specific challenges and needs of agunot. There is a special "agunah unit" in the Chief Rabbinate, an arm of, by, and for that establishment, supported by public funds. Jewish women deserve a real "agunah unit" in a consumer-oriented, communally funded, comprehensive effort dedicated to freeing agunot and ending iggun.

Unlike organizations, like Footsteps in the United States, or Leshinui/Out for a Change, or Israel Hillel in Israel, which assist haredi women and men wishing to leave religious observance, the goal of the agunah initiative must be to support women in the ability to leave get abuse and construct healthy, flourishing new lives—to enable *that* departure—while respecting and supporting their right to remain religious, if they so wish, however they define this. More pertinent models are the Jerusalem Open House, and the Bat Kol and Eshel organizations for LGBTQ Jews who are and wish to remain Orthodox.[15]

Iggun is a systematic Jewish problem. Only a systematic, woman-centered, agunah-centered, Jewish effort will end it. Since the problem transcends national boundaries and different civil legal systems, the communal initiative to end iggun must also be transnational and metadenominational, with active collaboration across Jewish communities, Diaspora and Israeli.

Iggun: Orthodox or Jewish Problem?

What call does women's marital captivity have on Jews outside of Orthodoxy or Israel?

Al ta'amod al dam re'ekha, the Torah (Leviticus 19:16) enjoins: Do not stand by as the blood of your companion is shed. A triumphalist stance about iggun, dismissing it as an Orthodox problem, is unworthy of communal sensibilities and responsibility. It is not even in the self-interest of those outside of Orthodoxy, whether they affiliate with other denominations or with none, or live outside of Israel, since people move ideologically and geographically and can find themselves or loved ones in a very different situation.[16] *Tikkun olam*, "repairing the world," is a shared value of Jews across denominations and with no denominational affiliation.[17] Marital captivity is an insidious abuse within our gates; as Netty C. Gross put it decades ago, "A horror story—ours."[18] We must recognize and act on it as a Jewish problem, whose resolution respects the religious beliefs, practices, and sensibilities of agunot, whatever these may be. Marital captivity, not religion or religious observance, is the target. Religious or political triumphalism—a version of the political exploitation of iggun in power struggles between denominations and within Orthodoxy, at women's expense as we have examined, is no model for ending iggun. We need to think outside such chains about Jewish community, broadly construed.

This point goes all the more for Jewish women. Whatever our differences, we share the predicament and challenge of Otherness in Jewish tradition, in which we are both insiders and outsiders. We have different ways of addressing that challenge but its dialectics and imperatives are our shared inheritance as Jews and women. That is our covenant, with this tradition and with one another.

We must engage this issue on the communal and intercommunal levels because if we do not, women's marital captivity will continue. And there will be no blaming it on bad husbands or bad rabbis.

Ending the Problem rather than Managing It

Ideally, we would see rabbinic courts act to free all agunot, using established halakhic methods. If it were clear that a husband's get refusal would be overridden swiftly by rabbinic courts without get extortion, get refusal would cease. But no such action is forthcoming by any rabbinic establishment, independent or Jewish-state-recognized. Iggun continues because there is powerful incentive for its continuation and no perceived benefit in ending it on the part of those who could do so. There are no consequences (for them) in perpetuating women's marital captivity and substantial interest, financial and political, in its continuation. Consequently, appeals to any variant of this system to act are not only futile but infuse the system with renewed legitimacy and vitality.

Ideally, agunah-advocacy organizations would focus on educating about kinyan and kiddushin as the source of iggun, about alternatives to them, and about the realities of prenups and their limits, rather than present these, much less postnups, as a solution ("a world without agunot," Mavoi Satum states about prenups). Ideally, they would educate about the range of halakhic alternatives to end dead marriages and would support and promote any rabbinic courts that use them, rather than affiliating with or being beholden to one rabbinic court or establishment. Ideally, they would cease appealing to and empowering anew with each such appeal the same systems that cause and perpetuate iggun. In short, they would shift from seeking to manage iggun—settling, as one activist openly puts it, for "fewer agunot"—to policies that end it.[19] This would mean operating independently, as consumer advocates for women. But this, too, is not to be expected. While collaboration would be ideal and some tactics can overlap—sending agunot to any rabbinic court likely to free them without extortion, if such exist—collaboration of agunah-advocacy organizations with the effort to end, rather than continue to manage, iggun is not to be expected.

Collusion with iggun from an unexpected source must also end. The Reform movement must recognize the problem of get-refusing men using its services for marriage and urge its rabbis to require proof from any couple or individual approaching them for marriage that any prior Jewish marriage has been ended with a get to the wife who wishes one, with the facts verified independently. Reform rabbis must not inadvertently participate in marital abuse by conducting the marriage of a man who has refused a get or is extorting for one. No rationalization, including the movement's position that civil divorce ends rabbinically enacted marriage, justifies such collusion; no body has the right to impose its ideology on unaffiliated others, in this case women whose position and sensibilities have not even been ascertained. The movement's own primacy on individual religious conscience mandates that its representatives ascertain and respect the woman's position about this. Get refusers who seek marriage through Reform auspices in order to evade pressure to give their wives a get express contempt for that movement, as well as their wives, using the movement to that abusive end. Reform rabbis need to think outside the chains about this, too.

Since Jewish marriage does not require rabbinic officiation, anyone conducting a Jewish marriage must make the same inquiry and condition. That will only happen if we so publicize the realities that no one remains ignorant of them, nor about behavior that, however unintended, colludes with marriage abuse.

Alternatives to Kinyan and Kiddushin

Since iggun originates in the husband's acquisition and sexual sanctification (kinyan and kiddushin) of the bride as the means of effecting marriage, preventing iggun necessarily involves other methods.[20] Here are two options, based on other aspects of rabbinic law. Others exist, and of course can be developed.

In her book *Engendering Judaism*, Rabbi Rachel Adler proposes an alternative based on halakhic partnership law, which treats both parties to the marriage as equals. Rabbinic partnership law, which is written, like all of halakha, by men, but unlike halakha regarding women, is intended for men, protects the rights and interests of both parties to the agreement equally, precisely what halakhic marriage does not do.[21]

In this ritual, the couple creates a partnership, into which both invest with a symbolic object (the ring in halakhic marriage is explicitly also symbolic, of nominal monetary value). Dissolution, should divorce be desired, would come from dissolving the partnership, which, like any partnership, can only continue with the active consent of both parties and ends if either party withdraws from it.

Dr. Tzemah Yoreh has proposed using the rabbinic laws of vows (*nedarim*) to establish marriage, and nullification of vows (*hatarat nedarim*) to end it.[22] Unlike marriage vows in other traditions, halakhic vows are not declarations of emotion and intent but legal instruments binding specified behavior until and unless the person making the vow undergoes formal release from it. Such release is enacted before a court of three knowledgeable Jews, usually rabbis; Yoreh's ceremony also allows for dissolution of the vow before a quorum of ten Jews. Either option means a formal act, public in nature, to end the marriage, just as such acts initiated it. Yoreh's marriage vow includes conditions under which the marriage can be terminated, so that doing so in the event of marital breakdown does not violate the vow but fulfills one anticipated application of it.

Halakhic alternatives to marriage via kinyan and kiddushin are nothing new. As noted, in 1997 Rabbi Meir Simcha Feldblum published an alternative that would obviate both iggun and mamzerut. His proposal remains unused but available for any who wish it.[23] His and other works have remained without effect because the problem is not legal—halakhic—but political and psychosocial—stemming from the failure of Jews to enact available solutions. Indeed, the problem, ultimately, is social, as is the solution.

The end of iggun starts with recognition that this will come only from Jews changing Jewish practice. This is how protections for women in marriage and divorce emerged in the past, and it is the only route to ending women's marital captivity now. Despite the Chief Rabbinate's official monopoly on marriage and divorce for Israeli Jews, options exist there, too—because Jews have taken the initiative in creating and using them. The organization Yisrael Hofshit (A Free Israel) offers webinars for engaged couples and their families, led by lawyers, about ways to marry outside the Chief Rabbinate or any rabbinate, and have an egalitarian wedding in ways that obviate the legal need for a get in case of desired divorce. This includes the critical guidance against registering any marriage with the Ministry of Interior, since such registration means that a legally recognized divorce can only be obtained in a rabbinic court. These seminars also give guidance about family members who press for a Chief Rabbinate or other halakhic ceremony.

Action on the Personal and Family Level

Prevention

The traditional formula the groom pronounces to the bride: "You are hereby sanctified to me with this ring, according to the laws of Moses and Israel," by which kiddushin is enacted and kinyan completed, has the advantage of antiquity and familiarity. It "feels" real and authentic, a prerequisite for successful ritual.[24] The vast majority of couples, of whatever religious background, orientation, or lack thereof, marrying in any Jewish ceremony including the most nontraditional, use these words without understanding their meaning in the moment or their consequences. Concerted effort addresses that ignorance and popularizes good alternatives.

One need not abandon all of halakha or create an entirely new, unrecognizable system, a commonly stated anxiety, in order to reject kinyan and kiddushin. The alternatives proposed by Meir Simcha Feldblum, Rachel Adler, and Tzemah Yoreh apply halakhic traditions in new ways. Programs in which all this is taught and discussed, hevruta- (learning-partner) and worskshop style, in forums like the Havurah Institute in the United States, the Hadar Institute in the United States and Israel, and BINA/the Secular Yeshiva in Israel, would encourage grassroots engagement in creating healthy Jewish marriage and divorce norms while simultaneously enhancing engagement with Jewish traditions. From such encounters, materials can be created and shared in all the ways that foster conversation, encouraging further conversation and process. With funding to cover at least expenses, participants in such encounters could go on teaching circuits, Lehrhaus-style, to further the grassroots process, which can also be facilitated through online presentations and discussions.[25]

In remarkably little time, new practices feel "old," natural, and right, as occurred, to cite but one example, in the relatively quite recent adoption across the Jewish religious spectrum, in the Diaspora and Israel alike, of birth and bat mitzva ceremonies for girls—change not decreed or even sanctioned from "above," but emerging from popular demand.[26] This will happen with rituals that enact equal, respectful, mutually responsible marital partnering.

Some couples use alternatives but do not make this known at the wedding for fear of distressing some family or guests. Without minimizing this consideration, the more couples use alternatives openly and without fuss, the sooner new norms spread and a new social reality is created in which iggun does not exist. Couples can present their chosen manner of enacting the marriage in programs handed out to guests or by the officiant under the huppah simply announcing: "A and B will solemnize their marriage in the following way."

Personally, I find very moving the statement in Genesis 1:27 that declares the creation of humans, female and male, to be in the Divine Image: "And God created the earth-creature [ha'adam] in the image of God; in the image of God, God created it; male and female God created them." This verse (almost always mistranslated),[27] so unlike the ones with which this book opened, has not been halakhized—turned into concrete imperatives and actions regarding women, despite the categorical, abstract pronouncement, so rare in Pentateuchal texts and emphasized in the repetition, that exhorts our attention and our covenant as Jews to translate values into practice.

The place to do this is at weddings, and the way to do it is openly. Women's creation in the Divine Image precludes treating women as sex objects or as wards of men—as anything other than equal, not in comparison with men but in our own right, not as Others to a male norm but as one manifestation of human existence. If cultural conditions in previous eras precluded that statement, attributed to the dawn of Creation, from coming to consciousness and implementation in religious commandment, it is available to us now, with the urgent call to act, and enact.[28]

To the possible critique that doing this would "politicize" the wedding ceremony: the existing, or any, ceremony is also "political," enacting a status change based on and reifying underlying cultural assumptions about power, privilege, and social arrangements, in this case gendered ones. Kinyan and kiddushin enact values—the sexual objectification and commodification of women and the enablement of marital captivity—that no woman, nor many men, maintain. If a potential marriage partner harbors such values, women should know that up front.

The acquisition–commodification model of enacting marriage is inherently degrading and abusive. Making it egalitarian by having the bride say the traditional words of acquisition to the groom, as is done in Reform weddings and some Conservative rabbis suggest, is no fix.[29] As we have seen in other instances, this is egalitarianism gone awry. Kinyan and kiddushin need to be retired, not reformed. The fact that most Jews have no idea what these rituals mean or do, regarding them merely as "traditional," "quaint," a "tolerable anachronism," or not "threatening," as some rabbis who enact them report, is no license to continue their use.[30] There is, first, the prohibition of placing "a stumbling block before the blind" (Leviticus 19:14). People also deserve to be treated honestly and with respect. Rather than riding on popular ignorance, we can see in the problem a kernel of opportunity, realized through education about and enactment of good alternatives.

The personal is political; there is no escaping that reality. The only question is what values are enacted under the marriage canopy, with what consequences.

It should be obvious from all said in this book that simply having Orthodox women rabbis adjudicate and apply halakha in these matters in the same manner as men have done and do—an egalitarian solution—will accomplish nothing worthwhile and arguably is worse than women not participating in adjudication. Among the difficult moments in research for this book was hearing a veteran agunah advocate in New York report that when she turned to an Orthodox woman rabbi about a case the rabbinic courts were not resolving, she heard from her exactly what these courts had said: Sorry, nothing I can do. Another such moment was hearing from a panel of Orthodox women rabbis in Jerusalem in 2019 that their goal as halakhists was to render rulings indistinguishable from those of men, only given with more expressed compassion. I heard this comment in response to a question I put about how these women halakhists would handle the case of an *isha katlanit*, a "murderous wife," two of whose husbands have died, whom halakha bars from marrying a third time—this, in a system that has no corresponding category for men who have had numerous wives die in childbirth, a situation, quite unlike that of the *isha katlanit*, directly attributable to the men.[31] More "compassion" while administering these and similar misogynistic rulings is no worthy goal. On the contrary, it is to be co-opted in the service of systematic injustice against women, the worse for giving this female legitimacy. It is only a matter of time until even those who oppose the ordination of women as Orthodox rabbis realize this benefit and proclaim it, since it absolves male Orthodox rabbis of the sin of patriarchy and misogyny, transferring this to women rabbis. Of course, exploiting the voices of women rabbis and appropriating this absolution from them surely will not be accompanied by any acknowledgment of the women's rabbinic authority.

Men need not be concerned with protecting themselves from degradation in the act of marriage or from the act's consequences. That onus is now, unfairly, entirely on women engaged to be married or on the women who care about protecting them. Women I have spoken with feel or are made to feel defensive and guilty, as spoilers at a happy occasion, as "difficult," not sufficiently committed or trusting, for raising the question of the marriage ceremony or even of a serious prenup. They fear offending their partner or his family, and thus they join Jewish marriage roulette and, however inadvertently, propagate iggun for others. Only a communal program can correct this structural disadvantage and relieve women from bearing individually what is a systemic, gendered disadvantage. Unapologetic, full premarital negotiating to protect women was the norm in premodern Jewish societies across the globe. The initiative takes traditional Jewish behavior, practiced by couples and families for more centuries than not in Jewish history, in all Jewish ethnicities, and makes it contemporary communal policy.

On the Communal Level: A Public-Awareness Campaign on Marriage-Ritual Alternatives

It will take time and sustained professional effort to address complicated concerns and facilitate a complex social process, so the communal initiative must be ongoing. Women in right-wing Orthodox and ultra-Orthodox communities are aware of and knowledgeable about social media and have been using these resources regarding get abuse,[32] a phenomenon significant enough to have caught mainstream attention.

While remaining independent and unaffiliated, the community initiative should be in conversation with and be a resource for such efforts.

Women's use of online media, even to launch and run successful businesses, let alone for protection from marital abuse, is under attack in haredi quarters. There have been mass assemblies, with tens of thousands of women bused in from ultra-Orthodox centers—Lakewood, Williamsburg, and Borough Park—to a stadium in New Jersey in June 2022 for *nekadesh* ("Let us sanctify") rallies. These assemblies railed against women's use of smartphones and all online media. One such rally was held in English; a more strident one was held in Yiddish, assumed inaccessible to outsiders. The organizers (the Technology Awareness Group, TAG) and their backers threatened mothers with expulsion of their children from their (Bais Yaakov) schools if the mothers failed to attend—at the cost of fifty-four dollars a ticket. They used guilt manipulation—mothers who use smartphones and any online media were selfish, spiritually inferior, and hurting their children. Attendees were told that "technology is a manifestation of Satan's efforts to spread rot in the world." In the Yiddish rally, one rabbi gave the cultlike directive to women "not to speak on the street, except in cases of emergency."[33] Of course, women accessing social media for information and support about marriage and divorce will be targeted vehemently and ruthlessly. As noted, isolation is a necessary component for ongoing abuse—hence the communal initiative's emphasis on facilitating access to information and on communication.

The "good news" about tactics of intimidation is that we know not just that they will be employed but what they will be: personal attacks, defamation, slurs, falsehoods, shaming, shunning, threats. Exposing such tactics must be part of the initiative's educational materials, with all needed support, including legal help, made available.

Stages and Concurrent Approaches

No problem as complex and embedded, and in Israel, legally authorized, as Jewish marital captivity can be ended quickly. The end of iggun can emerge only in stages. Different needs and solutions will exist simultaneously for some time.

Women who are already agunot and have been socialized by families and education, or in Israel, also by legal and social reality, need options different from those of girls on the cusp of dating or beginning to
date, and from those in serious relationships and planning marriage.
The communal initiative will need to compose materials appropriate to
different stages of life and direct them appropriately.

When concerted support enables increasing numbers of agunot to reject intimidation and use any rabbinic court that frees agunot, and then
date and remarry if they wish to, they will free themselves and help end
iggun for their daughters and granddaughters as well as themselves. The
initiative's agunah support groups can be most effective to this end. It
would be helpful if women freed in the Morgenstern–Rackman, Krauss,
and Sperber courts, and the few freed in Chief Rabbinate courts, spoke,
anonymously if desired, through the initiative's resources about having gone on with their lives. The chains of taboo about adultery and
mamzerut, allied with those of iggun, break in the face of such actions.

It would make solid emotional sense for agunot to proclaim in
writing—the template of which document, the initiative could help
compose—that when they became engaged and married, neither the officiant nor anyone else told them what kinyan and kiddushin mean; that
they never gave informed consent to becoming agunot under any circumstance as a danger inherent in the marriage; that they would never
have consented to their marriage had they known that their husbands
were capable of taking them extortive hostage if they sought divorce;
and that they were never informed that rabbinic courts would not treat
get withholding and extortion, or even violence by husbands, as grounds
for annulment of their marriages. They entered their marriages actively
denied full knowledge necessary to informed consent.

Another document, in which women state that they do not consent to
becoming marital hostages under any circumstance, and that no method
of Jewish marriage they use, including marital cohabitation, signals such
consent, should be popularized for use before weddings. Men should
sign this, as well as another document renouncing the right to withhold
a get from their wives under any circumstance, or extort to give one.
They should also sign a conditional divorce, which the wife can activate
without court processes in the event a husband is unable for any reason

to give a divorce or withholds one. These documents should be in the woman's possession, with copies provided to lawyers—treated as the ketubbah was in eras when it was legally actionable. Such documents may or may not be legally actionable, and that is not their point; they are certainly not directed to any rabbinic establishment for approval. There is no guaranteeing how systems or societies treat even legally recognized documents. Ultimately, it is for women and couples to resolve that, in the event of anyone rejecting their stated understandings, commitments, and intentions in dissolving their marriages, they will proceed on the basis of those agreements.

A get—a clear Jewish divorce to end what was a Jewish coupling, but equally, in the case of retroactive annulment, a document solemnizing the end of a relationship once considered a marriage—provides similar, critically needed clarity and closure.[34] The initiative should draw up templates of such documents, too, and publicize them.

Agunot needing freedom via expanded application of *mekah ta'ut*, *hafka'at kiddushin*, and/or *get zikui*, when most Orthodox rabbinic courts will not use these methods, are in the most difficult circumstances and need the initiative's resources if enacting their own emancipation is to be a true choice, tenable socially, religiously, and financially.

As noted, even in Israel Jews now have legal alternatives to marriage via kinyan and kiddushin, methods that obviate the need to obtain a get. To avoid embroilment with rabbinic courts in case of divorce, couples who marry in whatever method or location must not register as married with the Ministry of Interior because to do so is to land in rabbinic courts in case of divorce. Rather, they, and those who do common-law marriages (*yeduim ba'tsibur*), use lawyers to establish marital status for legal purposes during marriage and in case of its desired dissolution; Yisrael Hofshit provides such services, as do individual lawyers. The fees and effort involved are comparable to those entailed in marriage via the Chief Rabbinate but nothing compared to embroilment in rabbinic divorce courts. When a critical mass of couples sidestep the established system, religiously embedded abuse in marriage and divorce will diminish and disappear and healthy new practices will replace it.

With greater awareness of the realities of iggun, informed consumer behavior will lead to choosing marriage officiants who use alternatives to kinyan and kiddushin and, if the couples wish one, only the best prenup—that which ends a marriage automatically, after a limited, specified time, without payoffs or involvement of rabbinic courts.

The verses with which this work began testify that already-current practices of divorce in biblical times were reflected in the verses about divorce, which then became the basis for rabbinic law. The Babylonian Talmud (Berakhot 45a) gives voice to this principle in advice to rabbis:

—"פוק חזי מאי עמא דבר"

"Look around, see what people are doing; then, legislate." To the women faced with the difficult prospect of using halakhic and other solutions that their rabbis, families, or communities reject, know that law follows.

The personal is political. To accept the status quo is to perpetuate it, and this is as political an act as any that works to create new realities. To embrace the responsibility of forging new paths is to honor the Jewish past and the Jewish future, using our lives as opportunity.

On Not Knowing the Past and Perpetuating the Abuse

We know what does not work. Publicizing the abuse, dramatizing, or ritualizing it does not work. Such actions normalize women's marital captivity, contributing thereby to its perpetuation. People become inured to the seemingly inevitable "tragedy" of "the poor agunah"—to women as natural, normal victims, and wring their hands at news of the latest outrageous case, regularly reported in media across the Jewish world. Then the news passes, while the abuse continues. The passing outrage, or prayers on "Agunah Days," is reminiscent of the ritualized responses in the United States after the latest mass shooting, followed by no effective action against gun violence. More of the same will yield only more of the same.[35]

That goes for appealing to rabbis, or God, to act. Continuing to appeal to the rabbinic-court system, regardless of country, to deliver results other than those it has, is futile and craven. As Dahlia Lithwick says, "The problem with power is that there is no speaking truth to it when it holds all the cards."[36]

No man fears, or need fear, iggun happening to him. Male immunity from this problem underlies its persistence. Rabbi Dov Linzer, head of Yeshivat Chovevei Torah, told me that his father, also a rabbinic judge, asked him once how long these laws would last if men were subject to them. The answer: they would never have been written.[37]

There is no halakhic expedient to end iggun—none—that some rabbinic authority cannot invalidate. We have seen that again and again, against the actions that Rabbis Morgenstern, Rackman, and Sperber, and even the Chief Rabbinate's own court in Safed, took to free agunot. This does not mean that Jews who wish it should not use these expedients if they are available. Rituals serve critically important purposes in proclaiming intent, conveying meaning, and effecting transition between states, like "married" and "divorced." But couples must determine that in the event of their desire to end the marriage, they do not condition that termination on outside recognition or approval. Only behavior in accordance with the termination, enacted by get, annulment, or other measure, will end iggun.

When a problem is treated as intractable, that is what it becomes. That is what has happened with iggun. Perception and reality change through action.

This problem has a deep history. We need to study that history because without historical consciousness, each generation rediscovers and reexperiences iggun and reinvents arguments and expedients long proven useless, while the systemic abuse of women—in the act of marriage, whether or not they also become agunot, and certainly when they do—continues.

To this end, this book has put the abuse of iggun in historical perspective, the perspective of the distant and the recent past, in order to illuminate the contemporary problem so that we will cease repeating history while imagining that we are acting. So that we break out of learned helplessness and act effectively.

Jewish women have a history. They should know it. And apply its lessons.

Because we don't want to be having this same conversation in another hundred years. Or even one.

CONCLUSIONS

On July 24, 2022, the main evening TV news on Israeli Channel 13 carried the following story, conveyed through an interview with "Rivka," the victim of rabbinic political machinations that resulted in her reinstatement as an agunah by the same Chief Rabbinate court that had annulled her marriage after nineteen years of her husband's get refusal. Her husband had left Israel for England, where, through rabbinic release from the Ashkenazic prohibition of polygyny, he married a second wife. Following intense political pressure by other rabbis engaged in a promotion struggle with those of the rabbinic court that freed Rivka, *that court annulled its own annulment of her marriage and reinstated her to iggun.*[1]

Here is some of the Twitter feed of the Center for Women's Justice about this woman and the rabbis involved:[2]

> Center for Women's Justice Nov. 4, 2021
> A few months ago, an agunah of 19(!) years was finally given a judgement by the rabbinic court annulling her marriage and allowing her to remarry—a very rare . . . deal.
>
> Yesterday, due to political pressure, all three rabbinic court judges on the case recanted and declared the woman an "eshet ish gmura"—a woman who is still very much married and who is required to obtain a get from her husband.
>
> The original annulment had come after years . . . of levying . . . sanctions on the man, ordering him to be forced to give a get (kfiya—a very rare step), even jail. Nothing budged. FOR 19 YEARS.
>
> A few months ago, the main rabbinic judge on the case wrote a detailed psak din (judgment) explaining why the marriage could be annulled on grounds of "mekach ta'ut" (a halakhic flaw in the original marriage based on misinformed consent), making a get unnecessary.
>
> Cautious, he wrote in his judgement that it would go into effect if two other rabbinic court judges agreed to corroborate his psak. None other

than Chief Rabbi Lau found two other rabbinic court judges to agree, and the three of them signed it into being. The woman was free.

But . . . convening of the Committee to Appoint Rabbinic Judges fast approaches, and with it, the coveted promotions to the High Rabbinic Court. A group of rabbinic court judges launched a campaign against the one who issued the judgement freeing the woman.

They circulated an open letter among the community of [rabbinic judges]: "This mistaken judgement is incorrect from a halakhic stand-point and constitutes *a serious and dangerous precedent for the future*. . . . [my emphasis]. We call on the members of the rabbinic court to recant their erroneous judgement."

The original judgment . . . has not been made public, but that did not stop a number of prominent rabbinic court judges from signing on to the half-page letter condemning it. . . . The letter names the three "problem-atic" judges publicly.

. . . The purpose of the letter is clear: signaling to these judges, as well as any other judge who dares to be "creative" in freeing agunot, that this will cost them dearly. It is professional suicide. *A similar fate was suffered 7 years ago by the rabbinic judge who freed the infamous "Agunah of Tzfat," a woman whose husband had been in a coma for a decade. His career was quashed and to this day, he has not been promoted* (my emphasis).

This letter was circulated and signed by prominent rabbinic judges and an outcry was raised. Pressure mounted. Consequently, all three judges who had signed onto the judgement recanted yesterday. And just like that, the woman is once again an agunah.

. . . A court just rescinded its own judgement because of outside bul-lying and politics. . . .

. . . There are numerous halakhic problems . . . in calling a woman's free status into question after the fact, of exerting pressure on judges to influence their decisions, and . . . torturing this woman for political gain.

Women are more than just unfortunate collateral damage. Women's lives are the tool used by those in power, in mafia-like behavior, for per-sonal and institutional benefit and to threaten others into compliance with the patriarchal order.

This story is emblematic of the state of Jewish marital captivity in our day.

This news item, sure as day dawns to be followed by others egregious enough to catch media attention, just as such stories have populated the media for centuries, well sums up the futility of appealing to the rabbinic system to act rationally, honestly, or even competently regarding women, and in particular agunot. It also demonstrates why appeals to that system, or use of it, only feed and enable an irremediably corrupt and misogynist establishment in continued abuse of women, victimization necessary to the establishment's internal power struggles and material interests.

This book has labored to show that the active, proactive, creative, assertive, and transgressive behavior of women in the past delivered protections for women in marriage and divorce and relief for some marital captives. It has shown that such behavior, by entirely traditional women in premodern, traditional communities and societies, delivered results. This behavior was simultaneously rebellious and pious. It was pious because its practitioners understood and acted on the assumption, to them self-evident, that they were part of the Jewish system and therefore had a claim on it to serve their needs. By making that demand and using tough measures to support it, they indeed forced it to meet their needs. They changed reality for themselves and in the system itself, which was compelled to integrate changes that not only went beyond but violated Talmudic law yet became an integral part of traditional Jewish jurisprudence and practice. That practice functioned for centuries, until a rabbinic backlash terminated it. Even thereafter, as in the sixteenth-century examples we have discussed, women continued to act assertively and creatively to liberate themselves from threatened iggun, and sometimes succeeded.

The rulings of late medieval rabbinic decisors who enacted the backlash against reforms in marriage and divorce that had benefited women operate to this day in rabbinic courts in Israel, the United States, and elsewhere. To appeal to those courts to behave any differently than they have and do is delusive or the result of intolerable ignorance. This book is devoted to ending both ignorance and delusion.

It has sought to lay bare the failure and futility of any effort to work with or within the system, whether that of Israel or the United States. Such efforts guarantee that iggun will continue to be managed rather than ended. Whatever the intent, such efforts are part of the problem, not any solution to it. As with any pathology, accurate information and diagnosis are essential for effective solutions to be applied. There is a cure to the pathology of Jewish marital captivity and it begins with seeing the big picture, past and present, and telling the truth.

The origin of iggun is not bad husbands or bad rabbis, though both abound, but kinyan and kiddushin. To end iggun going forward, it must first be prevented through changed rituals of Jewish marriage that respect the human and Jewish dignity of women and treat both parties to the marriage as equal in status, obligations, and rights, with no power to chain the other in a marriage.

Only when women act as full agents in the Jewish system will the system be fully Jewish, that is, encompassing and responsible to all its constituents and not the preserve of male privilege and abuse and female subordination and victimization. Only when women act as agents and not as pitiful and pitiable victims will marital captivity end and captives be freed.

Women cannot do this individually, on their own. The problem is not individual but systemic, and the solution must also be systemic, enacted in community policy. In the premodern Jewish world, male as well as female kin acted to support women threatened with marital abuse because they perceived this as in their own interests. The premodern, male-led Jewish community saw women's welfare as a group concern because iggun meant poverty and agunot were a liability to the communal purse, as well as a perceived threat to social order. Although there were clear limits to what could be accomplished in an androcentric and patriarchal system, there was a community paradigm that saw women's liabilities in marriage and divorce as a problem demanding concrete solutions, like conditional and forced divorces. Women's welfare was a communal concern.

The call to end iggun and free agunot is a call to construct a contemporary communal Jewish paradigm, Diaspora and Israeli, that puts the marital and divorce rights of women front and center, in the spirit of a dynamic Jewish past and a just future.

That will happen when women demand this, accept no less, and act to bring it to fruition.

* * *

Figure C.1 "He who differentiates between darkness and light." Credit: Hila Karabelnikov Paz.

Figure C.2 Rachel's Tomb. Credit: Avraham Bar Adon.

This book has emphasized the power of images, verbal and visual, in both reflecting and shaping reality. I would like to close with two images to ponder.

One is the torso of a woman, illuminated in the fiery yellow light of a havdalah candle, used to demarcate the end of the Sabbath and the start of the new week. We do not see her face but we do see her hands, acting to ignite the flame of separation and creation. In the flame we see the face of a woman whom the artist, Hila Karabelnikov Paz, tells me represents a woman who had given another woman pivotal support.

The other image is a miniature of Rachel's Tomb. It shows Rachel in a seated, somewhat bent pose, hand to her forehead, recalling, of course, the famous lines in Jeremiah 31:15–17. We need not, however, limit ourselves to Jeremiah's description of lament and consolation in interpreting this image, but also see Rachel in the pose of Rodin's *Thinker*, contemplating effective action to lead from lament to redemption, and the lines, a few verses later, "Keep in mind the highway, the road that you have traveled."

I completed work on this book as we neared the holiday of Purim. Passover follows exactly a month after that.

As is well-known, God's name appears nowhere in the Book of Esther, which relates the Purim story. And Moses's name appears nowhere in the text of the Haggadah, recited and enacted at the Passover seder.

There is a lesson in both for anyone wishing to do something effective to end Jewish marital captivity.

God will not do that work. And neither will a man, or men. It is not, to cite another text, in the heavens, but in our hands.

"There has to be another way," my mother, z"l, said.

There is. It is up to us to make it, and take it.

תם ונשלם שבח לאל בורא עולם
ירושלים

ACKNOWLEDGMENTS

This book is the product of love and of pain.

The pain part is evident from what I say in the preface, and, I think, from the entirety of the book. That, and a desire to prevent future injury, first sparked its writing. There is no exorcising the pain of seeing a mother living with horrific loss, then victimized by people unworthy of her and of her belief, commitment, and trust. Completing this book comes with the usual gratification of a major project concluded but also with relived pain, to which there is some counterpoise in uncovering and telling the truth.

But love has also suffused this project. I am a historian of Jewish society and of Jewish women. I am very fortunate to have been able to pursue my passion for Jewish history and to have had superb mentors, models, colleagues, and the most wonderful students. However miserable the subject matter of this book, discovering and making sense of the material, realizing new insights, and synthesizing the story I tell here was a profound, sometimes thrilling experience for me as a historian.

My family history underlay this project but my professional training and career as a historian enabled my doing it. I have had many occasions to wish I could consult with Paula Hyman, to whom my debt continues for her inestimable example and support when I was a student and for conversations as colleagues. Deborah Dash Moore connected me to Jennifer Hammer and New York University Press, but her help extended well beyond that. She read and critiqued enough of this work to make a critical contribution to its presentation and coherence and to the accessibility of its arguments. She expressed her belief in the book's importance; her encouragement was a great gift. I thank Ivan Marcus for comments on the premodern material. I thank the manuscript's two anonymous readers for their comments and suggestions. Jennifer Hammer gave me the great gift of immediate interest in and support for the project, and the manuscript, her meticulous editorial attention. Brianna

Jean of NYU Press handled technical queries from me patiently, kindly, and with generosity. Valerie Zaborski gave the manuscript expert, meticulous attention during the copyediting phase. Great thanks to Agi Erdos for her expert and expeditious production of the book's index. Nurit Jacobs Yinon graciously helped in consulting about the book's cover image and with permission to use her compelling photography.

This project originated with the invitation of Rabbi Rachel Adler to write about agunot and iggun. Her enthusiastic response to an initial, article-sized version encouraged me to proceed on the larger one. Conversations with friends and colleagues—Margalit Shiloh, Rachel Elior, Katharina von Kellenbach, Phyllis Chesler, Marian and Abe Sofaer—gave confirming boosts of interest and helpful advice. Judith and Jeff Green hosted me in the most congenial of settings and gave me opportunities at their *shabbes* table to try out my findings on other guests. Jeff most generously offered help at a stressed time with Hebrew transliteration in the bibliography. Shana Roskies read an early version and aptly remarked, "You've been writing this your whole life, Shulamit." Daniel Price, librarian of the Shalom Hartman Institute in Jerusalem, extended pivotal help time and again in swiftly locating and sending materials, sometimes also in clarifying terms. He has my warm thanks and tremendous appreciation. Paul Serkin ("The PC Guy" indeed), several times saved "the last of the Luddites" from computer disasters. At a critical time, Tova Hartman and Marc Brettler expressed encouragement and support for the project and its atypical nature as a work of both scholarship and advocacy; Tova alerted me to an important text. Atara Ross and Yisrael Gale generously helped parse some responsa. Susan Weiss enabled tax-deductible fundraising that covered the cost of producing the book's index, thanks to the generosity of wonderful friends and family in the United States and Israel including, most movingly, former students. I thank Richie Lewis for conversations over years of research and writing as I untangled and grasped the implications of sources; for various valuable suggestions; for help several times about terms and texts; and for allowing me to use his collection as a lending library. For soulful singing and the best soup in Jerusalem at their *shabbes* table, my thanks to Avivah and Eric Zornberg. My ever-loving cousins, Amy Sporer Schiff and Julie Krigel, never failed to express their enthusiastic interest and support. My cousin, Al Sporer, z"l, gave steadfast love and support to me and to my projects, personal and professional, throughout my life. My children, Natan, Talya, Maya, and Roee, bring sunshine. They have all my love and boundless esteem.

Ruthie Sporer, Edie Gelles, Nancy Fuchs-Kreimer, Rose Gerszberg, Kathryn Hellerstein, Dinah Mendes, Charmaine Gruber, dear friends over many years and eras of my life, gave sustaining friendship, interest in this project, and encouragement. They have my loving thanks.

APPENDIX

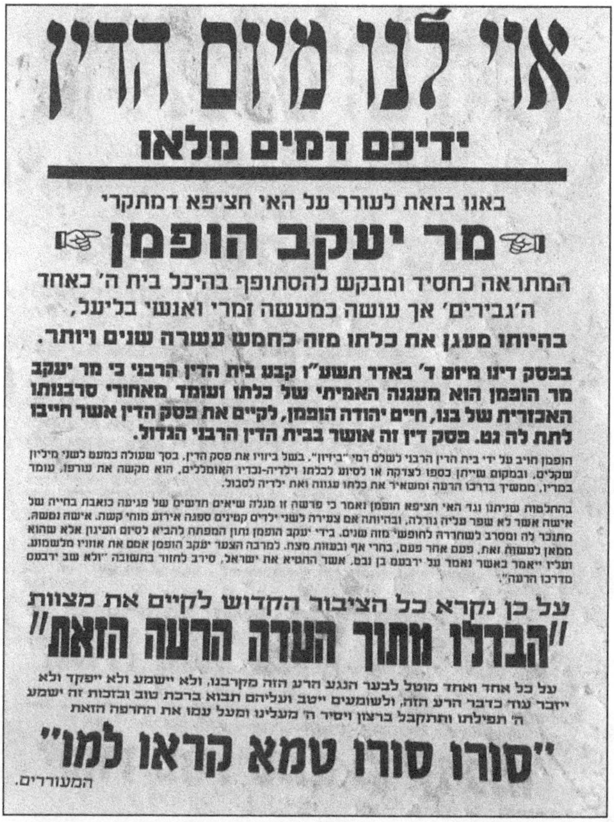

אוי לנו מיום הדין

ידיכם דמים מלאו

באנו בזאת לעורר על האי חציפא דמתקרי

מר יעקב הופמן

המתראה כחסיד ומבקש להסתופף בהיכל בית ה' כאחד
ה'גבירים' אך עושה כמעשה זמרי ואנשי בליעל,
בהיותו מעגן את כלתו מזה כחמש עשרה שנים ויותר.

בפסק דינו מיום ד' באדר תשע"ו קבע בית הדין הרבני כי מר יעקב
מר הופמן הוא מעגנה האמיתי של כלתו ועומד מאחורי סרבנותו
האכזרית של בנו, חיים יהודה הופמן, לקיים את פסק הדין אשר חייבו
לתת לה גט. פסק דין זה אושר בבית הדין הרבני הגדול.

הופמן חויב על ידי בית הדין הרבני לשלם דמי "ביזיון". בשל ביזויו את פסק הדין, בסך שעולה כמעט לשני מיליון
שקלים, ובמקום שייתן כספו לצדקה או לסיוע לכלתו וילדיה-נכדיו האומללים, הוא מקשה את עורפו, עומד
במריו, ממשיך בדרכו הרעה ומשאיר את כלתו עגונה ואת ילדיה לסבול.

בהחלטות שניתנו נגד האי חציפא הופמן נאמר כי פרשה זו מגלה שיאים חדשים של פגיעה כואבת בחייה של
אישה אשר לא שפר עליה גורלה, ובהיותה אם צעירה לשני ילדים קטינים ספגה אירוע מוחי קשה. אישה נפשה,
מתוכר לה ומסרב לשחררה לחופשי מזה שנים. בידי יעקב הופמן נתון המפתח להביא לסיום העיגון אלא שהוא
ממאן לעשות זאת, פעם אחר פעם, בחרי אף ובעזות מצח. למרבה הצער יעקב הופמן אטם את אוזניו מלשמוע.
ועליו ייאמר באשר נאמר על ירבעם בן נבט, אשר החטיא את ישראל, סירב לחזור בתשובה "ולא שב ירבעם
מדרכו הרעה".

על כן נקרא כל הציבור הקדוש לקיים את מצוות

"הבדלו מתוך העדה הרעה הזאת"

על כל אחד ואחד מוטל לבער הנגע הרע הזה מקרבנו, ולא יישמע ולא ייפקד ולא
ייזכר עוד כדבר הרע הזה, ולשומעים ייטב ועליהם תבוא ברכת טוב ובזכות זה ישמע
ה' תפילתו ותתקבל ברצון ויסיר ה' מעלינו ומעל עמו את החרפה הזאת

"סורו סורו טמא קראו למו"

המעוררים.

Figure A.1 Flyer circulating in Jerusalem neighborhoods, 2022, calling for shunning of a get refuser's father for abetting his son's fifteen-plus-year get refusal, against the rabbinic court's ruling.

Rabbinical Court of Greater Cleveland

בית דין צדק דקליבלנד

13967 Cedar Road - Suite 205, Cleveland, Ohio 44118
216-409-2020   Fax 216-397-9455

ראב"ד
הרב ישראל גרומער

דיינים קבועים
הרב יהודה בלום
הרב נפתלי בורשטיין
הרב משה גארפונקעל
הרב ברוך הירשפעלד
הרב דובער חייקין
הרב דניאל נייסטט

מנהל כללי
בנימין סווייבר

Rosh Beis Din
Rabbi Yisroel Grumer

Permanent Dayanim
**Rabbi Yehuda Blum
Rabbi Naphtali Burnstein
Rabbi Sholom Chaikin
Rabbi Moshe Garfunkel
Rabbi Boruch Hirschfeld
Rabbi Doniel Neustadt**

Executive Administrator
Binyomin Cweiber, Esq.

February 2005   אדר א' תשס"ה

Proclamation

We wish to hereby notify the Cleveland Jewish community and other concerned individuals that the Beis Din of Cleveland summoned Mr. Nathan Offenberg to come to a Din Torah (in front of the three undersigned Dayanim) to answer charges brought against him by Mr. Chaim Weiszner. Mr. Offenberg has contemptuously rejected the Beis Din's summons and refused to come. We therefore gave Mr. Weiszner permission to pursue the case in Civil Court.

We also wish to declare that Mr. Nathan Offenberg is in defiance and contempt of Beis Din (נברא דלא ציית דינא) as stated in Bava Kama 112b-113a and in Shulchan Aruch Choshen Mishpat 11 and Yoreh De'ah 334:43. Mr. Offenberg is, therefore, subject to all of the sanctions as prescribed in Shulchan Aruch Yoreh De'ah 334:2.

The above shall be in effect until he appears in Beis Din to partake in the Din Torah.

Rabbi Yisroel Grumer

Rabbi Yehuda Blum   Rabbi Moshe Garfunkel

The Meaning of this Declaration

According to the Shulchan Aruch cited above, a person who refuses a summons three times from a recognized Beis Din is placed in *Nidui*. Shulchan Aruch states: One who is in *Nidui*, you must not sit near him at least four amos (approx. 6 feet), you are not permitted to eat or drink with him nor enter his home ...

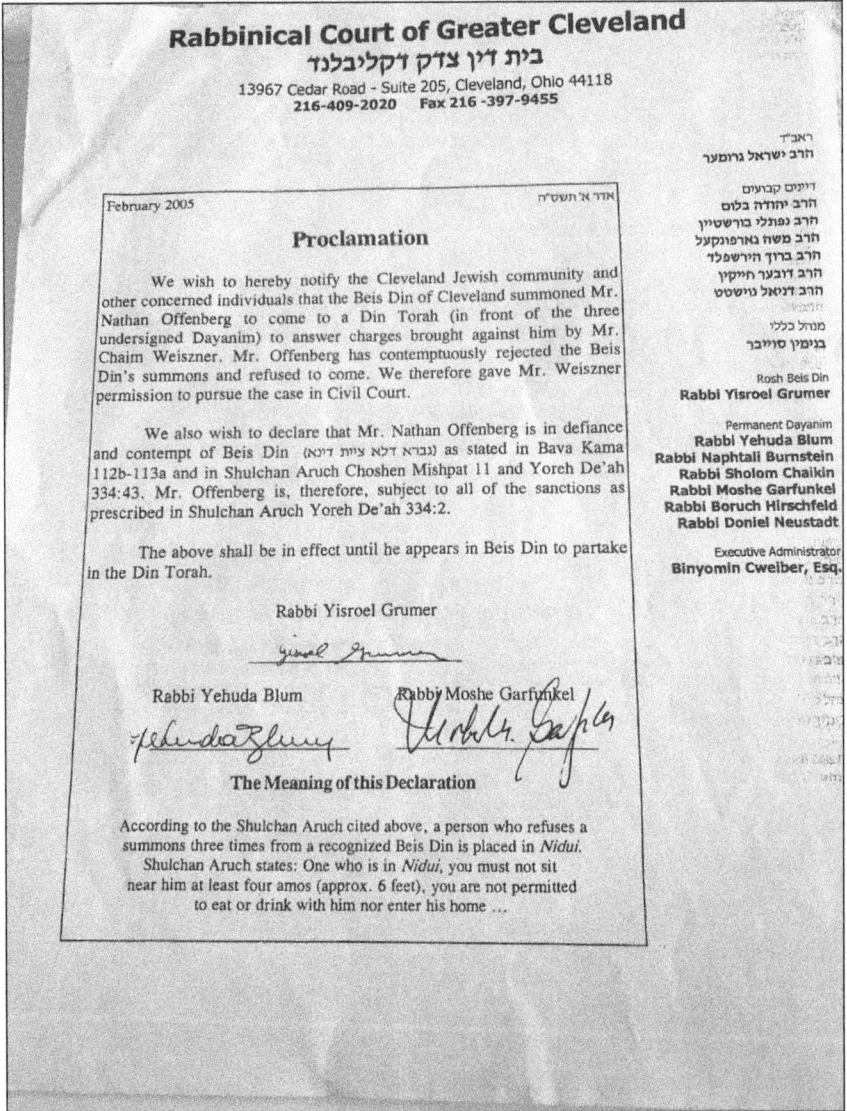

Figure A.2 "Proclamation" (2005) of a Cleveland, Ohio, rabbinic court summoning a man who has ignored the court's prior summons, authorizing sanctions against him for this defiance.

December 8, 1966

THE JOINT LAW CONFERENCE
OF
THE RABBINICAL ASSEMBLY AND
THE JEWISH THEOLOGICAL SEMINARY OF AMERICA

Dear Mr. C.,

The National Beth Din of the Jewish Theological Seminary of America and the Rabbinical Assembly was requested by Mrs. G to convene a court session to discuss her request for a Jewish divorce. It is our understanding that your marriage to Mrs. G. had been civilly terminated. The marriage *ketubah* agreement which you signed at the time of your wedding established a moral and legal obligation on each of you to appear before our court should either party of the marriage summon the other for such an appearance.

We are aware that there are often differences between marriage partners that ought to be aired, and that inequities are sometimes not brought before civil authorities and thus remain unresolved. We are an impartial court dedicated to helping Jews live within the framework of Jewish law and ethics and want to be of service both to you and Mrs. G.

We are holding a court session on Thursday afternoon, December 20, 1966, in room 301 in the Teacher's Institute Building of the Jewish Theological Seminary, 3080 Broadway...and are summoning you to attend. You may of course be represented by counsel.

Yours Truly,
Rabbi Morton Leifman
Secretary, National *Beth Din*

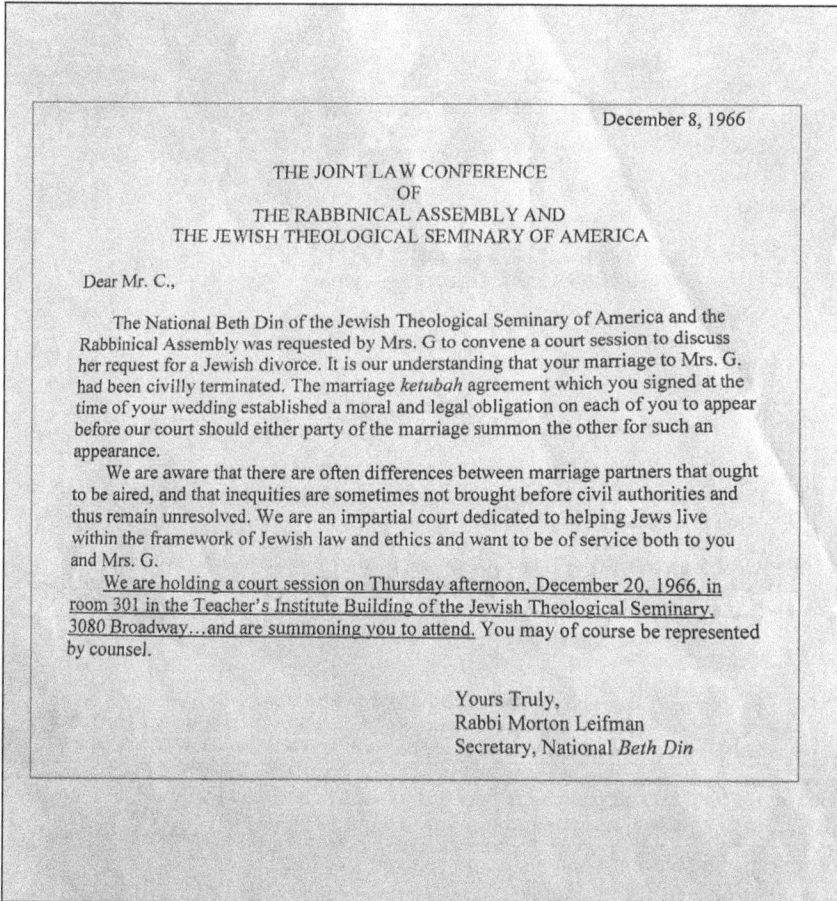

Figure A.3 Letter of the Joint Law Conference of the Rabbinical Assembly and the Jewish Theological Seminary of America (1966) requesting a man's attendance in its rabbinic court regarding his wife's request for a get.

Figure A.4 Natalie Lastreger and supporters as she awaits arrest by the Chief Rabbinate for seeking to use a haredi rabbinic court and not that of the Chief Rabbinate for her divorce. Credit: Shulamit Magnus.

NOTES

1 Thanks to Rabbi Hal Rudin-Luria for references to rabbinic commentaries on the verse "Justice, justice, you shall pursue."

PREFACE

1 This work is dedicated in honor of those who have fought for agunot, taken their plight personally, intervened, and made a difference—first, in not just throwing up their hands, citing impotence. It is dedicated in particular to those I have been privileged to know personally: Rivka Haut, z"l, Norma Joseph, Susan Aranoff, Susan Weiss, Nitzan Caspi Shiloni, Rabbi Daniel Sperber. This acknowledgment in no way implies their endorsement of what I write. This work preeminently is in honor of my mother, Libby Grossman Magnus, z"l, the best of Jews, who taught me the meaning of true piety, and about honesty.

2 The study of women's—and Jewish—history is predicated on rejection of assertions of scholarly "objectivity." See Magnus, "Ghetto"; Kelly, *Women*; Carroll, *Liberating*.

3 See Magnus, "Loving."

4 Magnus, "Agunot."

5 Cohen and Hyman, *Family*; Kraemer, *Family*.

6 Sarna, *American*; Shilo, *Princess*.

7 Diner and Lieff Benderly, *Works*.

8 Email, October 22, 2019.

9 Grossman, *Pious*; idem, *Pious* (Hebrew); Goldin, *Jewish Women*.

10 Baumgarten, *Piety*.

11 Lamdan, *Separate*; Rozen, *History*.

12 Adelman, *Marriage*.

13 Shashar, *Vanished*. See my review of Shashar, *American*.

14 H. Sperber, *Plight*; idem, "Agunot, 1851–1914"; idem, "Agunot"; idem, "Responsa"; idem, "Phenomenon."

INTRODUCTION

1 Labovitz, "Purchase," demonstrates the connection between rabbinic marriage altogether and slavery.

2 Ross, *Expanding*, 28, also makes this claim but offers no specifics to support it.

3 My previous publications were Magnus, "Thinking" and "Agunot."

4 Snyder, *Bloodlands*, 218.

5 See Parkes, *Conflict*; Baer, "Disputations"; Cohen, *Friars*; Gilman, *Self-Hatred*; Magnus, "Good."

6 See Grossman, *Pious* (Hebrew) 346–97; idem, *Pious*, 198–211; Goldin, *Jewish Women*, 26–47.

7 Jewish marital captivity also has cross-religious and cross-cultural, Christian, Muslim, and Hindu analogues; see Deogratias, *Trapped*. Marital captivity and its associated abuses (extortion, violence) also exist in communist China; see Wang and Dong, "China's 'Road-Trip Auntie,'" *New York Times*, August 2, 2024. This is not about religion per se but about male-gendered power.

8 See Spiro, "Jailed."

9 In 2022, of fifty cases appealed to the Supreme Court against actions of the Chief Rabbinate, the court agreed to hear one; Caspi Shiloni, "Judicial Upheaval."

10 Aranoff and Haut, *Wed-Locked*; Weiss and Gross-Horowitz, *Marriage*.

1. ORIGINS

1 This work addresses marriage and divorce of heterosexual couples. On legalities of rabbinic marriage and divorce law, see Elon, *Principles*.

2 All citations are to the Babylonian Talmud.

3 See Haut, *Divorce*, and Klein, *Guide*, 449–508, and reproduced texts and images of get documents there and in Freeze, *Jewish Marriage*, 143.

4 The categorical nature of Jewish men's ownership of their wives' sexuality is seen in the insistence, in antinomian Sabbatian circles, on the prerogative of husbands to permit or force wives to have sex with men other than their husbands—the flip side of anathematizing this. See Rapoport-Albert, *Women*, 38–39 and 84, n. 12.

5 On punishment of women accused of adultery and treatment of children born of illicit sex in among nineteenth- to mid-twentieth-century Libyan Jewry, see Simon, *Change*, 70.

6 E.g., see Deut. 21:13; Isaiah 62:4–5. The Hebrew conveys the meaning of male sexual penetration of the female as the act, simultaneously, establishing ownership/mastery of her and marriage. Halakha enacts the Hebrew meaning.

7 See Lamm, *Way*; Falk, *Matrimonial*. For treatment of the legal consequences of kinyan and kiddushin, see Labovitz, "With Righteousness and Justice," and Lubitch, "Force."

8 See the extensive treatment in Shashar, *Vanished*.

9 Deut. 25:5–10; Book of Ruth. If the deceased has no brothers, the widow is a regular widow. The "childlessness" operative in levirate situations is that of the deceased husband. If the widow had children from a prior marriage, she was obligated to levirate marriage. There is no corresponding biblical or rabbinic concern with perpetuating the "name" (memory) of a childless woman. About the inheritance of such women, halakha has much to say.

10 On the halitsa ritual, see Hezser, "Halitza."

11 See Finkelstein, *Self-Government*, and extensively, Grossman, *Pious*, and Goldin, *Jewish Women*.

12 For a full critique of the rabbinic marriage ceremony, see Adler, *Engendering*.

13 On the private–public tension in this strikingly immodest, indeed crass declaration at the wedding ceremony, see Greenstein, "Equality," 3.

14 See Kulp, "Enjoy."

15 Bleich, "Annulment," 114.

16 On the premodern kehilla in Europe and its demise, see Katz, *Tradition*; idem, *Ghetto*.

17 Examples are: Meiselman, *Jewish*; Lamm, *Jewish*; Lieberman, "Partnership"; Wolowelsky, *Women*. On such apologetics by Joseph B. Soloveitchik, see Attia, "Beast" (accessed on Academia.edu, June 11, 2020). See Ross, *Expanding*, 25–161, for exposition of such apologetics and responses to them.

18 See Friedman, *Jewish Marriage*, vol. 1; Epstein, *Marriage*; Hauptman, *Rereading*; Romney Wegner, *Chattel*.

19 Friedman, *Jewish Marriage*, vol. 1: viii, 2–3, 7. There is no complete formulary for the ketubbah in the Talmud; Friedman, 3.

20 See Lamm, *Jewish*, 197–206.

21 See Feldman, *Marital*, 46–59.

22 For instances of textual fluidity in the ketubbah and negotiations about its terms in modernity, see Lamdan, "Early," and Simon, *Change*, 58, 68.

23 See the extensive discussion in Hauptman, *Rereading*.

24 See Hauptman, *Rereading*, 114–21; Riskin, *Women*; Friedman, "Divorce"; idem, "Termination"; idem, *Jewish Marriage*.

25 See Polzer, "I Thought."

26 See Katz, *Tradition*, 63–155; Ben-Sasson and Levitats, "Community"; Baron, *Jewish Community*.

27 See Riskin, *Women*; A. Westreich, "Divorce"; E. Westreich, "Rise"; idem, "Rise" (Hebrew); Grossman, *Pious*, 239–44; Reiner, "Regulation"; idem, "Courts"; Furst, "Marriage."

28 Goldin, *Jewish Women*, 75–78, 100–116, argues that these ordinances were initiated in the twelfth century, well after Rabbenu Gershom, by Rabbi Eliezer ben Nathan (Raban), who attributed them to Rabbenu Gershom to establish their authority. Grossman, *Pious*, 70–72, differs about this dating. In any case, the ordinances became authoritative in Ashkenaz by the twelfth century.

29 Lamdan, *Separate*, 149.

2. WHY DID REFORMS HAPPEN?

1 See Cohen, *Crescent*; Rustow, "Jews"; Baumgarten, "Medieval"; Franklin and Margariti, *Jews*.

2 The seventeenth-century memoirs of Glikl Hamel depict children of both sexes participating in the economic life of the family as a matter of course. She began learning her business skills in childhood; her account shows that the same was true for the other females in her family. See *Glueckel*, trans. and ed. Abrahams; *Memoirs of Glueckel*, trans. Lowenthal; Turniansky, *Glikl*.

3 Baumgarten, *Mothers*, 184.
4 Kaplan, *Making*. For a perspective including working-class Jews in Europe and the United States, see Hyman, *Gender*; idem, "Gender."
5 Goldin, *Jewish Women*, 223–24.
6 Grossman, *Pious*, 111–12.
7 Grossman, *Pious*, 114. See, too, Tallan, "Medieval."
8 Goldin, *Jewish Women*, 22–23, 223–225.
9 Grossman, *Pious*, 117.
10 Goldin, *Jewish Women*, 223–24.
11 Grossman, *Pious*, 118; Goldin, *Jewish Women*, 223.
12 Grossman, *Pious*, 118.
13 Grossman, *Pious*, 119–20, notes that even hasidei ashkenaz, greatly concerned with women's "modesty," ignored the prohibition of women's seclusion with Gentile men because of the "great economic importance" of women's moneylending activities and their trust in women's piety. Goldin, *Jewish Women*, 224, observes similarly. See, too, Keil, "Public Roles."
14 Grossman, *Pious*, 122. See, too, Baumgarten, *Piety*, 130–31.
15 Goldin, *Jewish Women*, 99. See, too, Fram, *Ideals*, 79.
16 Cited in Fram, *Ideals*, 80.
17 Keil, "Roles," 5.
18 Grossman, *Pious*, 119; treated extensively in Baumgarten, *Mothers*.
19 Goldin, *Jewish Women*, 99.
20 On changes in rulings about trade with non-Jews, see Kanarfogel, "Halakhah and Mezi'ut," and Fram, *Ideals*, 67–105.
21 See S. D. Goitein, "Introduction," in *Mediterranean*, 9–74; unless otherwise noted, citations of Goitein's work are from the abbreviated edition; Marx, "Importance"; Ben-Sasson, "Cairo"; Cohen, *Poverty*; Krakowski, *Age*; Rustow, "Jews."
22 Friedman, "Marriage," 36; Goitein, *Mediterranean*, 378.
23 Cohen, *Poverty*, 15, states that "poverty constituted a substantial social problem" and cites Goitein's estimate that one-quarter of the Rabbanite (non-Karaite) Jewish population of Fustat in 1150, totaling about 3,300 souls, relied on the communal dole, estimating that the same proportion held eighty years later. Goitein spoke of the destitute; many more were economically marginal. As Cohen, 16, notes, the Geniza lists record only those seeking communal help; many sought private assistance. The well-to-do in this society were international traders.
24 Krakowski, *Age*, 160.
25 Krakowski, *Age*, 161.
26 Krakowsk, *Age*, 162. When teaching of, e.g., embroidery was not mother-to-daughter, teachers were paid so the activity registered in recordkeeping.
27 Goitein, *Mediterranean*, 377–78, 448–49.
28 Krakowski, *Age*, 198. Rabbanites followed rabbinic traditions; Karaites followed nonrabbinic, Karaite traditions. Each, with its own hermeneutics of biblical texts both considered Divine and authoritative, considered the other in error and

schismatic, but the two groups intermarried routinely. Karaites were an important segment of the Jewish population in medieval Middle Eastern Jewries. See Hofman, "Karaites."

29 Krakowski, *Age*, 199.

30 Krakowski, *Age*, 210 and 200–201.

31 See Friedman, "Marriage," 36; Goitein, *Mediterranean*, 370, 377.

32 Friedman, "Marriage," 36; Krakowski, *Age*, 255.

33 Goitein, *Mediterranean*, 449–51.

34 As Lewis, *Islam*, 6, notes, while Jews "managed to survive" in medieval Christendom, Muslims did not, driven out of Spain, Portugal, and Sicily.

35 On Augustinian doctrine about Jewish existence in Christendom, see Cohen, *Friars*, 19–32; Cohen, *Crescent*, 30–51; and Chazan, *Church*, 2–8.

36 See Rozen's summary, *History*, 16–28, of the rules and realities (in Istanbul) of dhimmi status, with important comments, 34–40, contrasting this status with that of Jews in Christian domains; and, for further such comparison, Cohen, *Crescent*, and idem, "Origins," 23–39; Stillman, *Jews*; Lewis, *Jews*.

37 Krakowski, *Age*, 255.

38 Krakowski, *Age*, 258, cites evidence "from surviving questions sent to Rabbanite jurists, which presume . . . that pledges in a marriage agreement increase women's legal claims to [the husband's payment to the wife in case of his death or their divorce]. . . . Relatives who worked to insert these stipulations into a daughter's marriage agreement did so . . . in hopes of giving her greater bargaining power against her husband during the marriage, but also in case it dissolved."

39 See Grossman, *Pious* (Hebrew), 137.

40 Grossman, *Pious*, 249–51, 291, n. 26, and 235–36; Grossman, *Pious* (Hebrew), 83 and 89. Grossman, *Pious*, 251, notes that "the family unit in most Jewish communities was not at all stable . . . idyllic descriptions . . . have no basis in fact"; see too, there, 74. Krakowski, *Age*, echoes this assessment for the Jews of Fatimid and Ayyubid (tenth to thirteenth centuries) Fustat (Cairo).

41 Grossman, *Pious*, 74, notes that the edict's stated limit indicates that men were routinely absent for longer than this.

42 Grossman, *Pious*, 249; idem, *Pious* (Hebrew), 142.

43 Krakowski, *Age*, 35–36. The Fatimids reigned from 909 to 1171; the Ayyubids from 1171 to 1260.

44 See Cohen, *Poverty*, 143. The term "widow of a living man" is Talmudic; see B. Ketubot 62:2.

45 See Rustow, "Jews," 91, for population estimates of Jews in medieval Ashkenaz and the Middle East.

46 Cohen, *Poverty*, 151–52.

47 It is quite clear that "the wife of the apostate living in the inn of Abu Thina, the only woman so designated in the Geniza, as Goitein remarks, is not a widow. Her husband's conversion to Islam would have left her abandoned, hence needy"; Cohen, *Poverty*, 152. See, too, Cohen, "Poverty."

48 Cohen, *Poverty*, 143.

49 Grossman, *Pious*, 250; idem, *Pious* (Hebrew), 130–32.

50 See Grossman, *Pious* (Hebrew), 118–73.

51 Grossman, *Pious*, 75, 80–83; see, too, idem, *Pious* (Hebrew),129–31 and 141–42; Friedman, *Jewish Polygyny* (Hebrew), 19–21, 34–36, 205–6; Keil, "Roles," 317–30.

52 Grossman, *Pious* (Hebrew), 141, 415.

53 Goitein, *Mediterranean*, 378.

54 Lamdan, *Separate*, 147; Rozen, *History*, 158–70; Adelman, "Custom," 107–25, and idem, *Marriage*, 113–22.

55 See Shashar, *Vanished*, 298–300, for discussions among decisors from the thirteenth to the sixteenth century about this expedient and its actual application.

56 Lamdan, *Separate*, 173.

57 Lamdan, *Separate*, 174.

58 Conditional divorce was also practiced by Jews in the Russian Empire; Freeze, *Jewish Marriage*, 200, 236, 364–65, n. 160.

59 See Krakowski, *Age*, 241–43, 249–52, and there, chapter 7; Cohen, *Poverty*, and on women who made such claims, 139–55.

60 Cohen, *Poverty*, 145–46.

61 Cohen, *Poverty*, 147; Krakowski, *Age*, 258.

62 Krakowski, *Age*, 114, 68, 160, and 258.

63 Krakowski, *Age*, 160; Goitein, *Mediterranean*, 3:195–205; Cohen, *Poverty*, 143.

64 Goitein, *Mediterranean*, 3:195–205, as Cohen, *Poverty*, 143, notes.

65 Krakowski, *Age*, 259–60.

66 Zinger, "Women."

67 Krakowski, *Age*, 260.

68 Krakowski, *Age*, 261.

69 Cohen, *Poverty*, 144.

70 Lamdan, *Separate*, 62–63, 158. Under halakha, mothers, wives, and daughters do not inherit in the first instance. In order to bequeath them property, men used wills, gifts formalized by legal deeds, and the Muslim institution of waqf, through which property "was endowed to a . . . charitable or religious institution, but family members, including women, were allowed to use it in perpetuity," Lamdan, "Encounters," 111; idem, "Mothers," 83 and n. 9, p. 83. Jewish, and specifically female, poverty was widespread in Ottoman Jewries; Lamdan, *Separate*, 159. Inheritance, of course, was a significant counter to poverty.

71 Lamdan, *Separate*, 34, 54–55, 116, who notes, 134, that men who agreed at the time of marriage to remain monogamous or to require the wife's consent in order to marry a second wife often tried to renege on these agreements and that disputes about this factored heavily in divorce cases—divorcing the first wife being a man's means to marry another. Men often succeeded in this quest despite formal agreements to bar it.

72 Lamdan, "Mercies," 60–61.

73 Lamdan, "Mercies," 63.

74 Reiner, "Rabbinical Courts," 303–4.

75 For abundant such dynamics in early modern Italy, see Adelman, *Marriage*; for but one example, 47.

76 For one case, see Adelman, *Marriage*, 148.

77 Goldin, *Jewish Women*, 74, citing Finkelstein, *Self-Government*, 168–70.

78 נחלה פניו [. . .] לעזור לקרב לה התועלת, כי בשלומה יהיה שלום לעיר אלדינו אשר ירדה פלאים, ולחכימא ברמיזה." Lamdan, *Separate*, 159–60 (my translation).

3. AGENCY AND AUTHORITY

1 Borrowing from Baumgarten, *Piety*, 128.

2 See Meiselman, *Woman*; Wolowelsky, *Women*. Such usages are not confined to apologetics. In Grossman, *Pious*, the terms "the Jewish woman" and "the woman" are ubiquitous. Such usage reflects terminology in halakhic sources, but the absence of awareness and clarification about this, and scholarly distance from it, are problematic. Despite the title, Nizri, " 'Living," omits agunot as a subject and distinguishes (63) between "a woman" and "another Jew" (meaning another Jewish husband, the two "Jews" being men). In Radzyner, "Halakha," Jews are men. Thus (279), Jews "who marry there [Morocco] know that their ability to marry a second wife is limited." Despite reliance on halakhic sources, Goldin, *Jewish Women*, speaks of "women"; as do Judith Baskin, "Women"; idem, "Separation"; and Berkovitz, *Women*.

3 Agunah advocates frequently cite the Talmud (Shabbat 55a) and the term there, "the cry of the wretched" (Hebrew: *za'akat dal*), in calls for compassion. The term is the title of several halakhic analyses of and progressive proposals about agunot; Sarna, *American*, 241, refers to "the poor anchored women," who got no benefit when the controversies regarding iggun of 1935 and 1953 between the Conservative and Orthodox movements worked to define their respective denominational boundaries. Generic Jews (meaning men) in victimized situations—pogroms, the Shoah—let alone in situations of abuse created by other Jews, are never referred to as "the poor Jews." The usage reflects the anchored association of agunot with permanent, normal, if pitiable, women's victimhood, and their otherness.

4 Illustration by Maureen Fain, also featured on the Schechter Institute's Jewish Law Watch- Case Study pamphlets, suggesting halakhic solutions to agunah cases unresolved in Chief Rabbinate courts.

5 The works of Ruth Lamdan and Minna Rozen are indispensable in laying the groundwork for study of agunot and iggun in the sixteenth-century Middle East. Their analyses of cases, however, reflect male, rabbinic perspectives on them.

6 Furst, "Marriage," 9 and 30. See, too, idem, "Right."

7 Berkovitz, "Women."

8 Friedman, *Jewish Marriage*, I: 326.

9 Cited in Baumgarten, *Piety*, 164. The historical question of halakhic responsiveness to changing circumstance has been and continues to be studied extensively; for one iconic work, see Katz, *"Shabbes Goy."* This question is not my interest in this work, but, rather, women's behavior regarding their own rights becoming enshrined in normative, rabbinic pronouncement, against other, articulated rabbinic norms.

10 Baumgarten, *Piety*, 167. See, too, Kanarfogel, "Rabbinic Attitudes."

11 Baumgarten, *Piety*, 171. See, too, Har-Shefi, "Women."

12 Baumgarten, *Piety*, 158; Labovitz, "Purchase."

13 Baumgarten, *Piety*, 145, 157, 168–69.

14 Baumgarten, *Piety*, 145.

15 Baumgarten, *Piety*, 215.

16 Baumgarten, *Piety*, 156–71. As she (169) writes, "This dynamism not only shows how gender constructed religion but how religious politics constructed gender and led to transformed definitions of man and woman and their traits."

17 See Graetz, "Wifebeating"; idem, Silence.

18 Krakowski, *Age*, 252.

19 Roth, "Strategy," 391.

20 Discussing Jewish autonomy under Ottoman rule, Benbassa and Rodrigue, *Sephardi*, 18–19, state:

> The leaders of [the Jewish, theocratic "micro-states," in which "temporal and spiritual authority merged"] had to place the people they administered into social . . . and juridical frameworks . . . without possessing the real power they would . . . have required to procure compliance with laws and regulations. . . . Jewish law and Jewish judges did not enjoy official recognition. Nor did the verdicts of non-Muslim courts have real legal status. . . . The only law officially recognized was Muslim law [though] the judgments of the Jewish courts, in principle, had the force of law for Jews. . . . The Jewish courts however, were impotent when faced with Muslim ones who might reject their authority.

They also note that "many legal cases involving Jews alone often came to be tried under Muslim jurisdiction. In view of the limited power of their own courts, Jews sometimes preferred to appeal to the kadi in matters relating to inheritance or commercial litigation."

21 Benbassa and Rodrigue, *Sephardi*, 19.

22 See Adelman, "Custom"; *Marriage*.

23 See, for example, Ackerman-Lieberman, "Woman's Right," about extensive machinations by a wealthy wife in sixteenth-century Safed vs. her husband, in and outside of rabbinical courts, to protect and maximize her economic interests through control of her son's prenuptial agreements.

24 Lamdan, *Separate*, 64–65.

25 Although Lamdan, *Separate*, 74, does not specify the community in which this case occurred, the one named rabbi who permitted the woman to marry without delay was Rabbi Meir Gavizon, who served in Safed and Cairo, in the latter as head of the rabbinical court; idem, 209.

26 Rozen, *History*, 141.

27 Lamdan, *Separate*, 148.

28 Lamdan, "Mercies," 63.

29 Rozen, *History*, 168; about immigrating to Israel giving the wife the right of divorce, see Ilan, "Patriarchy."

30 Lamdan, *Separate*, 165–66.

31 Rozen, *History*, 176–77; see, too, 158.

32 Lamdan, "Mercies," 56 and n. 26 there.

33 Rozen, *History*, 176–77.

34 Lamdan, *Separate*, 172. They ruled so in contrast to decisors in Salonika, see below. On the Iberian immigration to Palestine and the Levant during the sixteenth and seventeenth centuries, see Gerber, *Jews of Spain*, 15–175; Abraham, "Spanish Exiles"; Benbassa and Rodrigue, *Sephardi*, xviii–lxiii and 1–64; Fromm, "Hispanic"; and Dorn Sezgin, "Jewish Women," who cites (216) a figure of 50,000–150,000 Iberian Jews who came to Ottoman-ruled lands in the aftermath of 1492.

35 Lamdan, *Separate*, 172–73.

36 Lamdan, *Separate*, 165–66, 172.

37 See Lamdan, *Separate*, 170 and 175, n. 8.

38 See Lamdan, *Separate*, 170 and 175, n. 8; and Porgos, *She'elot u'teshuvot*, 24–25, including a copy of the document reproduced here: https://hebrewbooks.org /pdfpager.aspx?req=1840&st=&pgnum=23&hilite= Immense thanks to Daniel Price for locating this document.

39 Goldin, *Jewish Women*, 79.

40 Rozen, *History*, 157–60.

41 Rozen, *History*, 168.

42 Lamdan, "Mercies," 59.

43 Rozen, *History*, 161–62.

44 Lamdan, *Separate*, 171.

45 Adelman, "Custom," 112, speaking of Don Isaac Abravanel (1437–1508) and "his contemporary, the Italian kabbalist, Elijah Hayyim Genazzano."

46 Adelman, "Custom."

47 Lamdan, *Separate*, 170–72.

48 See Lamdan, *Separate*, 169–70.

49 Lamdan, *Separate*, 169–70.

50 Rozen, *History*, 171–72; see, too, Lamdan, "Mercies," 53–54.

51 Adelman, "Custom," 112–15.

52 Adelman, "Custom," 116–17.

53 Shashar, *Vanished*, 309, who reproduces the full text of the letter in the original Yiddish, with Hebrew translation. My translation.

54 See Chizhik-Goldschmidt, "Polarizing." The article's headline states: "The book, rooted in modern Christian fundamentalism, has captured the attention of this insular community." One would expect this Christian origination alone to invalidate and anathematize the book in Orthodox circles. The fact that this is not the case testifies to a need to uphold patriarchy against the threat of women's autonomy so overwhelming that it trumps normally definitive and sacrosanct dividing lines against other religions.

55 See Lauer, "Jewish Law"; Klein, "'Widow's Portion"; idem, "Splitting Heirs"; Siegmund, "Division"; Goldin, *Jewish Women*, 130, 138, 142, 152, 155, 159–60, 162, 163.

4. USING NON-JEWISH COURTS, AND RABBINIC COURTS

1 Zinger, "'She Aims," 161, see especially 166. About Jewish women who took their cases to Muslim courts and the preponderance of women among Jews doing this, see 170–71 and figure 1, p. 164. As Friedman, *Jewish Marriage*, vol. 1, 324–25, notes, the ordinance is cited in the responsa of several other geonim and "was practiced among Jewish communities of different lands for several hundred years." On women initiating divorce and evolving rabbinic practice about this from the Mishna through medieval Geniza documents, see there, 312–46.

2 Cited in Riskin, *Women*, 57–58; see, too, 73, 75.

3 Grossman, *Pious*, 241–42.

4 Goldin, *Jewish Women*, 161; Riskin, *Women*, 59–60. Friedman, *Jewish Marriage*, vol. 1, 335, cites a ban (herem) placed on an Egyptian Jewish woman in 1032 for bringing her husband "before the judge of the gentiles and divorc[ing] him by her desire, against his will;" see, too, there, 336, n. 78, on the opposition of Jewish authorities to recourse by Jews to non-Jewish courts.

5 Krakowski, *Age*, 68–69.

6 Krakowski, *Age*, 82.

7 Krakowski, *Age*, 158.

8 Krakowski, *Age*, 94 and 95.

9 See Goldin, *Jewish Women*, 78, 97, 130, 138, 142, 159–63.

10 Citations in Rapoport-Albert, *Women*, 103 and there, n. 61.

11 Adelman, *Marriage*, 144.

12 Rapoport-Albert, *Women*, 103.

13 See Katz, *Tradition*, 63–94.

14 See Lauer, "Jewish Law," 115–16, about recent scholarship on premodern Jewish use of Gentile courts for intra-Jewish disputes.

15 See Katz, *Tradition*.

16 See Lauer, "Defense."

17 Lauer, "Defense," 583.

18 Parush, *Reading*.

19 Lauer, "Jewish Law," 120.

20 See Roth, "'Precious.'"

21 Grossman, *Pious*, 120–22; see, too, 76–77.

22 Goldin, *Jewish Women*, 23; see, too, 121.

23 Cited in Fishman, "Gender-Specific," 213–14.

5. SOCIOECONOMIC AND HALAKHIC REALITIES IN EARLY MODERNITY

1 Lamdan, "Mothers," 84; idem, *Separate*, 23.

2 Lamdan, *Separate*, 97.

3 Lamdan, *Separate*, 97. Dorn Sezgin, "Jewish Women," 220–21, gives statistics for seventeenth-century Istanbul showing 15 percent of the Jewish population poor, 15 percent "extremely rich," and the vast majority petty shopkeepers. Women routinely produced goods, e.g., textiles and embroidered goods sold in such shops. The poorest women worked as servants in the homes of wealthy Jewish families, who could arrange their marriages, including provision of a dowry. This could be a leg out of poverty, dowries being commonly used to finance business ventures.

4 Rapoport-Albert, *Women*, 110, n. 7; Benbassa and Rodrigue, *Sephardi*, 38; Sezgin, "Jewish Women," 220; Fromm, "Hispanic," 154; Lamdan, "Jewish Women."

5 Lamdan, *Separate*, 96–97.

6 Lamdan, "Mothers," 84.

7 See Ackerman-Lieberman, "Woman's Right."

8 Lamdan, "Mothers," 86. Lamdan, whose sources are all rabbinic, mostly responsa, cites cases in which mothers advised sons against a levirate marriage but none in which women urged sons to refuse or extort for halitsa.

9 Lamdan, "Mothers," 87.

10 Lamdan, "Mothers," 89–90; see, too, idem, *Separate*, 78.

11 On use of the waqf, see above, chapter 2, n. 70; Lamdan, "Mothers," 83 and n. 9, there.

12 Lamdan, *Separate*, 96, and idem, "Women," 54–58.

13 Lamdan, *Separate*, 97–99.

14 Fishman, "Gender-Specific," 206.

15 Fishman, "Gender-Specific," 205.

16 Lamdan, "Jewish Women," 49.

17 Adelman, *Marriage*, 52–53, 109–11, 138–39.

18 Adelman does not define what "illiterate" in this case means; it is hard to imagine this woman conducting extensive business dealings while completely "illiterate."

19 As we have seen in other contexts, bequests were a means to bypass women's disabilities in rabbinicinheritance law; see Adelman, *Marriage*, 139–40.

6. BACKLASH

1 Lists of the victims of the Blois massacre show that the martyrs were primarily women, with women and children being the majority of those choosing death over conversion to Christianity, and most of those put to death for this refusal being girls; Goldin, *Jewish Women*, 66.

2   Goldin, *Jewish Women*, 66–68.

3   Cited in Grossman, *Pious*, 239; see, too, Grossman, *Pious* (Hebrew), 425–26, 429, 440.

4   Adelman, *Marriage*, 120.

5   Grossman, *Pious*, 242–43.

6   See Goldin, *Jewish Women*, 152–53; Lamdan, "Mercies," 57–58.

7   See Goldin, *Jewish Women*, 77–79.

8   Goldin, *Jewish Women*, 124.

9   Cited in Goldin, *Jewish Women*, 157; see, too, Reiner, "Rabbinical Courts," 312–13.

10 For a sense of Rabbi Tam's authority and the awe in which he was held by his rabbinical contemporaries and later followers, see Soloveitchik, "Halakhic Texts."

11 Grossman, *Pious*, 243; cf. Riskin, *Women*. The Rosh also accepted the assertion that earlier authorities intended the rebellious-wife ordinance to be temporary; see Goldin, *Jewish Women*, 161 and 156.

12 Cited in Grossman, *Pious*, 243.

13 Rabbenu Gershom Me'or Hagolah also ruled that a financial penalty be imposed on women who he ruled should get a get by rabbinic coercion of the husband; Goldin, *Jewish Women*, 153.

14 Grossman, *Pious* (Hebrew), 441; idem, *Pious*, 243. In the case of a wife who refuses to perform any of the labors deemed wifely obligations to a husband under halakha—behavior that would also get the woman labeled rebellious—Maimonides rules that "she may be coerced to do so, even with a whip;" Grossman, *Pious*, 219. Rabbi Meir ben Barukh, the Maharam of Rothenburg (1215–1293), ruled similarly against the rebellious-wife ordinance in principle and went further, ruling, against Talmudic law, that a "rebellious woman" was to have the possessions she brought with her into the marriage confiscated; Grossman, *Pious* (Hebrew), 445–46.

15 Goldin, *Jewish Women*, 127–28, 129.

16 Rozen, *History*, 157–92.

17 Grossman, *Pious*, 240–41.

18 Grossman, *Pious*, 242. See, too Friedman, *Jewish Marriage*, vol. 1, 325.

19 Goldin, *Jewish Women*, 99–116.

20 Goldin, *Jewish Women*, 126, 137.

21 Goldin, *Jewish Women*, 137.

22 Goldin, *Jewish Women*, 136–49.

23 Baumgarten, *Piety*, 138–149; Keil, "Roles," 3.

24 Cited in Baumgarten, *Piety*, 169, and Grossman, *Pious*, 244.

25 Grossman, *Pious*, 244.

26 As quoted in Baumgarten, *Piety*, 169; cf. Grossman, *Pious*, 244–45.

27 Cited in Baumgarten, *Piety*, 169.

28 Grossman, *Pious*, 244–45.

29 Grossman, *Pious*, 244–45; idem, *Pious* (Hebrew), 445–47. About the upsurge of rulings against "rebellious" women, Goldin, *Jewish Women*, 157–58, says:

"The responsa literature abounds with discussions . . . of the 'rebellious wife' . . . throughout the thirteenth century . . . the sages were attempting to restore the men to the superior economic position . . . while . . . punishing the 'rebellious' women. . . . The main protest voiced by the male writers was against the economic power and various advances achieved by women, as borne out, they believed, by the growing number of 'rebellious wife' cases."

30 Grossman, *Pious*, 246.
31 Grossman, *Pious*, 246; idem, *Pious* (Hebrew), 448–40, 452–56.
32 Grossman, *Pious*, 247.
33 Goldin, *Jewish Women*, 159, 163.
34 Goldin, *Jewish Women*, 161. Goldin, 139, also cites rabbinic fear that coercing women who refused levirate marriages into such marriages "might force them to turn for help to the Christians and even lead them to convert in order to free themselves from an undesirable husband."
35 Goldin, *Jewish Women*, 159–64.
36 Goldin, *Jewish Women*, 158.
37 Goldin, *Jewish Women*, 68.
38 Baumgarten, *Piety*, 169, in an apparent reference to Goldin's assertion.
39 On Medina/Maharashdam, see Zohar, "Sephardic," and "Shmuel de Medina, Maharashdam" (Hebrew), *Entsyklopedia Yehudit*, www.daat.ac.il.
40 Cited in Weiss and Gross-Horowitz, *Marriage*, 1–2.
41 Weiss and Gross-Horowitz, *Marriage*, 8.
42 Weiss and Gross-Horowitz, *Marriage*, 8, cite the devastating importance of what they term the "Mahardasham–Maharik rule," which states "that a husband cannot in any way be ordered or compelled to divorce his wife, even if theoretical grounds exist for so doing, if he claims that he is willing to give a get so long as his wife meets his demands that are, in the opinion of the rabbis, either justified (Maharik) or easy to fulfill (Maharashdam)," 168. For an apologetic assessment of Colon/Maharik, see Woolf, "Damsels."
43 Weiss and Gross-Horowitz, *Marriage*, 54.
44 Woolf, "Damsels," 108, n. 36.
45 Fram, *Ideals*, 80, n. 41. The upshot of Colon's ruling in sixteenth-century Poland, says Fram, is that, rather than there being an encompassing legal principle that women could undertake large-scale economic activities on their own authority (per the ruling of the twelfth-century Raban), husbands could now ask rabbinical judges to decide the matter. Even the possibility of such intervention impeded the wife's actions and economic and social agency. This ruling by Colon fits a broader pattern of his rulings unfavorable to women.
46 See Gerber, *The Jews*, 106–44.
47 Ben-Shalom, "Social Context," 178–79, 182, shows that this was established behavior: after mass conversions in 1391, following attacks on Jewish communities across Spain, widows needing halitsa or wives needing divorce sought this from converted men "within the Converso community according to Jewish law."

48 See Grossman, *Pious* (Hebrew), 362, 364.

49 Lamdan, *Separate*, 150; idem, "Mercies," 61.

50 On Jewish population growth in Salonika and the town's growing importance—by 1613 it was "one of the most important Jewish centers in the world and the leading Jewish city on the Mediterranean"—see Benbassa and Rodrigue, *Sephardi*, 9, 39; Gerber, *Jews of Spain*, 153–54, 179; Mazower, *Salonica*, 8, 10, 6, 56–63.

51 See Lamdan, *Separate*, 150–51.

52 Hacker, "Ibn Habib."

53 As noted, other decisors, in Istanbul, who were not Sephardi and therefore, according to Rozen, *Pathways*, 12–13, not moved by the same emotional considerations as Sephardi decisors, ruled differently than ibn Habib. Lamdan, "Mercies," 62, argues the opposite about the influence of ethnic background on the rulings of Sephardi decisors in Palestine and Egypt, who (Joseph Karo not among them) tended to leniency, albeit, she notes, possibly because relatively few such cases reached them. On manifold such problems reaching decisors of various Jewish ethnicities in this period and responses—all, obviously, only from male perspectives—see Rozen, *History*, 92–98.

54 Rozen, *Pathways*, 12–13; idem, *History*, 93–94; Lamdan, *Separate*, 149–50.

55 See Kanarfogel, "Changing Attitudes."

56 Benmayor, "Salonika." Benmayor does not name the rabbis in this "triumvirate"; presumably, it included Rabbis de Medina, Yosef Taitatsak, and Jacob ben Solomon ibn Habib. These converts would not have been accepted as valid witnesses in halakhic proceedings, including marriage ceremonies, one of the requirements for which, aside from being male, being strict observance of the Sabbath and other holidays and kashrut.

57 In his study of social relations between Jews, Christians, and conversos, Ben-Shalom, "Social Context," with one exception, writes of converts as men, with no consideration of the behavior of conversas. On conversas in Castile, see Levine Melammed, *Heretics*, which makes no mention of agunot, iggun, get, or halitsa.

58 Rozen, *History*, 99–105.

59 See Yerushalmi, *Spanish*, 1–50; and the excellent summary in Benbassa and Rodrigue, *Sephardi*, xvi–lxiii.

60 See Rozen, *History*, 99–105.

61 On the trauma of the Iberian refugees, Benabassa and Rodrigue, *Sephardi*, 13, state:

> The experience of exile had destroyed families, separated couples, and left many parents without their children. Forced conversions, disease, abductions, and exhaustion shattered the family nucleus. Some had remained in the peninsula, preferring conversion to departure. This explains why many arrived in the [Ottoman] Empire alone, without a family to support them in confronting the new reality. Various calamities such as epidemics and the death rate which ensued weighed heavily on the newcomers. . . . In this period, when the Jew remained attached to the faith, when, furthermore, the notion of "individual" as

we know it did not yet exist, the destruction of families meant above all a break in . . . continuity and a challenge to the survival of the Jewish people itself. See, too, 30, 34; and Rozen, *History*, 99–105.

62 On the national resonance of the Spanish Jewish catastrophe among other Jewish ethnicities, see Scholem, *Sabbatai Sevi*, and idem, *Major Trends*, 244–86.

63 On this migration, see Goldberg, "Family and Community"; Benbassa and Rodrigue, *Sephardi*, xviii–liv.

64 See Soloveitchik, "Halakhic Texts."

65 Cited in Ben-Shalom, "Social Context," 191.

66 Cited in Ben-Shalom, "Social Context," 192.

67 Cited in Ben-Shalom, "Social Context," 192.

68 Cited in Ben-Shalom, "Social Context," 192.

69 Cited in Ben-Shalom, "Social Context," 192.

70 Cited in Ben-Shalom, "Social Context," 192.

71 See de Medina, and ben Matanya, *Responsa*. On Maharashdam, see "Shmuel de Medina, Maharashdam" (Hebrew), *Entsyklopedia Yehudit*, www.daat.ac.il/. Great thanks to Daniel Price for sending me the texts of these *teshuvot*.

72 For a similar reading of another seemingly positive rabbinic ruling from a very different era, see Ilan, "Patriarchy."

7. "AGUNOT, HALAKHIC DECISORS, AND SUFFERING" IN MID-SEVENTEENTH TO MID-NINETEENTH-CENTURY EUROPE

1 Shashar's phrase, *Vanished*, 391.

2 Shashar, *Vanished*.

3 Shashar addresses the problems of historical use of responsa and other rabbinical materials extensively; see 228, 272, 353–63, as does Adelman, *Marriage*, 1–24, and throughout the book; see, too, Soloveitchik, *Responsa*; idem, "Halakhic Texts"; Washofsky, "Taking Precedent"; Furst, "Marriage," 21.

4 Shashar, *Vanished*, 90–128. On halitsa extortion in medieval Ashkenaz, see Goldin, *Jewish Women*, 137, 140, 142, 144; and in early modern Italy, Adelman, "Custom."

5 Shashar, *Vanished*, 108–10.

6 Shashar, *Vanished*, 115, 118.

7 Shashar, *Vanished*, 126–27.

8 Shashar, *Vanished*, 318. Kanarfogel, "Changing," 37, shows that medieval Talmudists debated Rashi's ruling that "a Jew who sins [meaning a convert] is still a Jew" for all halakhic purposes, including a levir's eligibility to give halitsa, but never questioned the convert's eligibility to give a get.

9 See Goldin, *Jewish Women*, 37, on converts in medieval Ashkenaz giving gittin.

10 Sinclair, "Halakhic."

11 Shashar, *Vanished*, 318, n. 131, my translation.

12 Shashar, *Vanished*, 319. On Perl's critiques of rabbis on these issues, see Sinkoff, "Maskil."

13 See Stampfer, "Gzeyres"; idem, "What Actually"; Raba, *Remembrance*.

14 Shashar, *Vanished*, 169–83, 353–54, n. 1

15 Shashar, *Vanished*, 232–35, shows that involvement of non-Jewish authorities investigating a man's death would hurt, not help, an agunah's chances in rabbinical courts.

16 Much of Shashar's book is devoted to this question; see especially 183, 205, and 233–34.

17 Shashar, *Vanished*, 379.

18 Shashar, *Vanished*, 345.

19 Grade, *Agunah*, 130.

20 Ginzburg, "Colon."

21 See Lamdan, *Separate*, 207–10, for decisors' biographical details.

22 Lamdan, *Separate*, 164 (my translation). On this case, see Dimitrovsky, "Vikuaḥ."

23 Lamdan, *Separate*, 164–65.

24 Lamdan, *Separate*, 165.

25 On the socioeconomic makeup of the Jewish community in seventeenth-century Istanbul, see Benbassa and Rodrigue, *Sephardi*, 32.

26 Shashar, *Vanished*, 216, 369–74.

27 Soloveitchik, *Rupture*, 9.

28 This is not at all to suggest that these were the only periods of increased numbers of agunot in the context of anti-Jewish persecutions. See, e.g., Grossman, *Pious*, 205, about "the large number of . . . husbands [who] converted to Christianity" [during violent persecution in the Crusades, eleventh to thirteenth centuries], and wives who "refused to join them, even though they were thus left . . . as 'chained wives.'"

29 For one example of such assertions, see Chigier, "Ruminations."

30 Freeze and Harris, *Everyday*, 220, n. 3. They also assert (226, n. 1), about halitsa, that "in contemporary Jewish practice as well [in apparent contrast to "in Russia"], levirate divorce was the much-preferred option." This statement omits mention of contemporary civil law outlawing polygyny as responsible for any such "preference," leaving the (mis)impression that halakhic benevolence (or embarrassment) motivated or motivates it.

31 Shashar, *Vanished*, 392.

32 Shashar, *Vanished*, 348, and there, n. 161.

33 Shashar, *Vanished*, 362, 407–12.

34 Shashar, *Vanished*, 366.

35 Shashar, *Vanished*, 369.

36 Wengeroff, *Memoirs*, vol. 1: 42–72.

37 On girls' traditional education, see Turniansky, *Glikl*, 1–60; Weissler, *Voices*; Eliav, *Education*; Rosman, "History"; Stampfer, "Gender"; idem, *Families*; Greenbaum, "Heder"; idem, "Girl's Heder"; Adler, "Educational Options"; idem, *Hands*; Parush, *Reading*; Ellenson, "German Orthodox"; Elior, *Grandmother*; Magnus, "Introduction"; Wengeroff, *Memoirs*, vol. 1: 1–75; Seidman, *Schenirer*.

38 On the dissemination of Lurianic kabbalah and Sabbatianism, see Scholem, *Major Trends, Sabbetai Sevi*; on petitionary prayers for women, see Weissler, *Voices*.

39 Shashar, *Vanished*, 373.

40 Shashar, *Vanished*, 374–75, and 375, n. 69; and 381.

41 Quoted in Zalkin, *Beyond*, 162. Woolf, "Damsels," 108, states that "appeals for support and confirmation from other halakhists were common in late medieval Ashkenaz"; he does not specify types of cases for which decisors sought supportive rulings from other decisors. About Joseph ben Solomon Colon (Maharik) of late fifteenth-century Italy, however, Woolf says that Colon rarely asked for such support—except in cases of agunot.

42 Maharashdam, *teshuvot, even ha'ezer, siman yud*. Thanks to Yisrael Gale, Atarah Ross, and Richie Lewis for their readings of this responsum.

43 Rozen, *History*, 158; Lamdan, "Mercies," 55–56.

44 Benbassa and Rodrigue, *Sephardi*, 34.

45 Shashar, *Vanished*, 385.

46 Shashar, *Vanished*, 172–79 and 383–85.

47 Shashar, *Vanished*, 384–85.

48 Shashar, *Vanished*, 386.

49 Shashar, *Vanished*, 386, my translations.

50 Shashar, *Vanished*, 401.

8. AGUNOT VS. IGGUN

1 Shashar, *Vanished*, 224–25.

2 See Dubin, "Women"; Berkovitz, "Women"; Shashar, *Vanished*, 286.

3 Shashar, *Vanished*, 287.

4 Under halakha, in case of the husband's death, or divorce, the dowry was to revert to a wife, though as we have seen it was often contested in both situations and could also be confiscated to punish "rebelliousness."

5 Shashar, *Vanished*, 250–51.

6 Shashar, *Vanished*, 27, and in detail, 250–88.

7 Quoted in Shashar, *Vanished*, 331.

8 Shashar, *Vanished*, 331–32.

9 Cited on the front page of all volumes of the journal *Polin*.

10 For Glikl, see chapter 2, n. 2 above. For Maimon, see *Autobiography*, from which all quotes are taken.

11 *Glikl*, Turniansky, ed., 427; *Glueckel*, Lowenthal, ed., 123–24.

12 My translation of Turniansky, 425–27.

13 My translation, from *Glikl*, Turniansky, ed., 425–45; see, in *Glueckel*, Lowenthal, ed., 184–87, 194–97; *Glueckel*, Abrahams, ed., 128–135.

14 *Autobiography*, 61, 81.

15 See *Autobiography*, 49–61; Maimon gives his wife's name as Sarah, 53.

16 *Autobiography*, 130–31, 140–42.

17 Shashar, *Vanished*, 381, 393.

18 Berkovitz, "Women," studies Jewish businesswomen's use of and reception in rabbinic and French courts in eighteenth-century Metz. He does not treat cases of iggun. Shashar assesses the records of the Metz beit din; they show no divergence from the larger pattern she documents.

19 Sarna, *American*, 241.

20 See Katz, "Orthodoxy"; Silber, "Orthodoxy"; Samet, "Beginnings"; Berkovitz, "Orthodoxy"; Sperber, "Paralysis"; Sinclair, "Methodology"; and further, below.

21 Keil, "Roles," 9–10. On medieval Ashkenazic women's presence in the synagogue, see Baumgarten, *Piety*, 21–50.

9. IGGUN IN MODERNITY

1 See Sarna, *American*; Jick, *Americanization*; Goren, *New York*; Endelman, *Georgian*; idem, *Britain*.

2 Freeze and Harris, *Everyday*, 33; see, too, Mendes-Flohr and Reinharz, *Jew*, 395–96, 879–84.

3 See Stampfer, "Patterns"; Freeze, *Marriage*, 158.

4 Sperber, "Agunot," 95; idem, "Agunot, 1851–1914," 108, and idem, *Plight*, 17.

5 Baker, "Voice"; Sperber, "Agunot, Immigration," 79–108; idem, "Phenomenon," 102–8; idem, "Agunot, 1851–1914," 107–35, and idem, *Plight*, 4–7; Zalkin, *Beyond*, 141–43.

6 Shilo, *Princess*, 191.

7 Freeze, *Marriage*, 233, 235; see, too, S. Friedman, "'Send'"; Hyman, "Gender"; idem, "America"; Igra, *Wives*, 14–15; Metzger, *Bintel Brief*, 15–16; Silverstein, "Harry."

8 Meir, *Kiev*, 120.

9 Cited in Freeze, *Marriage*, 201.

10 Freeze, *Marriage*, 231; see, too, Sperber, "Agunot," 114; Lederhendler, *Responses*; Gartner, *Immigrant*, 169 and there, n. 5.

11 See Bristow, *Prostitution*, 104, and Kaplan, *Feminist*, 116–17. See Sperber, "Agunot," 112, for other criminal exploitation of agunot.

12 Bristow, *Prostitution*, 217.

13 Freeze, *Marriage*, 237, see also 188.

14 Freeze, *Marriage*, 230–31.

15 Sperber, "Agunot, 1851–1914," 121.

16 Freeze, *Marriage*, 231–32.

17 Freeze, *Marriage*, 236.

18 Freeze, *Marriage*, 232, 285, 365–66, n. 171.

19 Freeze and Harris, *Everyday*, 224–26, who note (227, n. 8) another case of halitsa extortion.

20 Freeze and Harris, *Everyday*, 194–204.

21 Wengeroff, *Memoirs*, vol. 1: 117.

22 Wengeroff, *Memoirs*, vol. 2: 38–41.

23 Freeze and Harris, *Everyday*, 83.

24 Freeze and Harris, *Everyday*, 190–93 and 193, n. 3.

25 Shimoff, *Rabbi Isaac*, 93; Cf. Freeze, *Marriage*, 231; Eliach, *Once*, 730, n.9.

26 Freeze, *Marriage*, 231; see, too, Freeze and Harris, *Everyday*, 218–22, for several
    Spektor responsa on agunot. Responsa of earlier periods in the region's history
    are replete with mention of agunot; see Freeze, *Marriage*, 364, n. 144. Spektor is
    reported as having acted leniently about witnessing requirements to establish
    a husband's death in order to free agunot in specific situations; see Freeze and
    Harris, *Everyday*, 221–22, for one such ruling. In that case, however, the evidence
    found on the body indicating the dead man's identity was explicit, varied, and
    abundant, including an amulet with the man's full Hebrew name (his and that of
    his mother, used when praying for a sick person, when it was known that he had
    left home seeking a cure). It is hard to deem a ruling in this case "lenient," but this
    illustrates the standard otherwise applied. See Shimoff, Rabbi, 85–105, for Spektor
    rulings in other circumstances of iggun. Freeze and Harris also produce responsa
    showing Spektor allowing men to marry a second wife without divorcing the
    first; ibid, 194–204, 222–23; cf. multiple references to agunot and dispensation
    for bigyny in Shimoff, Rabbi. To my knowledge there has been no study of the
    frequency with which such dispensation for bigyny occurred, but it appears not to
    have been uncommon. See Freeze and Harris, *Everyday*, 194–204, about another
    such dispensation. About references to agunot in the responsa of other decisors,
    see Sperber, "Agunot," 116 and his table 3.
27 Freeze and Harris, *Everyday*, 467.
28 Quoted in Freeze and Harris, *Everyday*, 468, n. 1.
29 See Stanislawksi, *Toil*, 125–28.
30 See Baron, "Kritut"; Govrin, "Baron"; Jelen and Pinsker, *Hebrew*; Bernstein,
    "Wife"; idem, "Midrash"; Zierler, "World?"
31 Grade, *Agunah*. See the list of fictional writings about agunot by nineteenth-
    century Eastern European Jewish writers in Sperber, *Plight*, 66–67.
32 Shilo, *Princess*, 190.
33 Shilo, *Princess*, 197.
34 Shilo, *Princess*, 190–93, 195, 197.
35 See Shilo, "Feminism."
36 See Mendes-Flohr and Reinharz, *Jew*, "Appendix: Demography," 879–91.
37 On this history, see Weiss and Gross-Horowitz, *Marriage*.
38 For expressions of Orthodox fear of feminism and antagonism even (especially)
    to Orthodox feminism, see Meiselman, *Jewish Woman*; Feldman, "Halakhic";
    Wolowelsky, *Women*; and Elinson, *The Woman and Mitzvot*, especially vol. 3, *Man
    and His Wife*, endorsed by then (Sephardi) chief rabbi Ovadia Yosef. For a less
    defensive approach, see Berman, "Status."
39 Sperber, *Plight*, 13. On the Jewish press in the tsarist empire, see Orbach, *Voices*;
    Stein, *Making*; Soffer, *No Complicating*; Veidlinger, *Public*.
40 See Sperber, *Plight*, 4–13 and 18–19, about ads seeking disappeared husbands,
    some of whom married multiple times without divorcing any of the wives, whose
    assets they stole; ads about men who fraudulently claimed to act as a disappeared
    husband's messenger to deliver a get and sought donations to defray alleged

travel expenses; and about women who posted fraudulent ads about disappeared husbands.

41 Sperber, *Plight*, 14.

42 Freeze and Harris, *Everyday*, 47, 383.

43 Sperber, *Plight*, 16

44 Sperber, *Plight*, 18.

45 Gudefin, "Reforming," 56. See, too, Gudefin, "Creating."

46 See Kaplan, "Thorny," 64–67; Sperber, *Plight*, 74.

47 On the cited reasons for opposing the reforms, see Susskind-Goldberg and Villa, *Za'akat*, 138, 144, and Kaplan, "Thorny," 67–68. *Archives Israélites* (July 25, 1907), 235–36, published a letter by David Friedman, chief rabbi of Karlin and Pinsk, and Chaim Ozer Grodzinski of Vilna opposing the French proposals. Rabbi Judah Lubetzki, leader of the Eastern European Jewish immigrant community in Paris, who opposed the proposals, claimed that decades earlier the then chief rabbi of France, Zadoc Kahn, had raised conditional marriage with Rabbi Isaac Elchanan Spektor of Kovno, who had firmly opposed it, leading Rabbi Kahn to abandon the reform; see *Univers Israélite*, July 5, 1907, 495, and *Archives Israélites*, July 4, 1907, 212. Thanks to Geraldine Gudefin for these specifics, email of September 22, 2022; she notes Rabbi Lubetsky's tract, *There Is No Condition on Marriage* (1930), which lists the religious authorities who supported his position; available at "En tena'i be-niśu'in: kolel berur halakhah u-mikhteve meḥa'ah me-et gedole ziḳne ha-dor . . . ," 1976, https://lawcat .berkeley.edu/; on Spektor's relationship with Kahn, see Shimoff, *Rabbi*, 65-66. On tensions between acculturated and assimilated, native-born French Jews and traditionalist Eastern European Jewish immigrants, see Hyman, *Dreyfus*.

48 See Cohen-Albert, *Modernization*.

49 Employing Judeophobic stereotypes, Napoleon in 1806 ordered an "Assembly of Notables" and then a "Sanhedrin" to convene in order to confer rabbinic and communal sanction on measures directing French Jews to put loyalty to France and French law above any Jewish attachments, and certainly over any competing, much less conflicting, obligations under halakha. For succinct treatments, see Seltzer, *People*, 525–27; Efron and Weitzman, *Jews*, 273–75.

50 Kaplan, "Thorny," 64–66.

51 On relations between the Consistory and the state and implications that it was a co-opted institution, incapable of defending French Jews even during the Dreyfus Affair, see Marrus, *Politics*.

52 See Kaplan, *Feminist*, 10–13. The JFB was founded by middle-class German Jewish women seeking to transform traditional women's volunteer activities in the community into professional social work in childcare, youth, and old age homes, and in tuberculosis treatment centers run by women, also demanding women's suffrage in communal elections.

53 See Kaplan, *Feminist*, 117–45.

54 See Klier, "Pogroms"; Shtif, *Pogroms*; Veidlinger, "Fields"; Snyder, *Holocaust*, 23, 26.

55 Seidman, *Schenirer*, 30.

56 Bristow, *Prostitution*, 104. Bristow gives the date for the conference as 1929 but it took place in 1923; see World Congress of Jewish Women, Vienna, May 6–11, 1923, www.worldcat.org.

57 Bristow, *Prostitution*, 104.

58 Aranoff and Haut, *Wed-Locked*, 15. An online search for *heter iska* readily yields many resources for executing it: this rabbinic workaround to a biblical prohibition remains a very contemporary practice.

59 Quoted in Seidman, *Schenirer*, 40. See, too, Kaplan, *Feminist*, 116–17. The source of the twenty thousand number for agunot in Eastern Europe in 1929 is the Frauenbund's newsletter (*Blätter*) of 1936. On Pappenheim, see *Pappenheim*.

60 Seidman, *Schenirer*, 40.

61 Kaplan, "Innovation," 299; see, too, Bacon, *Politics*; idem, "Agudas"; idem, "Da'at Torah"; and Soloveitchik, *Rupture*, 31–36, 61, 72.

62 Pappenheim, 428.

63 My translation, with thanks to Katharina von Kellenbach for her input. In memory of the recently deceased Pappenheim, her letter to the Agudah was published in the *Blätter des Jüdischen Frauenbunde für Frauenarbeit and Frauenbewegung*, 12 (1936), 7/8 (Juli–August), 20–21. A Hebrew translation of it appears in *Pappenheim*, 429–30.

64 Seidman, *Schenirer*, 41–42.

65 Document of the Australian agunah-advocacy organization Unchain My Heart, www.facebook.com/unchainmyheartaus, citing halakhic expedients to circumvent both rabbinic and biblical prohibitions, despite the latter having sacrosanct, obligatory force in halakha, while claiming that there is no halakhic solution to a husband's get withholding. Thanks to Dr. Elana Sztokman for bringing it to my attention.

66 Greenberg, *Women*, 142. For proposals to mitigate iggun as of 1999, see Meacham, "Marriage."

67 Haruvi, "Bet Din."

10. THE PRESENT STATE OF JEWISH MARITAL CAPTIVITY

1 On the origins of the earliest agunah-advocacy organizations in the United States, see Nusan Porter, *Women*, xiii–xv. The following list does not claim to be comprehensive. In the United States: G.E.T. (Getting Equitable Treatment); Agunah International; Agunah, Inc.; ORA (Organization for Resolution of Agunot); Jewish Orthodox Feminist Alliance (JOFA); L'Maan B'nos Yisroel International; in Canada: Canadian Coalition of Women for the Get; in the UK: Agunot Anonymous Educational Foundation; Agunot Campaign; Getting Your Get; in Israel: Center for Women's Justice; ICAR (International Coalition for Aguna Rights); International Jewish Women's Human Rights Watch; Mavoi Satum; Ruth and Emanuel Rackman Center for the Advancement of Women's Status, at Bar-Ilan University; Yad La'isha—Monica Dennis Goldberg Legal Aid Center and Hotline for Agunot

(affiliated with the Ohr Torah Stone network); in Australia: Unchain My Heart, www.facebook.com/unchainmyheartaus. A modern Orthodox organization based in Israel, Chochmat Nashim, while not centered on iggun, has addressed it using traditional methods.

2 A defining difference between Orthodoxy and ultra-Orthodoxy lies in attitudes to secular knowledge, with modern Orthodoxy embracing this and committed to resolving the resulting tensions, and ultra-Orthodoxy suspicious of or hostile to secular learning. Modern Orthodoxy sees modernity as a necessary and fruitful, if difficult, challenge; ultra-Orthodoxy, as a danger and threat.

3 Batnitzky, *Judaism*. The following focuses on Jewish modernization in Western realms.

4 See Meyer, *Response*, which includes treatment of the creation of modern Orthodoxy in the nineteenth century. For full and evocative treatments of the demise of halakhic authority and the responses of *poskim*, see Katz, "Shabbes Goy," 121–58; and idem, *Ghetto*; and *Tradition*.

5 Aranoff and Haut, *Wed-Locked*, 2; Soloveitchik, *Rupture*, 32.

6 Regev, "Do Not See," cites a decrease of 11 percent in couples marrying via the state-recognized Chief Rabbinate between 2015 and 2018. See, too, Riskin, "Disintegration"; Shilkof, "Remote"; and Finkelstein and Goldberg, "Statistical," the latter of which, incomprehensibly, relies on the Chief Rabbinate reporting of the number of get-refusal cases and the duration of divorce proceedings, despite known distortion in such reporting, about which below.

7 See the websites of Chuppot, Huppa Pratit, Rabbanei Tzohar, and ITIM; Ettinger, "Without the Rabbinate"; and Fischer, "Defy." For a critique of Orthodox wedding ceremonies conducted by independent Orthodox rabbis, see Magnus, "Huppa."

8 Weiss, "Divorce," 58–59.

9 Weiss, "Divorce," 59.

10 Ettinger, "Man's Refusal."

11 See Aranoff and Haut, *Wed-Locked*, 161–71; Frank, "Agunah"; Kobrun, "Enforceability"; Fishbayn Joffe, "Negotiating"; Broyde, "Thoughts"; Zwiebel, "Tragedy"; Jacob, "Agunah." On the situation in Canada, see Baumel Joseph, "Jurisdiction."

12 Keene, "California." See, too, Macner, "Coercive."

13 Frot, "Top Rabbi." Although Hool is quoted using the passive tense in referring to the get being deemed coerced/invalid, given his position as a judge on the rabbinic court, any such grammatical dodge is disingenuous. In any case, he advised a get-withholding man against relenting to give it, which, of course, left the husband liable to penalties under civil law

14 Weiss and Gross-Horowitz, *Marriage*, 16.

15 Aranoff and Haut, *Wed-Locked*, 71.

16 "Getting a Get," March 30, 2021, 7:00 pm:

> What do I do now? Where can I turn? Who can help me? These are just some of the questions people facing divorce ask themselves. Rabbi Yacov Barber resides in New York and is a Dayan [judge] and Toen/Rabbinic

Advocate. For 18 years he was the Senior Dayan on the Melbourne Beis Din, overseeing more than 600 divorces. Rabbi Barber leaves no stone unturned in order to procure a get for his clients and help them receive a fair settlement. Being a Senior Dayan with 18 years of experience, Rabbi Barber's unique perspective, professionalism, and compassion have led to his impressive track record. He is ready to act as your advocate and guide in navigating the very challenging journey of divorce. For further information and consultation please contact Rabbi Barber on 9178188707 or yacovbarber@gmail.com.

17 For example, see 1–800-G-E-T-A-G-E-T-T.

18 Frank, "Agunah," 34–35.

19 Frank, "Agunah," 36, and Hellman,17

20 Because of Israel's experience of wars, there is one notable difference in types of agunah cases brought there: wives of soldier whose bodies were unidentifiable or not located. See Lieber, "Rav Ovadia," on the exceptional actions of the Sephardi chief rabbi at the time to free some one thousand agunot after the Yom Kippur War of 1973. No establishment rabbinic figure in any country has taken such action to free agunot refused or extorted for divorce.

21 Aranoff and Haut, *Wed-Locked*, 55–58, 66–69.

22 "רוב רובם של המקרים, אולי יותר מ-99% אחוז, נשים לא מקבלות כתובה. אולי יש יותר מקרים בישראל מאשר באמריקה, אבל זה עדיין מקרים ממש ממש ממש בודדים"; email of October 10, 2019.

23 Aranoff and Haut, *Wed-Locked*, 6.

24 Aranoff and Haut, *Wed-Locked*, 6.

25 Sanctions could include shunning, enacted by the offender's community; in Israel, this could also include state-enforced financial and legal penalties and imprisonment. Caspi Shiloni stresses the distinction between a rabbinical-court order to issue a get (*hiyuv get*) and a court-forced get. The former carries no sanctions, which, outside of Israel, cannot be enforced in any case (email of October 5, 2019). What both *hiyuv* and *kfiyat get* accomplish is to shift the focus from the woman in the case to the power struggle between the husband and the rabbinical court he is defying.

26 "חשוב להדגיש שגבר לא אשכנזי (ספרדי/תימני) לא צריך בכלל היתר מאה רבנים כדי להתחתן עם אישה שניה. החרם היה תקף רק באשכנז, ולכן גם היום בתי הדין לא דורשים היתר מאה רבנים אם הגבר לא אשכנזי. מספיק שתהיה החלטה של בית הדין כדי שהוא יוכל להתחתן (גם מבחינה חוקית. החוק הפלילי שאוסר על ביגמיה אומר במפורש שאם יש היתר מבית הדין—מותר לגבר להתחתן עם אישה שניה, שזה לא ביגמיה")." Email of Nitzan Caspi Shiloni, October 5, 2019.

27 See Caspi Shiloni, "שולי רנד נשוי לשתיים: על היתר מאה רבנים—והפער הבלתי נסבל בין נשים לגברים", www.ynet.co.il, November 11, 2021; Young, "Shuli Rand's Marriage"; updated: November 13, 2021. This article first appeared simply as a report about a celebrity wedding, with no mention of the fact that the marriage is bigynous. The update came following protests.

28 Brander, "Isakov."

29 Phone conversation, September 19, 2019; see Saar, "Husband."

30 Reported in Eisman-Lifschitz, "Women." Given the significant and growing problem of male spousal abuse in Israel, which worsened during the Covid-19 shutdowns and during the war that began in October 2023, the presentation on this subject by Rabbi Yuval Cherlow, a founder and leader of the Tzohar Rabbinical Organization, is disconcerting at best. Cherlow condemns such violence (while also diluting the problem by calling for attention to violence of all kinds, "regardless of gender," making violence against women a "starting point" for needed protection of "other victims as well"), and lauds mutual respect in marriage. But he utterly distorts the inherent power imbalance established in rabbinic marriage, let alone rabbinic divorce, stating counterfactually: "We . . . dismiss erroneous views . . . that the halachot surrounding marriage and divorce might indicate a sort of masculine ownership of the husband over the wife." His presentation is radically apologetic, inaccurate, and unhistorical. Cherlow, "Mutual Respect." See, too, Karmiel, "Invisible Violence."

31 Aranoff and Haut, *Wed-Locked*, 5–78.

32 See Radzyner, "Halakha."

33 Quoted in Radzyner, "Halakha," 295, and n. 133.

34 See, e.g., Radzyner, "We Act."

35 See, e.g., Reiner, "Rabbinical Courts"; and idem, "Adjudication."

36 Aranoff and Haut, *Wed-Locked*, 15.

37 Cited in Schwartz, "Court." Barack Fishman, *Breath*, 37, cites "scores of new agunot . . . in the United States each year, according to rabbinic figures," but does not cite her rabbinical source/s.

38 Aranoff and Haut, *Wed-Locked*, 13, 15.

39 Mavoi Satum website, accessed June 14, 2023.

40 Landesman, "Agunot," 132.

41 Mavoi Satum website. See, too, *Jewish Week* editors, "Agunot."

42 Cited in Sharon, "Rabbinical Court Statistics."

43 Caspi Shiloni, "Women Get Refusers."

44 Posted on the Facebook page of Center for Women's Justice, October 6, 2021.

45 *Jewish Week* editors, "Agunot."

46 Sharon, "Rabbinical Court Staistics." For another such manipulation, explicitly directed against "feminists," see Breitowitz, "Ask."

11. DIVORCE IN THE CONSERVATIVE/MASORTI AND OTHER MOVEMENTS

1 See Epstein, *Marriage*, and idem, "Solution."

2 See Epstein, "Hatsa'a."

3 Sarna, *American*, 240.

4 Sarna, *American*, 241.

5 See Rackman, "Political," who details (against denial expressed to me by one authority affiliated with the Rabbinical Council of America) Soloveitchik's

cooperation with Lieberman, albeit in cloak-and-dagger fashion, and approval of the proposed text, before reneging.

6 See Aranoff and Haut, *Wed-Locked*, 176; Shapiro, *Lieberman*.

7 See Cohen, *Birth*; Steiner, "Clause"; Bokser, "Ketubah"; Golinkin, "Approaches"; Schwartz, "Conservative"; Aranoff and Haut, *Wed-Locked*, 176–77; Greenberg, *Women*, 135–38; Lamm, "Additions"; Susskind Goldberg, "Using," 101–11. Frank, "Agunah," gives an excellent summary of halakhic solutions proposed in twentieth-century America to minimize iggun, and inter- and intradenominational disputes over them, and scores the role of feminism in spurring both attention to iggun and reactionary opposition to solutions; see, too, Meacham, "Marriage" and Meiselman, *Woman*, 103–15.

8 See Berkovits, *Conditions*; Villa, "Conditional," 119–49; and Riskin, *Women*, 133–42.

9 See Rackman, "Political"; Riskin, *Women*, 133–42; Meiselman, *Woman*, 103–15.

10 See Meyer, *Response*, 81–82, 187, 200, 210, 211, 256, 257; Ellenson, "Holdheim on the Legal Character"; idem, "Holdheim and Zacharias Frankel"; [no author cited] "A Reform Get" and "Agunot," in Jacob and Zemer, *Gender Issues*, 187–97; Rayner, "Gender"; Washofsky, *Jewish Living*.

11 Barack, *Breath*, 37, cites Orthodox agunah activist Rivka Haut complaining bitterly about this problem, which Riskin, *Women*, 133–42, also mentions. See, too, Frank, "Agunah."

12 Hirsch, "Progressive."

13 Aranoff and Haut's term, *Wed-Locked*, 178. See extensively in Susskind Goldberg and Villa, *Zaʿakat*, 3–100.

14 Aranoff and Haut, *Wed-Locked*, 177. Personal communication from the parents of one young woman, who married into a Yeshiva University family and used the RCA prenup: the parents, both of whom are attorneys and not from Orthodox backgrounds, held no illusions that this document would protect their daughter but felt no other option feasible in the wedding dynamics.

15 Joel Weissman, director of the RCA-affiliated Beith Din of America, quoted in Levine, "Many Agunot." For a withering critique, see Weiss, "Sign"; see, too, Susskind Goldberg and Villa, *Zaʿakat*, 14–17.

16 For defense of the RCA prenup against attacks from the right, see Broyde, "Analysis." Cf. the podcast by JOFA (2021), "The RCA Pre-Nup: $10,000 and Counting?" The moderator's introduction entices with news of two cases he says were adjudicated "successfully" by the RCA court, in one of which the court awarded the agunah $10,000. To the uninitiated, this suggests that the woman might actually have received that sum in compensation for the get refusal, in addition to the get and her ketubbah settlement, when no rabbinic court outside of Israel has enforcement power. This, aside from it being standard RCA policy to waive fines it assesses get-withholding men, including in cases, such as this one, where the husband violated his prenuptial agreement, causing litigation.

17 The Israeli government sworn in on December 29, 2022, has sought to enlarge the competency of rabbinic courts to handle civil matters unrelated to divorce if the

parties agree to this "voluntarily." Aside from concern about expansion of theocracy beyond personal status issues to financial ones, there is concern that women would be pressured into "voluntary" participation in rabbinic-court adjudication of civil matters.

18 See Jachter, "Gray Matter," in the section critiquing Rackman and Morgenstern.

19 Richie Lewis (personal communication, October 14, 2020) notes the important difference between the traditional ketubbah, about whose contents most women have no knowledge, and a prenup, in whose drafting they will have participated, meaning they will have been party to some discussions of the risks of rabbinic (or any) legal marriage. Frank, "Dependent," gives an excellent comparison between moderate ("modern") and right-wing Orthodox stances toward iggun in their communities.

20 See the Mavoi Satum website, entry opening with "Getting married soon? Mazal Tov!"

21 I asked Rabbi Daniel Sperber (phone conversation, June 2023) about this possibility, which would render useless any prenuptial agreement, even the best (which he developed), which entails automatic, retroactive annulment under specified conditions. He replied, "*Anan sahadei* cannot function halakhically when there is a contradiction to it. The prenuptial agreement declares, 'I am not married' [under specified circumstances]. It is like walking around with a sign that says, 'I am not married.'" However, Richie Lewis, halakhic adviser to the work *Za'akat*, says that this position could be disputed and the prenup dismissed as an *asmakhta* (written proof), with the argument that the couple did not mean it when they said they were not married since they subsequently lived together as if they were. His position is that the couple meant all they said at the time of their marriage—the intent to marry, and its dissolution under specified conditions. Personal communications, July 10, 2022. My point is that there is no halakhic ruling or document that cannot be disputed, which, in this case, would mean the woman's marital freedom contested; see below.

22 Goldberg, "Time a Gendered Affair?" 27; Rabbi Snir Gueta, quoted in Tirosh, "Rosh Hashanah."

23 JOFA website, accessed December 5, 2023. In the twenty-fifth-anniversary issue of JOFA's newsletter, published on that site, the organization sums up its history and accomplishments in several areas, of which agunah advocacy is one. Citing its conferences and lobbying, it claims that its efforts achieved recognition within Orthodoxy, against resistance, of the existence of a problem of marital captivity. It also implies that its actions were responsible for the RCA changing its position from not requiring use of its own prenup by its affiliated rabbis, in 2012, to requiring this, as of 2016. While JOFA does not recommend the RCA prenuptial agreement or its rabbinical court specifically (its site lists several Orthodox rabbinical courts), nor does it state the nature of its relationship to the RCA, JOFA clearly has at the least very close ties to the RCA. The latter has authoritative rabbinic status, including the power to approve of or disavow JOFA policy. JOFA has no such

power but is reliant on approval by Orthodox authorities for its activities to have perceived legitimacy among JOFA's constituents—Orthodox Jewish feminists.

24 It is important to note a case that Mavoi Satum and others have termed precedent-setting, in which Natalie Lastreger, in 2015, succeeded in getting the Chief Rabbinate to rescind its demand that she seek a get in its court rather than in a haredi court—the validity of whose gittin the Chief Rabbinate, of course, recognizes; this was purely a political maneuver in the Chief Rabbinate's institutional interests. Lastreger achieved this by daring the Chief Rabbinate to implement its threat to jail her and revoke her passport for refusing its demand; having had one get experience in a Chief Rabbinate court, she had made it a prenuptial stipulation that in case of divorce, the get would be done in a haredi court. Her husband reneged on the prenup and filed for divorce in a Chief Rabbinate court. Fearing possible Supreme Court involvement yielding a ruling to limit its powers, the Chief Rabbinate retreated, her husband lost his leverage, and Lastreger got a get in a haredi court. See Sharon, "'Precedent.'" I and some other supporters sat with Ms. (now Rabbi) Lastreger in a streetside café in Jerusalem, awaiting her arrest; see photo in the appendix. Lastreger is third from right in the bottom row in this photo.

25 Eisman-Lifschitz, "Women." See the video presentation and appeal for funds by Mavoi Satum, posted on the organization's Facebook page on December 18, 2022, מבוי סתום—עזרה למסורבות גט ועגונות—**Mavoi Satum**, including clips of agunot saying that they had no prior understanding of the situation they were facing until they were ensnared in iggun and rabbinic-court procedures, including being labeled there "separated" rather than as an "agunah" or a *mesorevet get*. On the spurious distinction between these categories, see chapter 10.

26 Weiss and Gross-Horowitz, *Marriage*, 8.

27 The same would hold if women rabbinic judges and not just "representatives" adjudicated according to these rules. Egalitarianism in this situation is no solution.

28 Gross, "Precedent."

29 See Kaplan Sommer, "Decades."

30 See Givati, "Yad La'Isha." The article, illustrated with an appalling image of women's victimized impotence, falsely asserts that a rabbinical court can never give a get on behalf of a husband. Courts can also annul marriages without a husband's consent.

31 See on the center's website, "Halakhic Marriage Prenup" for the document in Hebrew and English, and Weiss, "Prenups."

32 Weiss and Gross-Horowitz, *Marriage*, 136–37; see, too, 79–97 and 121–47.

33 For one instance, see the case of Natalie Lastreger, above, n. 24.

34 In 1978, a case, Avitzur v. Avitzur, was adjudicated all the way up to the Supreme Court of the United States. The husband in a couple that had used the Conservative movement's ketubbah with its Lieberman clause refused to honor it after a civil divorce and refused to give his wife a get. The New York State Court of Appeals upheld the civil validity of the clause. The husband appealed to the Supreme

Court, which refused to hear the case, allowing the lower court's ruling to stand; Frank, "Agunah," 31.

35 As a well-to-do groom told me at his wedding, conducted in Israel in the summer of 2021. This groom had signed the prenup of the modern Orthodox Tzohar organization but told me that its monetary fine was meaningless to him and would be no deterrent. His bride, with whom I also spoke during the engagement, did not wish to open the question of a more effective prenup because her fiancé wanted a Zohar rabbi to officiate, which meant a Zohar prenup.

36 See Weiss, "Misconceptions."

37 Weiss summarizes the critiques of prenups in "Prenups."

38 Email communications to me from Rabbis Chuck Davidson, December 5, 2022, and Abraham Shamma, December 13, 2022, the latter of whom wrote:

ארגון "חופות" עורך חופות כדת משה וישראל לבני זוג שבוחרים במסורת, אך
נרתעים מהמונופוליזם והפוליטיזציה של הרבנות. כמו כן הוא עורך חופות למי שיהדותם כשרה על
פי ההלכה, אך הרבנות דורשת מהם הוכחות יהדות שמעבר לדרישת ההלכה.
הארגון מחייב עריכת קידושין בליווי תנאי בקידושין לשם מניעת סרבנות גט וחליצה, סחטנות גט
וחליצה, או אי כשירות למתן גט וחליצה. בכך מסייע הארגון גם לצמצום ממזרות."

"The organization Chuppot conducts weddings according to the law of Moses and Israel for couples who choose tradition but are put off by the monopolizing and politicizing of the Chief Rabbinate. It also conducts weddings for those whose Jewish status is halakhic but from whom the Rabbinate demands proof exceeding halakhic requirements. The organization requires kiddushin accompanied by conditional kiddushin in order to prevent get and halitsa refusal or extortion or inability to give a get or halitsa. In this, the organization also assists in limiting mamzerut." Shamma claims over one thousand weddings conducted under its auspices as of late 2022; see, too, Chuppot's website. Another Israeli modern Orthodox organization, Beit Hillel, which also operates independently of the Chief Rabbinate, recommends but does not require a prenup.

39 Personal communications, December 13, 2022.

40 ICAR website.

41 See Sperber, "Private Rabbinal Court." Rabbi Sperber's court's ruling annulling Gorodetsky's marriage applied the halakhic principles of *umdenah de'mukhah* and *mekah ta'ut*. See, too, Ettinger, *Unraveled*, 218–20, and 278, n. 7.

42 On the Gorodetsky case, see Eglash, "Man"; Feldman, "Man"; Sharon, "Groundbreaking"; Newman, "Move"; Magnus, "No Aguna."

43 Cited in the&MG, "Hypocrisy."

12. INTRADENOMINATIONAL POLITICS AND RIVALRIES ABORT SOLUTIONS WITHIN ORTHODOXY

1 Feldblum, "Problem." On this proposal and Orthodox rejection of it, see Susskind Goldberg and Villa, *Za'akat*, 243–55.

2 Aranoff and Haut, *Wed-Locked*, 203, 216.

3 For halakhic details, see Susskind Goldberg and Villa, *Za'akat*, 310–32, and Aranoff and Haut, *Wed-Locked*, 209–10.

4 Aranoff and Haut, *Wed-Locked*, 203, 206–17; Brozan, "Annulling"; JTA, "Focus"; Jachter, "Gray Matter"; Rackman, "Letter"; idem, "Painful," 8; Rackman, "Annulment."

5 Aranoff and Haut, *Wed-Locked*, 213–15.

6 Aranoff and Haut, *Wed-Locked*, 208. See Broyde, "Review"; idem, *Marriage*. Rabbi Broyde is a member of the RCA's beth din and was its head during the Rackman-court controversy. He is a chief proponent of the RCA's prenup and a prominent critic of alternatives. See, too, Bleich, "Annulment" and idem, "Marriage?"

7 See "Agunah International" for a link to this document, and Aranoff, "Halakhic Principles."

8 Aranoff and Haut, *Wed-Locked*, 209.

9 Aranoff and Haut, *Wed-Locked*, 210.

10 Bleich, "Annulment," 114.

11 Aranoff and Haut, *Wed-Locked*, 212.

12 Magnus, "Sacks." See Rackman, "Political," who details (against denial expressed to me by one authority affiliated with the Rabbinical Council of America) Soloveitchik's cooperation with Lieberman, albeit in cloak-and-dagger fashion, and approval of the proposed text, before reneging.

13 Riskin, *Women*.

14 Aranoff and Haut, *Wed-Locked*, 207.

15 Aranoff and Haut, *Wed-Locked*, 201–3.

16 See Jachter, "Gray Matter."

17 Hacohen, *Tears*; Jackson, *Agunah*. Broyde, in "Review Essay," severely critiqued Hacohen's work; to which Weiss, "Response," replied.

18 Aranoff and Haut, *Wed-Locked*, 216–17. This volume was completed and published after Rivka Haut's death; we lack, therefore, her voice about her position.

19 Aranoff and Haut, *Wed-Locked*, 215.

20 Quoted in Schwartz, "Court."

21 Quoted in Schwartz, "Court."

22 Quoted in Schwartz, "Court." On other dimensions of the power struggle between the Chief Rabbinate and Tzohar, see Joffre, "Decision." For a partisan's presentation of the bitter disputes and ostracisms between religious-Zionist and haredi groups, see Meir, "Heaven."

23 On Rabbi Sperber's scholarly record, see Sperber, "Bibliography," 681–706. Since that list's compilation, he has published another two scholarly works.

24 בפעילות של אגף עגונות שוחררה מעגינותה אישה "נשואה" ''לשני גברים.
בית הדין הרבני שחרר לחופשי אישה עגונה שהייתה כבולה בקשרי אישות לשני גברים. בפעילות של אגף עגונות שוחררה האישה מעגינותה, זאת לאחר שנערכו לה חופה וקידושין ע''י בית דין פרטי בלתי מוכר על ידי המדינה לגבר נוסף מבלי שקיבלה קודם גט מבעלה הראשון.

25 Caspi Shiloni Facebook page, Nov. 8, 2021.

26 My translation.

27 Caspi Shiloni, "Smotrich."
28 Caspi Shiloni, "The Narrative."
29 Tessler, "'Excuse Me.'"
30 On use of "marriage counseling" by husbands and rabbinic courts to delay divorce proceedings, prolong cases, and extort get-seeking women, see Darel, "Women," and Weiss and Gross-Horowitz, *Marriage*.
31 In the above-noted egregious case of Shira Isakov, when her murderously violent husband, having refused to give her a get, finally agreed to do so, the rabbinic court required Isakov to be present in court and to herself receive the get from the same hands that beat and stabbed her nearly to death.
32 Sharon, "Rabbi"; Jewish Telegraphic Agency, "Get-Refuser"; Magnus, "Rabbi."
33 Nachshoni and Cohen, "Rabbinical Court," *Ynet*, December 3, 2020 (Hebrew ("בית הדין דחה את בקשת העגונה; ההלוויה ההמונית נמשכת"). This massively attended funeral occurred in defiance of corona restrictions. The community involved did not ask permission but proceeded; a lesson here for agunah activists, and for agunot.
34 Center for Women's Justice, Facebook post, October 2, 2019.
35 This is not to say that these have been the only cases of rabbinical courts restoring freed agunot into captivity.
36 Sharon, "Rabbinical Court to Reopen."
37 See Sharon, "Rabbinical Court Staistics"; Ettinger, "Wife"; idem, "Get"; Ungar-Sargon, "Woman."
38 See Sharon, "Defeat"; Jewish Telegraphic Agency, "Court"; Ungar-Sargon, "Woman"; "Israel Democracy Institute Scholar," January 11, 2017.
39 See Levinson, "Ruling."
40 See Ettinger, "Wife."
41 Kubovich and Ettinger, "Israeli"; Leibovitz, "Move."
42 Golinkin, "Study," 3. This publication examines "actual agunot cases that have languished for years in rabbinical courts. . . . In most instances, [these courts have not published their decisions on cases brought before them. . . . We present . . . 'halakhic directions,' which the rabbinical courts should have examined in order to free [the agunah]."
43 See, in brief, Wald, "Authority"; Adelman, "Authority"; Ross, *Expanding*, 60–70.
44 On *da'as toyre/da'at torah*, see Silber, "Emergence"; Kaplan, "Innovation"; idem, "Daas Torah"; Soloveitchik, *Rupture*, 34–37, 51, 109–10, n. 87; Ross, *Expanding*, 60–62.
45 See Meyer, *Response*; Ellenson, *Emancipation*; idem, "Reactions"; Katz, "Orthodoxy"; idem, "Society."
46 Sperber, "'Friendly,'" 2.
47 Sperber, "'Friendly,'" 2. See, too, idem, "Paralysis."
48 Chigier, "Ruminations," 82.
49 Ross, "Overcoming," 384. It is not true that all halakhic innovation in modernity has been in the direction of rigidity. Some poskim ruled leniently in some cases, explicitly in response to strict halakhic observance having become a minority be-

havior and in order to encourage wavering adherents to stay within the halakhic system; see Katz, 'Shabbes Goy,' 133-158. The behavior Katz cites resembles that which Krakowski (252) analyzes in her assessment of rabbinic calculations and concessions to attract Jewish claimants to their courts in medieval Egypt.

50 Lopes-Cardozo, *Law*; Rabbi Sperber, quoted there, in "Approbations," 8.

51 Kaplan, "Innovation," 306. For comments by an ex-insider about absolute haredi fealty to the authority of their "*gedolim*," not based on the strength of the arguments of the latter in any pronouncement but simply because of their source, see the Facebook post of Rabbi Chuck Davidson, November 15, 2024.

52 Aranoff and Haut, *Wed-Locked*, 202.

53 A well-known rabbinic judge who works with and through the Rabbinical Council of America told me that he frees more agunot than are freed through the efforts of any agunah-advocacy organization but that he does not make this known, in order to avoid unpleasant consequences; conversation in May 2024. When I expressed shocked dismay that withholding this information prevents other agunot from obtaining release, that argument was dismissed as "emotional."

54 One Israeli halakhic scholar and activist, who requires anonymity, who supports the position of rabbis who have established independent courts that freed agunot, told me that he could not behave similarly until he is retired and the youngest of his children, married—that is, not vulnerable to being harmed in marriage prospects by actions against the rabbi for his acts. We recall, too, that the other judges on Rabbi Sperber's court in actions to free agunot, men who lack his institutional independence, have remained anonymous.

55 Aranoff and Haut, *Wed-Locked*, 202. Natalie Lastreger clearly operated on this conviction; see above, n. 24 to chapter 11. Thanks to Richie Lewis for alerting me to the possible disparity in favor of haredi over modern Orthodox courts in the United States and to the implications of Rabbi Soloveitchik's view of halakha for rigidity about agunot exceeding that of traditional halakhic rulings. See Ross, *Expanding*, 66–68; Lawrence, "Philosophy"; Soloveitchik, *Halakhic*.

56 Rothkoff, "Soloveitchik."

57 Soloveitchik, *Harav*, 223–24; my translation. Thanks to Dr. Tova Hartman for alerting me to this passage.

58 Lopes-Cardozo, "Genius"; see, too, idem, *Law*, 418–20, 432–35; Singer, "Rackman"; Kaplan, "Cooperation"; Slifkin, "The Rav"; Rackman, "Soloveitchik," 65.

59 Rackman, "Painful," 8. One scholar with whom I spoke likened Soloveitchik's position to "flat earth-ism."

60 Soloveitchik expresses his radical essentialism about male and female in *Lonely*, in his reading of Genesis 1–3. Such pronouncements in other contexts would be read rightly as racism, of which sexism is a variant. For another remarkable instance of Soloveitchik's rabbinical ruling about women, see Ross, *Expanding*, 91.

61 Aranoff and Haut, *Wed-Locked*, 222.

62 Haut, "The Agunah," 188–200. It would not cheer Haut to read the plea decades later of Shira Pasternak Beeri of Jerusalem, "Picturing," which asks, as if for the

first time, "How can we explain that Judaism lets men withhold divorce as a . . . weapon?"

63 Quoted in Rosenbaum, "Rabbi," 6.

64 See Franzman, "Voice." Rabbi Krauss died in January 2022; Schachne, "Memories." While the article's header proclaims that Rabbi Krauss "fearlessly tackled thorny issues such as agunot," the article says not a word about this. Nor does Rabbi Krauss's successor at his Queens, New York, synagogue, quoted in the article praising Rabbi Krauss, say anything about continuing to operate a court that frees agunot. With his death, the Jewish world lost one of the very few rabbis to whom agunah advocates could send agunot with any hope of release ensuing. Apparently, even reporting about this is now off limits.

65 Aranoff and Haut, *Wed-Locked*, 51, 123–25, 128–30.

66 Email communication, September 2020.

67 Ross, *Expanding*, 236, and 304, n. 13.

68 See Leibovitz, "Move," about rabbinically sanctioned shunning of Oded Guez, which did not result in him giving a get. On other such tactics, about whose efficacy no statistics have been released by enthusiastic advocates, see, too, Keats-Jaskoll, "Taking."

69 "Brooklyn Man," *Jewish Voice*, March 14, 2021.

70 "Brooklyn Man." See, too, "Flatbush," *Yeshiva World News*; VINnews, "Watch."

71 The hashtags in "Brooklyn Man" are those of Shoshana Keats-Jaskoll and Rachel Stomel, founders of Chochmat Nashim, which advocates for a variety of reforms in Israeli Orthodox society regarding women. Its activists have promoted rabbinically authorized shaming events. From the group's website:

     Every year, Chochmat Nashim runs an Agunah Day campaign to reframe the public conversation. We advocate for the widespread use of halachic prenuptial and postnuptial agreements to prevent agunot [sic]. We partner with leading women's advocacy organizations and leverage our connections in the Knesset, courts and community leadership. We stay abreast of the latest developments on the agunah front to contextualize and understand the avenues most effective for progress, and then present this information to you. Enter your email and find out what YOU can do to end Get refusal!

     They post the following video, airing on youtube: https://youtu.be /zQjl3biBCzg. Rachel Stomel informs me that she left the organization and does not see shaming as an effective tool of agunah advocacy; emails, July 28–29, 2022.

72 See examples of shaming efforts against get refusers on the Facebook page of ORA, directed against Israel Meir Kin (referred to as "Meir"), posted on March 5, 2021; cf. ORA's post about "Meir" on its Facebook page, August 23, 2019; and on the Facebook page of Shoshana Keats-Jaskoll on December 19, 2022. Multiple examples of such shaming appear on the Facebook page of the Australian agunah-advocacy organization Unchain My Heart. And the Facebook page, "Flatbush Girl."

73 Post of ORA on its Facebook page, August 23, 2019, about the Kin case.

74 Weiss and Gross-Horowitz, *Marriage*, 175–76.

75 "Basic Laws," website of the Knesset, accessed January 31, 2024.

76 See Weiss and Gross-Horowitz, *Marriage*, 98–120, case of "The Accidental Agunah."

77 See Weiss and Gross-Horowitz, *Marriage*, 183–84, on Israeli rabbinical courts operating to extract get-extortion deals from women.

78 Frankel, "Rabbinical Ties."

79 Kampeas, "Afghanistan."

80 Times of Israel, "Jew."

81 Magnus, "Last Agunah."

13. THINKING OUTSIDE THE CHAINS TO END JEWISH MARITAL CAPTIVITY

1 On women choosing Orthodoxy and on constraints and threats keeping women born into ultra-Orthodoxy from leaving that world, see Kaufman, *Daughters*; Davidman, *Tradition*; Wellen Levine, *Mystics*; Fader, *Mitzvah*; Harris, *Holy Days*; Feldman, *Unorthodox*; Taylor-Guthartz, *Challenge*; Glass, *Kissing*.

2 See Ross, "Ex-Frum"; Deitsch, *Here*; Deen, *All*; Posen, "Modern"; and, about Henny Kupferstein: Amy Standen and Judy Campbell, "An Unorthodox Life," *KQED*, April 25, 2017, www.kqed.org/. Fear of loss of custody of her children is a central theme in Glass, *Kissing*, motivating many actions she was otherwise loath to take.

3 For one (unusually connected) agunah's testimony to her unwillingness to forgo ultra-Orthodox life to be free of an abusive marriage, and the resources she could marshal to that end, see Lewak, "Woman's."

4 Video on the website of Chochmat Nashim, "No More Sacrificing Women on the Altar of Agunah" (sic). The quoted segment starts at minute 3.31. In their ignorance of the legal or practical realities of rabbinic marriage and divorce, the comments of these women, in a video released in 2021, are no different from those by women a generation earlier, reported in Nusan Porter, "Introduction," and Lagnado, "Of Human Bondage," in Nusan Porter, *Women*, xi–xv and 3–13.

5 Cited in Coy, "Consent."

6 Blumberg, "Divorce."

7 See, for instance, this report, aired on Israeli television, in which Nitzan Caspi Shiloni describes her experience in rabbinic courts, including in the case of Tzviya Gorodetsky: https://youtu.be/3ZSZc8m5X5I, and this podcast by Lubitch and Caspi Shiloni, about kiddushin: https://open.spotify.com/episode/4t1Upj3PWJZM5paSodWsH8 (Hebrew).

8 See Frot, "Rabbi." There is clear rabbinic-court interest, regardless of nationality, in mooting civil legislation that punishes get withholding/extortion: if men reliably faced serious civil consequences for this behavior, it would wane to disappearance and with it, most of the rabbinic-court system as a legal and financial enterprise.

9 See Weiss, "Women." Rivka Lubitch innovated *mimzur*, a verb, to emphasize that "mamzerut" results from deliberate action; see Lubitch, "Courts" and "Canceling."

10 This project is called "Forum Tears of the Oppressed: Solutions to the Mamzer Problem." See Lubitch, "Time"; idem, "Religion"; idem, "Religion"; Weiss, "Women"; idem, "Stigma"; idem, "Stigma, todaʾa."

11 See Lopes Cardozo, *Law*, 248, 268, 269–71 and there, n. 25; 272–88, 290, 296–98, 401.

12 Laqueur, *Secret*, makes the important distinction between facts being available and being absorbed.

13 Book of Esther 4:14.

14 It is clear from Glass, *Kissing*, how crucial it is that women have not just legal representation but that of lawyers experienced in custody suits against women who run afoul of rabbinic courts and, equally important, who are knowledgeable about the judges where any such case will be heard.

15 See Bezalel, "Israel"; Cidor, "Haredim"; Levi, "Worlds"; Richler, "Finding"; Footsteps, website.

16 There is no foreseeable scenario for introduction of an option for civil marriage in Israel. See Nitzan Caspi Shiloni, "Looming judicial reform dominates the news—but what does it mean?" Facebook, January 18, 2023, www.facebook.com /Centerforwomensjustice/posts/pfbid0i9z4KuddZh3TFqU7imssWiinRjTteCZ jgyTPqmxvHBy1sreshfXcqFfgPQXUTKsGl; idem, www.facebook.com/groups /1125346724711592/posts/1241494729763457/; idem, "Plea"; idem, "Judicial Upheaval"; Darel, "They Want"; Weiss, "Agunot."

17 See Schindler and Seldin-Cohen, *Recharging*; Limmer and Pesner, *Resistance*; Taragin, "Orthodox"; Cohen, "Sudan"; Kaplan-Sommer, "Young."

18 Gross, "Horror Story."

19 Shoshana Batya Greenwald, listed as "Jewish educator," in the video "No More Sacrificing Women on the Altar of Agunah (sic)"; this comment appears at ca. minute 6:53. Greenwald pronounces herself "so disappointed that this [iggun] is still an issue." In his "Ruminations," after proposing halakhic actions that rabbinic authorities could (and don't) take to pressure get-refusing men to give gittin, Moshe Chigier admits, "Neither is it possible to find a solution to all and every Agunah problem. There were and will be difficult problems which defy any solution."

20 For cosmetic changes addressing some Orthodox women's discomfort with the halakhic marriage ceremony but that retain kinyan and kiddushin, see Koren, "Voice"; Linzer, "Ani Li." Koren's article and her interviewees mention iggun but approach the problem as aesthetic and subjective, rather than as inherently degrading and with legal consequences. The article's identification of "religious" and "Orthodox" is also problematic. Linzer pronounces authoritatively as an Orthodox rabbi and decisor about halakhic limits. He distinguishes between symbolic

acts with no halakhic effect, which he approves, and acts that would obviate kinyan or kiddushin, which he rejects. See Greenstein's critique, "Equality." For a learned critique of kinyan and kiddushin, see Lubitch, "Force." For alternatives to traditional kiddushin, see Labovitz, "Behold." For options, some cosmetic, to kinyan and kiddushin, some subverting them, see the website *The Kiddushin Variations*, http://alternativestokiddushin.wordpress.com/background/.

21 Adler, *Engendering*, 169–217, and for a critique, Greenstein, "Equality." On the antiquity of the partnership model in Jewish marriage, see Friedman, *Jewish Marriage*, vol. 1, viii: in Palestinian marriage contracts, "marriage was . . . a partnership. Husband and wife undertook mutual obligations, and each party was assured the right to terminate the marriage if he or she desired," and his findings throughout the volume.

22 Yoreh, "Shvu'at."

23 Feldblum, "Problem," 203–17. Bleich, "Marriage?" rejected Feldblum's proposal, as did the Masorti movement; see Pitkowsky and Susskind Goldberg, "Derekh," in Susskind Goldberg and Villa, *Za'akat*, 254.

24 See Orenstein, *Lifecycles*, 359–76; Magnus, "Ritual."

25 The Lehrhaus model, founded by Franz Rosenzweig (1886–1929), based on traditional *hevruta*-style study, put Jewish learning and teaching in the hands of participants seeking to engage texts and traditions directly. See Rosenzweig, *Learning*.

26 See Magnus, "Ritual."

27 See Trible, "Depatriarchalizing."

28 See Ross, *Expanding*, for application of Rabbi Abraham Isaac Kook's teaching about "successive hearings" of Torah to feminism.

29 See Herman, "Twelve"; Barmash, "Egalitarian"; cf. Labovitz, "Reflections."

30 Quoted in Labovitz, "Reflections."

31 Cases of *isha katlanit* are routine in Chief Rabbinate courts, since these interrogate women about their marital history; see Rosenblum, "Widows.'" On women rabbis becoming "honorary men," also a problem in service leading in egalitarian prayer groups, see Magnus, "Dybbuk."

32 See Satenstein, "Orthodox Women"; Chizhik-Goldschmidt, "Revolution"; Lambert Adler, "TikTok"; #agunot #agunah #agunahcrisis #jewish #judaism #frumwomenhavefaces #givehertheget #theget; the Facebook groups "I'm also fed up with the way women are treated in Orthodoxy," and "Flatbush Girl"; and #myorthodoxlife; www.vogue.com.

33 Hajdenberg, "Women."

34 See Hollander, "Weathering," and Cardin, "Ritual."

35 Wojakovsky, "Hope," shows no awareness of get abuse in rabbinical courts and cites halakhic prenups as a solution with no apparent awareness of their limits or variants; such reporting peddles and gives life to old, failed approaches, perpetuating the problem.

36 Lithwick, "Why I Haven't."
37 Conversation, summer 2018.

CONCLUSIONS

1 Ariela Sternbach, "'הקריבו אותי 'מסורבת הגט ששוחררה אחרי 18 שנה—והוחזרה לעגינות," Network 13, July 24, 2022.
2 Thanks to Rachel Stomel of the Center for Women's Justice for links and the Twitter feed, which she wrote. For a haredi source reporting on and applauding the woman's return to agunah status, see Weisberg, "Storm."

BIBLIOGRAPHY

RESPONSA

Alshikh, Moshe. *Responsa Maharam Alshikh*, ed. Yom Tov Porgos (Safed, Israel: Sifriyah Toranit Beit Yosef, 1975).

ben Matanya, Binyamin, *Responsa* (Jerusalem: Yad Harav Nissim, 1959).

Medina, Shmuel de. *Responsa Maharashdam, Even haezer, siman yud* (Salonika, 1595).

PUBLISHED PRIMARY SOURCES

Archives Israélites (July 25, 1907), pp. 235–36, letter by David Friedman, chief rabbi of Karlin and Pinsk and Chaim Ozer Grodzinski of Vilna, see *Univers Israélite*, July 5, 1907, p. 495, and *Archives Israélites*, July 4, 1907.

Frauenbund, Jüedischer, Bläetter des Jüdischen Frauenbunde füer Frauenarbeit und Frauenbewegung, XII (1936), 7/8 (Juli–August 1936): 20–21.

"Halakhic Marriage Prenup," website, Center for Women's Justice.

World Congress of Jewish Women, Vienna, May 6–11, 1923, www.worldcat.org.

WEBSITES

Center for Women's Justice

Chochmat Nashim

Chuppot

Danya Ruttenberg

Footsteps

Huppa Pratit

ITIM

JOFA

The Knesset

Mavoi Satum

Ohr Sameah

ORA (Organization for Resolution of Agunot)

Rabbanei Tzohar

Ritualwell

Yisrael Hofshit

FACEBOOK PAGES

Center for Women's Justice
Chochmat Nashim
Chuck Davidson
Flatbush Girl
Nitzan Caspi Shiloni
ORA
Shoshana Keats-Jaskoll
Susan Weiss
Unchain My Heart

PODCASTS

Allison Kaplan Sommer, "Young US Jews Believe that Judaism Is about Social Justice," *Haaretz*, April 21, 2024.

Center for Women's Justice podcast series, "Justice Unbound: Women, Religion and the State of Israel," https://bit.ly/JusticeUnbound2.

Rivka Lubitch and Nitzan Caspi Shiloni, about kiddushin: https://bit.ly/CWJkiddushin.

SECONDARY SOURCES

Abraham, David. "The Spanish Exiles in the Holy Land," in *Moreshet Sepharad: The Spanish Legacy*, ed. Haim Beinart (Jerusalem: Magnes, 1992), vol. 2: 183–204.

Ackerman-Lieberman, Philip. "The Woman's Right to Choose: An Unsigned Responsum from Ottoman Safed," *Jewish Studies Quarterly*, 17 (2010): 99–113.

Adelman, Howard Tzvi. *Women and Jewish Marriage Negotiations in Early Modern Italy: For Love and Money* (New York: Routledge, 2018).

———. "Authority, Rabbinic and Communal," in *Reader's Guide to Judaism*, ed. Michael Terry (Chicago: Fitzroy Dearborn, 2000), 51–54.

———. "Custom, Law, and Gender: Levirate Union among Ashkenazim and Sephardim in Italy after the Expulsion from Spain," in *The Expulsion of the Jews: 1492 and After*, ed. Raymond B. Waddington and Arthur H. Williamson (New York: Garland, 1994), 107–25.

Adler, Eliyana, "Educational Options for Jewish Girls in Nineteenth-Century Europe," *Polin*, 15 (2002): 301–10.

———. *In Her Hands: The Education of Girls in Tsarist Russia* (Detroit: Wayne State University Press, 2011).

Adler, Rachel. *Engendering Judaism: An Inclusive Theology and Ethics* (Boston: Beacon, 1998).

Aranoff, Susan and Rivka Haut. *The Wed-Locked Agunot: Orthodox Women Chained to Dead Marriages* (Jefferson, NC: McFarland, 2015).

———. "Halakhic Principles and Procedures for Freeing Agunot," *Jewish Week*, August 28, 1997.

Attia, Miriam. "She Is like the Beast That Speaks Not: Soloveitchik and the Silencing of Women," unpublished paper, accessed on Academia.edu, June 11, 2020.

Bacon, Gershon. *The Politics of Tradition: Agudat Yisrael in Poland, 1916–1939* (Jerusalem: Magnes, 1996).

———. "Agudas Yisroel," *YIVO Encyclopedia of Jews in Eastern Europe* (New Haven, CT: Yale University Press, 2008), vol. 1: 16–19.

———. "Da'at tora and the Birthpangs of the Messiah: On the Question of the Ideology of Agudat Yisrael in Poland" (Hebrew), *Tarbiz*, 52 (1983): 497–508.

Baer, Yitzhak. "The Disputations of R. Yehiel of Paris and Nachmanides" (Hebrew), *Zion*, 5 (1939): 1–44.

Baker, Mark. "The Voice of the Deserted Jewish Woman, 1867–1870," *Jewish Social Studies*, New Series, 2/1 (1995): 98–123.

Barack Fishman, Sylvia. *A Breath of Life: Feminism in the American Jewish Community* (Hanover, NH: University Press of New England/Brandeis University Press, 1993).

Barmash, Pamela. "On Egalitarian Marriage," *Nashim*, 43 (2024): 103–7.

Baron, Devorah. "Kritut," *Proyekt Ben Yehuda*, https://benyehuda.org/read/24690.

Baron, Salo W. *The Jewish Community: Its History and Structure to the American Revolution*, 3 vols. (Philadelphia: Jewish Publication Society of America, 1942).

Baskin, Judith. "From Separation to Displacement: The Problem of Women in 'Sefer Hasidim,'" *AJS Review*, 19 (1994): 1–18.

———. "Jewish Women in the Middle Ages," in *Jewish Women in Historical Perspective*, ed. Judith Baskin (Detroit: Wayne State University Press, 1991), 94–119.

Batnitzky, Leora. *How Judaism Became a Religion* (Princeton, NJ: Princeton University Press, 2011).

Baumel Joseph, Norma. "Civil Jurisdiction and Religious Accord: Bruker v. Marcovitz in the Supreme Court of Canada," *Studies in Religion*, (2011): 1–19.

Baumgarten, Elisheva. *Practicing Piety in Medieval Ashkenaz: Men, Women, and Everyday Religious Observance* (Philadelphia: University of Pennsylvania Press, 2014).

———. "Medieval Jews and Judaism in Christian Contexts," in *The Bloomsbury Companion to Jewish Studies*, ed. Dean Philip Bell (London: Bloomsbury, 2013), 85–143.

———. *Mothers and Children: Jewish Family Life in Medieval Europe* (Princeton, NJ: Princeton University Press, 2004).

Benbassa, Esther and Aron Rodrigue, *Sephardi Jewry: A History of the Judeo-Spanish Community, 14th-20th Centuries* (Berkeley: University of California Press, 2000).

Benmayor, Jacov. "Salonika," *Encyclopaedia Judaica* (Jerusalem: Keter, 1971), vol. 14: 699–704.

Ben-Sasson, Haim Hillel, Israel Levitats et al., "Community," *Encyclopaedia Judaica* (Jerusalem: Keter, 1972), vol. 5: 807–54.

Ben-Sasson, Menahem. "Cairo Geniza Treasures and Their Contribution to Historiography," *Bulletin of the Israeli Academic Center in Cairo*, 21 (July 1997): 3–12.

Ben-Shalom, Ram. "The Social Context of Apostasy among Fifteenth-Century Spanish Jewry: The Dynamics of a New Religious Borderland," in *Rethinking European*

Jewish History, ed. Jeremy Cohen and Moshe Rosman (Oxford: Littman Library, 2007), 173–98.

Berkovitz, Eliezer. *Jewish Women in Time and Torah* (Hoboken, NJ: Ktav, 1990).

———. *Conditions for Marriage and a Get* (Hebrew) (Jerusalem: Mosad Harav Kook, 1966).

Berkovits, Jay R. "Women before the Bet Din in Early Modern France: The Evidence from Metz," in *The Paths of Daniel: Studies in Judaism and Jewish Culture in Honor of Rabbi Professor Daniel Sperber*, ed. Adam S. Ferziger (Ramat Gan, Israel: Bar Ilan University Press, 2017), 47–75.

———. "Historicizing Orthodoxy," *AJS Perspectives* (2010): 12–15.

Berman, Saul. "The Status of Women in Halakhic Judaism," *Tradition* (Fall 1973): 5–28.

Bernstein, Marc S. " 'Like a Wife Forsaken' ": On the Story 'Agunah,' " in *Hebrew, Gender, and Modernity: Critical Responses to Dvora Baron's Fiction*, ed. Sheila E. Jelen and Shachar Pinsker (Bethesda: University Press of Maryland, 2007), 117–44.

———. "Midrash and Marginality: The 'Agunot' of S. Y. Agnon and Devorah Baron," *Hebrew Studies*, 42 (2001): 7–58.

Bezalel, Ronit. "In Israel, Orthodoxy Embraces Religious LGBTs—Partly," *The Times of Israel*, September 22, 2016.

Bilski, Emily D. and Nurit Jacobs-Yinon, eds. *Mamzerim: Labeled and Erased* [*Mamzerim: simun u'mehika*] (Jerusalem: Aluma Films, 2017).

Bleich, J. David. "Can There Be Marriage without Marriage?," *Tradition*, 33/2 (Winter 1999): 39–49.

———. "Kiddushei Ta'ut: Annulment as a Solution to the Agunah Problem," *Tradition*, 33/1 (Fall 1998): 90–128.

Blumberg, Ilana M. "When Divorce Isn't Democratic," *Haaretz*, August 11, 2023.

Bokser, Ben Zion. "The Ketubah and Conservative Judaism," *Jewish Frontier*, 21/12 (December 1954): 17–20.

Breitowitz, Yitzhak. "Ask the Rabbi: The Plight of the Agunah and a Summary of Possible Solutions," Ohr Sameah, accessed June 12, 2023.

Bristow, Edward J. *Prostitution and Prejudice: The Jewish Fight against White Slavery, 1870–1939* (New York: Schocken, 1983).

Brooten, Bernadette J., ed. *Beyond Slavery: Overcoming Its Religious and Sexual Legacies* (New York: Palgrave Macmillan, 2010).

Broyde, Michael J. "An Analysis of Rabbi Moshe Sternbuch's Teshuva on the Beth Din of America's Prenuptial Agreement," in *The Jewish Family*, ed. Harry Fox and Tirzah Firestone, *Jewish Law Association Studies*, 28 (2019): 41–55.

———. "Some Thoughts on New York Regulation of Jewish Marriage: Covenant, Contract, or Statute?," in *Marriage and Divorce in a Multi-Cultural Context: Multi-Tiered Marriage and the Boundaries of Civil Law and Religion*, ed. Joel A. Nichols (Cambridge: Cambridge University Press, 2011), 138–63.

———. "An Unsuccessful Defense of the Beit Din of Rabbi Emanuel Rackman," review of *The Tears of the Oppressed: An Examination of the Agunah Problem: Background and Halachic Sources*, by Aviad Hacohen, *Edah Journal*, 4/2 (Winter 2005): 1–28.

——. *Marriage, Divorce, and the Abandoned Wife in Jewish Law: A Conceptual Under-standing of the Agunah Problems in America* (New York: Ktav, 2001).

Brozan, Nadine. "Annulling a Tradition: Rabbis Stir Furor by Helping 'Chained Women' Leave Husbands," *New York Times*, April 13, 1998.

Cardin, Nina Beth. "A Ritual Acknowledging Separation," in *Lifecycles: Jewish Women on Life Passages and Personal Milestones* (Woodstock, VT: Jewish Lights, 1994), ed. Debra Orenstein, vol. 1: 206–10.

Carroll, Berenice A. ed. *Liberating Women's History* (Urbana: University of Illinois Press, 1976).

Caspi Shiloni, Nitzan. "The Judicial Upheaval Puts Women's Voices in Danger" (Hebrew), *Haaretz*, May 2, 2023a.

——. "My Plea to Israeli Women This Agunah Day," *The Times of Israel* (Blogs), March 6, 2023b.

——. "The Narrative That Turns Abuse of Three Decades into A Moving Story" (Hebrew), *Z'man Yisrael*, January 10, 2022.

——. "Smotrich, Chained Wives, and the Superman Effect," *The Times of Israel* (Blogs), April 27, 2021.

——. "More Women Get Refusers than Men Get Refusers? How the Rabbinic Court Distorts the Picture" (Hebrew), *Makor Rishon*, February 15, 2017.

Chazan, Robert. *Church, State, and Jew in the Middle Ages* (West Orange, NJ: Berhman House, 1980).

Cherlow, Yuval. "The mutual respect of true love (Day for the Elimination of Violence against Women)," *The Times of Israel* (Blogs), November 25, 2024.

Chigier, Moshe. "Ruminations over the Agunah Problem," in *Women in Chains: A Source-book on the Agunah*, ed. Jack Nusan Porter (Northvale, NJ: Jason Aronson, 1995), 73–76.

Chizhik-Goldschmidt, Avital. "How a Polarizing Best Seller Became Required Reading for Orthodox Jewish Women," *The Atlantic*, April 25, 2022.

——. "Is Social Media Fueling a Women's Rights Revolution in the Orthodox Jewish Community?," *Religion and Politics*, March 30, 2021.

Cidor, Peggy. "Haredim Who Want Out: Are We Giving Them the Help They Need?," *Jerusalem Post*, October 13, 2021.

Cohen, Arthur A. and Paul Mendes-Flohr, eds. "Authority," in *Contemporary Jewish Religious Thought* (New York: Free Press, 1987).

Cohen, Ilan. "Sudan Needs Our Help. Jews Should Not Turn Away," *Haaretz*, April 22, 2024.

Cohen, Jeremy. *The Friars and the Jews: The Evolution of Medieval Anti-Judaism* (Ithaca, NY: Cornell University Press, 1982).

Cohen, Mark R. "The Origins of Sephardic Jewry in the Medieval Arab World," in *Sep-hardic and Mizrahi Jewry: From the Golden Age of Spain to Modern Times*, ed. Zion Zohar (New York: New York University Press, 2005a), 23–39.

——. *Poverty and Charity in the Jewish Community of Medieval Egypt* (Princeton, NJ: Princeton University Press, 2005b).

——. *Under Crescent and Cross: The Jews in the Middle Ages* (Princeton, NJ: Princeton University Press, 1994).

Cohen, Michael R. *The Birth of Conservative Judaism: Solomon Schechter's Disciples and the Creation of an American Religious Movement* (New York: Columbia University Press, 2012).

Cohen, Steven M. and Paula E. Hyman, eds. *The Jewish Family: Myths and Reality* (New York: Holmes & Meier, 1986).

Cohen Albert, Phyllis. *The Modernization of French Jewry: Consistory and Community in the Nineteenth Century* (Hanover, NH: Brandeis University Press, 1977).

Coy, Peter. "What Does True Consent Look Like for Consumers?," *New York Times*, March 29, 2024.

Darel, Yael. " 'They Want to Set Women Back 500 Years': Israel's Rabbinical Courts Now Set to Enjoy 'Horrifying' Power," *Haaretz*, February 6, 2023.

Davidman, Lynn. *Tradition in a Rootless World: Women Turn to Orthodox Judaism* (Berkeley: University of California Press, 1991).

Deen, Shulem. *All Who Go Do Not Return* (Minneapolis: Graywolf, 2015).

Deitsch, Chaya. *Here and There: Leaving Hasidism, Keeping My Family* (New York: Schocken, 2015).

Deogratias, Benedicta. *Trapped in a Religious Marriage: A Human Rights Perspective on the Phenomenon of Marital Captivity* (Intersentia Online Publishing, 2020).

Dimitrovsky, C. Z. "A Controversy between Maran Joseph Karo and the Mabit" (Hebrew), *Sefunot*, 6 (1962): 71–123.

Diner, Hasia R. and Beryl Lieff Benderly. *Her Works Praise Her: A History of Jewish Women in America from Colonial Times to the Present* (New York: Basic Books, 2002).

Dorn Sezgin, Pamela. "Jewish Women in the Ottoman Empire," *in Sephardic and Mizrahi Jewry: From the Golden Age of Spain to Modern Times*, ed. Zion Zohar (New York: New York University Press, 2005), 216–35.

Dubin, Lois. "Jewish Women, Marriage Law, and Emancipation: A Civil Divorce in Late-Eighteenth-Century Trieste," *Jewish Social Studies*, 13/2 (2007): 65–92.

Efron, John and Steven Weitzman, eds. *The Jews: A History* (Boston: Pearson, 2009).

Eglash, Ruth. "Israeli Man Facing Criminal Charges after Refusing Wife Divorce for Twenty Years," *Washington Post*, September 14, 2018.

Eisman-Lifschitz, Kylie. "Women Judged by Men," *Jerusalem Post*, March 11, 2022.

Eliach, Yaffa. *There Once Was a World* (New York: Little, Brown, 1998).

Eliav, Mordechai. *Jewish Education in Germany in the Period of Emancipation and Enlightenment* (Hebrew) (Jerusalem: Sivan, 1960).

Elinson, Eliakim G. *The Woman and Mitzvot*, vol. 3, *Man and His Wife* (Hebrew) (Jerusalem: World Zionist Organization, 1990).

Elior, Rachel. *Grandmother Did Not Know How to Read and Write* [Hebrew]. (Jerusalem: Carmel, 2018).

Ellenson, David. "German Orthodox Rabbinical Writings on the Jewish Textual Education of Women: The Views of Rabbi Samson Raphael Hirsch and Rabbi Esriel Hildesheimer," *in Gender and Jewish History*, ed. Marion A. Kaplan and Deborah Dash Moore (Bloomington: Indiana University Press, 2011), 158–69.

———. *After Emancipation: Jewish Religious Responses to Modernity* (Cincinnati: Hebrew Union College Press, 2004a).

———. "Samuel Holdheim and Zacharias Frankel on the Legal Character of Jewish Marriage," in David Ellenson, *After Emancipation: Jewish Religious Responses to Modernity* (Cincinnati: Hebrew Union College Press, 2004b), 139–53.

———. "Traditional Reactions to Modern Jewish Reform: The Paradigm of German Orthodoxy," in David Ellenson, *After Emancipation: Jewish Religious Responses to Modernity* (Cincinnati: Hebrew Union College Press, 2004c), 154–83.

———. "Samuel Holdheim on the Legal Character of Jewish Marriage: A Contemporary Comment on His Position," in *Marriage and Its Obstacles in Jewish Law*, ed. Walter Jacob and Moshe Zemer (New York: Rodef Sholom, 1999), 1–26.

Elon, Menachem, ed. *The Principles of Jewish Law* (Jerusalem: Keter, 1975).

Endelman, Todd M. *The Jews of Britain, 1650–2000* (Berkeley: University of California Press, 2000).

———. *The Jews of Georgian England, 1714–1830: Tradition and Change in a Liberal Society* (Philadelphia: Jewish Publication Society of America, 1979).

Epstein, Louis M. "Proposal to Resolve Agunoot" (Hebrew), *Proceedings of the Committee of Jewish Law and Standards, 1927–1970* (New York: Rabbinical Assembly, 1997).

———. "A Solution to the Agunah Problem," *Proceedings of the Rabbinical Assembly of America*, 4 (1930): 83–90.

———. *The Jewish Marriage Contract: A Study of the Status of the Woman in Jewish Law* (New York: Jewish Theological Seminary of America, 1927).

Ettinger, Yair. *Unraveled: The Disputes That Redefine Religious Zionism* (Hebrew), (Hevel Modi'in, Israel: Kinneret, 2019).

———. "Man's Refusal to Divorce Wife Unless She Pays $131K 'Not Extortion,' Israel Court Says," *Haaretz*, October 14, 2016.

———. "Wife with Husband in Seven-Year Coma Gets Rabbinical Divorce," *Haaretz*, May 22, 2014.

———. "Without the Rabbinate, I'll Thee Wed," *Haaretz*, October 11, 2011.

Fader, Ayala. *Mitzvah Girls Bringing Up the Next Generation of Hasidic Jews in Brooklyn* (Princeton, NJ: Princeton University Press, 2009).

Falk, Ze'ev. *Jewish Matrimonial Law in the Middle Ages* (Oxford: Oxford University Press, 1966).

Feldblum, Meir Simcha. "The Problem of Agunot and Mamzerim: A Comprehensive Solution" (Hebrew), *Dine Yisrael*, 19 (1997–98): 203–17.

Feldman, Aharon. "Halakhic Judaism or Feminist Halakha?," *Tradition*, 33/2 (Winter 1999): 61–79.

Feldman, Ari. "Israeli Man Already in Jail for Refusing to Divorce Wife Facing More Prison Time for Same," *Forward*, September 14, 2018.

Feldman, David. *Marital Relations, Birth Control, and Abortion in Jewish Law* (New York: Schocken, 1978).

Feldman, Deborah. *Unorthodox* (New York: Simon & Schuster, 2012).

Ferziger, Adam S., ed., *The Paths of Daniel* (Hebrew) (Ramat Gan, Israel: Bar-Ilan University Press, 2017).

Finkelstein, Ariel and Ayala Goldberg. "Statistical Report on Religion and State in Israel: New Chapters," *The Israel Democracy Institute*, https://en.idi.org.il/, April 16, 2023.

Finkelstein, Louis. *Jewish Self-Government in the Middle Ages* (New York: Feldheim, 1964).

Fischer, Elli. "Why I Defy the Israeli Chief Rabbinate," *Jewish Review of Books*, Winter 2016, 1–5.

Fishbayn Joffe, Lisa. "Negotiating Divorce at the Intersection of Jewish and Civil Law in North America," in *Love, Marriage, and Jewish Families: Paradoxes of a Social Revolution*, ed. Sylvia Barack Fishman (Waltham, MA: Brandeis University Press, 2015), 240–55.

Fishman, Talya. "A Kabbalistic Perspective on Gender-Specific Commandments: On the Interplay of Symbols and Society," *AJS Review*, 17/2 (Fall 1992): 199–246.

"Flatbush: Dibo (Jeff) Hafif Gives Wife a Get after 17 Years as Movement Grows to Pressure Husbands," *Yeshiva World News*, March 14, 2021.

Fram, Edward. *Ideals Face Reality: Jewish Law and Life in Poland 1550–1655* (Cincinnati: Hebrew Union College Press, 1997).

Frank, Laura R. "The Agunah and the Secular State," *Conversations*, 23, Institute for Jewish Ideas and Ideals (undated, online source): 1–47.

Franklin, A. and R. E. Margariti, eds. *Jews, Christians and Muslims in Medieval and Early Modern Times: A Festschrift in Honor of Mark R. Cohen* (Leiden: Brill, 2014).

Franzman, Seth. "A Voice in the Wilderness: An Exclusive Interview with Rabbi Simcha Krauss," *Jerusalem Post*, October 22, 2015.

Freeze, ChaeRan Y. *Jewish Marriage and Divorce in Imperial Russia* (Waltham, MA: Brandeis University Press, 2002).

Freeze, ChaeRan Y. and Jay M. Harris, eds. *Everyday Jewish life in Imperial Russia: Select Documents, 1772–1914* (Waltham, MA: Brandeis University Press, 2013).

Friedman, Mordechai A. "Marriage as an Institution: Jewry under Islam," in *The Jewish Family: Metaphor and Memory*, ed. David Kraemer (New York: Oxford University Press, 1989), 30–45.

———. *Jewish Polygyny in the Middle Ages: New Documents from the Cairo Geniza* (Hebrew) (Jerusalem: Bialik Institute, 1986).

———. "Divorce upon the Wife's Demand as Reflected in Manuscripts from the Cairo Geniza," *Jewish Law Annual*, 4 (1981): 103–28.

———. *Jewish Marriage in Palestine: A Cairo Geniza Study*, 2 vols. (Jerusalem: Daf-Chen, 1980). Tel Aviv, 1980.

———. "Termination of the Marriage upon the Wife's Request: A Palestinian Ketubba Stipulation," *Proceedings of the American Academy for Jewish Research*, 37 (1972): 29–55.

Friedman, S. R. " 'Send Me My Husband Who Is in New York City': Husband Desertion in the American Jewish Immigrant Community, 1890–1926," *Jewish Social Studies*, 44/1 (Winter 1982): 1–18.

Fromm, Annette B. "Hispanic Culture in Exile: Sephardic Life in the Ottoman Balkans," in *Sephardic and Mizrahi Jewry: From the Golden Age of Spain to Modern Times*, ed. Zion Zohar (New York: New York University Press, 2005), 145–66.

Frot, Mathilde. "Top Rabbi Reportedly Admits He Stopped a Get which A Man Had Agreed to Give," *Jewish Chronicle*, July 16, 2021.

Furst, Rachel. "The Right to Light: Jews, Christians, and Shared Legal Practices in Medieval Ashkenaz," *Jewish Studies Quarterly*, 31 (2024): 136–59.

———. "Their Husbands' Agents: Talmudic Theory and Lived Law," *Dine Yisrael*, 38 (2024): 57–76.

———. "Marriage before the Bench: Divorce Law and Litigation Strategies in Thirteenth-Century Ashkenaz," *Jewish History*, 31 (2017): 7–30.

Gartner, Lloyd. *The Jewish Immigrant in England, 1870–1914* (Detroit: Wayne State University Press, 1960).

Gerber, Jane S. *The Jews of Spain: A History of Sephardic Experience* (New York: Free Press, 1992).

Ginzburg, Louis. "Colon, Joseph b. Solomon," *Jewish Encyclopedia* (1906), accessed via *Jewish Encyclopedia.com* (2002–2021).

Givati, Sharon. "Yad La'Isha, Jerusalem Center Fighting Trapped Marriages," *Jerusalem Post*, March 11, 2023.

Glass, Sara. *Kissing Girls on Shabbat: A Memoir* (New York: Atria/One Signal, 2024).

Glikl. *Memoirs, 1691–1719*, trans. and ed. Chava Turniansky (Jerusalem: Mercaz Zalman Shazar, 2006).

Glueckel of Hameln: The Memoirs of, trans. Marvin Lowenthal (New York: Shocken, 1977).

Glueckel of Hameln: The Memoirs of, Written by Herself, trans. and ed. Beth-Zion Abrahams (New York: Yoseloff, 1963).

Goldberg, Harvey E. "Family and Community in Sephardic North Africa: Historical and Anthropological Perspectives," in *The Jewish Family: Metaphor and Memory*, ed. David Kraemer (New York: Oxford University Press, 1989), 133–51.

Goldin, Simha. *Jewish Women in Europe in the Middle Ages: A Quiet Revolution* (Manchester: Manchester University Press, 2011).

Greenbaum, Avraham. "Girls' Heder and Girls in Boys' Heder in Eastern Europe in the Pre–World War I Era," in *Education and History: Cultural and Political Contexts* (Hebrew), ed. Rivka Feldhay and Immanuel Etkes (Jerusalem: Shazar, 1999).

———. "The Girls' Heder and Girls in Boys' Heder in Eastern Europe before World War I," *East-West Education*, 18/1 (Spring 1997): 55–62.

Greenberg, Blu. *On Women and Judaism: A View from Tradition* (Philadelphia: Jewish Publication Society of America, 1981).

Greenberg-Kobrun, Michelle. "Civil Enforceability of Religious Prenuptial Agreements," *Columbia Journal of Law and Social Problems*, 32 (1999): 359–97.

Greenstein, David. "Equality and Sanctity: Rethinking Jewish Marriage in Theory and in Ceremony," *G'vanim*, 5/1 (5769/2009): 1–36.

Goitein, S. D. *A Mediterranean Society: An Abridgement in One Volume*, rev. and ed. Jacob Lassner (Berkeley: University of California Press, 1999a).

———. *A Mediterranean Society: The Jewish Communities of the Arab World as Portrayed in the Documents of the Cairo Geniza*, 5 vols. (Berkeley: University of California Press, 1999b).

Goldberg, Sylvia-Anne. "Is Time a Gendered Affair? Category and Concept: 'Woman' and 'Mitzvah,'" in *Memory, Community, and Gender in Medieval and Early Modern Jewish Societies* (Hebrew and English), ed. Elisheva Baumgarten, Amnon Raz-Krakotzkin, and Roni Weinstein (Jerusalem: Mosad Bialik, 2011), 15–28.

Golinkin, David, ed. "Approaches of the Masorti (Conservative) Movement toward Solution of the Problem of Agunot in the Twentieth Century," in *The Woman in Judaism: Deliberations*, ed. Tova Cohen, nos. 4–5 (2000a): 71–80.

———. "Case Study Number One," in *Jewish Law Watch: The Agunah Dilemma* (Jerusalem: Schechter Institute, 2000b).

Goren, Arthur A. *New York Jews and the Quest for Community: The Kehilla Experiment, 1908–1922* (New York: Columbia University Press, 1970).

Govrin, Nurit. "Baron, Devorah," *YIVO Encyclopedia of Jews in Eastern Europe* (New Haven, CT: Yale University Press, 2008), vol. 1: 127–28.

Grade, Chaim. *The Agunah*, trans. Curt Leviant (New York: Menorah, 1974).

Graetz, Naomi. "Wifebeating in Jewish Tradition," in *Jewish Women: A Comprehensive Historical Encyclopedia* (Jerusalem: Shalvi, 2005) (digital).

———. *Silence Is Deadly: Judaism Confronts Wifebeating* (Northvale, NJ: Jason Aronson, 1998).

Gross, Judah Ari. "In Precedent, Court Says Divorce Refuser's Family Can't Be Buried in Israel," *The Times of Israel*, September 6, 2022.

Gross, Netty C. "A Horror Story—Ours," in *Women in Chains: A Sourcebook on the Agunah*, ed. Jack Nusan Porter (Northvale, NJ: Jason Aronson, 1995): 39–41.

Grossman, Avraham. *Pious and Rebellious: Jewish Women in Medieval Europe* (Waltham, MA: Brandeis University Press, 2004).

———. *Pious and Rebellious: Jewish Women in Europe in the Middle Ages* (Hebrew) (Jerusalem: Merkaz Zalman Shazar, 2001).

Gudefin, Geraldine. "Creating Legal Difference: The Impossible Divorce of Russian Jews in Early Twentieth-Century France," *Nashim* (2017a): 11–36.

———. "Reforming Jewish Divorce: French Rabbis and Civil Divorce (1884–1907)," in *Gender, Families and Transmission in Contemporary Jewish Context*, ed. Martine Gross and Sophie Nizard (Newcastle upon Tyne: Cambridge Scholars, 2017b), 50–61.

Hacker, Joseph. "Ibn Habib, Jacob Ben Solomon," *Encyclopaedia Judaica* (Jerusalem: Keter, 1972), 1176–78.

Hacohen, Aviad. *The Tears of the Oppressed* (Jersey City, NJ: Ktav, 2004).

Hajdenberg, Jackie. "US Orthodox Women Built Businesses and Friendships Online, Now They Are Being Told to Sign Off," *Jerusalem Post*, July 5, 2022.

Harris, Lis. *Holy Days: The World of a Hasidic Family* (New York: Summit Books, 1985).

Har-Shefi, Bitkha. "Women and Halakha in the Years 1050–1350: Between Law and Custom," PhD diss., Hebrew University of Jerusalem, 2002.

Haruvi, Yuval. "The Great Bet Din of Tunisia Dealing with Marital Problems and 'Get' (Divorce Writ) Refusal, 1898–1921." Unpublished paper delivered at the "Conference on the Jewish Family Confronting Crisis in Modern Times," Western Galilee College, March 8–9, 2017.

Hauptman, Judith. "Women and Jewish Law," in *Women and Judaism: New Insights and Scholarship*, ed. Frederick E. Greenspahn (New York: New York University Press, 2009).

———. *Rereading the Rabbis: A Woman's Voice* (Boulder, CO: Westview, 1998).

Haut, Irwin H. *Divorce in Jewish Law and Life* (New York: Sepher-Hermon, 1983).

Haut, Rivka. "The Agunah and Divorce," in *Lifecycles: Jewish Women on Life Passages and Personal Milestones*, ed. Debra Orenstein (Woodstock, VT: Jewish Lights, 1994), vol. 1: 188–200.

Hellman, Peter, "Playing Hard to Get," in *Women in Chains: A Sourcebook on the Agunah*, ed. Jack Nusan Porter (Northvale, NJ: Jason Aronson, 1995), 15–23.

Herman, Jane E. "Twelve Rituals You May See at a Jewish Wedding," ReformJudaism .org, accessed June 12, 2023.

Hezser, Catherine. "The Halitza Shoe: Between Female Subjugation and Symbolic Emasculation," in *Jews and Shoes*, ed. Edna Nahshon (Oxford: Berg, 2008).

Hirsch, Richard. "Progressive Approaches to Jewish Divorce," *Ritualwell* (website), accessed June 12, 2023.

Hofman, Sholomo. "Karaites," *Encyclopaedia Judaica* (Jerusalem: Keter, 1972), vol. 10: 761–85.

Hollander, Vicki. "Weathering the Passage: Jewish Divorce," in *Lifecycles: Jewish Women on Life Passages and Personal Milestones*, ed. Debra Orenstein (Woodstock, VT: Jewish Lights, 1994), vol. 1: 201–5.

Hyman, Paula, E. "Does Gender Matter? Locating Women in European Jewish History," in *Rethinking European Jewish History*, ed. Jeremy Cohen and Moshe Rosman (Oxford: Littman, 2014), 54–71.

———. "America, Freedom, and Assimilation," in *Gender and Assimilation in Modern Jewish History: The Roles and Representations of Women*, ed. Paula Hyman (Seattle: University of Washington Press, 1995a), 93–133.

———. *Gender and Assimilation in Modern Jewish History: The Roles and Representations of Women* (Seattle: University of Washington Press, 1995b).

———. "Gender and the Immigrant Jewish Experience in the United States," in *Jewish Women in Historical Perspective*, ed. Judith Baskin (Detroit: Wayne State University Press, 1981), 222–42.

———. *From Dreyfus to Vichy: The Remaking of French Jewry, 1906–1939* (New York: Columbia University Press, 1979).

Igra, Anna R. *Wives without Husbands: Marriage, Desertion, & Welfare in New York, 1900–1935* (Chapel Hill: University of North Carolina Press, 2007).

Ilan, Tal. "Patriarchy, the Land of Israel and the Legal Position of Jewish Women in Rabbinic Literature," *Nashim*, 1(1998): 42–50.

"Israel Democracy Institute Scholar Responds to High Court Deliberations on the 'Agunah of Safed.'" *Israel Democracy Institute*, https://en.idi.org.il/, January 11, 2017.

Jachter, Chaim. *Gray Matter* (Teaneck, NJ, 2000–2012), published online, unpaginated, accessible via Sefaria.

Jackson, Bernard. *Agunah: The Manchester Analysis* (Liverpool: Deborah Charles, 2011).

Jacob, Marvin E. "The Agunah Problem and the So-Called New York State Get Law: A Legal and Halachic Analysis," in *Women in Chains: A Sourcebook on the Agunah*, ed. Jack Nusan Porter (Northvale, NJ: Jason Aronson, 1995), 159–84.

Jacob, Walter. "Agunot," in *Gender Issues in Jewish Law: Essays and Responses*, ed. Walter Jabob and Moshe Zemer (New York: Berghahn, 2001a), 195–97.

———. "A Reform Get," in *Gender Issues in Jewish Law: Essays and Responses*, ed. Walter Jacob and Moshe Zemer (New York: Berghahn, 2001b), 191–94.

———. "Reform Judaism and Divorce," in *Gender Issues in Jewish Law: Essays and Responses*, ed. Walter Jacob and Moshe Zemer (New York: Berghahn, 2001c), 187–90.

Jacob, Walter and Moshe Zemer, eds. *Gender Issues in Jewish Law: Essays and Responsa* (New York: Rodef Sholom, 1999).

Jelen, Sheila E. and Shachar Pinsker, eds. Hebrew, Gender, and Modernity: Critical Responses to Dvora Baron's Fiction (Baltimore: University Press of Maryland, 2007).)

Jewish Week, editors. "Agunot: 469 Too Many," October 25, 2011.Jick, Leon A. *The Americanization of the Synaogue, 1820–1871* (Hanover, NH: Brandeis University Press, 1992).

JOFA Newsletter (Tishrei 5784/Fall 2023), www.jofa.org.

Joffre, Tzvi. "Minister Kahana's Decision to Recommend Tzohar Rabbi to Head Conversion Authority Infuriates Orthodox Religious Leaders," *Jerusalem Post*, January 7, 2022.

Jewish Telegraphic Agency. "Alleged Get-Refuser Whose Mother's Burial Delayed Denies He Changed His Mind," August 22, 2019.

———. "Supreme Court Ends Israeli Woman's Marriage to Comatose Husband," March 31, 2017.

———. "Focus on Issues: Orthodox Groups Attack 2 Rabbis Who Set Up Court to End Marriages," November 18, 1998.

Kampeas, Ron. "Last Afghanistan Jew's Would-Be Jewish Rescuers Save Afghan Women Soccer Team," *The Times of Israel*, August 29, 2021.

Kanarfogel, Ephraim. "Halakhah and Mezi'ut (Realia) in Medieval Ashkenaz: Surveying the Parameters and Defining the Limits," *Jewish Law Annual*, vol. 14 (2003): 193–224.

———. "Understanding the Uneven Reception of Rabbenu Tam's Taqqanot," in *Polemical and Exegetical Polarities in Medieval Jewish Cultures: Studies in Honor of Daniel J. Lasker*, ed. Ehud Krinnis, Nabih Bashir, Sara Offenberg, and Shalom Sadik (Berlin: De Gruyter, 2021), 437–66.

———. "Changing Attitudes toward Apostates in Tosafist Literature, Late Twelfth–Early Thirteenth Centuries," in *New Perspectives on Jewish–Christian Relations: In Honor of David Berger*, ed. Elisheva Carlebach and Jacob J. Schacter (Leiden: Brill, 2012), 297–327.

————. "Rabbinic Attitudes toward Nonobservance in the Medieval Period," in *Jewish Tradition and the Non-Traditional Jew*, ed. Jacob J. Schachter (Northvale, NJ: Aronson, 1992), 3–35.

Kaplan, Lawrence. "From Cooperation to Conflict: Rabbi Professor Emanuel Rackman, Rav Joseph B. Soloveitchik, and the Evolution of American Modern Orthodoxy," *Modern Judaism*, 30/1 (February 2010): 46–48.

————. "Halakhic Innovation," in *The Jewish Political Tradition*, ed. Michael Walzer, Menachem Lorberbaum, and Noam Zohar (New Haven, CT: Yale University Press, 2000), vol. 1: 299–306.

————. "Rabbi Joseph B. Soloveitchik's Philosophy of Halakha," *Jewish Law Annual*, 7 (1998): 139–97.

————. "Daas Torah: A Modern Conception of Rabbinic Authority," in *Rabbinic Authority and Personal Autonomy*, ed. Moshe Z. Sokol (Northvale, NJ: Jason Aronson, 1992), 1–61.

Kaplan, Marion A. *The Making of the Jewish Middle Class: Women, Family, and Identity in Imperial Germany* (New York: Oxford University Press, 1991).

————. *The Jewish Feminist Movement in Germany: The Campaigns of the Juedischer Frauenbund, 1904–1938* (Westport, CT: Greenwood, 1979).

Kaplan, Zvi Jonathan. "The Thorny Area of Marriage: Rabbinic Efforts to Harmonize Jewish and French Law in Nineteenth-Century France," *Jewish Social Studies*, 13/3 (Spring–Summer 2007): 59–72.

Kaplan Sommer, Allison. "After Two Decades, America's Best-Known Agunah Is Still Fighting for Freedom," *Haaretz*, September 14, 2022.

Karmiel, Tirza, "The Invisible Violence of Divorce Refusal," *The Times of Israel* (Blogs), Novermber 24, 2024.

Katz, Jacob. *Tradition and Crisis: Jewish Society at the End of the Middle Ages* (New York: Schocken, 1993).

————. *The "Shabbes Goy": A Study in Halakhic Flexibility* (Philadelphia: Jewish Publication Society, 1992).

————. "Orthodoxy in Historical Perspective," *Studies in Contemporary Jewry*, 2 (1986): 3–17.

————. "Traditional Jewish Society and Modern Society," in *Jewish Societies in the Middle East*, ed. S. Deshen and W. P. Zenner (Washington, DC: University Press of America, 1982), 33–47.

————. *Out of the Ghetto: The Social Background of Jewish Emancipation* (New York: Schocken, 1978).

Kaufman, Debra Renee. *Rachel's Daughters: Newly Orthodox Jewish Women* (New Brunswick, NJ: Rutgers University Press, 1993).

Keats-Jaskoll, Shoshanna. "Taking the Matrimonial Bull by the Horns," *Jerusalem Post*, December 11, 2015.

Keene, Louis. "California Ruling Deemed Step Forward for Jewish Women Stuck in Abusive Marriages," *Forward*, April 21, 2022.

Keil, Martha. "Public Roles of Jewish Women in 14th and 15th–Century Ashkenaz: Business, Community and Ritual," in *The Jews of Europe in the Middle Ages*

(Tenth to Fifteenth Centuries), ed. Christoph Cluse (Turnhout, Belgium: Brepols, 2004), 1–12.

Kelly, Joan. *Women, History, and Theory* (Chicago: University of Chicago Press, 1984).

Klein, Elka. "Splitting Heirs: Patterns of Inheritance among Barcelona's Jews," *Jewish History*, 16 (2002): 49–71.

———. "The Widow's Portion: Law, Custom and Marital Property among Medieval Catalan Jews," *Viator*, 31 (2000): 147–64.

Klein, Isaac. *A Guide to Jewish Religious Practice* (New York: Ktav, 1979).

Klier, John. "Pogroms," *YIVO Encyclopedia of Jews in Eastern Europe* (New Haven, CT: Yale University Press, 2008), vol. 2: 1375–81.

Knesset, The. "Basic Laws," https://main.knesset.gov.il/.

Koren, Irit. "'The Bride's Voice': Religious Women Challenge the Wedding Ritual," *Nashim*, 10/2 (Fall 5766/2005): 29–52.

Kraemer, David, ed. *The Jewish Family: Metaphor and Myth* (New York: Oxford University Press, 1989).

Krakowski, Eve. *Coming of Age in Medieval Egypt: Female Adolescence, Jewish Law, and Ordinary Culture* (Princeton, NJ: Princeton University Press, 2018).

Kubovich, Yaniv and Yair Ettinger. "Israeli Who Refuses to Grant Wife Divorce Arrested in Belgium for Using Fake Passport," *Haaretz*, July 28, 2016.

Kulp, Joshua. "'Go and Enjoy Your Acquisition': Virginity Claims in Rabbinic Literature Re-Examined," *Hebrew Union College Annual*, 77 (2006): 33–65.

Labovitz, Gail. "Reflections on 'With Righteousness and with Justice,'" *Nashim*, 43 (2024): 107–15.

———. "With Righteousness and Justice, with Goodness and with Mercy: Options for Egalitarian Marriage within Halakha," Rabbinical Assembly, Jewish Law Committee, May 2023, www.rabbinicalassembly.org.

———. "With Righteousness and with Justice: To Create Equitable Jewish Divorce, Create Equitable Jewish Marriage," *Nashim*, 31 (2017): 91–122.

———. "Behold You Are [Fill in the Blank] to Me," in *Love, Marriage, and Jewish Families: Paradoxes of a Social Revolution*, ed. Sylvia Barack Fishman (Waltham, MA: Brandeis University Press, 2015), 221–39.

———. "The Purchase of His Money: Slavery and the Ethics of Jewish Marriage," in *Beyond Slavery: Overcoming Its Religious and Sexual Legacies*, ed. Bernadette J. Brooten (New York: Palgrave Macmillan, 2010), 91–101.

Lagnado, Lucette, "Of Human Bondage," in *Women in Chains: A Sourcebook on the Agunah*, ed. Jack Nusan Porter (Northvale, NJ: Jason Aronson, 1995), 3–13.

Lambert Adler, Rivka. "We TikTok, but Not on Shabbat," *Jerusalem Post Magazine*, August 19, 2022.

Lamdan, Ruth. "Mothers and Children in Ottoman Jewish Society as Reflected in Hebrew Sources of the Sixteenth to Eighteenth Centuries," in *Mothers in the Jewish Cultural Imagination*, ed. Marjorie Lehman, Jane L. Kanarek, and Simon J. Bronner (Oxford: Littman, 2017), 77–101.

———. "Jewish Encounters in Muslim Courts: The Ottoman Empire, Sixteenth to Seventeenth Centuries," in *Jewish Law and Its Interaction with Other Legal Systems*, ed. Christine Hayes and Amos Israel-Vleeschhouwer (Liverpool: Deborah Charles, 2014), *Jewish Law Association Studies*, 25: 105–19.

———. "Jewish Women as Providers in the Generations following the Expulsion from Spain," *Nashim*, 13 (2007): 49–67.

———. "An Early 17th Century Ketubah from Sefer Tikun Sofrim by Rabbi Yitzhak Sabakh," *Early Modern Workshop: Jewish History Resources*, vol. 3: *Gender, Family, and Social Structures*, Wesleyan University, 2006, 86–96.

———. "The Mercies of the Court: Jewish Women Seeking Divorce in Sixteenth-Century Palestine, Syria, and Egypt," *Nashim*, 1 (1998): 51–69.

———. *A Separate People: Jewish Women in Palestine, Syria, and Egypt in the Sixteenth Century* (Hebrew) (Tel Aviv: Beytan, 1996).

Lamm, Maurice. *The Jewish Way in Love and Marriage* (New York: Harper & Row, 1982).

Lamm, Norman. "Recent Additions to the Ketubbah: A Halakhic Critique," *Tradition*, 2/1 (Fall 1959): 93–118.

Landesman, Leib. "Agunot: Is the System Working? A Beit Din Responds: Yes," in *Women in Chains: A Sourcebook on the Agunah*, ed. Jack Nusan Porter (Northvale, NJ: Jason Aronson, 1995), 131–38.

Laqueur, Walter. *The Terrible Secret: Suppression of the Truth about Hitler's Final Solution* (New York: Penguin, 1982).

Lauer, Rena N. "In Defense of Bigamy: Colonial Policy, Jewish Law, and Gender in Venetian Crete," *Gender and History*, 29/3 (November 2017): 570–88.

———. "Jewish Law and Litigation in the Secular Courts of the Late Medieval Mediterranean," *Critical Analyses of Law*, 3/1 (2016): 114–32.

Lederhendler, Eli. *Responses to Modernity: New Voices in America and Eastern Europe* (New York: New York University Press, 1994).

Leibovitz, Liel. "In Rare Move Rabbinic Court Annuls Divorce Refuser's Marriage." *Tablet*, June 19, 2018.

Levi, Sarah. "Between Worlds: Former Orthodox Jews Speak Out," *Jerusalem Post*, January 13, 2018.

Levine, Talia. "For Many Agunot, Halachic Prenups Won't Break Their Chains," Jewish Telegraphic Agency, November 27, 2013.

Levine Melammed, Renee. *Heretics or Daughters of Israel?: The Crypto-Jewish Women of Castile* (Oxford: Oxford University Press, 1999).

Levinson, Chaim. "In Rare Ruling, Wife of Comatose Man Granted a Rabbinic Divorce," *Haaretz*, October 4, 2018.

Lewak, Doree. "An Orthodox Woman's 3-Year Divorce Fight," *New York Post*, November 4, 2013.

Lewis, Bernard. *Islam and the West* (New York: Oxford University Press, 1993).

———. *The Jews of Islam* (Princeton, NJ: Princeton University Press, 1984).

Lieber, Chavie. "Rav Ovadia Yosef's Mission to Free Agunot," *Forward*, October 7, 2013.

Lieberman, Philip I. "Partnership, Equity, and Traditional Jewish Marriage," in *The Jewish Family*, ed. Harry Fox and Tirzah Meacham, *Jewish Law Association Studies*, 28 (2019): 73–93.

Limmer, Seth M. and Jonah Dov Pesner, eds. *Moral Resistance and Spiritual Authority: Our Jewish Obligation to Social Justice* (Chicago: CCAR Press, 2022).

Linzer, Dov. "Ani Li [sic] Dodi vi [sic] Dodi Li: Towards a More Balanced Wedding Ceremony," *JOFA Journal* (Iyar 5763/Summer 2003): 4–7.

Lithwick, Dahlia. "Why I Haven't Gone Back to SCOTUS since Kavanaugh," *Slate*, October 30, 2019.

Lopes Cardozo, Nathan. "The Genius and Limitations of Rabbi Joseph Ber Soloveitchik," David Cardozo Academy, www.cardozoacademy.org, August 2020.

———. *Jewish Law as Rebellion: A Plea for Religious Authenticity and Halachic Courage* (Jerusalem: Urim, 2018).

Lubetsky, Judah. *There Is No Condition on Marriage* (Hebrew) (1930), https://lawcat .berkeley.edu.

Lubitch, Rivka. "On the Force of Kinyan of a Woman in Kiddushin" (Hebrew), *Akdamut*, 31 (2019): 97–116.

———. "Canceling the Black List" (Hebrew), *Makor Rishon*, March 22, 2017.

———. "Religion and State against the Mamzer: Cost and Solution" (Hebrew), in *Mamzerim: Labeled and Erased*, ed. Emily D. Bilski and Nurit Yakobs-Yinon (Jerusalem: Aluma Films, 2017), 127–31.

———. "Religion and State versus the Mamzer: Costs and Solutions," in *Mamzerim: Labeled and Erased*, ed. Emily D. Bilski and Nurit Yakobs-Yinon (Jerusalem: Aluma Films, 2017), 165–74.

———. "Time to Face and Solve the Issue of Mamzer," "Fresh Ideas from HBI," *HBI Blog*, www.brandeis.edu/hbi/blog, May 23, 2014.

———. "The Courts Fight, the Child Comes Out a Mamzer" (Hebrew), *Ynet*, February 5, 2009.

Macner, Esther. "Coercive Control: A Legal Definition of 'Get' (Jewish Divorce) Abuse," *Jewish Journal*, https://jewishjournal.com/, July 28, 2020.

Magnus, Shulamit S. "Agunot," *Shalvi/Hyman Encyclopedia of Jewish Women* (digital).

———. "Noa Shashar, Gevarim ne'elamim" (review), *American Association for Polish-Jewish Studies*, October 2022.

———. "The Last Agunah of Afghanistan," *The Times of Israel* (Blogs), September 20, 2021a.

———. "Ritual," in *Jewish Women in America: An Historical Encyclopedia* (digital; rev. ed. 2021b).

———. "Jonathan Sacks Was a Beloved Leader. Yet His Stance on Marriage Captivity Belied His Ethics," *Forward*, November 19, 2020a.

———. "Thinking outside the Chains to Free Agunot and End Iggun," "Fresh Ideas from HBI," *HBI Blog*, January 2020b.

———. "Chief Rabbi Lets Corpse of Woman Rot to Free an Aguna," *The Times of Israel*, August 20, 2019a.

———. "Dybbuk, or Voice? On Women's Ordination in Orthodoxy," *The Times of Israel*, Featured Post, September 3, 2019b.

———. "Loving a Mentally Ill Parent," *The Times of Israel* (Blogs), January 31, 2019c.

———. "Huppa Pratit: Good, Necessary, but Not Sufficient," *Jerusalem Post*, July 5, 2018a.

———. "No Aguna Day," *Jerusalem Post*, March 1, 2018b.

———. "Good Bad Jews: Converts, Conversion, and Boundary Redrawing in Modern Russian Jewry: Notes toward a New Category," in *Boundaries in Jewish Identity*, ed. Susan A. Glenn and Naomi B. Sokoloff (Seattle: University of Washington Press, 2010), 132–60.

———. " 'Out of the Ghetto': Integrating the Study of Jewish Women into the Study of 'the Jews,' " *Judaism*, 39/1 (Winter 1990): 29–36.

Maimon, Solomon. *The Autobiography of Solomon Maimon*, trans. J. Clark Murray (London: East and West Library, 1954).

Marrus, Michael R. *The Politics of Assimilation: The French Jewish Community at the Time of the Dreyfus Affair* (Oxford: Clarendon, 1980).

Marx, Alexander. "The Importance of the Cairo Geniza for Jewish History," *Proceedings of the American Academy of Jewish Research*, 16 (1946–47): 183–204.

Mazower, Mark. *Salonica, City of Ghosts: Christians, Muslims, and Jews, 1430-1950* (New York: Knopf, 2005).

Meacham, Tirzah. "Marriage, Freedom, and Equality: Can the Three Go Together? A Review of the Conference at Bar-Ilan University, June 21–22, 1999," *Jewish Law Annual Review*, 28 (2019): *The Jewish Family*, ed. Harry Fox and Tirzah Meacham, 265–86.

Meir, Aryeh. " 'For the Sake of Heaven': On Charedim and Religious Zionism," *HaMizrachi*, 5/3 (Tisha B'av 5782) (no secular date listed).

Meir, Natan M. *Kiev, Jewish Metropolis: A History, 1859–1914* (Bloomington: Indiana University Press, 2010).

Meiselman, Moshe. *Jewish Woman in Jewish Law* (New York: Ktav, 1978).

Mendes-Flohr, Paul and Jehuda Reinharz. "Appendix: The Demography of Modern Jewish History," in *The Jew in the Modern World: A Documentary History*, ed. Paul Mendes-Flohr and Jehuda Reinharz (New York: Oxford University Press, 2011), 879–91.

Mendes-Flohr, Paul and Jehuda Reinharz, eds. *The Jew in the Modern World: A Documentary History* (New York: Oxford University Press, 2011).

Metzger, Isaac, ed. *A Bintel Brief: Sixty Years of Letters from the Lower East Side to the Jewish Daily Forward* (New York: Doubleday, 1971), 15–16.

Meyer, Michael. *Response to Modernity: A History of the Reform Movement in Judaism* (New York: Oxford University Press, 1988).

Murray, J. Clark, trans. *The Autobiography of Solomon Maimon* (London: East and West Library, 1954).

Nachshoni, Koby and Gilad Cohen. "Rabbinical Court Rejects Agunah's Request; Funeral Proceeds with Mass Attendance" (Hebrew), *Ynet*, December 3, 2020.

Newman, Marissa. "In Rare Move, Private Rabbinical Court Sets 'Chained' Woman Free after 23 Years," *The Times of Israel*, June 5, 2018.

Nizri, Yigal S. " 'Living as Widows': Narrating the Agunah in Maghrebi Rabbinic Texts," in *The Jewish Family*, ed. Harry Fox and Tirzah Meacham, *Jewish Law Association Studies*, 28: (2019): 57–72.

Nusan Porter, Jack, ed. *Women in Chains: A Sourcebook on the Agunah* (Northvale, NJ: Jason Aronson, 1995).

Orbach, Alexander. *New Voices of Russian Jewry: A Study of the Russian Jewish Press of Odessa in the Era of the Great Reforms* (Leiden: Brill, 1980).

Orenstein, Debra, ed. *Lifecycles: Jewish Women on Life Passages and Personal Milestones* (Woodstock, VT: Jewish Lights, 1994), vol. 1: 359–76.

Pappenheim, Bertha. *Bertha Pappenheim—a Woman's Right: Writings on Feminism and Judaism*, ed. Natalie Naimark-Goldberg (Hebrew) (Jerusalem: Carmel, 2019).

Parkes, James. *The Conflict of the Church and Synagogue: A Study in the Origins of Antisemitism* (New York: Atheneum, 1969).

Parush, Iris. *Reading Jewish Women: Marginality and Modernization in Nineteenth-Century Eastern European Jewish Society* (Waltham, MA: Brandeis University Press, 2004).

Pasternak Beeri, Shira. "Picturing the Plight of Agunot," *The Times of Israel* (Blogs), March 22, 2021.

Pitkowsky, R. M. and Monique Susskind Goldberg. " 'Derekh Qiddushin' instead of Qiddushin," in Monique Susskind Goldberg and Diana Villa, *Za'akat Dalot: Halakhic Solutions for the Agunot of Our Time* (Jerusalem: Schechter Institute, 2006), 254.

Polzer, Natalie. " 'I Thought I Could Endure Him but Now I Cannot'—Gendered Sensory Landscapes in M Ketubot 7.7–10 and Parallels," *Women in Judaism: A Multidisciplinary Journal*, 12/1 (2015): 1–63.

Posen, Izzy. "Modern Orthodoxy Must Sever All Ties to Charedim," *The Times of Israel* (Blogs), July 11, 2017.

Rackman, Emanuel. "A Painful Chapter," *Jewish Press*, November 29, 1996.

———. "Political Conflict and Cooperation: Political Considerations in Jewish Interdenominational Relations, 1955–1956," in *Comparative Jewish Politics*, vol. 2: *Conflict and Consensus in Jewish Political Life*, ed. Stuart A. Cohen and Eliezer Don-Yehiya (Ramat Gan, Israel: Bar-Ilan University Press, 1986), 118–27.

———. "Soloveitchik: On Differing with My Rebbe," *Sh'ma: A Journal of Jewish Responsibility*, 15/289 (March 1985): 65.

Rackman, Michael I. " 'Kiddushei Ta'ut' Annulment as a Solution to the Aguna Problem," *Tradition*, 33/3 (Spring 1999): 102–7.

Radzyner, Amihai. "Halakha, Law, and Worldview: Chief Rabbis Goren and Yosef and the Permission to Marry a Second Wife in Israeli Law," *Dine Israel* (2018): 261–304.

———. "'We Act as Their Agents' and the Prohibition of Judgment by Laymen: A Discussion of Babylonian Talmud, Gittin 88b," *AJS Review*, 37/2 (November 2013): 257–83.

Rapoport-Albert, Ada. *Women and the Messianic Heresies of Sabbatai Zevi, 1666–1816* (Oxford: Littman, 2011).

Raynor, John D. "The Gender Issue in Jewish Divorce," in *Gender Issues in Jewish Law: Essays and Responses*, ed. Walter Jacob and Moshe Zemer (New York: Berghahn, 2001), 33–57.

Regev, Uri. "What They Do Not See," blog of the president of *Hiddush*, January 18, 2019.

Reiner, Avraham (Rami). "The Adjudication of Fines in Ashkenaz during the Medieval and Early Modern Periods and the Preservation of Communal Decorum," *Dine Yisrael*, 32 (2018): 159–88.

———. "Regulation, Law, and Everything in Between: The Laws of Gitin as a Reflection of Society" (Hebrew), *Tarbiz*, 82 (2013–14): 139–69.

———. "Rabbinical Courts in France in the Twelfth Century: Centralisation and Dispersion," *Journal of Jewish Studies*, 60/2 (Autumn 2009): 298–318.

Richler, Jennifer. "Finding a New Path: Israel Wakes Up to the Needs of Ex-Haredim," *Tablet*, November 16, 2018.

Riskin, Shlomo. "The Disintegration of the Chief Rabbinate," *Jerusalem Post*, July 4, 2018.

———. *Women and Jewish Divorce: The Rebellious Wife, the Agunah and the Right of Women to Initiate Divorce in Jewish Law, a Halakhic Solution* (Hoboken, NJ: Ktav, 1989).

Rocker, Simon. "Coercive Control Private Prosecution 'New and Powerful Weapon' for Women Denied Religious Divorces," *Jewish Chronicle*, January 15, 2020.

Romney Wegner, Judith. *Chattel or Person: The Status of Women in the Mishnah* (Oxford: Oxford University Press, 1988).

Rosenbaum, Alan. "The School Rabbi, the Scholar, and the Spiritual Leader: Women Leaders in Israel's Orthodox Sector, Part II," *Jerusalem Post Magazine*, August 6, 2021.

Rosenblum, Irit. "On Israel's 'Black Widows,'" *Haaretz*, February 3, 2012.

Rosenzweig, Franz. *On Jewish Learning*, ed. N. N. Glatzer (New York: Schocken, 1955).

Rosman, Moshe. "The History of Jewish Women in Early Modern Poland: An Assessment," *Polin* (18): 25–56.

Ross, Tamar. "Overcoming the Epistemological Challenge," in *Jewish Philosophy for the 21st Century: Personal Reflections*, ed. Aaron Hughes and Hava Tirosh Samuelson (Leiden: Brill, 2014), 372–90.

———. *Expanding the Palace of Torah: Orthodoxy and Feminism* (Waltham, MA: Brandeis University Press, 2004).

Ross, Tova. "How Ex-Frum Memoirs Became New York Publishing's Hottest Trend," *Tablet*, January 7, 2014.

Roth, Pinchas. "'My Precious Books and Instruments': Jewish Divorce Strategies and Self-Fashioning in Medieval Catalonia," *Journal of Medieval History* (2017): 1–14.

———. "Legal Strategy and Legal Culture in Medieval Jewish Courts in Southern France," *AJS Review*, 38/2 (November 2014): 375–93.

Rothkoff, Aaron. "Soloveitchik, Joseph Dov," *Encyclopaedia Judaica* (Jerusalem: Keter, 1972), vol. 15: 132–33.

Rozen, Minna. *A History of the Jewish Community in Istanbul: The Formative Years, 1453–1566* (Leiden: Brill, 2010).

———. *On the Pathways of the Middle East: The Sephardi Jewish Diaspora in the 16th–18th Centuries* (Hebrew) (Tel Aviv: Tel Aviv University Press, 1993).

Rustow, Marina. "Jews and the Islamic World: Transitions from the Rabbinic to Medieval Contexts," *The Bloomsbury Companion to Jewish Studies*, ed. Dean Philip Bell (London: Bloomsbury, 2013), 90–120.

Saar, Tsippi. "Your Husband Pursued You with a Knife? You're Still Not Entitled to a Get," *Haaretz* (Hebrew), June 5, 2019.

Samet, Moshe. "The Beginnings of Orthodoxy," *Modern Judaism* 8/3 (1988): 249–69.

Sarna, Jonathan. *American Judaism: A History* (New Haven, CT: Yale University Press, 2004).

Satenstein, Liana. "How Orthodox Women Are Using Social Media to Liberate Each Other from Dead Marriages," *Vogue*, May 5, 2021.

Schachne, Erica. "Memories of Rabbi Simcha Krauss," *Jerusalem Post Magazine*, February 4, 2022.

Schereschewsky, Ben-Zion. "Agunah," in *The Principles of Jewish Law*, ed. Menachem Elon (Jerusalem: Keter, 1975), 409–14.

Schindler, Judith and Judy Seldin-Cohen. *Recharging Judaism: How Civic Engagement Is Good for Synagogue, Jews, and America* (Chicago: CCAR Press, 2021).

Scholem, Gershom. *Sabbatai Sevi, the Mystical Messiah, 1626–1676* (Princeton, NJ: Princeton University Press, 1973).

———. *Major Trends in Jewish Mysticism* (New York: Schocken, 1969).

Schwartz, Sidney H. "Conservative Judaism and the Agunah," in *Women in Chains: A Sourcebook on the Agunah*, ed. Jack Nusan Porter (Northvale, NJ: Jason Aronson, 1995), 195–203.

Schwartz, Yaakov. "Jerusalem Rabbinical Court Refuses to Grant Couple a 'Get' until Prenup Voided," *The Times of Israel*, August 31, 2017.

Seidman, Naomi. *Sarah Schenirer and the Bais Yaakov Movement: A Revolution in the Name of Tradition* (Oxford: Littman, 2019).

Seltzer, Robert M. *Jewish People, Jewish Thought* (New York: Macmillan, 1980).

Shapiro, Marc B. *Saul Lieberman and the Orthodox* (Chicago: University of Chicago Press, 2006).

Sharon, Jeremy. "Chief Rabbi Prevents 10-Year Divorce Refuser from Burying His Mother," *Jerusalem Post*, August 20, 2019.

———. "Groundbreaking Ruling in Rabbinical Court Frees 23-Year 'Chained Woman,'" *Jerusalem Post*, June 5, 2018.

———. "Defeat for Chief Rabbi Yosef in High Court Ruling on 'Agunah from Safed,'" *Jerusalem Post*, March 30, 2017a.

———. "Rabbinical Court Statistics on 'Agunot' Being Disputed," *Jerusalem Post*, February 14, 2017.

———. "Rabbinical Court to Reopen Divorce Case after Two Years," *Jerusalem Post*, November 20, 2016.

———. "'Precedent-Setting' Case Allows Woman to Divorce in Independent Rabbinical Court," *Jerusalem Post*, December 1, 2015.

Shashar, Noa. *Vanished Men: Agunot in the Ashkenazi Realm, 1648–1850* (Hebrew) (Jerusalem: Carmel, 2020).

Shilkof, Shira. "Can Remote Civil Marriage Break the Chief Rabbinate's Monopoly?," *Jerusalem Post*, July 16, 2022.

Shilo, Margalit. "Feminism and Orthodoxy: The Council for the Amelioration of the Legal Position of the Jewess" (Hebrew), *Zion* (2006): 203–24.

———. *Princess or Prisoner? Jewish Women in Jerusalem, 1840–1914* (Waltham, MA: Brandeis University Press, 2005).

Shimoff, Ephraim. *Rabbi Isaac Elchanan Spektor: Life and Letters* (New York: Balshon, 1959).

"Shmuel de Medina, Maharashdam" (Hebrew), *Entsyklopedia Yehudit*, www.daat.ac.il/.

Shtif, Nokhem. *The Pogroms in Ukraine, 1918–1919: Prelude to the Holocaust*, trans. Maurice Wolfthal (Cambridge, UK: Open Books, 2019).

Siegmund, Stefanie B. "Division of the Dowry on the Death of the Daughter: An Instance in the Negotiation of Laws and Jewish Customs in Early Modern Tuscany," *Jewish History*, 16 (2002): 73–106.

Silber, Michael. "Orthodoxy," *YIVO Encyclopedia* (New Haven, CT: Yale University Press, 2008), vol. 2: 1292–97.

———. "The Emergence of Ultra-Orthodoxy: The Invention of Tradition," in *The Uses of Tradition: Jewish Continuity in the Modern Era*, ed. Jack Wertheimer (New York: Jewish Theological Seminary, 1994), 23–84.

Silverstein, Andrew. "Harry Schimmelman: We Know Your Wife Didn't Die of Influenza," *Forward*, June 26, 2024.

Simon, Rachel. *Change within Tradition among Jewish Women in Libya* (Seattle: University of Washington Press, 1992).

Sinclair, Daniel. "Halakhic Methodology in the Post-Emancipation Period: Case Studies in the Responsa of R' Yechezkel Landau," *Le'ela: A Journal of Judaism Today* (April 1988): 16–22.

Singer, David. "Emanuel Rackman: Gadfly of Modern Orthodoxy," *Modern Judaism*, 28/2 (May 2008): 134–48.

Sinkoff, Nancy. "The Maskil, the Convert, and the Agunah: Joseph Perl as a Historian of Jewish Divorce Law," *AJS Review*, 27/2 (2003): 281–99.

Slifkin, Nathan. "The Rav and the Immutability of Halacha," *Rationalist Judaism*, November 7, 2011.

Snyder, Timothy. *Black Earth: The Holocaust as History and Warning* (New York: Duggan, 2015).

———. *Bloodlands: Europe between Hitler and Stalin* (New York: Basic Books, 2010).

Soffer, Oren. *No Complicating This! The Newspaper "Hatsefirah" and the Modernization of Political Discourse* (Hebrew) (Jerusalem: Mosad Bialik, 2007).

Soloveitchik, Haym. *Rupture and Reconstruction: The Transformation of Modern Orthodoxy* (London: Littman, 2021).

———. *Responsa as Sources of History* (Hebrew) (Jerusalem: Mercaz Zalman Shazar, 1990).

———. "Can Halakhic Texts Talk History?," *AJS Review*, 3 (1978): 153–96.

Soloveitchik, Joseph B. *Halakhic Man* (Philadelphia: Jewish Publication Society of America, 1983).

Soloveitchik, Yosef Dov Halevi. *Harav: Aloneness and Togetherness: A Selection of Hebrew Writings* (Hebrew), ed. Pinhas Pel'i (Jerusalem: Orot, 1972).

Sperber, Daniel. "Why I Established a Private Rabbinical Court" (Hebrew), *Kipa*, July 31, 2018.

———. "'Friendly' Halakha and the 'Friendly' Posek," *Edah Journal*, 5/2 (Sivan 5766/2006): 2–36.

———. "Paralysis in Contemporary Halakha," *Tradition*, 36/3 (2002): 1–13.

Sperber, David. "Bibliography: Complete List of Rabbi Professor Daniel Sperber's Writings (English and Hebrew)," in *Darkhei Daniel*, ed. Adam S. Ferziger (Ramat Gan, Israel: Bar-Ilan University Press, 2017), 681–706.

Sperber, Haim. *The Plight of Jewish Deserted Wives, 1851–1900: A Social History of East European Agunah* (Brighton: Sussex Academic Press, 2023).

———. "The Agunot Phenomenon from 1851 to 1914: An Introduction," *Annales de démographie historique*, 136/2 (2018): 107–35.

———. "Agunot, Immigration, and Modernization, from 1857 to 1896," in *Mishpachah: The Jewish Family in Tradition and in Transition* (Studies in Jewish Civilization, vol. 27), ed. Leonard J. Greenspoon (West Lafayette, IN: Purdue University Press, 2016), 79–108.

———. "Responsa Books as a Source for the Investigation of the Phenomenon of Agunot," *Quntres: An Online Journal for History, Culture, and the Art of the Jewish Book*, 2/1: 47–58.

———. "The Agunot Phenomenon in Eastern European Jewish Society during 1857–1896 as Reflected in the Jewish Press" [Hebrew], *Kesher*, 40 (2010): 102–8.

Spiro, Amy. "He Was Jailed for Threats to Kill His Wife. A Rabbinic Court Wants to Reconcile Them," *The Times of Israel*, March 13, 2023.

Stampfer, Shaul. *Families, Rabbis and Education: Traditional Jewish Society in Nineteenth-Century Eastern Europe* (Oxford: Littman, 2010).

———. "Gzeyres Takh Vetat," *YIVO Encyclopedia of Jews in Eastern Europe* (New Haven, CT: Yale University Press, 2008), vol. 1: 644–47.

———. "What Actually Happened to the Jews of Ukraine in 1648?," *Jewish History* 17/2 (2003): 207–27.

———. "Patterns of Internal Migration in the Russian Empire," in *Jews and Jewish Life in Russia and the Soviet Union*, ed. Yaacov Ro'i (Portland, OR: Frank Cass, 1995), 28–47.

———. "Gender Differentiation and Education of the Jewish Woman in Nineteenth-Century Eastern Europe," *Polin* 7 (1992): 63–87.

Stanislawksi, Michael. *For Whom Do I Toil: Judah Leib Gordon and the Crisis of Russian Jewry* (New York: Oxford University Press, 1988).

Stein, Sarah A. *Making Jews Modern: The Yiddish and Ladino Press in the Russian and Ottoman Empires* (Bloomington: Indiana University Press, 2004).

Steiner, Benjamin. "The Lieberman Clause Revisited," *American Jewish Archives Journal*, 69/1 (2017): 41–70.

Stillman, Norman A. *The Jews of Arab Lands: A History and Source Book* (Philadelphia: Jewish Publication Society of America, 1979).

Susskind Goldberg, Monique. "Using the Ketubbah to Prevent Igun," in Monique Susskind Goldberg and Diana Villa, *Za'akat Dalot: Halakhic Solutions for the Agunot of Our Time* (Jerusalem: Schechter Institute, 2006), 101–11.

Susskind Goldberg, Monique and Diana Villa. *Za'akat Dalot: Halakhic Solutions for the Agunot of Our Time* (Jerusalem: Schechter Institute, 2006).

Taragin, Moshe. "Orthodox Jews and 'Tikkun Olam,'" *Jerusalem Post Magazine*, January 13, 2023.

Taylor-Guthartz, Lindsey. *Challenge and Conformity: The Religious Lives of Orthodox Jewish Women* (London: Littman Library, 2021).

Tessler, Yitzhak. "'Excuse Me, Who Are You?' After Thirty Years a Father Meets His Daughter in the Rabbinic Beit Din in Jerusalem" (Hebrew), *Mynet*, January 6, 2022.

the&MG. "The Hypocrisy of Thoughts & Prayer concerning Mass Shootings," *Medium*, March 23, 2023.

Times of Israel, Staff. "Last Jew out of Afghanistan Set to Land in Israel This Week," *The Times of Israel*, October 17, 2021.

Tirosh, Yofi. "Rosh Hashanah," *Haaretz*, October 2, 2024.

TJV. "Brooklyn Man Finally Gives Wife Get after 17 Years." *Jewish Voice*, March 14, 2021.

Trible, Phyllis. "Depatriarchalizing in Biblical Interpretation," in *The Jewish Woman*, ed. Elizabeth Koltun (New York: Schocken, 1976), 217–40.

Ungar-Sargon, Batya. "Jewish Woman Granted Divorce from Comatose Husband," *Tablet*, May 23, 2014.

Veidlinger, Jeffrey. "The Killing Fields of Ukraine: Massacres of over 100,000 Jews between 1918–1921 Paved the Way for the Nazi Holocaust by Bullets," *Tablet*, March 1, 2022.

———. *Jewish Public Culture in the Late Russian Empire* (Bloomington: Indiana University Press, 2009).

Villa, Diana. "Conditional Marriage,"/ "T'nai be'nissu'in," in Monique Susskind Goldberg and Diana Villa, *Za'akat Dalot: Halakhic Solutions for the Agunot of Our Time* (Jerusalem: Schechter Institute, 2006), 119–49.

VINnews, Editor. "Watch: Flatbush Man Who Withheld Get for 17 Years Arrested for Domestic Violence," *VINnews*, March 11, 2021.

Wald, Stephen. "Authority," in *Contemporary Jewish Religious Thought*, ed. Arthur A. Cohen and Paul Mendes-Flohr (New York: Free Press, 1987), 29–34.

Wang, Vivian and Joy Dong. "China's 'Road-Trip Auntie' to Husband: Bye-Bye," *New York Times*, August 23, 2024.

Washofsky, Mark. "Taking Precedent Seriously: On Halakha as a Rhetorical Practice," in *Re-examining Progressive Halakhah*, ed. Walter Jacob and Moshe Zemer (New York: Berghahn Books, 2002), 1–70.

———. *Jewish Living: A Guide to Contemporary Reform Practice* (New York: Behrman House, 2001).

Weisberg, Moshe. "A Huge Storm: Rabbinic Greats against a Precedent-Setting Ruling" (Hebrew), *Behadrei hadarim*, November 3, 2021.

Weiss, Susan M. "Agunot Are Not the Only Vulnerable Ones in the Jewish State," *The Times of Israel* (Blogs), March 5, 2023.

———. "Five Misconceptions about Jewish Law's Chained Women," *The Times of Israel* (Blogs), March 6, 2022.

———. "How to Make a Tort of Marital Captivity: The Israeli Experience," in *Marital Captivity: Divorce, Religion, and Human Rights*, ed. Susan Rutten, Benedicta Deogratias, and Pauline Kruiniger (The Hague: Eleven International, 2019), 283–308.

———. "Prenups Meant to Solve the Problem of the Agunah: Toward Compensation, Not 'Mediation,'" *Nashim*, 31 (Spring–Fall 2017a): 61–90.

———. "Stigma, Critical Consciousness and the State's Responsibility to Its Citizens: Comparing the 'Untouchables' of India and 'Mamzerim' in Israel," in *Mamzerim: Labeled and Erased*, ed. Emily D. Bilski and Nurit Jacobs-Yion (*Mamzerim: simun u'meḥika*, Hebrew) (Jerusalem: Aluma Films, 2017b), 99–104.

———. "Stigma, toda'a biqortit veaḥrayut hamedinah leezraheiha: bein 'hatemeim' behodu lamamzerim beyisrael," in *Mamzerim: Labeled and Erased*, ed. Emily D. Bilski and Nurit Jacobs-Yion (*Mamzerim: simun u'meḥika*, Hebrew) (Jerusalem, 2017c), 71–75.

———. "Women, Divorce, and Mamzer Status in the State of Israel," in *Love, Marriage, and Jewish Families: Paradoxes of a Social Revolution*, ed. Sylvia Barack Fishman (Waltham, MA: Brandeis University Press, 2015), 256–84.

———. "From Religious 'Right' to Civil 'Wrong': Using Israeli Tort Law to Unravel the Knots of Gender, Equality, and Jewish Divorce," in *Gender, Religion, and Family Law: Theorizing Conflicts between Women's Rights and Cultural Traditions*, ed. Lisa Fishbayn Joffe and Sylvia Neil (Waltham, MA: Brandeis University Press, 2013), 119–36.

———. "Response to Rabbi Broyde's Critique of Aviad HaCohen's 'Tears of the Oppressed,'" *Edah Journal* (Tammuz 5765/2005): 1–5.

———. "Israeli Divorce Law: The Maldistribution of Power, Its Abuses, and 'Status' of Jewish Women," in *Men and Women, Gender, Judaism and Democracy*, ed. Rachel Elior (Jerusalem: Urim, 2004), 58–59.

———. "Sign at Your Own Risk: The 'RCA' Prenuptial May Prejudice the Fairness of Your Future Divorce," *Cardozo Women's Law Journal* (1999): 49–102.

Weiss, Susan M. and Netty C. Gross-Horowitz, *Marriage and Divorce in the Jewish State: Israel's Civil War* (Waltham, MA: Brandeis University Press, 2013).

Weissler, Chava. *Voices of the Matriarchs: Listening to the Prayers of Early Modern Jewish Women* (Boston: Beacon, 1998).

Wellen Levine, Stephanie. *Mystics, Mavericks, and Merrymakers: An Intimate Journey among Hasidic Girls* (New York: New York University Press, 2003).

Wengeroff, Pauline. *Memoirs of a Grandmother: Scenes from the Cultural History of the Jews of Russia in the Nineteenth Century*, trans. with introduction, notes, and commentary by Shulamit S. Magnus, 2 vols. (Stanford, CA: Stanford University Press, 2010, 2014).

Westreich, Avishalom. "Divorce on Demand: The History, Dogmatics, and Hermeneutics of the Wife's Right to Divorce in Jewish Law," *Journal of Jewish Studies* (2011): 340–63.

Westreich, Elimelech. "The Rise and Decline of the Law of the Rebellious Wife in Medieval Jewish Law," *Jewish Law Association Studies* (2002): 207–18.

———. "The Rise and Decline of the Wife's Right to Leave Her Husband without Fault in Medieval Jewish Law," ([Hebrew]), *Shenaton ha-Mishpat ha-Ivri; Annual of the Institute for Research in Jewish Law*, 21 (1998–2000): 123–47.

Wojakovsky, Nadine. "A Year of Hope for Chained Wives," *Jewish Chronicle*, December 23, 2020.

Wolowelsky, Joel B. *Women, Jewish Law, and Modernity: New Opportunities in a Post-Feminist Age* (New York: Ktav, 1997).

Woolf, Jeffrey. "Damsels in Distress: Jewish Women in the Responsa of Rabbi Joseph Colon," in *Memory, Community, and Gender in Medieval and Early Modern Jewish Societies*, ed. Elisheva Baumgarten and Amnon Raz-Krakotzkin (Jerusalem: Bialik, 2011), 103–17.

Yerushalmi, Yosef Hayim. *From Spanish Court to Italian Ghetto* (Seattle: University of Washington Press, 1981).

Yoreh, Tzemah. "Shvu'at Zugiyyut: An Oath Model for Jewish Marriage Ceremonies," *Jewish Law Journal* (2019): 15–24.

Young, Eve. "Shuli Rand's Marriage of Additional Wife Highlights Inequality— Women's Orgs," *Jerusalem Post*, November 13, 2021.

Zalkin, Mordechai. *Beyond the Glory: Community Rabbis in Eastern Europe* (Berlin: De Gruyter, 2021).

Zierler, Wendy. "'In What World?': Devorah Baron's Fictional Exile," *Prooftexts*, 19/2 (May 1999): 127–50.

Zinger, Oded. "'She Aims to Harass Him': Jewish Women in Muslim Legal Venues in Medieval Egypt," *AJS Review*, 42/1 (April 2018): 159–92.

———. "Women, Gender and Law: Marital Disputes according to Documents from the Cairo Geniza," PhD diss., Princeton University, September 2014.

Zohar, Zvi. "Sephardic Jurisprudence in the Recent Half-Millenium," in *Sephardic and Mizrahi Jewry: From the Golden Age of Spain to Modern Times*, ed. Zion Zohar (New York: New York University Press, 2005), 167–95.

Zwiebel, Chaim Dovid. "'Tragedy Compounded': The Aguna Problem and New York's Controversial New 'Get' Law," in *Women in Chains: A Sourcebook on the Agunah*, ed. Jack Nusan Porter (Northvale, NJ: Jason Aronson, 1995), 141–57.

INDEX

Page numbers in italics indicate Figures.

abandonment, of wife, 46, 85, 127; concerns and problems with, 7, 40, 153; economic incentives for, 125, 134; husbands threatening, 50; increase in cases of, 134–35; premodern, 51, 140–41; rabbinic inaction on, 151

Abravanel, Don Isaac, 107

abuse, 13, 15, 69, 115, 164, 246, 249; Domestic Abuse Act of 2021 and, 162, 231; get extortion/refusal as, 14, 163, 227, 240; halakhic marriage and, 33, 54, 225, 230, 234, 254; marital, 14, 29, 63, 67, 89, 153, 161, 170, 177, 189, 216, 290n30; sexual, of children, 7, 167; of women in rabbinic courts, 228–29, 234. *See also* violence

acquisition, of woman in marriage. See *kinyan*

Adelman, Howard, xxiv, 60, 68, 70, 85, 89

Adler, Hermann, 144

Adler, Rachel, xiii, 14, 240, 242, 260

adultery, 23, 29, 43, 51, 96, 140, 191, 226, 247

Afghanistan, 219–21

Africa. *See* Cairo Geniza; Egypt; North Africa

aginut. See *iggun*

Agnon, Shmuel Yosef, 139–40

Agudath ha Rabbanim, 174

Agudath Israel (Agudah), 147, 149, 172, 179, 191, 207

Agunah, Inc., 190

agunah/agunot (woman/women "chained" in marriage), 6, 14, 55, 117; advocacy,
142–43, 157, 169, 179, 180, 190, 194, 195, 205–6, 213, 230, 236, 238, 239, 287n1, 287n65, 297n53; apostasy of, 5, 64, 65, 67–68, 98; childlessness of, 139, 149; definition of, 1, 171–72, 293n25; husbands sought in newspaper ads by, 135, 141, 143, 285n40; isolation/loneliness of, 2, 107, 130, 139, 237, 246; *mesorevet get* and, 171, 172, 201, 293n25; number of, 10, 64–65, 112, 116, 134, 168, 282n28; poverty among, 41, 42–43, 125, 130, 135, 136, 146–47, 149, 254; prayers for, 180, 185, 189; rabbinic indifference to, 139, 151; rabbinic power struggles use of, 108, 113–15, 120, 133, 167–68, 196–97, 251–52; resourcefulness, strategies of, 5, 49, 61, 63, 64, 67, 71, 79, 118, 120, 124, 235, 253; sex slavery and, 146–47; after Spanish expulsion, 101; support for, 72, 135, 150, 235, 247; victimization of, xxii, 11, 104, 125, 131, 144, 204, 227, 273n3. *See also iggun*; release (*heter*) of agunot; widows; women; *specific individuals and topics*

agunah/agunot, rulings on: lenient, 2, 64, 114, 116, 280n53, 285n26; not publicized, 16, 206–7, 209, 210, 231; stringent, 101, 104, 114, 115, 118, 120

Agunah Day, 185, 189, 249, 298n71

"Agunah of Safed/Tzfat" (court case), 16, 197, 205–8, 209, 231, 252

"agunah problem," politicization of, 11, 12, 143–44, 167–68

Agunah Research Unit, 194
Alfasi, Isaac, 90
Algeria, 10–11, 144
Altona-Hamburg-Wandsbeck (Ashkenazi community), 118, 125–26
American Judaism (Sarna), xxiii
anan sahadei ("We are witnesses") (Talmudic principle), 179, 292n21
anchor (*oggen*), 25
annulment, marriage, 145, 175, 182, 197, 206–7, 247, 251; automatic, 177, 179, 180–81, 184, 211–12, 228; for Gorodetsky, 186, *187–88*, 204, 231; *mekah ta'ut* principle and, 190–91, 193, 211–12, 214, 228, 248, 251
Antelman, Moshe, 214
anuss (forced conversions), 9–10, 64, 101, 103–5. *See also* apostasy
apologetics, halakhic, 28, 59
apostasy (renunciation of religion): of agunah/agunot, 5, 64, 65, 67–68, 98; of husband leading to *iggun*, 1–2, 42, 51, 64, 102–3, 111. *See also* conversion
Aranoff, Susan, 147–48, 158, 163, 164, 168, 190, 192, 194, 195, 213, 219, 232
Archives Israélites (newspaper), 144
armalat al-hayat ("widows of living husbands"), xxiv, 42
arrests: of get refusers, 206, 216; of Lastreger, *266*, 293n24
artists, women, *255, 256*
Asher ben Yehiel (Rosh), 75, 88, 90, 93–94, 95, 98
Ashkenaz, medieval, 6, 40, 52, 99, 126; polygyny prohibited in, 30, 59, 88, 97–98, 137, 165, 251; rabbinic backlash against "rebellious" wives in, 88, 101, 115, 130, 253, 278n29; "rebellious" wives in, 75, 88, 94–95, 98, 101, 115, 130, 212, 253, 278n29; women in, 4, 31, 58, 79–80, 94, 130, 278n29
Ashkenazi, Gershon, 112
Ashkenazi communities, 118, 125–26

Augustinian doctrine, 38
Australia, 142
Austria, 122–23, 146, 147
authorities, non-Jewish, 60, 127; divorce and, 29; efficacy of help from, 53; women seeking help from, 11, 42, 46, 50, 61, 75, 90, 111, 124, 136, 145, 162
authorities, rabbinic, 47, 58, 101, 110, 121–22, 136, 152, 174–75, 178, 205, 209–10, 213; agunah problem denied by, 169, 193, 199; financial independence of, 208; *iggun* perpetuated by, 12, 162–63, 178, 192, 199, 231, 236, 239; infallibility of, 149, 207, 208. *See also* decisors
authority: of husband, 24, 179; of kehilla, 77, 80, 134, 157, 158
authority, rabbinic, 56, 57, 79, 125, 149, 151, 168, 236, 250; affirmed through stringency, 115–16, 121–22; in dynamic play with circumstances, 60, 73, 78, 130; as limited, 12, 47, 53, 60, 65, 77, 131, 153, 178–79, 274n20; in Orthodoxy, 207–8, 225–26; prenup override by, 179; subverting, 64, 65, 233; weakening of, 121–22, 130, 144, 178–79
autonomy, Jewish, 38, 39, 56, 60, 77, 78, 134, 274n20; abolished by modern state, 11, 28, 123, 145, 153, 157–58. *See also* community, Jewish
Ayyubid, Egypt, 76

baal (rabbinic term for husband), 24–25, 27
Babylonia. *See* Iraq
Bacharach, Yair, 33
Balkans, 146
Barber, Yacov, 163
Baron, Devora, 140
batei din. See courts
baths, ritual (mikva/mikvaot), 61–62, 86
Baumgarten, Elisheva, xxiv, 31, 58, 88, 94, 95, 132

behavior, of women defending their rights, 5, 9, 124; assertive, 6, 64, 65–67, 80–81, 85, 129, 197, 253; transgressive, 8, 33, 61, 63, 73, 118, 235

beit din. See courts, rabbinic

Beit Din Tsedek Le'Ba'ayot Agunot, 190

Ben Avraham, Isaac (Rizba), 92

Benbassa, Esther, 60, 121

Benderly, Beryl Lieff, xxiii

Ben Hillel, Mordechai/Mordekhai, 81, 96

Ben Meir, Samuel (Rashbam), 81, 90

Ben-Shalom, Ram, 106

Ben Yehiel, Asher (Rosh), 75, 88, 90, 93–94, 95, 98

Ben Yitzhak, Hayyim (Or Zaru'a), 96

Ben Zimra, David (Radbaz), 61, 63, 67, 68, 69, 84

Berav, Yaacov, 50

Berkovits, Eliezer, 175–76, 190, 207

Berkovits, Jay R., 57, 130

Berlin, Germany, 145

Berlin, Hayim, 144

Berlin, Naphtali Tzvi Yehuda (Netziv), 139, 144

Berman, Saul, 193

Beth Din of America, 177, 191, 216

the Bible, Hebrew, 21, 22, 24

bigyny, 49, 167, 204, 212, 216, 285n26, 289n27

Bin-Nun, Yoel, 215

birkat erusin (marriage ceremony blessing), 26–27

blackmail. *See* extortion, get

Bleich, J. David, 27, 192, 215

blood libel, 88

Blumberg, Ilana M., 228–29

Bnos Agudath Israel, 147

bnot horin (independent women), 215

The Book of Marital Laws (*Sefer Hukkei Ha'ishut*), 122–23, 131

The Book of the Pious (*Sefer Hasidim*), 96

Breslau, Germany, 128

Brill, Yehiel, 143

Britain, 134, 142, 168

brother-in-law. *See* levir

Broyde, Michael, 295n6

burial, withheld, 182, 203–4

Byzantine communities, 9

Cairo Geniza, xxiv, 2, 6, 35–37, 125; prenuptial contracts from, 45, 46–47, 60, 271n38

Canada, 169

Candia, Crete, 64, 79

captivity, marital. See *iggun*

Caspi Shiloni, Nitzan, 164, 166, 171, 186, *187–88*, 197, 230

Castile, Spain, 103, 107

Catalonia, Spain, 79

Center for Women in Jewish Law, 207

Center for Women's Justice (CWJ), 160, 164, 182, 184–85, 197, 204, 230, 232, 251–52

"chained" woman. *See* agunah/agunot

change, halakhic, 34–35, 59, 73, 157–58, 274n9

Charney, Baruch, xv

Cherlow, Yuval, 290n30

chief rabbi: Sephardi, in Israel, 205, 289n20; of UK, 207

Chief Rabbinate, Israel, 167, 179, 193, 203, 228, 250; agunah reinstatement by, 251; "agunah unit" of, 237; divorce approach in, 13, 16, 142, 170–71, 228; halakhic incompetence in, 189, 204; Jerusalem Rabbinical Court of, 170, 196, 204; Lastreger arrest by, *266*, 293n24; "mamzer" lists of, 231–32; marriage alternatives to, 241–42; marriage fees with, 248; monopoly on Jewish marriage and, 181, 241; shaming get refusers, 215; wedding officiation by, objections to, 229–30; women lack of power in, 159, 214. *See also* courts, rabbinic

Chigier, Moshe, 208

children, 28, 105, 232, 269n2; custody of, 25, 26, 161, 167, 183, 226, 237; marriage without, 2, 10, 44, 110, 139, 149, 268n9 (chap. 1); sexual abuse of, 7, 167; women as guardians of, 34, 38, 83, 84. See also *mamzer/mamzerim*

Chmielnicki rebellion, 112, 116

Chochmat Nashim, 227, 298n71

Christianity: conversion to, 5–6, 10, 64, 78, 98, 102, 136, 279n34; courts (non-ecclesiastical) and, 4, 73, 76–78, 85, 97

Chuppot, 159, 184, 294n38

Cohen, Haim, Judge, 160

Cohen, Mark, xxiv, 6, 42, 45, 46, 47

Cohen, Stephen M., xxiii

Colon, Joseph (Maharik), 45, 70, 100, 101, 113, 279nn42

commerce, 40; medieval women in, 32–34, 82

communication: of information about and strategies against *iggun*, 236–37, 239, 245–46, 254; between women, 8–9, 98, 118–20. See also networks

community, Jewish (kehilla), 12, 17, 28, 143, 194, 241; Ashkenazi, 118, 125–26; authority of, 77, 80, 134, 157, 158; Gentile pressure on, 4, 80; medieval, 38, 52, 79, 130; of Middle East, 5, 29, 35, 39, 82; Romaniot, 9, 82, 84–85; women and agunot in, 7, 45–46, 135, 146, 197, 234, 247

community paradigm, 31, 52, 126, 130, 235, 254

Conservative (Masorti) Judaism, 12, 13, 159, 174–75, 190, 194, 207, 244

Consistory, in France, 145, 168

"contempt of court" (*seruv*), 215–17

control, rabbinic, over women's marital freedom, 13, 94, 96, 105, 162

conversion: of agunot, 5, 64, 65, 98; to Christianity, 5–6, 10, 64, 78, 98, 102, 136, 279n34; forced, in Spain, 9–10, 64, 101; forced (*anuss*) conversions, 103–5; to Islam, 67–68, 74; of Jewish husband, 1, 9–10, 29, 42, 51, 64, 102, 111, 116; to Judaism, 23; rebellion through, 5–6, 64, 67–68, 74, 98, 279n34

Corfu, Greece, 115

costs, of litigation, 16, 51, 110, 128, 129, 169, 177–78

counseling, mandated by rabbinic courts, 15, 201, 296n30

courts, 79; Christian (non-ecclesiastical), 4, 73, 76–78, 85, 97; Muslim, 4, 46, 48, 50, 60, 73–76, 84; secular, 161

courts, non-Jewish: divorce cases taken to, 4, 5, 11, 29, 48, 50, 57, 61, 73, 78–79, 124, 162; rabbinic law in, 73, 78–79; women's use of, 4–5, 47, 48, 57, 73, 75–77, 124, 145

courts, rabbinic, 4, 60, 75, 76, 168, 169, 180, 249; abuse of women in, 228–29, 234; "Agunah of Safed/Tzfat" case in, 16, 197, 205–8, 209, 231, 252; counseling mandated by, 15, 201, 296n30; *hiyuv get* in, 165, 215, 217, 289n25; in Israel, 13, 15, 100, 101, 142, 159, 167, 178, 205–6, 208, 210, 214, 218–19, 252; judging *iggun* cases, 12, 110, 160, 190, 206, 215; limited power of, 47, 49, 53, 77, 130, 153, 178, 191, 274n20; male rule in, 142, 157, 159; *pinkassim* of, 117; *seruv* in, 215–17; summons from, 264–65; Supreme Rabbinical Court of Israel, 205–6, 252

Crete, Greece, 64, 78–79, 115

The Cry of the Wretched (*Za'akat Dalot*) (Susskind-Goldberg and Goldberg, D.), 55, 55–56, 194

custody, of children, 25, 26, 161, 167, 183, 226, 237

custom, halakhic, 65, 84, 96

CWJ. See Center for Women's Justice

Cyprus, 159

Czech Republic, xiv, 118

da'at Torah (concept), 149, 207, 208

Damascus, 43, 63

Davidson, Kalman Pesach, 185

death: burial withheld after, 182, 203–4; of husband, 1, 8, 25. *See also* levirate marriage; widows

decisors (*poskim*), xxv, 57, 103, 104, 108, 133, 138–39, 280n53; agunah cases reluctance from, 118, 208; agunot used by, for personal goals, 101, 111, 113–15; medieval, negating reforms benefitting women, 3, 98, 99; modern, veto attempts at marriage reform, 145; Orthodox, 149, 151, 152, 190, 208; Orthodox, female, 244–45; overruling other *poskim*, 100, 101; property ownership privileged over women's fidelity to Judaism, 105–7; requiring concurrence of other decisors, 112–13, 115, 118, 120–21, 129, 283n41; *rishonim* title for, 69, 168; rulings on agunot not publicized by, 16, 206–7, 209, 210, 231; sanction get/halitsa extortion, 101, 110, 160–63, 171, 199–200, 219, 231, 239; shopping for, 124; stringency of, 116, 118, 120, 208

defect (*p'gam*) in get, 114

de Medina, Samuel (Maharashdam), 100, 101, 102, 120–21, 279n42

denominations, Jewish, 12, 17, 122, 133, 158, 175, 176, 190, 196, 215, 227, 238, 240, 273n3

Deri, Aryeh, 195

desertion, by husband. *See* abandonment, of wife

dhimmis (non-Muslim classification), 39, 46, 271n36

Diena, Azriel, 77

Diner, Hasia R., xxiii

disappearance, of husband. *See* husband, disappearance of

disputes, Jewish, 37, 49, 52, 60, 83, 84, 105–7; Gentile courts for, 4, 5, 53, 73, 74, 124; marital, 39, 53, 125

divorce, 14, 23, 25, 202, 249, 266; on behalf of husband (*get zikui*), 191, 205, 214, 248, 293n30; cases taken to Gentile courts, 4, 5, 11, 29, 48, 50, 57, 61, 73, 78–79, 124, 162; civil, xvii, 10, 144, 153, 170, 176; civil, lacking in Israel, 13, 142, 159, 229, 241; coerced, 29, 30, 50, 70, 88–89, 90, 92, 98, 100, 161–62, 165, 183, 216, 231, 254; conditional, 7, 44, 60, 62–63, 212, 247, 254, 272n58; costs of, 16, 51, 110, 128, 129, 141, 169, 177–78; grounds for, 28, 29, 40, 63, 68, 70, 88–89, 92, 93, 95, 100, 205; halakhic alternatives to, 239; high rate of, in Middle Ages, 40, 96, 97; husband pressured for, 29, 30, 63, 88–89, 90, 92, 136, 138, 161–62; initiated by wife, 29, 57, 72, 74, 88, 92, 95, 97, 98, 212; initiated by wife, economic sanctions for, 92, 97, 98; in Israel, 3, 6, 13, 159, 160, 228–29; rights of men in, 8, 250; rights of women in, 9, 13, 38–40, 197; stringency in cases of, 101, 104, 114, 115, 118, 120, 208; against wife's will, prohibited in Ashkenaz, 30, 88, 93. *See also* Chief Rabbinate; get; "rebellious" wives

divorcee, 7, 8, 25, 29, 42, 45–46, 62, 180, 254

divorce reforms, medieval, xxii, xxiv, 3, 7, 11, 28, 31, 44, 48, 96, 129; rabbinic backlash against, 88, 101, 115, 130, 253; Talmud violations in, 39, 40, 80

Domestic Abuse Act (2021), 162, 231

domestic labor, of women, 36, 37, 278n14

dowry, 38, 47, 86, 96, 125, 137, 283n4

drug addiction, 191, 193

Dunner, Joseph Hirsch, 145

Duran, Shimon ben Tsemah (Rashbats), 76, 105, 106

duties, wife's domestic, 29, 93, 278n14

earnings, medieval women's, 35, 38, 40
economics: abandonment of wife and,
    125, 134; interests in marriage, 7–8,
    95, 278n29; politically engaged, 4,
    80, 129; women's, in Middle Ages,
    31, 35, 129; women's role in, 4, 29,
    31–38, 79–80, 82, 83, 86, 97, 101, 130,
    276n54; women using, to protect self-
    interests, 4, 80, 129
economic sanctions, against women, 92,
    97, 98, 106
education: of girls, 31, 118–19; on iggun,
    239, 244, 246
Egypt, 36, 37, 40, 42, 74–75, 115; Ayyubid,
    76; Fustat in Old Cairo, 41, 43, 47,
    270n23; Ottoman, 82–85; prenuptial
    contracts in, 45, 46–47, 60, 271n38. See
    also Cairo Geniza
Eisman-Lifschitz, Kylie, 181
Eleazar of Worms (Rokeah), 81
Eliezer ben Nathan of Mainz (Raban), 34,
    90, 101, 269n28
elite, rabbinic, 8, 58, 59, 66, 77, 119
engagement contracts. See prenuptial
    agreement
England. See United Kingdom
enlightenment movement, Jewish (Haska-
    lah), 111, 126–28, 139
Ephraim of Bonn, 88
Epstein, Louis M., 174, 175, 190
erusin, 24, 26, 27
Eshel, 237
Europe, Eastern, 11, 38, 99, 134, 135, 144,
    146. See also Ashkenaz, medieval;
    specific locations
"the evil decrees of 1648–1649" (gezerot
    takh va'tat), 112
expulsion, from Spain, 64–65, 101–2, 121
extortion, get, 15, 18, 25, 100, 142, 153, 172,
    177, 181, 201, 247; as abuse, 14, 163, 227,
    240; decisors-sanctioned, 101, 110,
    160–63, 171, 199–200, 219, 231, 239;
    halitsa and, 26, 44, 69, 70, 71, 86, 101,
    102, 110–11, 137, 144, 160–63, 171,
    199–200, 219, 231, 239

family, wife's: cutting off wife's contact
    from, 39–40; support from, 7–8,
    39–40, 42, 45, 46, 51, 61, 65, 72, 85, 98,
    235, 254
Fatimid rule, 74, 76
fear: of mamzerut, 232–33, 247; rabbis, of
    being labelled lenient, 115–16, 121, 124,
    168, 209; of rabbis, 3, 123; of rejecting
    rabbinic authority, 233; of women's
    power, 94, 96, 97, 197, 276n54, 278n29
Feinstein, Moshe, 190, 193, 206, 209
Feldblum, Meir Simcha, 190, 207, 232, 241,
    242
feminism, xx, 5, 142–43, 234, 285n38,
    291n7
feminists, xiii, xx–xxii, 5, 152, 176, 180, 195,
    215, 292n23
Ferrara, Italy, 89
financial officers (parnassim), 52–53, 121
fines: on agunot taking lovers, 43; on
    recalcitrant husband, 30, 47, 177, 182,
    184, 196, 294n35; on wife deserter, 41.
    See also sanctions
Fishman, Talya, 85
Flatbush Girl (social media persona), 230
Footsteps (organization), 237
forced conversions (anuss), 9–10, 64, 101,
    103–5
foreigners, marrying local women, 7, 43
Forverts (newspaper), 136
Fram, Edward, 131
France, 10–11, 43, 88, 144, 286n47; Consis-
    tory in, 145, 168; Provence, 35, 60, 90,
    91
Frank, Tzvi Pesach, 205
Frankfurt am Main, Germany, 118
Frankfurt an der Oder, Germany, 72
Freeze, ChaeRan, 136, 139
Friedman, David, 144
Friedman, Mordechai A., 35

fringed ritual garment (*tzitzit*), women wearing, 58, 94

Froyen Shtim (*Women's Voice*) (publication), 151

Furst, Rachel, 56, 88

Fustat, in Old Cairo, Egypt, 41, 43, 47, 270n23

Geniza. *See* Cairo Geniza

geonim, 57, 88

Germany, 11, 32, 43; Ashkenazi communities in, 118, 126; Berlin, 145; Breslau, 128; Frankfurt an der Oder, 72; Hamburg, 127; Regensburg, 94–95, 97, 100

Gershom, Rabbenu, 30, 40, 90, 93, 94, 212, 269n28

Get Free, 163

get/gittin, 1, 9, 22, 108, 174, 177, 202, 245, 265, 293n24; on behalf of husband, 191, 205, 214, 248, 293n30; coerced, 70, 88–90, 92, 98, 100, 161–62, 165, 183, 216, 231, 288n13; *hiyuv get* and, 165, 215, 217, 289n25; medieval reforms in laws of, 3, 44, 48, 79, 80, 88, 101, 129, 130, 253; *mesorevet get* and, 171, 172, 201, 293n25; *p'gam* (defect) in, 114; ultra-Orthodoxy and, 176; validity of, challenged, 25, 102, 112, 114, 205. *See also* divorce; extortion, get; get refusal/refusers; *get zikui*

Get Jewish Divorce Justice, 161

get refusal/refusers, 16, 145, 153, 160, 171–72, 198, 214, 230; as abuse, 14, 163, 227, 240; arrests of, 206, 216; polygyny among, 17, 137, 165–66, 204, 216, 251; sanctions against, 30, 161, 175, 177, 179, 182, 184, 186, 196, 201, 203, 204; shaming of, 215–18, *263*. *See also* husband, recalcitrant

get zikui (divorce on behalf of husband), 191, 205, 214, 248, 293n30

gezerot takh va'tat ("the evil decrees of 1648–1649"), 112

girls, 36, 243, 269n2; education of, 31, 118–19

gittin. *See* get

Glikl Hamel, 126, 269n2

Goitein, S. D., xxiv, 6, 37, 38, 45

Goldberg, Diana, 55–56, 194

Goldberg, Jessica, 76

Goldberg, Sylvie Anne, 179

Goldin, Simha, xxiv, 33, 35, 52, 80, 88, 90, 92, 94, 98, 126, 130

Golinkin, David, 207

Gordon, Judah Leib, 139

Goren, Shlomo, 167

Gorodetsky, Tzviya, 186, *187–88*, 204, 231

Grade, Chaim, 113, 140, 227

Greece: Corfu, 115; Crete, 64, 78–79, 115; Larissa, 84; Ottoman, 82–85; Salonika, 84, 85, 100, 102, 121, 280n50

Greenberg, Blu, 152, 163

Gross-Horowitz, Netty, 17, 101, 183, 218–19, 238

Grossman, Avraham, xxiv, 5, 33, 40, 79, 80, 88, 89, 90, 92, 95, 203

guardianship, of children, 34, 38, 83, 84. *See also* custody, of children

Guez, Oded, 206, 217, 298n68

HaAretz (newspaper), 161

HaCarmel (newspaper), 143

Hacohen, Aviad, 194

Hadar Institute, 242

hafka'at kiddushin, 145, 175, 210–11, 214, 248

halakha (Jewish law), 6, 149, 236; as abusive to women, 33, 54, 225, 230, 234, 254; androcentric view of women in, 54–55, 226; apologetics, 28, 59; Center for Women in Jewish Law, 207; change in, 34–35, 59, 73, 157–58, 274n9; Chief Rabbinate incompetence with, 189, 204; compliance with, voluntary, 12, 15, 28, 134, 157–58, 225; custom, 65, 84, 96; *iggun* and, 1, 3, 55, 167–68, 174–75, 214;

halakha (*continued*)
Jews equated with men under, 54, 104, 105, 254; loop of mutual influence in premodern, 5, 57, 58, 73, 78, 130; of marriage and divorce, 3, 8, 64, 69, 88, 101, 116, 280n53; *nimukim* and, 16, 206; politics in, 167–68, 174–75; rabbinic law distinction with, 5, 54, 56; rabbinic sources and, 55, 110, 194; women loyalty to, 102, 105, 144, 146, 150. *See also* leniency, halakhic; responsa
halakhic basis for ruling (*nimukim*), 16, 206
HaLevanon (newspaper), 143
Halevi, Zerahiah, 90, 91
halitsa, 2, 10, 18, 25, 68, 108; coerced, 65–67, 69, 71, 212; document, 67; get extortion and, 26, 44, 69, 70, 71, 86, 101, 102, 110–11, 137, 144, 160–63, 171, 199–200, 219, 231, 239; levir demanding payment for, 69–70, 102, 110–11; premodern prenuptial agreement on, 71, 86; refusal to perform, 69–70, 110–11, 136–37, 145–46; repulsiveness of husband as grounds for, 29, 70, 71, 89, 90, 92, 93, 95, 100
Halperin-Kaddari, Ruth, 170
Hamabit (Moshe Mitrani), 50, 69, 70, 113–14
Hamagid (newspaper), 135
Hamburg, Germany, 127. *See also* Altona-Hamburg-Wandsbeck
HaMelitz (newspaper), 143
haredim. *See* ultra-Orthodox
Haruvi, Yuval, 153
Haskalah (Jewish enlightenment movement), 111, 126–28, 139
hatarat nedarim (nullification of vows), 241
Haut, Rivka, 147–48, 158, 163, 164, 168, 194, 213, 219, 232, 234
Havurah Institute, 242
HaZefira (newspaper), 143

Hazon Ish (Avraham Yeshaya Karelitz), 205
herem (ostracism), 11, 30, 69, 76, 77, 78, 145, 174, 276n4
heter, for agunot. *See* release of agunot
heter iska (rabbinical document), 148, 149, 151, 152, 287n58
heter meah rabbanim (polygyny ban), 26, 152, 212. *See also* bigyny
"He who differentiates between darkness and light" (artwork), 255, 256
High Rabbinic Court. *See* Supreme Rabbinical Court
history, of *iggun*, xxii, xxiii, 2, 6, 11, 99, 199, 250
hiyuv get (court order to issue a get), 165, 215, 217, 289n25. *See also* husband, recalcitrant
Hoffman, David Zvi, 145
Hool, Jonathan, 162, 231, 288n13
humra/humrot. See stringency
hunger-strike vigil, at Knesset, 186, 187
huppa (wedding ritual), 15, 26, 27, 108
husband, 32, 34; absence of, on business, 7, 40, 52, 62, 126, 128; agunot seeking, through newspaper ads, 135, 141, 143, 285n40; apostasy of, leading to *iggun*, 1–2, 42, 51, 64, 102–3, 111; *armalat al-hayat* and, xxiv, 42; authority of, 24, 179; *baal* term for, 24–25, 27; conversion of Jewish, 1, 9–10, 29, 42, 51, 64, 102, 111, 116; criminal conviction of, 166, 177, 193; death of, 1, 8, 25; divorce inability for, 25, 89, 205; divorce on behalf of, 191, 205, 214, 248, 293n30; impotent, 68, 92, 95, 100; *mesarev/mesarevet get* and, 172, 201, 215; obligations of, 28, 38, 125; pressure on, for divorce, 29, 30, 63, 88–89, 90, 92, 136, 138, 161–62; repulsiveness of, as grounds for divorce/halitsa, 29, 70, 71, 89, 90, 92, 93, 95, 100; succumbing (*skhiv mira*) to divorce, 44; violent, 15,

89, 90, 164–66, 170, 177, 186, 191, 192, 198, 201–2, 216, 290n30; wife acquired through unilateral actions, 14, 25, 214, 240. *See also* abandonment, of wife; extortion, get; *kiddushin*; *kinyan*

husband, disappearance of, 8, 25, 285n40; *iggun* due to, 1, 40–42, 63, 64, 111, 112, 123, 125, 126–27, 147, 172; ketubbah payment avoidance and, 41–42, 125, 134, 153. *See also* abandonment, of wife

husband, recalcitrant, 14, 16, 17, 127–28, 137, 160, 171–72, 191, 206, 214, 240; compulsion order against, 208; fines on, 30, 47, 177, 182, 184, 196, 294n35; sanctions against, 30, 161, 175, 177, 179, 182, 184, 186, 196, 201, 203, 204; shaming of, 215–18

Hyman, Paula E., xxiii

Iberia. *See* Spain

Ibn Adret, Solomon (Rashba), 60

Ibn Habib, Jacob ben Solomon, 84–85, 102–3, 109, 116, 121

Ibn Habib, Levi (Ralbach), 69, 103, 104, 109

Ibn Yahya, Tam, 70

ICAR. *See* International Coalition for Agunah Rights

iggun (marital captivity), 24, 207, 232, 268n7 (intro), 273n3; as avoidable, 3, 54, 55, 173, 194–95, 209; circumstances leading to, 10, 64, 65, 99, 102, 111, 112, 134, 136; as communal responsibility, 42, 46, 51, 130, 143, 194, 234, 245–46, 254; communication of strategies against, 236–37, 239, 245–46, 254; ending compared with managing, xiii, xxiii, 14, 17, 143, 168, 181, 186, 189, 190, 197, 208, 217, 225, 233, 246, 250, 253; halakha and, 1, 3, 55, 167–68, 174–75, 214; halitsa refusal creates, 69–70, 110–11; history of, xxii, xxiii, 2, 6, 11, 99, 199, 250; husband's apostasy

leading to, 1–2, 42, 51, 64, 102–3, 111; husband's disappearance leading to, 1, 40–42, 63, 64, 111, 112, 123, 125, 126–27, 147, 172; as Jewish (not Orthodox or Israeli) concern, xiii, 13, 54, 174, 235, 237–38, 241 254; marriage alternatives for avoiding, 239, 248; perpetuation of, 12, 14, 15, 56, 163, 173, 178, 189, 192, 199, 225, 231, 236, 239, 249, 253; political and social problem of, 125, 192, 241, 249; politics behind, 12, 143–44, 251; poverty and, 42–43, 125, 130, 135, 149, 254; proposals to mitigate/prevent, 10–11, 174, 190; prostitution and, 136, 146–48, 150; rabbinic authorities perpetuating, 12, 162–63, 178, 192, 199, 231, 236, 239; rabbinic courts judging cases of, 12, 110, 160, 190, 206, 215; rabbinic marriage as cause of, 3, 14, 23, 25, 27, 123, 162, 194, 197, 199, 215, 228, 230, 239, 254; rabbinic sources on, 55, 110, 194; reinstated after agunah's release, 16–17, 162, 204–5, 230–31, 251; release from, 112, 117, 118, 127, 186, 205, 214; as social norm, xiii, 10, 55, 91, 104–5, 129, 143, 192, 194–95, 209; as systemic problem, 230, 236, 238, 245, 254; Talmud on, 2, 22; upsurge in, 9, 10, 64–65, 112, 116, 134; vulnerability caused by, 2, 46, 149; women's pious acceptance of, 125, 168; worsening of, 3, 99, 101. *See also* agunah/agunot; *kiddushin*; poverty; *specific topics*

iggun, rulings on: lenient, 2, 64, 114, 116, 280n53, 285n26; not publicized, 16, 206–7, 209, 210, 231; stringent, 101, 104, 114, 115, 118, 120, 208

"important woman" (*ishah hashuva*), 80–81

impotence, as grounds for divorce, 68, 92, 95, 100

independent women (*bnot horin*), 215

industrialization, 31, 32, 134

inheritance, 23, 25, 73, 74; rabbinic law of, 8, 29, 34, 49, 52, 148, 153, 268n9; by women, 37, 49, 75, 84, 86, 94, 97, 272n70
Inquisition, 2, 108
institutions, premodern, 8, 46, 47, 49
intercessors with non-Jewish world (*shtadlaniot*), 82
intercourse, sexual. *See* sex
interests, economic. *See* economics
International Agunah Day, 185, 189, 249, 298n71
International Coalition for Agunah Rights (ICAR), 185
International Conference for the Protection of Jewish Girls and Women, 148
Iraq, 37, 42, 57, 74, 75
ishah hashuva ("important woman"), 80–81
isha katlanit ("murderous" wife), 67, 244–45, 301n31
Isidor, Lazare, 145–46
Islam, conversion to, 67–68, 74
Israel, 12, 15, 17, 40, 63, 100, 158, 195; civil marriage or divorce lacking in, 13, 142, 159, 229, 241; divorce in, 3, 6, 13, 159, 160, 228–29; family courts in, 162, 167, 169, 183; millet system in, 142; Ministry of Interior, 159, 242, 248; personal status in, 123, 142, 159, 160, 206; Sephardi chief rabbi in, 205, 289n20; Supreme Court, 16, 159, 160, 182, 205–6, 268n9 (intro); Supreme Rabbinical Court, 205–6, 252. *See also* Chief Rabbinate, Israel; courts, rabbinic; Safed, Israel
Israel Hillel, 237
Istanbul, Turkey, 44, 63, 64, 67, 82, 100, 115, 121
Italy, xxiv, 44, 60, 68–69, 70, 77, 85; Ferrara, 89; Sicily, medieval, 35; Venice, 71, 115; Verona, 86

Jackson, Bernard, 194
Jerusalem, 52–53, 63, 140–41

Jerusalem Open House, 237
Jerusalem Post (newspaper), 172
Jerusalem Rabbinical Court, 170, 196, 204
Jewish enlightenment movement (Haskalah), 111, 126–28, 139
Jewish Orthodox Feminist Alliance. *See* JOFA
Jewish Telegraphic Agency, 219
Jewish Theological Seminary of America, 175, *265*
The Jewish Voice (newspaper), 216
Jewish Week (newspaper), 172
Jewish Women in America, xxiii
JFB. *See* Jüdische Frauenbund
JOFA, 180, 193, 195, 230, 292n23
Joint Law Conference of the Rabbinical Assembly, *265*
Joseph II of Austria, 122–23
Judaism, xxi, xxii, 9–10, 66, 157; denominations of, 12, 17, 122, 133, 158, 175, 176, 190, 196, 215, 227, 238, 240, 273n3; Hebrew Bible and, 21, 22, 24; rabbinic, misogynistic, 3, 28, 132, 133, 245, 253; *tikkun olam* in, 13, 238. *See also specific topics*
Jüdische Frauenbund (JFB), 146, 148, 149, 286n52
jurisdictions, Jewish compared with other, 123, 157–58, 160, 170, 274n20
justice (*mishpat*), xx

kabbalists, 68, 119
Kahana Dror, Batya, 170, 205–6
Kahn, Zadoc, 286n47
Kanievsky, Haim, 205
Kaplan, Lawrence, 208
Kaplan, Marion, 32
Karabelnikov Paz, Hila, 255, 256
Karaites, 37, 43, 270n28
Karelitz, Avraham Yeshaya (Hazon Ish), 205
Karo, Joseph, 7, 63, 65, 69, 113–14, 116, 119; *Shulhan Arukh*, 120, 131

Katz, Jacob, 78, 131

Katzenellenbogen, Meir (Maharam of Padua), 120

kehilla. *See* community, Jewish

Keil, Martha, 34, 88, 94, 132

ketubbah (Jewish marital agreement), 35, 59, 84, 85, 174–75, 248, 292n19; husband's disappearance to avoid paying, 41–42, 125, 134, 153; introduced to protect women, 28, 29, 245; payment denied to women initiating divorce, 74, 92, 96, 97; as prenuptial agreement, 28, 29, 185; settlement and payment of, 28–30, 41, 47, 72, 74–75, 86, 92, 96–97, 106, 128, 134, 137, 153, 164; for widows, 29, 67, 68

Ketubbot 5:5 (tractate), 29

kiddush hashem. See martyrdom

kiddushin (sanctification), of woman in marriage, 24, 108, 181, 184, 189, 191, 240; *al tnai*, 11, 145, 175; *iggun* origination with, 14; vulnerability with, 2

Kin, Israel Meir, 26, 166, 182, 203–4, 217, 298n72

kinship protection. *See* family, wife's

kinyan (acquisition), of woman in marriage, 24, 181, 184, 189, 199, 214, 240; *iggun* origination with, 14; vulnerability with, 2

Kira/Kyra/Kiera (medieval Jewish women), 82–83

Klayman, Yonatan, 216

Kluger, Shlomo, 139

Knesset, 167, 168, 185–86, *187*

Kol Mahazikei HaDat (newspaper), 143

Krakow, Poland, 118

Krakowski, Eve, xxiv, 7, 36, 37, 42, 45, 46, 60, 75, 76

Krauss, Simcha, 209, 214, 298n64

Krochmal, Menachem Mendel (Tzemach Tzedek), 122

Kurdistan, 44

Kyiv, Ukraine, 135

Kyra. *See* Kira/Kyra/Kiera

Labovitz, Gail, 215

Lamdan, Ruth, xxiv, 44, 68, 69, 82, 85, 115, 121

Landau, Yehezkel, 111, 116, 122–23, 131

Landesman, Leib, 169

Larissa, Greece, 84

Lastreger, Natalie, *266*, 293n24, 297n55

Lau, David, 200, 201, 252

Lauer, Rena, 78, 79

law, 57, 144, 153, 274n20; Jewish, distinct from rabbinic, 5, 54, 56, 87; rabbinic, 13, 78, 145, 157–58, 238. *See also* halakha; responsa

leadership, rabbinic. *See* authority, rabbinic

League of Jewish Women, 146

Lebanon, 42

le'humra. See stringency

leniency, halakhic, 8, 10, 69, 103, 296n49; in agunah/agunot rulings, 2, 64, 114, 116, 280n53, 285n26; *mekel* term for, 115–16, 121, 209; rabbis fear of, 115–16, 121, 124, 168, 209; Talmud and, 114, 117, 120, 211

Leshinui/Out for a Change (organization), 237

Levin, Yehuda, 163

levir (brother-in-law), 2, 7, 10, 25, 44, 64, 65, 68; demanding payment for halitsa, 69–70, 102, 110–11; sexual repulsion of woman toward, 29, 70, 71, 89, 90, 92, 93, 95, 100

levirate marriage (marriage to levir), 11, 44, 67–68, 145; widows and, 7, 25, 64, 65, 94

LGBTQ Jews, 237

Liberal Jews, 13

Libya, 114

Lieberman, Saul, 175, 190

Linzer, Dov, 250, 300n20

literature. *See* memoirs; novels

Lithwick, Dalia, 249

loop mechanism, of premodern halakha, 5, 57, 58, 73, 78, 130

Lopes Cardozo, Nathan, 208, 211
loyalty, of women to halakha and Judaism, 102, 105, 144, 146, 150
Lubitch, Rivka, 230, 232

Macner, Esther, 161, 162
Magnus, Shulamit, *187*
Maharam (Meir of Rothenburg), 94
Maharam of Padua (Meir Katzenellenbogen), 120
Maharashdam (Samuel de Medina), 100, 101, 102, 120–21, 279n42
Maharik (Joseph Colon), 45, 70, 100, 101, 113, 279nn42
Maharil (Jacob Moellin), of Mainz, 57–58
Maharitz (Yomtov Zahalon), 50
Mahazikei HaDat, 143
Maimon, Salomon, 126, 127
Maimonides, 33, 43, 74, 90, 92
Majorca, Spain, 105–6
mamzer/mamzerim (child born under forbidden union), 17, 23, 25, 98, 113, 125, 163, 179, 183, 191, 226, 237; act of creating (*mamzerut*), 90–91, 115, 140, 190, 232–33, 239, 247, 294n38, 300n9; Chief Rabbinate lists of, 231–32; rabbinic ruling (*mimzur*) on, 91, 232–33, 300n9
Manoah of Narbonne, 81
marital captivity. See *iggun*
marital contract. See ketubbah; prenuptial agreement
marital reserve (*yibbum*), 2, 68–69
Marranos (male converts in Iberia), 10, 103–4. See also conversion
marriage, 4, 24, 49, 160; abuse and halakhic, 33, 54, 225, 230, 234, 254; adultery and, 23, 29, 43, 51, 96, 140, 191, 226, 247; alternative forms of, 8, 14, 190, 232, 240, 241–42, 248; annulment, automatic, 177, 179, 180–81, 184, 211–12, 228; annulment of, 145, 175, 182, 186, *187–88*, 190, 197, 206–7, 247, 251; childless, 2, 10, 44, 110, 139, 149,

268n9 (chap. 1); civil, 145, 153, 159; civil, lacking in Israel, 13, 142, 159, 229, 241; common-law, 248; conditional, 11, 145, 175, 179, 184, 286n47; conversos witnessing halakhically invalid, 108, 120; economic interests in, 7–8, 95, 278n29; to foreign Jews, 7, 43; levirate, 7, 11, 25, 44, 64–68, 94, 145; *mekah ta'ut* principle of invalid, 190–91, 193, 211–12, 214, 228, 248, 251; men's privileges in, 8, 23, 195; as method of tying converso men to community, 10, 103; modern reforms proposed in, 145, 147–48, 239; as political act, 243, 244, 249; rabbinic, as source of *iggun*, 3, 14, 23, 25, 27, 123, 162, 194, 197, 199, 215, 228, 230, 239, 254; rabbinic, objectifying women, 14, 214, 244; rights of men in, 8, 250; rights of women in, 9, 13, 38–40, 197. See also annulment, marriage; halitsa; *kiddushin*; *kinyan*; *specific topics*
marriage ceremony, 15, 108, 229–30, 240, 254; blessing (*birkat erusin*), 26–27
marriage contract. See ketubbah
martyrdom, 6, 88, 106, 124, 277n1 (chap. 6)
Masorti (Conservative) Judaism, 12, 13, 159, 174–75, 190, 194, 207, 244
matriarchal system, 23
Mavoi Satum, 169, 170, 179, 181, 205–6, 229, 230, 239
media: reporting on agunot, 200, 202–3, 206, 251, 252; social, 215, 236, 245–46. See also newspapers
medieval era. See Middle Ages
Mediterranean, 2, 5, 9, 31, 73, 76, 97, 131
Meir of Rothenburg (Maharam), 94
mekah ta'ut (halakhic principle of invalid marriage), 190–91, 193, 211–12, 214, 228, 248, 251
mekel. See leniency, halakhic
memoirs, 119, 126, 138, 139, 226, 269n2
men, 28, 44, 54, 107, 125, 170; desire for "legitimate" progeny, 23, 123; networks

of, 7, 47–48; premodern, protected female kin, 7, 8, 40, 45, 46, 51, 61, 65, 66, 85, 235, 254; rights of, in marriage and divorce, 8, 250. *See also* patriarchal system; patriarchy, Jewish

Mendelssohn, Moses, 127

mesarev/mesarevet get (husband get refuser), 172, 201, 215. *See also* get refusal/refusers

meshumadim. See apostasy; conversion

mesorevet get (woman denied get), 171, 201, 293n25; as deceptive term for agunah, 172. *See also* extortion, get; get refusal/refusers

Metz, 57, 118, 130, 284n18

Middle Ages, xxiv, 2, 26, 37, 126, 135, 153, 168; decisors negating reforms benefitting women, 3, 98, 99; divorce in, 30, 40, 96, 97; get reforms in, 3, 44, 48, 79, 80, 88, 101, 129, 130, 253; Jewish community in, 38, 52, 79, 130; Kira women of, 82–83; male converts in, 10, 103–4; poverty among Jews in, 39, 270n23, 277n3; in Sicily, 35; women in commerce in, 32–34, 82; women's earnings in, 35, 38, 40; women's economic activity in, 31, 35, 129. *See also* Ashkenaz, medieval; divorce reforms, medieval

Middle East: agunot in, xxiii, xxiv, 42, 140, 221; Jewish communities of, 5, 29, 35, 39, 82

midwives, 35, 36

migration, 10, 64, 65, 99, 102, 134, 136

mikva/mikvaot (ritual baths), 61–62, 86

millet system, in Israel, 142

mimzur (rabbinic ruling on *mamzer*), 91, 232–33, 300n9

Mishna (Oral Torah), 22, 29, 276n1

mishpat (justice), xx

misogyny, rabbinic, 3, 28, 132, 133, 182, 198, 218, 219, 226, 229, 245, 253

Mitrani, Moshe (Hamabit), 50, 69, 70, 113–14

mitzvot (religious duties), women practicing, 58, 94

Modena, Leon, 71

modernity, 12, 28, 143, 153

Modern Orthodoxy, 12, 159, 177, 190, 193, 195, 288n2

modesty, 32, 33, 37, 88–89, 95, 132, 270n13

Moellin, Jacob (Maharil), of Mainz, 57–58

moneylending, 32, 33, 35; women's involvement in, 40, 82, 86, 97, 270n13

mor'dot. See "rebellious" wives

Morgenstern, Moshe, 12, 16, 178, 190, 207, 209, 210, 214, 232, 250

mothers, 36, 83–84, 98, 100, 118–19, 277n8

motivation, of men to protect women, 45–46, 51, 61

"murderous" wife (*isha katlanit*), 67, 244–45, 301n31

Muslim (sharia) courts: Jewish women appealed to, 4, 46, 48, 50, 60, 73–76; son suing mother in, 84

Muslim religious charitable trust (waqf), 49, 84, 272n70

Natanson, Shaul, 139

National Council of Hebrew Charities, 135

National Council of Young Israel, 191

Nebenzahl, Avigdor, 196

Netherlands, 108

networks: female, of mutual support, 7, 8, 62, 67, 98, 118–20; male, in Jewish institutions, 7, 47–48

Netziv (Naphtali Tzvi Yehuda Berlin), 139, 144

newspapers, 10, 136, 151, 161, 172, 216; "the agunah problem" addressed in, 143–44; husbands sought by agunot through ads in, 135, 141, 143, 285n40; *Times of Israel*, 219–20

nimukim (halakhic basis for ruling), 16, 206

North Africa, 5, 40, 42, 75, 82, 92, 105, 114, 142; Algeria, 10–11, 144; Tunisia, 153

novels, 136, 140, 227. *See also* memoirs
nullification of vows (*hatarat nedarim*), 241
Nuremberg, Germany, 100

oaths, 33, 34, 44–45
oggen (anchor), 25
ORA. *See* Organization for Resolution of Agunot
Oral Torah (Mishna), 22, 29, 276n1
ordinance, benefiting "rebellious" wives, 49, 57, 71, 74, 94, 96. *See also* reforms
ordinances, rabbinic. See *takkanot*
Organization for Resolution of Agunot (ORA), 169, 185, 215, 230
organizations, women's, 10, 147, 157, 169, 179, 227, 237, 287n1
orphans, 36, 46
Orthodoxy, xix, 13, 131, 133, 142, 151, 174–75, 197, 208; conflicts within, 190, 194, 195, 207; modern, 158, 177, 181, 190, 193, 195, 210, 288n2; other denominations and, 215, 227, 234, 238; Tzohar and, 12, 195–96, 290n30; women choosing to remain within, 225–26; women rabbis in, 244–45. *See also* denominations, Jewish; ultra-Orthodox
Or Zaru'a (Hayyim Ben Yitzhak), 96
ostracism (herem), 11, 30, 69, 76, 77, 78, 145, 174, 276n4
Otherness, of women, 55, 104, 107, 146, 235, 238, 243, 273n3
Ottoman Empire, 7, 9, 30, 44, 49, 60, 65, 82–85, 92, 102, 125, 276n54
Out for a Change/Leshinui (organization), 237

Pale of Settlement, 122, 135, 136, 138, 139, 147
Palestine, 7, 42, 45, 65, 74, 115, 139, 140; Ottoman, 82–85
Paperno (Paperna), Avraham, 139
Pappenheim, Bertha, 148–49, 208
parnassim (financial officers), 52–53, 121
partnership law, rabbinic, 240–41, 301n21

Parush, Iris, 79
patriarchal system, 8, 30, 107, 111, 130, 133, 134, 252, 254; marriage in, 22, 29; premodern, 35, 39, 42, 46, 47, 49; rabbinic, 54, 62, 66, 87, 99, 101, 102, 123, 132, 162
patriarchy, Jewish: dynamic character of, 48–49, 73, 130; men in marriage and divorce privileged by, 8, 30, 160, 195; protections for women in, 8, 39, 45, 51, 61, 66, 254; women's power causing anxieties for, 3, 94, 96, 97, 197, 276n54
Perl, Yosef, 111
persecution, 9, 64, 65, 88, 99, 112, 116
p'gam (defect) in get, 114
pinkassim (protocols) of rabbinic courts, 117
Poland, xiv, 11, 112, 116, 136, 147; Krakow, 118
politics: in halakha, 167–68, 174–75; *iggun*, 12, 143–44, 251; in marriage, 243, 244, 249; women and, 4, 80, 81, 94, 129
polygyny, 6, 39, 43, 85–86; bigyny, 49, 167, 204, 212, 216, 285n26, 289n27; among get refusers, 17, 137, 165–66, 204, 216, 251; *heter meah rabbanim* (ban) on, 26, 152, 212; prohibited in Ashkenaz, 26, 30, 59, 88, 97–98
Portugal, 65, 102
poskim. *See* decisors
postnup, 184, 239
poverty: of agunot, 41, 42–43, 125, 130, 135, 136, 146–47, 149, 254; *iggun* and, 42–43, 125, 130, 135, 149, 254; of Jews in Middle Ages, 39, 270n23, 277n3; trafficking and, 136, 146–47
power: of rabbinic court, limitations, 47, 49, 53, 77, 130, 153, 178, 191, 274n20; struggles, rabbinic, 113–15, 120, 167–68, 174–75, 180, 238, 251–52. *See also* authority; politics
power, of women, 150; fear of, 94, 96, 97, 197, 276n54, 278n29; Jewish patriarchy's anxieties over, 3, 94, 96, 97, 197, 276n54; men threatened by, 92,

276n54, 278n29; rabbinate backlash against, 88, 94, 96, 97, 101, 115, 130, 253

Prague, 118

Prato, 77

prayers, for agunot, 180, 185, 189

prayer shawl (tallit), women wearing, 58, 59, 94

prenuptial agreement, 12, 44–45, 85, 86, 177, 249, 292n19; limited efficacy of, 14, 179, 180–82, 189, 213, 218, 239, 291n14; Orthodox struggle around, 195. *See also* ketubbah

prenuptial agreement, premodern, 6, 59, 61, 245; to avoid polygyny, 85–86; Cairo Geniza, 45, 46–47, 60, 271n38; regarding halitsa, 71, 86; protective clauses in, 46–47, 271n38; Talmudic law contradicted in, 39, 40

press, Jewish, 10, 135, 136, 141, 143, 151. *See also* media; newspapers

pressure: Gentile, on kehilla, 4, 80; on husband for divorce, 29, 30, 63, 88, 89, 90, 92, 136, 138, 161–62; on rabbis, by community, 60–61, 143, 207, 213

property, 68, 110; decisors on, ownership, 105–7; women and, 37, 38, 49, 82, 84, 86, 94, 97, 99, 272n70

property law, rabbinic, 8, 49, 52

Proshansky, Leah, 151

prostitution, 43, 98, 136, 146–47

protection, of women's interests, 4, 235; communal priority of, 52, 130; extra-Talmudic, 45, 49, 50, 86; by men, 39, 45–46, 49, 51, 61, 66

protocols (*pinkassim*) of rabbinic courts, 117

Provence, France, 35, 60, 90, 91

qadi, 50, 75, 84

Raban of Mainz, 34, 90, 101, 269n28

Rabbanites, 37, 43, 270n28, 271n38

Rabbenu Tam, 40, 51, 58, 76, 90

rabbinate, 10–11, 105, 195, 206; freed agunot restored to captivity by, 16–17, 162, 204–5, 230–31, 251; *heter iska* and, 148, 149, 151, 152, 287n58; hostility towards women in, 88, 94–95; *iggun* ending proposals in, 174, 190; *iggun* solution not coming from, 236; inaction/indifference of, 139, 151, 207–8; misogyny within, 3, 28, 132, 133, 182, 198, 218, 219, 226, 229, 245, 253; partnership law, 240–41, 301n21; power struggles within, 113–15, 120, 167–68, 174–75, 180, 238, 251–52; property law, 8, 49, 52; stringency of, 64, 101, 104, 116–17, 121–22, 185, 208; women's power and backlash from, 88, 94, 96, 97, 101, 115, 130, 253. *See also* authorities, rabbinic; authority, rabbinic; Chief Rabbinate, Israel; courts, rabbinic; *takkanot*

Rabbinical Council of America (RCA), xvi, 169, 175, 177–78, 196, 207, 291n16, 292n23, 295n6

rabbinic pleaders, women (*to'anot rabbaniot/to'enet rabbanit*), 159, 181–82, 214

Rachel's Tomb (miniature), 256, *256*

Rackman, Emanuel, 12, 16, 178, 190, 207, 209, 211–12, 250

Rackman Center for the Advancement of Women, 170

Radbaz (David Ben Zimra), 61, 63, 67, 68, 69, 84

Ralbach (Levi Ibn Habib), 69, 103, 104, 109

Ralbag, Lonna, 26, 182, 203–4

Rand, Shuli, 165–66

rape, 24, 66, 103, 112

Rapoport-Albert, Ada, 77

Rashba (Solomon Ibn Adret), 60

Rashbam (Samuel ben Meir), 81, 90

Rashbats (Shimon ben Tsemah Duran), 76, 105, 106

Rashi (Shlomo Yitzhaki), 32

RCA. *See* Rabbinical Council of America

rebellion, through conversion, 5–6, 64, 67–68, 74, 98, 279n34

"rebellious" wives, 80, 88, 98, 212; number of, increases in, 94–95, 101; ordinance benefiting, 49, 57, 71, 74, 94, 96; rabbis and men fear of, 89, 91, 94, 96, 97, 278n29. *See also* reforms

reconciliation (*shalom bayit*) counseling, 15, 201

Reconstructionist movement, 176–77

Reform movement, 5, 122, 159, 176, 240, 244

reforms: benefiting women, xxii, 3, 44, 60–61, 79, 80, 96, 98, 99, 129; get, in Middle Ages, 3, 44, 48, 79, 80, 88, 101, 129, 130, 253; in Jewish marriage and divorce, xxiv, xxv, 28, 48; modern proposals for, 145, 147–48, 174; regression of, 88, 99, 129; Talmudic law violated by, 39, 40, 51, 73, 80, 86. *See also* divorce reforms, medieval

Regensburg, Germany, 94–95, 97, 100

release (*heter*) of agunot, 112, 117, 118, 127, 186, 205, 214; *iggun* reinstated after, 16–17, 162, 204–5, 230–31, 251

religious duties (mitzvot), women practicing, 58, 94

relocation, to Land of Israel, 40, 63

remarriage, 61, 114, 116

renunciation, of religion. *See* apostasy; conversion

"repairing the world" (*tikkun olam*), 13, 238

responsa: court rulings distinct from, 116–17; rabbinic, xxv, 110, 113, 125, 131, 138, 141, 193, 285n26

rights: of men in marriage and divorce, 8, 250; regression in, xxiv, 9, 88, 99, 101, 122, 129–30; of women in marriage and divorce, 9, 13, 38–40, 197. *See also* behavior, of women defending their rights

rishonim (title for decisors), 69, 168

Riskin, Shlomo, 182, 193

rituals, xviii–xix; baths (mikva/mikvaot), 61–62, 86; garments for, women wearing, 58, 94; wedding (huppa), 15, 26, 27, 108

Rizba (Isaac ben Avraham), 92

Rodrigue, Aron, xxiii, 60, 121

Rokeah (Eleazar of Worms), 81

Romaniot communities, 9, 82, 84–85

Rosh (Asher ben Yehiel), 75, 88, 90, 93–94, 95, 98

Rosh Hashanah, 58

Ross, Tamar, 208

Rozen, Minna, xxiv, 64, 67, 68, 70, 92, 121

rulings: decisors overruling other *poskim* on, 100, 101; on *mamzer/mamzerim*, 91, 232–33, 300n9; *nimukim* and, 16, 206; rabbinic, 59, 91, 193, 232–33, 300n9; responsa distinct from, 116–17; Talmud and leniency in, 114, 117, 120, 211. *See also* agunah/agunot, rulings on; *iggun*, rulings on

Russian Empire, 134, 136, 272n58

Sabbatianism, 119, 268n4

Sacks, Jonathan, 193

Safed, Israel, 7, 8, 44, 50, 65, 119, 121; agunah of, 16, 197, 205, 209, 231, 252; premodern group of agunot in, 63, 113–14, 116

Salonika, Greece, 84, 85, 100, 102, 121, 280n50

Samuel ben Ali Gaon, 75

sanctification, of woman in marriage. See *kiddushin*

sanctions, 110; economic, against women, 92, 97, 98, 106; against get refusers, 30, 161, 175, 177, 179, 182, 184, 186, 196, 201, 203, 204

Sanhedrin, Napoleonic, 144–45, 286n49

Sarna, Jonathan, xxiii, 130, 174, 175

Schechter Institute of Jewish Studies, 194

Sefer Hasidim (The Book of the Pious), 96

Sefer Hukkei Ha'ishut (The Book of Marital Laws), 122–23, 131

Segal, Ayelet, 214

Seidman, Naomi, 148, 151

Sephardi chief rabbi, in Israel, 205, 289n20

seruv ("contempt of court"), 215–17. See also get refusal/refusers

sex, 27, 61–62, 64, 67, 92, 95, 191, 226; intercourse, 28, 89, 231–32

sex slavery, agunah/agunot and, 146–47

sexual organ, lacking, 70

sexual repulsion, of woman toward husband/levir, 29, 70, 71, 89, 90, 92, 93, 95, 100

sexual violence: toward children, 7, 167; toward women, 24, 66, 103, 112

Shafran, Avi, 179

shalom bayit (reconciliation) counseling, 15, 201

shaming, of get refusers, 215–18, 263

sharia courts. See Muslim courts

Shashar, Noa, xxiv, 2, 9, 72, 110, 112, 115, 129, 130

Shas Party, 195

Sherira Gaon, 57, 74–75, 76, 92

Shilo, Margalit, xxiii, 135, 140, 141

shipwreck, 63, 113–14, 116

shmad. See apostasy; conversion

shtadlaniot (intercessors with non-Jewish world), 82

shul (synagogue), xv–xvi, 215, 226; services and rituals, xviii–xix, 59; women innovating practices for, 59; women's exclusion from, 132

Shulhan Arukh (Karo), 120, 131

Sicily, medieval, 35

Silber, Michael, 131

Simantov, Zebulon, 219–21

Simhah ben Samuel of Speyer, 66, 90, 91

skhiv mira (husband succumbing to divorce), 44

Smotrich, Bezalel, 199–200

social media, 215, 230, 236, 245–46

Soloveitchik, Haym (Vilna Gaon), 116, 158

Soloveitchik, Joseph B., 1, 167, 175, 177, 191, 210, 297n60

Sompo, Esty, 204, 217

South America, 142, 146, 169

Spain, 2, 32, 35, 40, 43, 79, 97; Castile, 103, 107; expulsion from, 64–65, 101–2, 121; forced conversions in, 9–10, 64, 101; iggun increase in, 9, 64, 65, 116; Majorca, 105–6; Marranos (male converts) in medieval, 10, 103–4

Spektor, Yitzhak Elhanan, 138–39, 144, 285n18, 286n47

Sperber, Daniel, 12, 182, 186, 187–88, 197–98, 204, 207, 208, 209, 214, 250, 292n21

Sperber, Haim, xxiv, 135, 136, 139, 144

Star, Keshet, 216

Stav, David, 196

Steinman, Aharon Leib, 205

stigmatization, 13, 17, 23, 25, 115, 226, 227, 231–33

stringency: in agunah/agunot rulings, 101, 104, 114, 115, 118, 120; of decisors, 116, 118, 120, 208; in divorce and iggun, 101, 104, 114, 115, 118, 120, 208; rabbinic, 64, 101, 104, 116–17, 121–22, 185, 208; rabbinic authority affirmed through, 115–16, 121–22

Supreme Court of Israel, 16, 159, 160, 182, 205–6, 268n9 (intro)

Supreme Rabbinical Court of Israel, 205–6, 252

Susskind-Goldberg, Monique, 55, 55–56, 194

synagogue. See shul

Syria, 42, 45, 84

taboo, 23, 51, 90, 140, 226, 233, 247. See also stigmatization

takkanot (rabbinic ordinances), xxv, 59, 77; benefiting "rebellious" wives, 57, 74–76, 88, 96; Gershom, benefiting women, 30, 40, 90, 93, 94, 212

tallit (prayer shawl), women wearing, 58, 59, 94

Talmud, 27, 34, 249; *anan sahadei* principle of, 179, 292n21; on *iggun*, 2, 22; leniency in rulings and, 114, 117, 120, 211; rabbinic measures contravening, 96, 98, 107, 120; violated in premodern practice, 39, 40, 49, 50, 73, 80, 86

"Tefillah for Agunot" (prayer), 180

tefillin (phylacteries), women wearing, 58, 59

Tendler, Mordechai, 191, 193–94, 206, 209

teshuvot. See responsa

Tessler, Yitzhak, 200–201, 202

tikkun olam ("repairing the world"), 13, 238

Times of Israel (newspaper), 219–20

to'anot rabbaniot/to'enet rabbanit (women rabbinic pleaders), 159, 181–82, 214

Torah, Oral (Mishna), 22, 29, 276n1

tosaphists, 33–34, 40, 91, 103

Trabot, Azriel, of Ascoli, 89

tractate (Ketubbot 5:5), 29

trade. *See* commerce

tradition-friendly women, 13, 17, 140, 227, 234

trafficking, of poor women and agunot, 136, 146–47

Trani, Isaiah di, 84

trauma, of Spanish expulsion, 121, 133, 280n61

travel, 40, 41, 62, 126, 128, 134

Tripoli, Libya, 114

Tunisia, 153

Turkey, 44, 63, 64, 67, 82, 100, 115, 121

Tzemach Tzedek (Menachem Mendel Krochmal), 122

tzitzit (fringed ritual garment), women wearing, 58, 94

Tzohar (Orthodox organization), 12, 195–96, 290n30

UK. *See* United Kingdom

Ukraine, 135, 147

Ulm, Germany, 100

ultra-Orthodox (haredim), 12, 13, 142, 149, 158, 159, 179, 191, 193, 195, 196, 198, 205, 207, 210, 237, 245–46, 288n2

Unchain My Heart (agunah-advocacy organization), 230, 287n65

United Kingdom (UK), 35, 134, 142, 168, 207, 231

United States, 12, 17, 134, 141, 142, 158, 163, 168, 190, 293n34, 297n55

Univers Israélite (newspaper), 144

Venice, Italy, 71, 115

Verona, Italy, 86

Vienna Women's Conference, 147

Vilna Gaon (Haym Soloveitchik), 116, 158

violence: marital, 15, 89, 90, 164–66, 170, 177, 186, 191, 192, 198, 201–2, 216, 247, 290n30; sexual, toward children, 7, 167; sexual, toward women, 24, 66, 103, 112

vows, nullification of (*hatarat nedarim*), 241

vulnerability, of women, 2, 46, 55, 149

waqf (Muslim religious charitable trust), 49, 84, 272n70

war, as cause of *iggun*, 136

"We are witnesses" (*anan sahadei*) (Talmudic principle), 179, 292n21

wedding ritual, traditional (huppa), 15, 26, 27, 108

Weinberg, Noam, 217

Weiss, Susan, 101, 160, 162, 183, 218–19

Weissler, Chava, 119

Wengeroff, Pauline, 119, 138

white-slaving, 146–47, 148

widows, xxiv, 32, 42, 51, 62, 83, 114; inheritance of, 94, 272n70; ketubbah payment for, 29, 67, 68; levirate marriage and, 7, 25, 64, 65, 94

"widows of living husbands" (*armalat al-hayat*), xxiv, 42

wife: acquired by unilateral actions of man, 14, 25, 214, 240; clothing provided for, 38, 40; divorced against her

will, 30, 88, 93, 212; domestic duties of, 29, 93, 278n14; dowry of, 38, 68, 86, 96, 125, 137, 283n4; earnings of, 35, 38, 40; inheritance of, 84, 86, 94, 97, 272n70; "murderous," 67, 244–45, 301n31; "rebellious," 49, 57, 71, 74, 88, 212, 278n29; sexual repulsion toward husband/levir, 29, 70, 71, 89, 90, 92, 93, 95, 100; "temporary," 43. *See also* abandonment, of wife; agunah/agunot; family, wife's; *kiddushin; kinyan; specific topics*
WIZO. *See* Women's International Zionist Organization
women, 14, 24, 59, 78, 91, 132; androcentric view of, in halakha, 54–55, 226; assertiveness of, 6, 64, 80–81, 85, 95, 118, 119, 129, 197, 253; in business, 32, 82, 83, 101, 130, 270n13, 284n18; as children's guardians, 34, 38, 83, 84; communal support of, 7, 45–46, 135, 146, 197, 234, 247, 254; CWJ work for, 160, 164, 182, 184–85, 197, 204, 230, 232, 251–52; earnings of, 35, 38, 40; economic clout used to protect self-interests of, 4, 80, 129; economic role of, 4, 29, 31–38, 79–80, 82, 83, 86, 97, 101, 130, 276n54; economic sanctions against, 92, 97, 98; haredi, use social media, 245–46; Judaism fealty of, 102, 105, 111, 150; martyrdom of, 6, 88, 124, 277n1 (bottom); migration of, after Spanish expulsion, 102; mitzvot practiced by, 58, 94; oaths taken by, 33, 34; organizations of, 10, 147, 157, 169, 179, 227, 237, 287n1; as Orthodox rabbis, 244–45; Orthodoxy chosen by, 225–26; Otherness of, 55, 104, 107, 146, 235, 238, 243, 273n3; pious and rebellious, 5, 80, 253; as political players, 80, 81, 94, 129, 168; property and, 37, 38, 82, 84, 86, 94, 97, 99, 272n70; protected by kin, 7, 8, 39, 40, 42, 45, 46, 51, 61, 65, 72, 85, 98, 235, 254; rabbinic hostility towards, 94–95, 278n29; recourse to Gentile and Jewish

courts by, 4–5, 47, 48, 57, 73; regression in status of, xxiv, 99, 101, 122, 129; rights of, in marriage and divorce, 9, 13, 38–40, 197; role in marriage and divorce, 5, 56, 57, 62–63, 67, 89, 118; self-interest protections by, 4, 39, 61, 86, 97, 119, 124, 129–30, 197, 235, 253; as *shtadlaniot*, 82; support networks of, 8, 9, 62, 67, 98, 118–20; tradition-friendly, 13, 17, 140, 227, 234; transgressive behavior of, 8, 33, 61, 63, 73, 118–19, 235. *See also* agunah/agunot; divorce; marriage; power, of women; *specific topics*
women rabbinic pleaders (*to'anot rabbaniot/to'enet rabbanit*), 159, 181–82, 214
Women's International Zionist Organization (WIZO), 147
Women's Voice (Froyen Shtim) (publication), 151
work, in premodernity, 31–32, 277n3
World Conference of Jewish Women, 147
World Congress of Jewish Women, 147, 149
World War I, 136, 147, 227
World War II, 141

Yad La'isha (organization), 182, 201
Yerusalimsky, Moshe Nahum, 135
yibbum (marital reserve), 2, 68–69. *See also* levirate marriage
Yisrael Hofshit, 241, 248
Yitzhaki, Shlomo (Rashi), 32
Yoreh, Tzemah, 14, 241, 242
Yosef, Ovadia, 167
Yosef, Yitzhak, 205

Za'akat Dalot (The Cry of the Wretched) (Susskind-Goldberg and Goldberg, D.), 55, 55–56, 194
Zahalon, Yomtov (Maharitz), 50
Zalkin, Mordechai, 122
Zilberman, Eliezer Lipman, 143
Zinger, Oded, 47, 74

ABOUT THE AUTHOR

SHULAMIT S. MAGNUS is Professor Emerita of Jewish Studies and History at Oberlin College. She is the author of *Jewish Emancipation in a German City: Cologne, 1798–1871*; *Pauline Wengeroff, Memoirs of a Grandmother Scenes from the Cultural History of the Jews of Russia in the Nineteenth Century* (2 vols.); *A Woman's Life: Pauline Wengeroff and Memoirs of a Grandmother*; and numerous articles. She is the recipient of a National Endowment for the Humanities Fellowship and the winner of a National Jewish Book Award, among other honors. She publishes about contemporary issues in *The Forward*, *The Times of Israel*, and other venues.

www.ingramcontent.com/pod-product-compliance
Lightning Source LLC
Chambersburg PA
CBHW031536260326
41914CB00032B/1826/J